Gordon Thomas and Max Morgan-Witts are the authors of nine previous books whose total global sales exceed 36,000,000 copies in all editions. Five of their books have been made into major motion pictures, including the Academy Award-winning *Voyage of the Damned*, *The Day the Bubble Burst* and *Enola Gay*. Their previous number one bestseller on Vatican affairs, *Pontiff*, has now been published in nineteen countries.

By the same authors

GORDON THOMAS AND MAX MORGAN-WITTS

The Year of Armageddon

The Pope and the Bomb

PANTHER
Granada Publishing

Panther Books
Granada Publishing Ltd
8 Grafton Street, London W1X 3LA

Published by Panther Books 1985

First published in Great Britain by
Granada Publishing 1984

Copyright © Gordon Thomas and Max Morgan-Witts
Productions Ltd 1984

ISBN 0-586-06059-6

Printed and bound in Great Britain by
Collins, Glasgow

Set in Plantin

'I declare it's marked out just like a large chess-board!' Alice said at last. 'There ought to be some men moving about somewhere – and so there are!' she added in a tone of delight, and her heart began to beat quick with excitement as she went on. 'It's a great huge game of chess that's being played – all over the world – if this *is* the world at all, you know.'

LEWIS CARROLL,
Through the Looking Glass and What Alice Found There

'The pope is like a spiritual Hercules trying to keep the super-powers apart, trying to avert nuclear Armageddon. Understanding that is crucial to grasping all else which is happening in this pontificate.'

MGR EMERY KABONGO, private secretary to His Holiness, Pope John Paul II, in conversation with the authors, 12 April 1983

Contents

1
By the Way . . .

One, or both of us, has reported on the papacy since the closing months of John XXIII's pontificate in 1963. We went on to record the election of Paul VI, the early promise and then disillusion during the latter stages of his fifteen-year reign which ended with his death in 1978. The same year saw the thirty-three-day pontificate and funeral of his successor, the first John Paul, and an end to the 455 years of Italian domination of the papacy with the emergence of Poland's Karol Wojtyla as John Paul II.

As social historians, we continue to monitor the workings of the Vatican and his pontificate, and have done so without interruption from that moment, five-eighteen p.m. on Wednesday, 13 May 1981, when Mehmet Ali Agca almost succeeded in assassinating John Paul.

In 1983 we released our initial research in a work entitled *Pontiff*. The book drew comforting critical acclaim from important Roman Catholic and secular commentators in the nineteen countries where *Pontiff* was published. But even before then, a follow-up work had been suggested. Trusted aides like Mgr Emery Kabongo, the first black to serve as a pope's personal secretary; Mgr John Magee, who exchanged the role of papal private secretary for the yet more exalted one of Master of Ceremonies; Mgr Crescenzio Sepe, a permanent civil servant in the Secretariat of State with ready access to Cardinal Casaroli; Fr Lambert Greenan, the waggish, waspish, hard-headed and straight-talking editor of the English-language edition of *L'Osservatore Romano*: these were among the priests who indicated to us there was an equally important book to be written about events which place the papacy at the very centre of the world's stage. Kabongo, not for the first time, synthesized matters in a memorable statement: 'The pope is like a spiritual Hercules trying to keep the superpowers apart, trying to avert nuclear Armageddon. Understanding that is crucial to grasping all else which is happening in this pontificate.'

The decisive moment, when we knew we had to write *The Year of Armageddon*, came when John Paul said in January 1983 that from then on, more than ever, he would spare no effort to avert war, *any* war, let alone a Third World War.

Today, as never before, papal diplomacy is governed by the same essential factors which control all secular international contact. The Vatican – or more accurately the Holy See, for Vatican State is the shell of temporal sovereignty which enables the Holy or Apostolic See not only to regulate the religious lives of currently a billion Catholics but also to maintain diplomatic relations the world over – is prepared to confront if coexistence fails; to co-operate if possible; to compromise if feasible. This blend of principles and expediency virtually guarantees that papal diplomacy is frequently looked upon with suspicion not only in Moscow but also Washington and London.[1]

Of all the secrets, those of diplomacy are the most guarded. Documentary literature on papal politics is scarce: popes do not publish their memoirs, and nuncios – unlike their secular counterparts – seldom produce accounts for public consumption about their years in papal diplomatic service.[2] There is almost nothing of value written on the 'policies' of the present pontificate; the role of the Holy See in current international affairs – apart from acting as an influential advocate of the universal yearning for peace – is often seen as being no more than to establish the kingdom of God among men by buttressing the practice of the faith where it is weak or crumbling.[3] That, we discovered, is touchingly out of touch.

The Vatican is an enigmatic place which gives up its secrets grudgingly. Some of its staff are by nature evasive, and a small handful habitually resent any attempt, however impartial, to portray their work. Even after our experience of researching and writing *Pontiff*, the place produces a ready unease in us, partly because of the Vatican's obsession with secrecy and partly because of a genuine reluctance among those of us who work in the human sciences to risk professional confrontation with an organization so powerful. These additional constraints challenged our long-held determination to maintain a properly disciplined receptivity towards professed truths.

As with our previous books, *The Year of Armageddon* is based on an amalgam of first-hand observations and that essential lode for any serious investigation: contemporaneous notes, memoranda, diary entries, logs, reports, calendars and correspondence, both official and private.

During 1982–3 we made, between our researchers and ourselves, literally hundreds of visits to the Vatican to study paperwork and conduct interviews.[4] Research visits were also made to England, the United States, Canada, West Germany, Austria, France, Belgium and both Northern and Southern Ireland. More than 300 persons were interviewed, some repeatedly.

All interviews were for the record – in the sense anything said could be used – but on the understanding that the identity of a source would, if requested, be protected. In view of the sensitive nature of certain material, this guarantee was essential: much of the information we obtained would not otherwise have been available to us.

The actual criteria we applied to interviews were those we have used for the past eighteen years and which have passed the scrutiny of that experienced research organization, the *Reader's Digest*, with whom we collaborated for over a decade. Every important fact provided should have at least one corroborating source, if possible two. Whenever feasible, interviewees were to be recorded on tape from which transcripts could be typed and indexed. Interviewees were afterwards free to amend any factual errors inadvertently made in their statements and we were free to make further contact for supplementary information or clarification, if necessary. When reporting on meetings, we were almost always able to speak to some of those who had been present or, if not, to those to whom the participants spoke subsequently. This also held good in those cases when there were meetings between only two persons.

Researching John Paul's pontificate is in some respects easier than previous administrations. The Italian influence, while not to be underestimated, is no longer overpowering: it is possible to obtain a great deal of genuine information without having to speak to a single Italian curialist. The Poles – no great surprise – have established themselves throughout the Vatican as reliable barometers on the mood swings of the papacy: they know what initiatives are under way, what proposals have been scrapped. The Irish continue to maintain their tenacious grip: they are good at minutiae, they have the knack of picking up and remembering with accuracy the barbed asides and throwaway lines which sometimes mean a priest's career in the Church is over; it was largely the Irish who provided what one of them, editor Lambert Greenan, calls the 'sort of revelations which are the blood and guts of a good papacy'. The American connection is better than before, largely because the US hierarchy has stronger links with John Paul than it had with his immediate predecessors. The German and French connections to the papacy remain good and consequently are reliable conduits for news, as are the Spanish and Latin American. In the main the rest do not amount to very much.

To develop these contacts we set up a network of secure restaurants in Rome; priests normally reticent within the confines of the Apostolic Palace and its environs felt able to relax when they could not be overheard.

No single motive can be ascribed to those who were of assistance. Some freely admitted they did so out of a sense of frustration: they were the ones who said it really is very tedious sitting in a Curial cubby hole watching the world pass by in an endless stream of memoranda and State papers. The frustration becomes acute, one civil servant said, when he feels he is simply a 'human rubber stamp', reading and initialling but having 'nobody above' interested in his opinion. The chance we gave him to talk, to explain his own views on where papal diplomacy should be going, was gratefully received. Some had a keen eye on the main chance: they wanted to leak information because in one way or another it would benefit them or their masters, often a bishop or cardinal. The intention of still others was more straightforward: they believed the world should know what John Paul was trying to achieve. At times there was a shiny fervour about them which made us uncomfortable.

To the end the motives of a few remain obscure. They were the ones who frequently expressed resentment against the rigid caste system they had chosen to live in; yet they were beneficiaries, not victims, of that system. Was it vanity, boredom, a compulsion to run risks (revealing Vatican secrets can be a serious offence, punishable by dismissal from church service and even excommunication), or just kicking over the traces? We shall probably never know for certain. Perhaps it does not matter.

Our Vatican connections have absolutely nothing to do with the Press Office which the city-state maintains to fob off the world's media. We have put most store on information from those who have access to the pope: men with real knowledge of what is happening to Holy See initiatives. They know the fluctuations on what papal secretary Kabongo has called 'the scales of Armageddon'.

Choosing how to tell the story proved more difficult than anticipated. While wishing to retain the style of our previous books – reproducing events as they unfolded – we concluded that with all the vagaries of papal manoeuvring, the criticism could arise that hindsight had allowed us a portrayal which was too conveniently twenty-twenty. The decision to recount a year in the history of papal initiatives and their attendant ramifications eventually dictated our approach. We cast ourselves as diarists, recording events as

11

they actually happened, or as soon as possible afterwards. This enabled us to show the decision-making process as it occurred, to reveal the problems, real or contributory, as they arose. In that sense *The Year of Armageddon* is unadulterated history in the making.

While using the format of a diary, we relied upon an increasingly recognized and acceptable means of writing modern non-fiction: a true story can be presented with all the texture and style of the novel. This approach is especially fitting for describing the circuitous ambiguity of papal politicking. Equally, we have made every effort to exclude embellishment, to present the realities while dispensing with the myths about the way a modern pope goes about putting the world to his rights.

We decided to exclude the burgeoning scandal surrounding the so-called 'P-2 Masonic lodge' of Arezzo, near Florence. While it has indeed raised serious financial questions which impinge upon the pontificate of John Paul – even tarnishing it – the machinations of P-2 have little bearing on the strict brief we set ourselves: to write a contemporary study of papal politics – to examine the present role of what Harold Laski called the problem of sovereignty in its acutest phase: that of Church and State.

While John Paul plays a more direct role in Vatican diplomacy than any of his recent predecessors, Holy See initiatives remain part of a system established over 400 years ago. Then as now, papal politics embody the truism that Church and State can never be entirely separate, in the sense that either side wishes to or can ignore the other.

Under John Paul's aegis papal policies continue to act and interact, are influenced and exert influence. There is, we discovered, sometimes no rational explanation for the way Vatican diplomacy works. Indeed, many regard it as a paradox and an anachronism. Others see it as a phenomenon which is truly baffling; an inexplicable deviation from the normal ways of International Law; a form of political life described as 'a regrettable retrogression in the march of progress towards a future when troublesome questions joining religion and politics no longer intrude'.[5]

But they do – often providing the key to the vexing question of Church-State relations. The pope is the visible apex of a unique diplomatic service. But, as we shall show, what is involved in papal politics is something far more than the mere 'moral authority' of a spiritual leader whose world 'prestige' commands respectful attention.

We decided to include the ongoing controversy, and mystery, surrounding Mehmet Ali Agca's attempt on the pope's life, for, while dealing largely with papal policies as they flow outwards from the Vatican, we concluded we could not ignore the reverse: a politically motivated act directed against the pope and the papacy, which, when all the facts become known, may have potentially disastrous political and diplomatic – ultimately perhaps even military – consequences for the world.

Finally, in *Roman Responses*, we ourselves appear within the text: reporting on our movements and meetings with intelligence officers and others who helped us; describing our feelings – and adventures – during the quest for truth within the strangely complex and multi-faceted organization of the Vatican.

Its people continue to surprise, dismay, intrigue, amuse and rivet us. And sometimes even frighten.

2

VATICAN CITY
Friday
Early Morning

Habit and training make him walk slowly. That is why Camillo Cibin allows himself on this damp Roman morning, as on any other, a full twelve minutes to walk the three-quarter circle encompassing Bernini's colonnades – the overpowering twin structures of 284 columns and 88 pilasters, themselves supporting 162 statues each twelve feet high – which form part of the limits of the tiny city state of which Cibin is chief of the Ufficio Centrale di Vigilanza. At Rome city police headquarters, in the offices of DIGOS, the national anti-terrorist squad, and in those of its bitter rival, the Italian Secret Service, as well as the local stations of foreign intelligence services – in all these places Cibin is known as *Hotshot*, his codename on the special emergency radio frequency which would be activated the moment an incident happens threatening the safety of the pope.[1]

Cibin knows he can trigger an immediate response that includes hundreds of uniformed police, detectives and the agents of a dozen secret services rushing to the vast expanse of St Peter's Square, around which he is still walking. All he need do is open his expensive trench coat and pull from a jacket pocket of his custom-made steel-grey suit a powerful walkie-talkie radio. One punch on the central of three buttons on the handset will instantly activate what the CIA Station Chief at the American Embassy in Rome calls *Pope Alert*, code words meaning John Paul has finally fallen victim of another assassination attempt.

During the twelve years, three months and five days Cibin has been head of Vatican security, ultimately it has been his responsibility to accept, revise and sometimes to reject the advice on how to protect the pope that the police forces and security agencies of a dozen western nations

14

regularly submit him to. The West German Bundeskrimi-
nalamt (BKA) proposal that the special squad of blue-
suited *vigili* directly responsible for guarding the pope
should receive extra training from BKA officers was swiftly
accepted. Welcomed too was the offer from Scotland Yard
to make available its expertise in crowd control. One of the
many difficulties Cibin had faced in the wake of the
shooting was clearing St Peter's Square fast enough to allow
essential police work to begin. As it was, Mehmet Ali Agca's
accomplices escaped and remain free.

Though almost two years have passed since that sunny
late afternoon in May 1981 when Agca pumped three bullets
into John Paul at close range, the memory of Cibin's feeling
of helplessness, and what he afterwards told a West
German secret serviceman was 'impotent rage', continues
periodically to engulf the police chief, deepening the worry
lines around his mouth and eyes, sometimes adding a
nervous tic to his upper lip.[2] This is why he listens most
carefully to even the most outlandish advice his peers in
other forces offer.

A Chicago policeman has suggested equipping the Swiss
Guards with stun-grenades. A senior Tokyo detective urged
the papal *vigili* squad should be trained in the martial arts.
A Paris policeman proposed the pope should be totally
encased at all times in public within a bullet-proof glass
dome; in design it looked like a gigantic botanical specimen
jar.

In the past year Cibin has received over a dozen memoranda sharply critical of what John Paul already considers too
restrictive protection, especially during his regular Sunday
visits to the parishes of Rome. On these occasions, the pope
has once written, he was a priest visiting his parishioners
and it was 'inappropriate' to encircle him with a phalanx of
blue-suited *vigili*. Both papal secretaries – the abrasive
Stanislaw Dziwisz, a tall and tightly wound Pole who has
been with the pope for seventeen years, and Emery Kabongo, a gentle-voiced black from Zaire, just a year in papal

service – have warned the security chief that the more John Paul feels penned in, the more he will protest.[3]

The natural curve of Bernini's colonnade brings Cibin to where he can stand in the lee of one of the giant columns – chipped and defaced by the mindless graffiti of some of the millions who yearly visit this most famous square in the western world. He indulges in a piece of tradecraft in which he is proficient. He discreetly observes the city of Rome policemen whose task it has been to guard St Peter's Square since the days of Mussolini.

Cibin does not care for the policemen. They had failed to spot Agca. Why should they not fail again? Besides, for the fastidious and withdrawn Vatican police chief who has made self-effacement a byword, these Romans are too flashy and self-assured in the way they tote their Uzi machine-pistols or regularly mutter into their handsets, reporting all is quiet to the mobile control van parked in a nearby side street. There is a clone-like quality about them – the same swarthy, hard-lined youthful faces, rumpled uniforms, scuffed shoes – as though they had been plucked from a police academy conveyor belt and plonked down in the square with but a single order: look menacing. Cibin still feels a sense of inner shock when they refer to the pope as *il bersaglio*, The Target.

The security chief does not doubt they are right: John Paul remains the one real target for assassination among the 3,294 persons who work within the Vatican.

What worries Cibin is the ability of these patrolling policemen, and their superiors, to provide adequate warning of a new threat to the pope's life. The men in the square, for all their bravado, have, Cibin knows from talking to them on other occasions, no particular interest in John Paul as a person, let alone his theology, philosophy, political acumen or pastoral ability. A number belong to Italy's thriving Communist Party, itself openly opposed to the ideas of the pontiff they are here to protect.

For all these policemen a spell of duty in the square is

looked upon with small favour. In Cibin's view this could, in a crisis, affect their responses. There is nothing he can do; he has no jurisdiction over them except during an emergency, and then only until a ranking Rome police *capo* arrives on the scene. It's a bad deal, the men at the CIA Rome Station have told him. It's Italian, Cibin has replied.

In some ways the Americans disturb him more than the patrolling policemen.

Cibin remains astounded how firmly the CIA retains its hold as the Vatican's chief adviser from the world of secular intelligence.[4]

As he walks slowly towards the Bronze Doors, the imposing entrance to the Apostolic Palace, he knows the sheer tenacity of the American intelligence agency, as much as its past close links to the Vatican, saved it in the débâcle following Agca's shooting of the pope.

It wasn't every day that the full fury of the Holy See was unleashed on a friendly superpower like the United States. But seventy-two hours after John Paul was shot, and while he still hovered between life and death in an intensive-care suite in the Gemelli Hospital in Rome, Cardinal Secretary of State Agostino Casaroli had demanded the CIA station in Rome should be swept clean. In the end some senior officers were posted to other US embassies or recalled to headquarters at Langley, Virginia.

The CIA should have known, Casaroli continued to fume for weeks afterwards; it, more than any other agency, was the one which we trusted. The CIA should have known about Agca, the KGB, the entire plot.

Later, Cibin was one of the first to pose the startling question: what if the CIA *had* known something before the attack, and just how much does the agency know *now* about the full ramifications of the plot?

Cibin knows it is not the first time the CIA has aroused such suspicions in its long and chequered dealings with the Vatican.

* * *

17

Long before Cibin came to the Vatican, when he had been a gangling teenager in post-war Italy, gawking at the Allied occupation, American intelligence had successfully penetrated the Holy See.[5] It had not been difficult. The wartime Office of Strategic Services (OSS) – the forerunner of the CIA – was welcomed, in the words of the head of the Rome Station in 1945, James Jesus Angleton, 'with open arms'. Pius XII and his Curia enlisted the OSS to gerrymander the Christian Democrat Party into power and to help the Church's militant anti-Communist crusade. Angleton, a practising Catholic, knew how to exploit the situation. The Vatican already had an unparalleled information-gathering service in Italy through the Jesuits who, from 1945 onwards, had a standing brief from the pope to report on the clandestine activities of Italian Communists and their relations with Moscow. Angleton arranged that anything important should be passed to him; he sent it on to Washington.

By 1952, when the Rome Station was being run by another good Catholic, William E. Colby – who went on to mastermind the CIA's infamous operations in Vietnam – American intelligence had established a network of informers and contacts among Vatican priests which extended to the Secretariat of State and included every key Sacred Congregation and Tribunal.

Linked by common cause – ridding Italy and the world of Communism (throughout the 1950s it was often expressed as crudely as that) – the CIA enjoyed the closest of ties with the papacy. More and more priests collaborated, not only in Rome, but wherever the Church writ ran. In Latin America, in Asia and Africa missionaries were recruited and threw themselves enthusiastically into the world of secret intelligence.

By 1960, the CIA could count another triumph. Milan's Cardinal Montini – three years later to become Paul VI – freely passed on a windfall: a treasure trove of files about the Italian Episcopate and 'the activities of the parish priests of

Italy'. This bounty enabled the CIA to be even more effective in its campaign to discredit priests deemed soft on Communism, and to reward those prepared to toe the agency line.

The CIA had a vast slush fund – called 'project money' – which enabled it to make generous contributions to Catholic charities, schools and orphanages and even pay for the restoration of church buildings. Holidays were given to co-operative priests and nuns; expensive altar artefacts were purchased. On a lower scale cardinals and bishops were wined and dined in an Italy slow to recover from the ravages of war. This was a halcyon time for the CIA; its succession of station chiefs were regarded in the Vatican as being of more importance than US ambassadors to Italy, or the 'personal representatives' that American presidents appointed to maintain indirect diplomatic ties with the Holy See.

But times were a-changing. John XXIII felt the crusade against Communism had largely failed; there was a need for a more accommodating approach. He ordered the Italian bishops to become politically neutral and to cease automatically endorsing the Christian Democrats. It was a command which left the Italian Episcopate in hopeless disarray. The CIA was alarmed. The pope began to nurture the seeds of an embryonic Ostpolitik. A mood of black panic gripped the CIA. John started a cautious dialogue with Khrushchev; there was an exchange of friendly letters. The CIA's worst fears were confirmed: the Vatican was no longer totally committed to the American system. From Washington came the anguished order to the then station chief in Rome, Thomas Hercules Kalamasinas, to regard the Vatican as 'hostile', and to observe its activities 'in that light'. Another phrase – 'dangerous left-wing drift' – began to creep into CIA reports from Rome.

The agency's director, John McCone, considered the situation sufficiently serious to place discussion on it near the beginning of his daily briefings. CIA analysts prepared exhaustive assessments with such grandiose titles as *The*

Links Between The Vatican and Communism and *The Catholic Church Reassesses Its Role in Latin America*. Other agency experts evaluated the impact of papal policies in every sphere of American influence.

There was little comfort for the conservative-minded McCone. John's pontificate was committed to liberalizing, to social change and, if needs be, political realignment in those very areas where the CIA had striven so hard; agency expertise had supported right-wing military juntas, stamping firmly on the first whiff of Communism. His staff told McCone the United States could expect the pope would increase his criticism of US-supported juntas while extending more open sympathy to such left-wing opposition groups as Salvador Allende's party in Chile; that on the horizon – indeed looming ever larger – was a new type of militant-minded cleric, men like the Brazilian Bishop Helder Camara who outspokenly supported the underprivileged. All the signs, ran the CIA consensus, suggested the Vatican and the Church were relinquishing their traditional position of being a pillar of the establishment.

McCone ordered every effort be made to improve the CIA 'intelligence capability' in the Vatican. More money and men were made available to execute a policy which regarded the Vatican as displaying an 'unfriendly ambience' rather close, in the CIA's estimation, to that exhibited towards the US by the Soviet Union.

Ironically this position was covertly continued by the Kennedy administration. John F. Kennedy, the first Catholic to become president, was determined to distance himself from the papacy. On the campaign trail he had found that his religious beliefs were often a key issue, especially in such strongly Protestant states as Indiana, Oklahoma and Mississippi. And many millions of other Americans feared that a devout Catholic in the White House was but a step from having the pope running America; that the election of Kennedy meant the end of the hitherto inviolate principle of keeping Church and State separate.

Shrewdly recognizing this concern within the nation, as well as the need to diffuse a potent political threat to his presidency, Kennedy deliberately remained remote from the American hierarchy while at the same time, so far as the public was concerned, positively ignoring the pope.

This visible posturing was a smokescreen. It hid clandestine assignations between members of the Kennedy administration and the papacy. Senior State Department officials frequently met the pope's apostolic delegate in Washington. In Rome the political officer at the American Embassy to Italy made equally discreet visits to the Vatican. Simultaneously the seven CIA officers assigned to the Rome Station probed and pried and plied their sources with gifts. Using every kind of 'acceptable leverage' to obtain information about the pope's policies, the CIA grew increasingly alarmed at his growing contacts with Moscow.

In the spring of 1963, the CIA's Director of National Estimates, James Spain, submitted a 'most secret' fifteen-page report to Kennedy castigating the pope's burgeoning Ostpolitik. It was an astounding document, filled with hyperbole and unsupported accusations. The pope was charged with advancing the 'specific theory that fundamental change is taking place in the Soviet Union'; that 'Marxism is losing its force within the USSR'. The pope was hell-bent on pushing an 'open door' towards Communism; at every opportunity he was selling short The Great American Dream.

The CIA's appraisal of papal policies was given a priority reading within the Kennedy administration. The document rang alarm bells throughout Washington.

Kennedy personally approved McCone's request that the CIA should intensify its activities in and around the Vatican. Money – never a problem for the agency – was made even more available in ever greater quantities to buy, bribe and reward. One helpful monsignor regularly received a crate of vintage champagne (in 1983 he was still able to open a bottle and toast 'the good old CIA'). A lowly priest working in the Holy Office who provided information accepted sufficient payment to buy a complete – and very expensive – wardrobe of clerical garb from the pope's tailors, the House of Gammarelli. Another, working in the Secretariat of State, filched a document which suggested the pope was anxious not to do or say anything which could be construed as anti-Soviet. The priest's reward was a Fiat.

By these means the CIA in Rome built their case of a deepening relationship between the Vatican and the Kremlin. In the late spring of 1963 came the nadir. Rome Station reported the Holy See was about to establish full diplomatic relations with Russia.

The normally placid McCone was galvanized. He sought, and obtained, an immediate meeting with Kennedy. Afterwards, armed with full presidential authority, he caught the next plane to Rome. Ten hours later he confronted the pope in his office.

McCone did not waste time on small talk – he was blunt, brutally and deliberately so. The president of the United States had commanded him to say that the Church should stop its drift towards Communism. It was both dangerous and unacceptable to dicker with the Kremlin. Communism was a Trojan Horse, as the evidence following the recent Italian left-wing election victories indicated: in office the Communists had dismantled many of the policies Catholic parties supported. Above all, American Catholics were dismayed. John's predecessor, Pius XII, had ordered that Catholics who joined the Communist Party should be excommunicated. Now the papacy was being increasingly criticized for its 'Communist sympathies'.

John did not speak until McCone finished. For a moment the old pope studied his tall, ascetic visitor with the piercing grey eyes and carefully groomed hair. What could this epitome of the American Good Life – John would later repeat to an aide – know about the realities of the world which preoccupied the pope? The world of abject poverty, denial of human rights, of slum dwellings, shanty towns, brutal racism of a kind modern America had almost forgotten. What could McCone know about this?

Speaking softly, the pope began to explain that the Church he led had an urgent duty, a sacred commitment, to make its presence felt in underdeveloped countries, to promote social reform in Europe and South America, to ease the plight of Catholics within the Soviet bloc by discussing matters directly with Moscow. This, he insisted, was how to meet the challenge of Communism: face up to it with reasoned argument, recognize its godlessness but not become blinded by ideological differences. In short, concluded John, to be realistic. He reminded McCone that as pope, 'I bless all people and I withhold my trust from no one.'

McCone was unimpressed. He replied angrily the CIA possessed ample evidence that even as the Church pursued détente with Moscow, Communism was actually persecuting Roman Catholic priests in Russia, Asia and South America.

John looked at his visitor, his eyes clouded with sadness. Did not McCone realize that his evidence, which he already knew to be unhappily true, was another reason to seek a better relationship with the Communists?

McCone returned to Washington convinced the pope was leading the Church into Moscow's camp. He recommended that the Kennedy administration sever its secret contacts with the Vatican. At the same time the CIA would attempt to nullify anything perceived as a threat to America's position in the world.

John's not unexpected death – he had a rapidly progressing cancer – provided a sense of deep relief for McCone.

In a report – TDCS BD 3/654,973 – Rome's then CIA station chief accurately predicted early in June 1963, weeks before Conclave, that Montini of Milan, the cardinal who had obligingly handed over to the agency all those revealing files on Italy's parish priests, would be the next pope.

Washington could relax.

Two days after Montini was crowned Paul VI he received Kennedy in private audience.

The meeting clearly demonstrated the president's dependency on the CIA in all matters relating to the Vatican. The agency had advised the time was now 'appropriate' for a visit. On the eve of the audience Kennedy suddenly realized he did not know what to wear for the meeting. Instead of having an aide call the protocol office at the State Department, Kennedy asked the CIA for details of the right attire. The swift response was: white tie and tails.

Before going to the Vatican Kennedy took a final look at the CIA's profile of Paul and the agency's list of suggested topics to discuss. They included requesting that the pope recall his apostolic delegate in Washington, because he 'presents a distorted view of the United States to the Vatican', and suggesting that Paul order the Vietnam hierarchy to pressurize Buddhist monks to end their anti-war stance in Vietnam, 'and stop setting fire to themselves in Saigon streets, an action which only misinterprets the position of the United States in Vietnam'.

In the event these issues were not raised during the thirty-minute audience. Both men were cautious, aware of the underlying tensions behind the meeting; each was anxious not to appear to wish to make capital out of a historic occasion.

Kennedy's assassination in Dallas in November 1963 and Lyndon Johnson's assumption of the presidency did nothing to improve Washington's relationship with the Vatican. When Paul visited New York to address the United Nations in 1966, Johnson paid a fleeting visit to the pope's Manhattan hotel, making clear there would be no invitation to the White House for the pontiff, let alone a state banquet.

For by now the CIA's briefings of the president only confirmed what was patently, and very publicly, obvious. Paul – the cardinal who had been so helpful to the agency during his days in Milan – had done one of his anguished, Hamlet-like reassessments. He believed not only that Johnson's escalation of the war in Vietnam was wrong, but that the Holy See should be allowed to play the role of peacemaker. Johnson left office still resisting the idea of Vatican involvement in what he saw, correctly, as a proposal which would effectively end US influence in south-east Asia.

Richard Nixon felt the same when he became president. Three months after entering the White House, he received a briefing from CIA Rome which included revealing – and accurate – details about Paul's personal habits, his current physical and mental state. It was a document altogether more thorough than the station had prepared for Kennedy; it reflected the new status CIA Rome had been given by Nixon before he flew to Rome to meet Paul. The President sat in Paul's study and without ado told him he proposed to increase America's commitment in Vietnam. Paul's role as peacemaker was effectively dead.

The CIA briefing suggested that after Nixon had delivered this hammer blow, he should offer, as a palliative, something to stop an already ailing pope from plunging into another of the debilitating depressions which had started to overcome him, giving Paul a martyred look in public. Nixon said he would appoint Henry Cabot Lodge as his personal representative to the Holy See. Lodge was a former ambassador to Vietnam.

The Nixon years, for members of the CIA station in Rome, were good years. They worked out of a comfortable annexe of the American Embassy on the Via Veneto: they had their regular tables at the nearby Excelsior Hotel – if not the best, then the city's most expensive hostelry. From time to time Langley sent inexperienced officers to Rome for on-the-job training. In reality Paul's leaking pontificate was 'a turkey shoot' for even raw intelligence officers. There was not a secret or a paper the CIA could not quickly obtain. In the closing months of the Nixon regime, Paul, already physically weakened and mentally moribund, roused himself sufficiently to urge the president to put an end to the CIA using priests as informers.

From the White House came the immediate assurance that, 'if this has been happening', it would be stopped.

By then Nixon had become adept at lying over Watergate on American network television and radio.

Nixon eventually went and the caretaker president, Gerald Ford, arrived. His promise to cleanse the American nation of its contaminated feeling did not extend to curbing the CIA activities around the Vatican. The Rome station flourished as before. The reporting was remarkably accurate: Paul's pontificate was grinding to a halt; he was taking Mogadon sleeping tablets and a mysterious elixir for his crippling arthritis, he was at loggerheads with his staff, he was increasingly obsessed with his death. The assessments were harsh: the CIA painted the pope as giving moral support to guerrillas and left-wing parties in Latin America; as the pontiff who looked benignly on Castro's Cuba; as the Holy Father who still clung to the idea that America was largely responsible for the horrors of Vietnam while never himself uttering a word of protest in public about the suppression of the Church in Hungary, Romania and Czechoslovakia. Even more than John, Paul had allowed his office to be exploited by the Communists. So said the CIA.

The arrival of the Carter administration was marked in Rome by the installation of new high-speed teleprinters and sophisticated surveillance devices, developed at Langley.

During the winter of 1977–8, the CIA, through some of its priest-agents in the Vatican, was able to plant six bugging devices in the Secretariat of State offices, Vatican Bank and the Governorate building. The bugs were sufficiently powerful to enable conversations to be overheard within buildings with walls thick enough to withstand artillery fire. Working from 'safe houses' close to the Vatican perimeter – usually apartments rented on short leases and changed frequently to avoid raising suspicions – CIA operatives were able to record often highly confidential discussions about papal plans.

It has been Camillo Cibin's outstanding triumph to have helped uncover the bugs.[6]

* * *

As he climbs the steps leading to the Bronze Doors, studiously ignoring the first of the day's tourists photographing the Swiss Guards guarding the entrance with their ceremonial halberds, Cibin can, if asked, vividly recall that day in May 1978 when he led two counter-surveillance experts from the Italian secret service past the doors and into the Apostolic Palace. The men, posing as estimators pricing an overhaul of the city-state's electrical system, spent a week in the Vatican. All told, they had unearthed not only the six CIA bugs but a further five of Soviet manufacture.

A sympathetic SIS officer based at the British Embassy in Rome – a man who, on Sundays, lends his pleasant voice to singing in the choir of the city's Anglican All Saints Church – had no need subsequently to inform Cibin that the sweep was a pointless exercise; there was, the security chief had already come to realize, no way he could keep every bug out of the Vatican.

Cibin is not alone in finding it remarkable how the CIA has recovered from that low point following the attempt on the pope's life; it is still the talk of Rome's foreign intelligence community. Officers working under diplomatic cover regularly tell Cibin – and sometimes to his chagrin will do so at formal Vatican receptions, edging him into a corner, offering him new snippets, hoping to draw him out but generally failing – their version of a story he knows well: how the American agency came to have such strong ties to John Paul's pontificate.

The links date back to that November day in 1978 when the pope had been in office for less than a month. He had received in very private audience – so secret that unusually no minutes were made – the head of the CIA station in Rome. The officer carefully explained the services the agency was eager to offer the pope: regular analysis of Russian intentions in Central Europe, with particular regard to Poland; a frequently up-dated over-view of the remainder of the Soviet bloc, with emphasis on matters of

27

specific Church interest, such as new impending threats to religious freedom or the expected arrests of priests who had become too outspoken; a general briefing on the volatile Middle East; selected briefings on any other sensitive areas the pope wished to be informed about.

John Paul asked for time to consider. He consulted Casaroli and other senior members of the Curia. Some were strongly opposed; others took the view that the CIA was an important source of reliable information. In any event rejection would not stop the spying.

Early in December the station chief returned to see the pope. John Paul wasted no time accepting the package.[7]

After the difficult years of John and then Paul, the agency was back in full papal favour. It had become the new pontificate's main source of secular intelligence. The CIA knew, and expected, that from time to time the Vatican would consult other secret services, notably Britain's SIS and West Germany's BND. But its own position was, for the foreseeable future, assured as a major influence in forming John Paul's view of the world.

The station chief who pulled off this great coup had been posted to Rome from Teheran; before that he was in Saigon and Chile. In all these places he had unfailingly gone to mass every morning. On learning of this John Paul invited him to attend Christmas 1978 mass in the pope's private chapel. It was, in the words of an envious officer of a rival intelligence service, 'the whipped walnut dressing topping the cream that comes with the strawberries'.[8]

This close and cosy relationship survived until Agca shot the pope. Soon afterwards Casaroli received evidence that almost a month before the assassination attempt on Paul John, the DIGOS office in Rome received news that 'a possible terrorist squad' was in Perugia, not far from the Italian capital. The source was MOSSAD, one of the two Israeli intelligence services. Their teletype identified the squad as including 'Mehmet Ali Agca alias Faruk Ozgun'.

Casaroli was mortified to learn that DIGOS had not given

the MOSSAD teletype a high priority because the Italian agency did not always trust the Israelis. DIGOS ran only perfunctory checks in Perugia, failing to pick up Agca's trail.

But what shattered Casaroli was to be told by a senior West German intelligence officer that it would be 'almost automatic' for the MOSSAD warning to have been copied to the CIA. Why had the American agency not informed the Vatican? Casaroli had confronted its chief official in Rome: the man was evasive, merely insisting the CIA had no prior knowledge and that Agca was 'a loner'. Casaroli was unimpressed. His fury boiled over. The CIA was out.

Four months later, having made a remarkable recovery, John Paul again took full control of his pontificate.

In October 1981 he received a very senior CIA emissary.[9] Details of the discussion between pope and spymaster remain secret. But the upshot was that shortly afterwards the agency resumed submitting reports, often directly to John Paul. The data was authoritative: the pope learned a full week beforehand that the Polish trade union, Solidarity, would be outlawed and its leader, Lech Walesa, arrested. The CIA cautioned there was nothing John Paul could – or should – do about these events. This was impressive foreknowledge, and the pope was properly impressed. The CIA brought him the first news, in November 1982, that Russia's President Brezhnev was actually dead – so ending days of speculation – and that Yuri Andropov had taken his place. It is the CIA's profile of the man who had been head of the KGB at the time the pope's death was planned that John Paul regularly reads.

Increasingly his decisions, his policies, his speeches and pronouncements take into account the CIA briefings he receives. They give him a political over-view no other pope has enjoyed. They may also add to the possibility that another attempt on his life could be made.

Now, as Cibin passes the Bronze Doors, he knows what the tourists photographing the pair of Swiss Guards on duty cannot know: the fear of a new attack on the pope has turned the Vatican into an extraordinarily defended citadel.

Behind the massive doors are Uzi machine-pistols, capable of firing 650 rounds a minute. The Swiss Guards will use them if any serious attack is made on this entrance to the Apostolic Palace.

Cibin goes to the guardhouse behind the Bronze Doors. One of his *vigili* is on duty, seated behind a high-fronted mahogany counter, the kind seen in the charge room of a police station. Beneath the counter is a loaded Uzi and several spare magazines. The *vigile* is middle-aged, wearing an unmatched jacket and trousers. On the counter, beside one of two telephones, is a small transistor radio. It is tuned to Vatican Radio's four-language early morning news programme, *Quattrovoci*. The guard has listened to the Italian segment of the newscast but has left the radio on to hear, although unable to understand, the English-speaking voice, Clarissa McNair.[10]

She is a tall, vivacious 35-year-old with an engaging grin and a following all over the world. McNair is a Protestant, married but separated from her Canadian husband. She has worked at Vatican Radio for almost a year, before that being employed by the CBC in Canada on an award-winning television exposé of organized crime in Canada.

Cibin knows she has clashed with a CIA operative in Rome known as The Mad Mentor. He has criticized her broadcasts for being 'anti-American'. She had brushed the accusation aside; the agent warned 'things' could get 'difficult' for her.

Cibin's concern is whether The Mad Mentor has been trying to recruit McNair as another informer in Vatican Radio. He suspects the station already has several moles, reporting to one foreign intelligence agency or another. He will now keep an eye on The Mad Mentor to see what further moves he may make towards McNair or anyone else at the station.

Cibin continues on his way, leaving the poky guardhouse

to climb an imposing staircase, wide enough to take a car or, as Napoleon once did, allow a squadron of mounted horse to clatter up its marble steps.

The security chief walks up the staircase and eventually reaches the courtyard of San Damaso. Here, in this large cobbled area, John Paul used to stroll between his endless round of meetings. The CIA has now advised against that, just as it frowned upon the pope jogging through the Vatican grounds at the end of a long day; the agency reportedly fears that rifles with scopes could shoot him from a mile away.

There is a Swiss Guard at the double doors leading on to the courtyard. He also has an Uzi within handy reach. Standing around the courtyard are more *vigili*. They all carry small arms.

Cibin continues his measured tread across the cobbles, heading for the Doorway of John XXIII. Yet another Swiss Guard stands there.

Cibin enters an elevator and emerges into a long, empty corridor. His feet echo on marble floors over which a hundred popes have trod. The security chief reaches a pair of closed double doors. He opens them and passes into an audience room, dominated by a throne; here the pope receives the credentials of new ambassadors to the Holy See. Cibin crosses this room, opens another pair of doors and enters a smaller reception room. It has green-painted walls and a frescoed ceiling. Though it is day, the heavy drapes are drawn and soft lighting gives the room a funereal feeling. There are icons on the walls, high-backed antique chairs, a pair of medieval refectory tables, a large chest and a statue of a Polish saint. There are also two rubber plants. The room is occupied by a court chamberlain and a *vigile* seated at a desk in a corner near the plants. A guard is always on duty here, day and night, week in, week out. He carries no visible arms. In the desk drawer is a loaded Browning pistol – identical to the one Agca used to shoot the pope. The *vigile* will use it as the last line of defence against an attack on the pope, who is already at work in his nearby study.

Nobody used to believe any attacker could ever penetrate this far into the papal apartment. But not any more. That is why the CIA have persuaded John Paul to accept yet another form of defence.

Cibin opens a door and enters a narrow corridor. At the end is another elevator. Normally it is reserved only for the pope, but Cibin has special permission to use it.

The elevator takes him up to the pope's private garden on the roof of the Apostolic Palace. It is a pleasing place of criss-crossing paths and flower beds. The whole area has been cleverly closed-in so that it is visible only from the air. No unauthorized flights are permitted over the Vatican.

Yet it is the fact that the garden is open to the sky which brought Cibin here every morning for the past forty-six days, from that day following the elevation of Yuri Andropov to head of state of the Soviet Union. Twenty-four hours after Andropov took office, CIA technicians came to the garden and installed detector devices capable of locating any approaching aircraft or helicopter. Italian airforce fighters are on standby to scramble in pursuit of such intruders.

John Paul has been told he is in danger each time he steps out on to this roof, either from a Kamikaze bomb attack or a snatch squad of terrorists who might swoop down and take him hostage.

Among Cibin's daily tasks is ensuring that the detectors are fully functional. The security chief frequently glances into the sky as he goes about his work.

Palazzo Di Giustizia, Rome
Same Day: Afternoon

The approach of dusk makes the Palace of Justice seem even more forbidding. The edifice is out of proportion in a district of nondescript buildings. The unrelieved severity of its exterior conceals cheerless corridors, stains around the floor drains in the washrooms, flickering fluorescent lights and a pervasive feeling of guilt. It is a place of endless questions and challenged answers. Strangers can easily get lost but for the armed guards posted strategically to check passes and provide escorts from one office to another. The men who occupy these offices seem cut from a pattern of dark suits and short haircuts. They radiate the authority of those who have heard all the excuses and know how to pick suspects clean to the bone. They are specialists in every kind of crime in a nation which has developed a finesse for it. Nothing surprises them about Italian society or its recalcitrant members.[11]

Yet on this New Year's Eve a mood of amazement permeates the fourth floor of the palazzo. The investigators here deal only with the most serious crimes: politically motivated murders, high-ransom kidnappings, large bank robberies, offences which display skilled planning and boldness. Even more than their colleagues in other areas of this vast building, they are determined to let nothing ruffle their professional masks.

The occupant of a comfortable but unpretentious office near the elevator on this floor has managed to do so. Judge Ilario Martella has astounded his peers over the way he is conducting his investigation into the assassination attempt on John Paul.

Agca had been convicted of the crime in July 1981, after a trial which produced no evidence of his motive. Many observers felt the court took care to ensure his reasons for shooting the pontiff should not be probed. Agca was sentenced to life imprisonment and told he would be eligible for parole in the year 2009.

There, legally speaking, the matter might have ended but for John Paul. Faced with information provided by the CIA and other intelligence agencies, the pope remains determined that the full truth about the assassination should surface, including, if necessary, making public any evidence of direct involvement by Yuri Andropov. This attitude, with all the emotional undertow which has come to mark John Paul's responses to the shooting, continues to create a sharp division within the Vatican. There are those who insist that to implicate Andropov would only exacerbate the already serious problems between the Vatican and the Soviet bloc.

The pope remains unconvinced by such arguments.

His feelings were originally made known to the CIA station chief in Rome, who informed Washington. The resulting discussions in Washington coincided with the deepening chill between the Holy See and the Polish regime.

Of all current papal diplomatic concerns, Poland predominates. That the same Russian guiding hand which menaces his country may previously have directly threatened him only fires the pope's wish to see the background to his attempted murder explored fully.

The CIA – recognizing the value to be gained from at minimum embarrassing the Soviet leadership, while at the same time having no public part in the matter – has encouraged the Vatican to press the Italian Ministry of Justice to resume enquiries.

In an inspired choice, Martella was appointed to head a new investigation.[12]

For weeks he has worked in the utmost secrecy on the fourth floor, reviewing files of evidence.

Martella's reputation is based on meticulous preparation. It enabled him to uncover the great scandal of the mid-1970s – Italian involvement with the Lockheed aircraft corporation. This turned out to be a sordid tale of wide-ranging corruption and bribery in the aviation industry. Martella's enquiries led to the resignation of Italy's president and the imprisonment of certain politicians.

He has just delivered his first bombshell in his investigation into the papal assassination attempt: he has issued warrants against seven persons. Five are Turks, two Bulgarians. All will be charged with playing a part in helping

Agca conspire to shoot the pope. The Bulgarian Connection has taken root.

In the Italian Parliament, supported by evidence from Martella, the Defence Minister has developed Bulgaria's involvement: the Italian counter-intelligence service, monitoring Bulgarian secret service transmissions, discovered 'unusual traffic around the time of the shooting of the pope, especially in the days prior'; three Bulgarian diplomats attached to the Bulgarian embassy in Rome were 'accomplices' of Agca in the attack on the pope: the trio had left Italy, returning to Sofia under diplomatic cover; Italy had recalled its ambassador and Bulgaria was about to reciprocate. Over it all, implied the minister, was an even darker force; Bulgaria was subservient to Moscow.[13]

It is not just the resulting world publicity which caused Martella's colleagues to whisper and shake their heads. Nor the fact Martella has once more mingled pure crime and murky politics with devastating results. What most concerns his fellow investigators is the way Martella treats Agca.

The first year of Italian prison life has blunted Agca's mind, left his intellect moribund, his outlook incurious. To his guards and fellow prisoners he was a primal and primitive inmate whose very philosophy made any rapport with them impossible. In that environment he became a special object of hatred; no opportunity was lost to strip away the last psychological supports which sustained him. He was verbally abused and occasionally physically assaulted. He bore it all stoically, as if he drew some strange inner pleasure from his suffering.

Later, at Martella's insistence, Agca was given special status. No longer does he languish forgotten, his only visitors intelligence officers and a prison service psychiatrist. He was moved to a new cell – still in solitary for his own safety – and allowed a television and radio. He was given Turkish books and newspapers to keep in touch with home, and facilities for study.

Fluent now in Italian, Agca is learning German. Such treatment for a convicted terrorist – let alone one who tried to kill the pope – has no precedent.

This afternoon Martella has once more arranged to see Agca.

Martella is forty-eight but looks older; Agca is twenty-three but appears younger. Both are lean men. Agca's build comes from a debilitating illness, anorexia nervosa, an ailment normally found in teenage girls. Martella's trim figure is the result of careful dieting and regular exercise. Each man comes from a country background: Agca was born in the remote Turkish village of Yesiltepe in Malatya province; Martella in Corsano, a small town nestling in the heel of Italy's boot. Agca has never lost his country-boy mannerisms; Martella radiates city sophistication. Yet despite these differences, there is a kind of bond between the two men.[14]

Undoubtedly this is nurtured in part by the almost endearing fatherly way Martella unfailingly addresses Agca as 'Ali'. The magistrate speaks with quiet sincerity, then allows Agca to talk without interruption before following up a point with a low-keyed rationality which seems to take so much into account. The self-evident authority in Martella's manner suggests there is no sense Agca wasting time on pointless argument; argument, in fact, would destroy the air of sweet reasonableness Martella invariably displays towards the prisoner.

It is there as he listens attentively to Agca explaining the strength he draws from reciting passages from the Koran during the first morning prayer before sunrise, the appointed moment when, runs Muslim writ, 'a black thread is visibly different from a white one when held at arm's length'. The same patient understanding is present when Agca adds that his religious beliefs allow him to exclude any feeling of original sin; that *Insh' Allah,* God's will, and *Jihad,* Holy War, remain two of the pillars of his personality. A third is another Koran tenet: 'God Gives and God Takes Away'.

Martella's own knowledge of the Koran – acquired after he took on the case, and hard won after many long nights of study – has enabled him to develop a relationship with Agca, unusual enough constantly to intrigue the prosecution's aides and colleagues.

Martella is not concerned about their reaction. He has grasped a fundamental fact from the psychiatrists who have probed Agca for over a year. The doctors have told him Agca is desperate to establish a meaningful relationship with what, for simplicity's sake, they call a father-figure; somebody Agca can respect and trust, and perhaps even cherish. These were feelings he did not have for his own father – long dead, but still the object of Agca's loathing. Win his confidence and affection, and you will win his mind, the psychiatrists informed Martella.

They also explained that Agca's mental state requires everything be done with the greatest of care. Agca suffers from melancholia and schizophrenia, mental diseases created by emotional shocks and little-understood inner conflicts. They manifest themselves in the way – and the psychiatrists can think of no simpler way of putting it – Agca dissociates part of his ego from himself. There are his diverse sexual needs: female prostitutes and homosexual dalliances. There are clinically speaking entire aspects of Agca which have become alienated from each other. He likes to people his secret world with those parts of his personality which he fears, loves or hates; this produces in him inner trauma of such fearsome complexity he is frequently unable to express himself in normal language.

During these periods surface his thought disorders; his regression to infantile behaviour; his many fixations; his lack of insight and his denial of his emotional needs.

The psychiatrists have warned Martella that Agca is far less interested in the difference between fact and fiction than he is by his own inventions, flights of imagination, mystery, sometimes poetry and, more often, caprice.

Using all this knowledge, Martella continues to build a

causeway across which he is careful to go only so far, beckoning Agca to come and meet him in this uncertain psychological no man's land. Step by step Martella has enticed Agca forward, often doing so by surprising the Turk with his insights into Islam, inviting Agca to challenge and then debate them. It has been a masterly performance by the magistrate, in part made possible through the support of the psychiatrists. For weeks now one of them has been trying to rebuild Agca mentally, to give him new emotional security, to provide him with a carefully planted sense of purpose, to make him feel in the end a need to explain the full ramifications behind the papal assassination attempt.

It is a slow process, but Martella is a patient man. He continues to listen carefully as Agca, on the eve of festivities for the new Christian year, speaks about Ramadan, the Islamic month of fasting. There is no detectable rhythm to Agca's monologue, yet it has a logic Martella has learned to decipher. Ramadan leads Agca to describe his time in Middle East training camps, recalling how the instructors would scream out *Galaat!* – pray – and the recruits would chant specially composed invocations for victory against Zionism or western imperialism. He speaks of the harsh punishments meted out by the *quadis*, the judges who preside over the camp tribunals; he explains the underlying philosophy of the camps: *smile at your enemy if you can't kill him – but always try and kill him.*

Martella has been given one other important piece of guidance from the psychiatrists. He must not prolong any session with Agca excessively, otherwise there is a risk of undoing the psychological restructuring.

It is late afternoon when the prosecutor summons an aide to request that the *carabinieri* have the bombproof truck ready to take Agca back to prison.

The assistant is leaving the office when he is startled to overhear Agca say he wants to write to the pope.

Martella promises he will help Agca compose a suitable letter after they have spoken a little more.

When this news percolates through the fourth floor there is more tongue-wagging and head-shaking.

What can Martella be up to?[15]

THE APOSTOLIC PALACE, VATICAN CITY
Same Day: Late Night

One of the heavy wrought-iron gates of the Arch of the Bells is closed – a prelude to the nightly ritual of locking up all the entrances to the Vatican on the stroke of midnight – when the dark blue Fiat limousine arrives. It bears a Vatican registration. Even so, no chances are taken; similar cars and false number plates are easy to obtain in Rome. A Swiss Guard, blue-caped against the cold, steps cautiously forward. Behind him the two *vigili* he has been talking to purposefully separate, ready to fire into the car's tyres should it attempt suddenly to force its way past the Renaissance-costumed Swiss Guard. He carefully scrutinizes the driver.[16]

The chauffeur is impatient. The flight he met at Rome's Fiumicino airport was late, delayed by bad weather over northern Europe; traffic into the city was heavy, with revellers already making driving conditions dangerous. The chauffeur is eager to join them; he can barely contain his irritation when the Swiss Guard leans further into the car for a better look at the dimly outlined figure in the rear.

There is a growled command from the passenger for the chauffeur to drive on. Almost simultaneously the driver releases the brake and the Swiss Guard steps swiftly back, managing both to salute the passenger and wave the *vigili* aside.

The Fiat speeds forward, skirts St Peter's Basilica, passes under another archway and bounces across the cobblestones of San Damaso Courtyard, halting at the main entrance to the Secretariat of State.

A small muscular figure emerges from the car and sniffs the air. It is the first thing he always does on arrival back at the Vatican. Even he does not know how many times he has done this during the past year; perhaps a hundred times, maybe more. For Archbishop Luigi Poggi – *Nunzio Apostolico con incarichi speciali* since 7 February 1975 – is the pope's extraordinary envoy at large, the Holy See's diplomatic troubleshooter, the natural heir to the world of very secret papal politics previously conducted by the willowy figure who now almost wafts forward to greet him – Secretary of State Agostino Casaroli.[17]

While the driver follows with Poggi's valise, the two men cover the last few steps of the dozen gruelling journeys Poggi has survived in the past few days: the nuncio now has merely to ride up in the elevator to the third floor of the Apostolic Palace where he has an office. Poggi is the only papal diplomat with a permanent private office in the Vatican in addition to his main one abroad – in Warsaw. His Vatican telephone numbers – 693-3817/4464 – are deliberately published in the *Annuario Pontificio*. Poggi knows that all kinds of people with information to impart study the Vatican yearbook, and gathering information is very much his business.

He has returned with a trawl of sufficient importance for Casaroli to meet him personally. Poggi has been to Geneva, Moscow, Bonn, Paris and Warsaw. It is a circuit the nuncio has already travelled many times this year: he occasionally jokes he spends more time dozing in aircraft seats than sleeping in bed; that he can recite the in-flight food of a dozen airlines; that he could find his way blindfolded around most major airports in Europe – East and West.

Few recent trips can match in importance what Poggi has gleaned this past week. At the Russian Mission in Geneva, a palatial nineteenth-century mansion stocked with the vodka and caviare Poggi likes, the chief negotiator, Yuli Kvitsinsky, indicated that a compromise in the Soviet position over limiting nuclear arms may be possible.

The issue is one of the most emotionally charged on the international scene.[18] It centres on whether NATO will install in Europe 572 US-built nuclear missiles to counter Soviet atomic-warhead-carrying missiles currently pointing at every NATO country in Western Europe.

In Geneva, Kvitsinsky made clear that President Reagan's 'zero option' remains unacceptable to the Russian leadership. This American proposal, Casaroli and Poggi now believe, is unrealistic because it requires that the Soviets destroy too many of their missiles.

But Kvitsinsky has agreed the Soviet Union will *withdraw* some SS20s, now aimed at Western Europe, to further inside its territory if NATO cancels plans to install its new weaponry.

Poggi had gone on to Moscow. In the Kremlin – he tells Casaroli – there is talk of as many as a hundred Russian missiles, each with three warheads, being moved. But, adds the nuncio, the Russians insist that the Americans will have to 'show willing'; NATO, too, must make 'certain concessions'.

Poggi learned in Bonn that while the West German government was refraining from public comment, there was disappointment over Reagan's view that the Soviet position was not 'adequate' and would leave the West 'at a considerable disadvantage'.

In Paris the nuncio found the mood cautious. The Mitterand administration is careful publicly to support the American position. But behind the scenes there is a feeling that perhaps something could be worked out; that a compromise might yet be found acceptable to both Washington and Moscow.

Finally, in Warsaw, Poggi learned that in spite of the Reagan administration's increasing coolness towards the carefully controlled trickle of information the Russians continued to disperse, there is a mood of maturing hope among western diplomats. Warsaw has long been a reliable sounding board for gauging Soviet attitudes; this time, trial balloon or not – 'up for grabs' one US diplomat has put it to the nuncio – the feeling is that the new Soviet offer augurs well. Casaroli continues to listen carefully. Poggi has that ability, rare even among diplomats, to produce a balanced and rapid assessment of material from a dozen sources. His voice is soft, his brown eyes watchful, lips purse before developing a new point. This careful, neutral and composed appearance almost never changes.

Both Casaroli and Poggi know the perils involving the Holy See beyond its present heavy commitments in trying to establish whether this new Soviet proposal indicates a genuine desire to reduce nuclear tensions and, if it does, in discreetly but actively promoting it.

Paul's unsuccessful intervention in the Vietnam war damaged papal diplomatic plausibility in many world capitals, not only because it failed but because it was seen so obviously to fail. In the aftermath of that débâcle Casaroli said that nothing must give the impression the Vatican was willing to reach accommodations with Communism 'at any price'. Under his guiding hand the Holy See, wherever possible, structures its attitudes towards the Soviet bloc on those prevailing in the West, taking its cue from Washington, Bonn, Paris and London.[19]

This attitude applies especially to the nuclear issue.

Undeniably the Holy See has a role to play there, and has since March 1970 when Casaroli travelled, for the first time, to Moscow to place his signature, on behalf of the pope, on the nuclear Non-Proliferation Treaty agreed between the superpowers.

Casaroli and Poggi are having this late-night meeting to explore how best the Holy See can continue to keep the United States and the Soviet Union from tearing up that agreement – and perhaps destroying the world.

42

3
THE PAPAL APARTMENT
Saturday
Dawn

For the pope's benefit the most important events of the world, as decided by his senior civil servants, on this New Year's Day are confined within a buff-coloured folder on his desk in the study which adjoins John Paul's bedroom. The file cover bears two words. Stamped in the centre in bold red lettering is SOMMARIO, Summary; in the top right-hand corner, SEGRETO, Secret.[1]

The file has been prepared in the Secretariat of State, with contributions from various 'desks', often small departments, each having a specific responsibility for monitoring an area of the globe. The submissions from the various desks for this Summary file are short, rarely more than a page. What they lack in literary style they more than make up by content. The Summary file often includes the first warning the pope gets of a current crisis worsening or a new one in the offing.

The file contained the prediction that Britain would go to war over the Falklands; that Israel would invade Lebanon. The file once included the first horrific details of how Israeli troops sealed off the Chatilla and Sabra refugee camps in West Beirut and allowed Lebanese Christian militiamen to slaughter at will hundreds of Palestinian refugees, mostly women, children and the elderly.

Kabongo, for one, believes this 'daily diet of tragedy' contributes to the physical changes in the pope. John Paul's face has become more creased. There are moments when pain clouds his eyes – inexplicable, says his devoted secretary, 'unless the Holy Father's suffering for the world is remembered'.

The physical effects have had almost inevitable mental ones. John Paul no longer reads at the same high speed;

43

often he goes back over a document. In the end he is usually as decisive as ever. But it takes longer. It is a textbook example of the effect of unremitting pressures on the natural process of ageing.

The contents of the file on this first day of the new year indicate how the papacy has changed and evolved during the past twelve months. A year ago the folder was bulkier, containing wide over-views of the world. Increasingly, reflecting John Paul's wishes, the file now concentrates on Central Europe and Soviet intentions there; the slightest indication of Russian plans in the area, especially in Poland, is included.

John Paul has developed a number of strong convictions about his pontificate. In particular he believes it must be devoted to studying and acting against forces which quell freedom: it must alert those who accept without question Soviet declarations of peace or who have become docile from fear of Russian strength. In public he is careful not to identify the Soviet Union specifically. Then, he alludes to the adversary as 'many men', 'many nations', 'many systems' and the way they use their economic and military power to threaten the less strong. But in the papal apartment, John Paul does not hide his feelings: the main enemy is Soviet Communism, and the challenge of preventing war can be met only by making the Russians realize that vigilance is always going to thwart aggression. He drills this thought into his staff at every opportunity.

During the first months of his pontificate the pope had remained largely aloof from the machinations of secular politics, preoccupying himself with consolidating his grip on the Curia. Gradually he began to ponder the intricate international stage. And finally, Poland – more riven and on the verge of bloody confrontation than it had been for years – eventually ensnared him. Given his background, an adult life in the Polish Church opposing Communism at every turn, this could hardly have been otherwise. The future of

44

the struggle between Church and State in his homeland continues to hold him in thrall.

To understand better how bleak the prospects might be, John Paul has learned a language unfamiliar to other popes. He knows when to use the nonce-words of modern nuclear strategists: he can speak to them on their terms about confidence-building measures designed to disguise war-like intentions; of the political exploitation of military force; of nuclear weapon free zones. John Paul is now as familiar with the acronyms of atomic arms – ICBM, MIRV, LRINF – as he is with the Creed. None of this lightens his mood. He is growingly convinced that if war does come between the superpowers it will almost certainly involve Poland. All he has read and been told indicates that the Soviet Union – like Israel – favours a short-war strategy: the Russians would not wish logistically to over-reach themselves, preferring a first-strike offensive in Europe in order to achieve a bargaining position. This, John Paul now fears, would almost certainly provoke a swift NATO response which could unleash a nuclear Armageddon involving Poland.

Should this frightening scenario occur, it will come close to confirming the prediction of the late Padre Pio, a priest in southern Italy who bore the stigmata. The mystic allegedly prophesied John Paul's reign would be short and end in bloodshed. Agca almost succeeded in making true the forecast. The pope believes only the miraculous intervention of the Virgin Mary had then saved him; he has already made a pilgrimage to the Shrine of Our Lady of Fatima in Portugal to give thanks for his recovery from a lengthy period of physical and mental struggle. After Portugal he told his closest aides that, having been spared, he felt impelled to perform a special mission – trying to save the world from destroying itself.

This morning, when he was awoken at five o'clock, his first action, as it is every morning, was to kneel on the *prie-dieu* near his bed and pray before an icon of the Blessed Virgin for guidance on how best to fulfil the momentous task God, through her, has given him. At seven o'clock, as another part of his daily habit, he offers a second such prayer while he celebrates Mass in his private chapel in the apartment.[2]

Then he hurries to his study to scrutinize the Summary before breakfast.

The study bookshelves offer a further clue to the many changes which have occurred in the pope's personality during the past year. Where once there were only uniform rows of leather-bound editions of the classics and the works of theologians and philosophers, these have now been joined by copies of the *International Defence Review* and the *Defence Management Journal,* as well as books with such arresting titles as *The Problems of Military Readiness, Military Balance* and *Surprise Attack: Lessons for Defence Planning.* Beside his encyclicals bound in white calf – they include the original draft of *Laborem Exercens* (On Human Work), a powerful evocation of the right to meaningful employment under just conditions, including the right to organize unions – is a scrapbook of letters from Solidarity members in Poland saying what a comfort they found the encyclical. John Paul has long known that it continues not only to provide comfort for Polish trade unionists but also to infuriate their Communist rulers. He does not mind; he believes such a response is an integral part of the difficult journey he is taking on the high road of faith, justice, peace and human dignity.

Close to the encyclicals are books dealing with a subject that now rivets the pope: eschatology, the study of biblical teachings which argues that God will inaugurate His Kingdom on earth through a series of 'happenings' to close an age. John Paul believes with a fervour which sometimes astonishes even his personal staff that, possibly before the end of the century, something 'decisive' may sweep the world. Could it be pestilence, a second Black Death? Or drought or famine on an unimaginable scale? Or nuclear war? He frequently now fears the latter; perhaps, he has been known to ponder, he has been cast in the role of head of the Church during what could be the final decade of the world before it is permanently blighted by a nuclear holocaust.

The need to purify and unify the Church before this awesome time of final judgement occurs helps to explain why John Paul has felt it a pressing duty to make so many arduous trips outside Italy, bringing his message to over 100 million people on five continents. He has expounded the great themes of Christianity, generated trust and goodwill even among non-believers and made himself the very visible foremost Christian leader of the age; an astute amalgam of priest, storyteller and missionary.

The pope is well aware that the Church is steadily losing ground to Marxist Communism, Socialism and, in western nations such as Germany and Holland, to secularism.[3] Drawing upon his own experiences as a priest under Communism he understands not only the great issues at stake for the Church but also the possible consequences for all mankind. In one way or another, whether he glosses it with a parable from the Scriptures, disguises it in obtuse diplomatic language or, as he chooses to be in the papal apartment, blunt and uncompromising, his overriding fear remains the same. Time may be running out for the world. He is convinced that it is presently on a collision course which could literally see rival systems destroy each other – unless a way can be found to stop them.

It is this concern, more than any other, which has affected the pope both mentally and physically.

Away from public scrutiny he is now more hunched. Agca's bullets not only shattered bone and tissue; they produced trauma whose residue remains. He has become more introspective and at times even morose. Whereas he used always to lead a discussion he now frequently prefers to listen; after a meeting he spends time alone taking his own counsel.

But, if anything, his workload has increased. Even the

Summary file before him this morning contains, as usual, a great deal to digest. It is deliberately designed to give the pope a taste of the current world situation and its problems. John Paul can flag anything which especially interests him. Then the Secretariat of State will send over position papers and experts to brief him further. There are some members of the Curia who see drawbacks in this decision-making system: they fear that from the file the pope could get an initially skewed view of a situation or problem; again, those who make submissions may be tempted to offer John Paul the sort of presentations they think he wants to see, leaving out important data which they believe he may not be particularly concerned about.

Poggi's report, written in the nuncio's sloping hand, is at the top of the file. [4] The pope flags it for further discussion with Casaroli. He makes a note on a scratch pad that he also wants to see Poggi. Later the pad will be collected by one of the papal secretaries, its notes typed-up into memos which are swiftly circulated. The papacy has become marked by a paper trail of these crisply worded commands.

While Poggi continues to have ready access to the pope, John Paul keeps at arm's length some of his other Italian advisers. Poles and eastern Europeans he has brought into the Vatican in increasing numbers are a different matter: the more senior of them come and go from the papal apartment virtually as they please, often seeing the pontiff without an appointment. But this deliberate distancing of himself from many in the still predominantly Italian Curia means the pope often misses the important early arguments for either side of a case because he is not privy to policy discussions at the lower levels; they are either muffled or glossed over without him even being aware of differences. Most of his civil servants have come to accept this system. Those who do not accept it find themselves moved out of the papal decision-making arena. [5]

Beneath Poggi's memorandum is the latest appraisal from the Polish Desk on an issue always uppermost in John

Paul's mind: a second triumphant pilgrimage home. The Polish regime is developing increasing confidence. Warsaw may soon be willing to accept such a visit. But the Polish Desk summary contains news that Walesa is once more being harassed. He fears he may be arrested again, just two months after John Paul completed a momentous personal initiative to have the trade unionist freed. The pope scribbles another note on his scratch pad. He wants Josef Glemp, Archbishop of Warsaw, to take soundings – and to report personally on what is happening to Lech Walesa.

While fully recognizing the humanitarian aspect behind the intervention, the pope's relationship with Walesa worries some of his civil servants.[6] Several clerics who have already displayed an ability to take a long view believe the pope is making a serious mistake by continuing to associate himself so forcefully with a man who is anathema to the Polish authorities, and will remain so. For John Paul to lend his authority so publicly in support of Walesa, runs the argument, only militates against what the pope so badly wants – the freedom for Polish workers he spelled out in his encyclical, *Laborem Exercens*. The civil servants fear Walesa is the pope's blind spot, one which was there from the outset of their unusual relationship.

It began with two letters.[7] On 5 July 1979 Walesa wrote to the pope asking whether he approved of the name 'Solidarity' for what Walesa wanted to be the first Polish trade union with real bite and power. He had selected 'Solidarity' from John Paul's encyclical *Redemptor Hominis*, whose message includes an appeal for 'acting together'. The significance was not lost on the pope.

Ten days later he sent a handwritten reply to Walesa, addressing him as 'my dear brother in Christ', in which he expressed his full approval for the use of the word Solidarity for the fledgling trade union that would soon prove such a powerful challenge to the Polish regime. This was the most direct indication so far that John Paul was ready to involve the papacy in the internal secular affairs of a nation.

49

He did not stop with the letter. Throughout the remainder of 1979, despite a gruelling schedule, the pope found the time to telephone frequently from the papal apartment to Walesa's home in Gdansk, a Polish industrial city, to learn of the progress of Solidarity. The conversations were brief and innocuous; the pope saw them as the sort a parish priest might make to a distant parishioner. But their object was obvious. John Paul wanted Walesa to know he had a very powerful friend looking over his shoulder from Rome. Equally, the pope wished to serve notice on the Polish authorities that he was decidedly in favour of Solidarity being created.

As a matter of routine the calls between pontiff and trade unionist were recorded by the Polish security police. They passed on details to the KGB. Moscow became aware of John Paul's attitude.

In February 1980, using the Castro regime as an intermediary to inform the papal pro-nuncio in Havana of his feelings, President Brezhnev warned the pope that his behaviour could lead to serious consequences.

John Paul continued to make telephone calls to Walesa. They had become, he told his secretary, Dziwisz, during the papal visit to France in the spring, almost an article of faith. To those around him the pope spoke glowingly of Walesa lighting a beacon for workers' freedoms not only in Poland but eventually throughout the Soviet bloc.[8]

Just as he had ignored the warning from Moscow, so John Paul chose largely to reject the restraint urged by those near him. Later Casaroli suggested the pope should at least limit the calls to Walesa. The trade unionist was becoming bolder in his challenge to the Polish regime; in Casaroli's estimation Walesa's increasing daring was in direct proportion to the number of papal telephone contacts made.

Reluctantly John Paul agreed to write to Walesa and ask him to moderate his public statements. But he insisted his letter should also confirm that papal support would continue. Poggi couriered the letter to Poland. On 11 June he returned to Rome with Walesa's reply: the trade unionist would try and be more temperate in his statements, but there was no way he would, or could, stop the momentum of what was happening.

Walesa's reaction made the matter of prime concern to the pope's most senior advisers. Casaroli and his *sostituto* (deputy), Eduardo Somalo Martinez, a gifted Spaniard, had regular consultations. The Secretariat's staff were alerted that Poland was on the brink of events which could engulf the Church in its biggest crisis since World War II.

Another approach was made to the pope asking that he urge Walesa, even at this late stage, to swerve from the path which increasingly looked like it would lead to bloody confrontation. John Paul resisted. He argued, like Walesa, that the outcome of events in Poland would justify his position.

At a fateful meeting in the pope's study later that June of 1980, there was a lengthy discussion over the question of a Soviet response to Walesa and the pope's determination to see Solidarity born. Not for the first time John Paul played to good effect his CIA card: the agency's analysts believed that for all its rumbling, the Soviet Union would not go so far as to invade Poland. Nothing should therefore be done by the Vatican to halt what was happening.

The pope visited Brazil. There, at the end of his twelve-day tour, a triumph of stamina, he received news, again from the CIA, that they had urgently revised their position in the light of Walesa's just-announced call for a national strike unless he got what he wanted – full status for Solidarity. CIA agents in Eastern Europe had learned the proposed strike was too great a challenge for Moscow to ignore: either the Polish Army would crush Solidarity on behalf of the Kremlin or the Red Army would. The spectre of war once more engulfing his country faced John Paul.

A final plea by Casaroli was made. The pope should ask Walesa to call off the proposed strike.

Instead, John Paul chose another and even more dramatic

course. On 4 August 1980, he wrote probably the most agonizing letter any pontiff has ever written. It was addressed to Brezhnev. On a single handwritten page of stationery bearing his coat of arms, the pope first expressed his concern over the possibility of Soviet action in Poland. He then added a final unprecedented paragraph: if the Russians invaded, the pope would give up the Throne of St Peter and return to lead a resistance movement in Poland.

John Paul wrote two identical letters. One would remain locked in a drawer of his desk in the papal study. The other was delivered to Brezhnev.[9]

The pope continues to believe his calculated gamble paid off. Russia did not invade Poland.

Nor will he take into account – while accepting it is likely – that as a result of writing the letter he became a target for the KGB, and probably remains one.[10]

And, in spite of continuous pressure from the Secretariat of State, he will not relinquish his support for Walesa.

During the long painful months of recovery after the attempt on his life, the pope had been sustained by the undoubted dignity Walesa displayed under onerous conditions. When the Polish regime finally banned Solidarity they arrested Walesa and subjected him to all kinds of psychological pressures which often stopped little short of torture. Yet Walesa never flinched. Through his brief permitted contacts with the Polish Church hierarchy in 1982, the trade unionist repeatedly sent messages of support and good wishes for John Paul's recovery; in one, Walesa explained that in captivity he was sustained by reciting from memory whole passages of *Laborem Exercens*. He promised the pope he would never give up the fight and he relished the day that John Paul would be strong enough once more to lend his voice of encouragement.

When he did return to the Vatican the pope made it a priority to have Walesa released. Bypassing, except for the most essential matters, his Secretariat of State the pope began another of his individual, secret and quite extraordinary initiatives to have Walesa freed. Working through Glemp, John Paul began a dialogue with the new Polish regime. He offered nothing but reason backed by the moral authority of his office; there could be no question of any compromise in his commitment to improving conditions for the Church under Communism. The Polish regime, understandably bemused by what was happening, referred the matter to Moscow: it was, after all, not every day that a pope intervened on behalf of an individual. The Kremlin was preoccupied with a more immediate drama. Brezhnev was dying and Yuri Andropov had virtually taken control. In a bitter twist of fate, John Paul found himself to all intents and purposes dealing with the man who as head of the KGB may have approved of his death.

Swallowing his deep distaste for what he must do – maintain civil contact with Andropov – the pope had continued to work towards having Walesa freed and martial law lifted in Poland. At times he was close to despair. Then, the very day Andropov formally took office, came news from Warsaw that Walesa would be released.

John Paul reportedly wept openly when Glemp telephoned to confirm it was true.

The pope makes a third note on the scratch pad. He asks Casaroli to explore the possibility of finding a lay position in the Church for Walesa, one where he could receive a red-covered Holy See passport, a document which would effectively place him beyond the harassment of the Polish authorities.

The request is another indication that he regards his involvement with Solidarity and Walesa as consistent with the radically new direction he is taking papal diplomacy. Like his immediate predecessors, he knows he is confronted by extremely sensitive national-religious problems in an atheist-ruled Eastern Europe.[11] But he has come to the conclusion that where they had felt it was possible to separate religious questions from political issues, it would be wrong for him to do so. The two are interlocked. They needed tackling in tandem. To achieve this the pope has begun a 'true dialogue', based on 'the real application of religious liberty which is guaranteed in every eastern European constitution yet invariably remains restricted in practice'.[12]

Not only is he going to continue to speak out for freedom of religious worship but he will pursue a more internationally active and individual style of papacy than ever before.

Poland will remain the test bed for his policies.[13] There is no alternative but to combine diplomatic initiatives and the papacy's moral-religious mission; they will remain inseparable. If this strategy proves successful in Poland it might work elsewhere within the Soviet bloc. That is why the prospect of returning home is such a heady one for John Paul.

For the moment though, there is nothing he can do. He needs more of what he thrives on – information: facts, opinions, indications, even a whiff of something which comes close to street rumour. Only after he has weighed it all will he know whether it really is feasible for him to go home and, if so, how he should act when he gets there.[14]

THE BULGARIAN EMBASSY, ROME
Monday
Noon

First Secretary Vassil Dimitrov feels as though he is about to take a long dive, the way he always does when he has to convey more bad news to the Foreign Ministry in Sofia. His watery brown eyes are bloodshot and heavy-lidded from lack of sleep.[15] Of late he has hardly seen his bed in the annexe across the courtyard and whenever he tries to doze in his office he seems to be disturbed by the telephone or called to the telex to answer yet more questions from the ministry.

Closer, Dimitrov can sense the endless speculation and hostility just beyond the high walls of the Bulgarian Embassy high up on the Via Monti Parioli in a district of Rome which contains the homes of many of the city's *nouveaux riches* and the ageing *nouveaux pauvres* as well as the embassies and residences of foreign diplomats and their families. It is a green pleasant haven around which Dimitrov formerly liked to stroll and drop in on colleagues at the nearby Polish and Yugoslav Embassies. But all that has stopped. The embassy's security officer, seconded from DS, Bulgaria's equivalent of the KGB, has ordered staff not to make trips outside unless they are absolutely necessary.

The DS man wants to avoid exacerbating an already tense situation: he does not wish any of the diplomats he is responsible for to be confronted by those who come and peer at the complex; some of the younger Italians – Dimitrov calls them 'hotheads on hot motor bikes' – frequently shout insults such as 'You tried to kill the pope', and 'This is the start of the *Pista Bulgara*'.

Since this began diplomats in other Soviet bloc embassies have found it prudent to give the Bulgarian complex a wide berth, helping to increase the tensions and apprehension inside.

Equally, Dimitrov can sense a change of atmosphere in Sofia. This disturbs him most of all. More than any other Bulgarian official in Rome, he has been the most closely associated with the whole wretched business. It is his advice his superiors in Sofia had sought – and which he gladly gave. They still call him. But there is a change of mood, and Dimitrov is sufficiently sensitive to grasp the meaning behind the nuances: nobody is happy with the way things have developed.

At first there had been bluff confidence that Bulgaria could ride out the storm; that the Bulgarian Connection was just another of those tiresome tales cooked up by the Italian authorities to mask their own incompetence in nailing down the truth about the plot to kill the pope. Surely no one would doubt Bulgaria's claim the assassination attempt was solely the work of Moslem fanatics, not one of whom had ever so much as set foot inside Bulgaria? Dimitrov still claims this is the true story – and will continue to expound it to anyone who will listen.

Almost nobody does. Perhaps, he has started to muse, he should write-off the entire shambles as yet another example of how the western press operates: 'without care for the truth'. It would be a relief to do that – to bring to an end the unremitting pressures of the past weeks.

Dimitrov can now only dimly recall how well it all started. He had positively relished preparing his embassy's first news releases on the matter. His rebuttal on behalf of Bulgaria was filled with the phrases he likes to air: this time it was the Italians who had been duped into becoming 'lackeys of imperialism'; the accusations were 'a serious political provocation against Bulgaria, the Soviet Union and all Socialist states'; the whole potage was 'the handiwork of western intelligence agencies'. Dimitrov thinks it 'typical' that the Italian press and the Rome-based correspondents of foreign media pay scant heed to his rhetoric.

He now recognizes this attitude should have alerted him to warn-off Sofia from their plan to scotch the entire Bulgarian Connection in one grand gesture. The idea had been hatched following the arrest of Sergei Antonov, the manager of Balkanair's office in Rome, and the naming of other Bulgarians as being co-conspirators with Agca in the plot to kill the pope.

Dimitrov had telexed to Sofia the story from *Newsweek*[16] as a prime example of 'western media calumny'.

The report galvanized the Foreign Ministry to go ahead with its plan. Bulgarian Embassies were instructed to invite journalists to Sofia to attend a press conference in late December.

Looking back on the event, which had occurred less than three weeks ago – though to an exhausted Dimitrov it now seemed light years away – the gangling First Secretary realizes he should have been further alerted by the few positive responses he received from Rome's press corps to his invitation. Many reporters flatly declined to make the trip, claiming the evidence already in their possession was too strong for Bulgaria to refute.

In the end 270 journalists from around the world had been found who were willing to cram into the Moskva Park Hotel in Sofia.

For the past week Dimitrov has been collating their accounts. The coverage stunned him. Hoped-for exoneration has turned into a crushing failure which ranges from the mockery of *Newsweek* – their account of the press conference is headlined, 'Anyone Here Know Mr Agca?'[17] – to the censorious tone of Britain's *Economist:* 'enough has surfaced to make the idea that the attempted murder of the pope 19 months ago was motivated by the Soviet government at least a working hypothesis'.[18]

That report finally brought home to Dimitrov the full magnitude of the disaster in which he had participated. It was bad enough to see Bulgaria ridiculed in the eyes of the world; worse was that the Russians were bound to react in their own particular way to being publicly dragged deeper into the papal plot. There was a Soviet procedure in such situations that Dimitrov well understood. Initially an angry denial by Tass with perhaps a letter of protest delivered from the Kremlin to certain western ambassadors. There, outwardly, the matter would end, regarded as another hiccup in the endless cut and thrust of modern diplomacy. But behind the scenes repercussions would continue.

The Soviet Foreign Ministry's direct lines to its counterpart in Sofia were doubtless busy with questions. Who had thought up the press conference? What were the names of the Bulgarian diplomats who helped in its preparation? What precautions, if any, had been taken to ensure the Soviet Union was not linked to the affair?

Such insistent questioning would go on until suitable scapegoats were identified. Then, for those hapless individuals, a career in the service of Socialism would, at the very minimum, be over. There might be an even harsher fate, one which diplomats like Dimitrov do not like to contemplate. If the Russians so wished he could be plucked from the comfort and freedom of Rome to a secret labour camp in the hinterland of Sofia. It had happened to others.[19]

The prospect is enough to make Dimitrov's eyes more watery. Knowing there is little he can do to influence his future, he continues to snip the press reports. The growing stack of clips on his desk has already convinced him the Bulgarian Connection is not going to go away.

SECRETARIAT OF STATE: VATICAN CITY
Same Day: Late Afternoon

Soutane swishing gently, the unrelieved blackness of the cloth only a shade darker than his skin, Monsignor Emery Kabongo steps out of the elevator which has brought him down from the papal apartment to the third floor of the Apostolic Palace.[20] The entire area is the overcrowded, artificially lit and inadequately ventilated headquarters of the papal diplomatic corps – the only foreign service in the world whose members regularly pray either to God or the Virgin Mary (Secretariat wags say John Paul gives them the choice) to help solve many of the world's more serious difficulties.[21]

Kabongo's presence signifies that the Bulgarian Connection has reached the status of Poland and Soviet intentions in Central Europe: the pope wishes to be informed immediately of any new *Pista Bulgara* development. Kabongo is here to collect the day's news on the Bulgarian Connection. It is not strictly part of his duties as the junior of the two papal secretaries: there are ample messengers who could do this.

But Kabongo relishes the chance to visit the third floor and sample the daily trawl of information. The mass of highly varied reporting is continuously processed: routed to the right department, sifted and analysed, moved from in-trays to out-trays, interpreted at each stage, edited, notated, initialled, recommended for action and referred back up the line.

Less than a year ago Kabongo himself was one of the sources for information flowing into the Secretariat round the clock: in terms of volume it receives almost as much paperwork as Britain's Foreign Office, the US State Department or other major foreign ministries; it is a measure of the Holy See's ever expanding world-wide diplomatic interests.

For four years Kabongo had contributed with regular reports he prepared in the nunciature, the papal embassy, in Seoul in South Korea.[22] There he gained valuable insights into the problems of the Third World, and how unworkable were many of the solutions offered by the West; he also learned first-hand how exploitative Communism could be. His suggestions helped promote ambitious Church goals for South Korea. From the other side of the world Kabongo had sent reasoned pleas that South Korea was no place for 'religious pacifism', but a place 'where the power of Jesus Christ should be known fully and totally'. Such highly motivated language was not lost on the priest-diplomats in the Secretariat.

Kabongo was tagged as a rising star. He was switched to another important Holy See posting, the nunciature in Brasilia. For the next three years he immersed himself in the problems of Brazil: overpowering wealth in the hands of a few and the masses close to starvation. He reported frankly on this unfair distribution. His views, when they reached the Secretariat, had been deemed sufficiently important to be included in the pope's brief for his visit to Brazil.

When John Paul visited that country Kabongo played a part – one he will not discuss – in helping the pope confirm what the CIA was saying: events in Poland were on the verge of boiling over.

The pontiff was so impressed by Kabongo he resolved to

make another staff change. He had already moved many in the Vatican, banishing some to distant parishes, bringing others closer to him; only Pius XI had scoured the Curia more thoroughly. This time he decided to promote John Magee to Master of Ceremonies from the position of English-language papal personal secretary: it was an open secret Magee and Dziwisz did not always get along.[23] Magee's elevation created an opening which was filled by Kabongo.

Now, more than ten months later, the 41-year-old secretary continues to attract comment in the gossipy Apostolic Palace because he is the first black ever appointed to the post. With his glistening moon of a face, crinkly black hair, almond-shaped eyes which for all their brightness require strong reading-glasses, set in solid gold frames; in the way he talks and walks; in his gentleness and unfailing courtesy: in these and other ways Kabongo evokes the rain forests of his beloved Zaire.

But people have come to realize they should never underestimate or trifle with Kabongo. His intellect is formidable; he graduated from the Pontifical Ecclesiastical Academy for Vatican diplomats with notably high marks. He speaks not only the major Zaire dialects, including the tongue-twisting Swahili, but is also fluent in several European languages. He is an astute professional, a tough bargainer behind his good manners.

His is the voice of liberalization in this papacy. He is an authentic New African: articulate, 'politically aware', not overly impressed by much of what he sees from his privileged vantage point.[24] Position and power by themselves do not impress him – as he has made clear to more than one cardinal and foreign diplomat who have tried to best him. Then a rock hardness sets in; his voice becomes as flinty as a veldt stone. People have learned it is not wise to arouse him to this point.[25]

He openly adores the pope; in a lesser man this would be maudlin sentiment. For Kabongo it is perfectly appro-

60

priate: his deep affection does not seem out of place with the athlete's stride which propels him from one office to another in the Secretariat as he drops in to catch up with the network – the generic term of the nuncios, pro-nuncios and apostolic delegates who report weekly, daily and, in a crisis, hourly by coded telegram or telex or by telephone, the calls sometimes in Latin to confuse phone-tappers.[26]

Today the network is fully extended reporting reaction to the pope's latest message that nuclear disarmament cannot be unilateral.[27] Equally, Armageddon, he implies is already on the launch pad.[28] Kabongo has 'a powerful feeling of big trouble if the world does not listen'.[29]

His first stop is at the Africa Desk, whose responsibilities extend from the Mediterranean to the Cape of Good Hope.[30]

From the nunciature in Pretoria, Archbishop Edward Cassidy has sent the South African government's response. Cassidy has a brief to establish how entrenched South African thinking is on an important issue: that the Reagan administration in Washington would not allow South Africa to go the way of Rhodesia; that the United States could not permit white domination to end in southern Africa because it might jeopardize the Cape sea routes Washington needs as part of the United States' own global strategy for survival.

For months Cassidy has been sending coded reports – impregnable enough he hopes to resist even the most sophisticated South African decoders – on the growing feeling in Pretoria's inner government circles that in the final analysis the United States would come to the defence of South Africa. Cassidy believes the pope's words have strengthened this conviction.

From the banana-tree-shaded nunciature in Luanda has come a very different response. During eight tumultuous years, the apostolic delegate to Angola has seen the revolution come, watched Portugal's old order finally swept away and the new revolutionary leaders set up open-house for their Soviet masters. The papal envoy, who speaks several bush dialects, knows his telephone – Luanda 30532 – is tapped; he can hear the clicks of recording apparatus switching on when he makes calls. He sends his reports to the Vatican by diplomatic pouch, sealing each bag with wax sent from the Secretariat. He hopes even the Angolans would not be so crude as to tamper with diplomatic mail. In recent months his reports have contained details of the deepening Soviet penetration into southern Africa.

He has also been given a special task by the Africa Desk: to try and discover whether the Russians are attempting to push Angola's Marxist regime into a conventional war against South Africa, and how deep are the fears in Luanda's revolutionary circles that South Africa would retaliate with the weapon which the Secretariat now knows it possesses, a nuclear bomb. That particular piece of disturbing news had come into the Vatican from the CIA, who were passing it on from Mossad Letafkidim Meyouchadim, Israel's espionage service, whose own connections with South African intelligence are the closest. The question which concerns the Secretariat's senior officials is this: do Angola's rulers include in their calculations the ultimate possibility of a nuclear response when they plot how far they will carry revolution into South Africa? If they do not they are more naïve than had been imagined; if they do, they are more dangerous than is already feared.

From Accra in Ghana; from Nairobi in Kenya; from Tananarive in Madagascar; from Maputo in Mozambique; from Lagos in Nigeria; from Dar-es-Salaam in Tanzania; from Kampala in Uganda; from Kinshasa-Gombe in Zaire; from Lusaka in Zambia; from Harare in Zimbabwe: from all these places papal diplomats have reported how the local administrations have regarded John Paul's plea for peace.

Already a discernible point of view is emerging. Across the African continent there is both a general welcome for the pope's appeal and the fear it may already be too late. More than one nuncio has conveyed the opinion of the government to which he is accredited that their views –

although vocalized in the United Nations – carry too little weight in the Pentagon and the Kremlin.

The responses will be ceaselessly analysed before being included in the pope's daily brief. A year ago Africa Desk summaries were relatively rare, perhaps no more than one or two a week. Since Kabongo's arrival they have increased substantially. It is a further sign of the influence he has.

Another is the warm welcome he always gets from the desk responsible for collating the South American communications.

The Brazilian government has called the pope's message a statesmanlike contribution to easing global tension. From further down the sub-continent, the nuncio to Argentina has sent an evaluation which clearly reflects his standing brief – to warn of any Soviet moves to exploit the persisting bitterness in Argentina over its humiliation by Britain in the short-lived Falklands War.

The pope's bleak warning that the entire world could be heading towards the brink of nuclear confrontation has stirred a strong emotional chord in the Argentinian psyche. Commentators who previously criticized John Paul for going ahead in 1982 with his visit to Britain at the height of the conflict are now full of praise for the pope's words. In the opinion of the nuncio any attempt by the Soviet Union to deepen the wounds between Britain and Argentina could back-fire; there is a mood in the country of pacifism, and the first genuine stirrings in Buenos Aires' business community of a wish to re-establish normal relations with their old trading partners in London.

Kabongo knows the pope will be encouraged to hear this. The Falklands War had profoundly troubled John Paul – far more than the protagonists realized. He had failed in his public and private peace appeals to Prime Minister Margaret Thatcher and the Argentinian dictatorship.[31] He had weighed most carefully the advice of Cardinal Hume in London and Cardinal Aramburu in Buenos Aires.[32] Eventually the pope had been left in no doubt that neither side was prepared to back away without a fight. He had been as much distressed by Argentina's initial illegal invasion as by Mrs Thatcher's exultation in victory. Equally, John Paul is convinced that ultimately there must be renewed negotiations which will probably lead to the islands becoming more closely associated with – if not part of – Argentina. The news from Buenos Aires can, Kabongo hopes, only bring closer that day.[33]

Elsewhere in this sprawl of offices, registries, libraries and communication rooms, yet other priests are assembling responses for the pope.

From Vienna has come the first hint of a Soviet response. The nuncio there reports that Moscow is furious, though nothing has been said officially. The Kremlin views the pope's words as no more than support for the hard-line attitude emanating from Washington. The nuncio is not surprised. A few days ago he had alerted the Secretariat to a bitter attack in a Communist magazine accusing the pontiff of being 'subversive', 'anti-Socialist', 'reactionary' and 'aiding Solidarity to subvert the Polish government'.

The papal diplomat in the Austrian capital is usually one of the first to hear of such attacks. In a city of intrigues, his residence is one of the acknowledged centres of real information. Baroque furniture, fine wines and the best of Viennese cooking provide a pleasing background for his guests to brief him. As well as fellow diplomats those around his dining table are often the men and women of secret intelligence services; those who run the spies and, sometimes, spy themselves. As a result of the papal envoy's connections, the Holy See is often more quickly aware of what is happening in Warsaw, Moscow and elsewhere in the Soviet bloc than are the superpowers. Increasingly Casaroli uses his man in Vienna to check on CIA estimations. In recent months they have tallied more than ever before, presenting a common view of a Kremlin growing increasingly more paranoid about the West.

Part of the reason rests with the ever accumulating and

very public evidence being gathered by the priest Kabongo has come to see. The man is an over-worked monsignor in the Secretariat's Extraordinary Affairs Section – responsible for implementing the foreign policy of the Holy See. He has been given the extra task of monitoring every development on the *Pista Bulgara*. He is in touch with Martella, CIA Rome and other foreign intelligence agencies. He has become, in effect, a papal spy. And just as the nervous Bulgarian, Dimitrov, in his embassy on the far side of the Tiber is mournfully snipping press reports, so the monsignor is collating similar clippings sent in by the network.

From Havana, Cuba the pro-nuncio has sent a fresh batch of articles claiming that Agca, far from being a KGB assassin, was actually a CIA-trained hitman and the entire papal plot is really a diabolical scheme by the United States to discredit Russia. The stories, as usual, are long on hyperbole and short on fact.

But Kabongo knows that Cibin is now not the only person in the Vatican who is beginning to ask questions about the exact role of the CIA before and after John Paul was shot. Copies of the Cuban articles will eventually find their way to the in-trays of Casaroli, Poggi and several other senior priests.

The Havana diplomat believes the articles to be another Soviet-inspired attempt to escalate Cuba US tension. It happens all the time. But he cannot be certain whether this is simply a further round of propaganda-mongering or whether, in fact, it is something more sinister – the earliest of early warnings that the Russians are preparing to move on other fronts, perhaps foment additional trouble in El Salvador or Nicaragua or some other flash-point in Central America. Cuba, in Secretariat parlance, is 'the distractor', a headline-catcher which will allow Russia to strike elsewhere while attention is focused on the antics of the Castro regime. That is why Cuba is a key listening post. Outlandish though the newspaper reports from Havana are, they will on that basis be carefully studied.

From Paris, from one of the most impressive addresses of any nunciature, Avenue du Président Wilson, the fastidious papal nuncio, Archbishop Angelo Felici, has sent not newspaper clips but a transcript of a French radio broadcast. It contains the highly intriguing report that French Intelligence sources, who, according to the transcript have 'close connections of an unspoken kind' with the KGB (not so fanciful as it seems since intelligence agencies often transcend national borders in their contacts), are beginning to say that the manner in which Yuri Andropov is being openly linked with the attempt on John Paul's life is a deliberate move to destabilize the new Soviet leader's position in the Politburo – from *within* the Politburo. The story runs that Andropov is seen as a growing embarrassment for having approved the attempt in the first place: he had not thought it through; his action has come to remind his colleagues of the bad old days of Stalin. Their hope is to drive him from office, and they want the help of world opinion to do it. So claims this transcript.[34]

The communication from Paris is careful to point out this is all speculation. But experts in the Secretariat believe there may possibly be a grain of truth in the allegations.

West German interest in the aftermath of the assassination runs high twenty months later – at least on the evidence of the latest bundle of articles sent by Nuncio Guido del Mestri in Bonn. He has been one of the first foreign diplomats to establish close ties with Chancellor Helmut Kohl's new government. The archbishop uses the connection to assist him to judge some of the more colourful German reporting. Just as his contacts allow him to comment authoritatively on the role of the Green Party in the Federal Republic, the growing anti-nuclear movement and the subtleties of German-Soviet relations in these areas, so Mestri is able to dismiss the articles he has sent as mostly sensational nonsense.

But the pope, Kabongo reminds himself, wants to see everything published about the attempt on his life. Though

66

Kabongo would never dream of uttering such a disloyalty, there are people in the Secretariat who believe that, as with Lech Walesa and Poland, John Paul is becoming obsessed with Agca, Andropov and the *Pista Bulgara*.[35]

ASCOLI PICENO PRISON, EAST OF ROME
Same Day: Night

Even as Italian gaols go, this maximum security prison is a place to be feared.[36] Its inmates are among the most dangerous in all Italy, the guards the toughest. The daily routine is harsh, the food poor: conditions are designed to punish not to rehabilitate.

Tonight there are undoubtedly prisoners here who believe it would be infinitely preferable to run the risk of being shot by the guards while trying to escape than to spend another minute in Ascoli Piceno.

It is equally certain the solitary inmate in cell 47 will make no attempt to leave.[37] He knows that even if he could break through the heavy-gauge steel door of his cell or the reinforced concrete walls and somehow get past the electrically locked cell-block gates, he would almost certainly never survive long beyond the prison perimeter. Out there, on the road to Rome, along which two thousand years ago the legions of Caesar had marched, he would assuredly be killed by any one of all those who trained or financed him: the KGB, the Bulgarian Secret Service, the Libyans, the PLO. At one stage or another each helped Agca along his route to St Peter's Square in May 1981 to murder the Pope. Agca believes now that because he failed it has made him, in their eyes, worthless, and, because he has betrayed them, a marked man for the rest of his life.

This fear made him come to terms with Ascoli Piceno. In a perverse way he actually likes prison life. He relishes the knowledge that he is the most notorious criminal incarcerated here, the only inmate constantly written about. Whenever he leaves to see Martella, Agca knows there will be a mob of reporters waiting outside the Palace of Justice to glimpse him as his bullet-proof truck roars up. He is a celebrity: the psychiatrist who sees Agca every weekday has told him so. It was another boost to Agca's ego, just as the doctor intended.

Far from missing contact with other inmates, Agca enjoys his special solitary status. His cell, twelve by ten, is in a prime position with easy access to the prison yard. Unlike other prisoners who are herded into the yard in groups, Agca exercises alone, jogging for an hour every morning and evening around the yard under the eyes of an escort who never leaves his side whenever he steps from his cell. There is a constant fear that during one of his walks through the prison corridors, a fellow convict will try and kill him – paid to do so by one of the organizations which Agca has fingered. Every inmate and cell is regularly searched at Ascoli Piceno for concealed weapons. This knowledge further boosts Agca's self-importance.

Physically he is fitter than he has ever been. As well as jogging he exercises two hours daily in his cell. His slender frame has become straighter and the muscles in his arms and legs firm. When he is not doing press-ups he shadow boxes, feinting and lunging at imaginary opponents, sometimes spitting out their names in the thick Patois of Malatya province he has not lost.

Other times he sits for hours listening to the radio or watching television; both are on a table in a corner of his cell. In another is an old bureau bookcase with a wooden writing flap. In the evenings, after eating, Agca sits on a chair and writes. Writing is something the psychiatrist has encouraged: he has told Agca to record his every impression of the day, his thoughts on any visitors; to put on paper anything which comes into his head. As well as keeping this diary, Agca has written scores of letters to his mother, the widow Muzzeyene, to his younger brother, Adnan, and his sister, Fatma. They are all at home in Yesiltepe, 465 miles due east of Ankara.

Agca carefully seals the letters and hands them to a prison officer who unfailingly assures him they will be in the next mail to Turkey.

The letters first go to Martella's office. The magistrate often has a number of them on his desk. Attached to each is a psychiatrist's report evaluating Agca's mood at the time of writing.

The lack of response from his family to his letters is neatly explained. Agca has been told their letters have no doubt been intercepted by the Turkish authorities.[38] He accepts this.

The bureau shelves contain a selection of books. There is a copy of the Koran, Italian and German language primers, a handful of paperbacks with lurid covers. From these Agca learned how to curse in Italian. When he is annoyed he uses his favourite word, '*vaffanculo*'. It amuses the guards.

Modest though the collection of books is, Agca has been told by the psychiatrist it further sets him above the other inmates: not a book is allowed in any other cell.

There are some things Agca does not like about his conditions. There is the unironed burlap-like cover on the cot and the bedding is rough enough to chafe his skin. He refused to wear the prison grey underwear and socks because they have been used before by other inmates. Above all he dislikes the brown soap which smells of the same carbolic that is in the bottom of the night soil bucket at the foot of his cot. He has been promised by Martella that later there could be improvements. This has been left deliberately vague at the suggestion of the psychiatrist.

Apart from the doctor's daily call and intermittent visits from other psychiatrists, Agca's days are further occupied by the arrival of intelligence officers, both Italian and foreign. For an entire year they did not come to question him; it was that period when, after his trial, Agca was left to rot in a cell on the other side of this prison. With the appointment of Martella the officers had suddenly returned.

He finds them, he has confided to his diary, different from Martella and the doctors. They are not so warm or sympathetic. But they are attentive, writing down his every response or, in the case of the American, recording him on a cassette.[39]

Agca does not know their names, nor do they say where they are from. This, too, is deliberate.

At first Agca had been incurious about his visitors. He answered their questions with an exaggerated show of indifference. A psychiatrist had adjusted Agca's daily drug dosage. He became more lively in his responses. He began to ask questions. Was the American from the CIA? Was another man from the BND or BKA? A third from his own country's MIT? Was a fourth from the agency he most fears, Israel's MOSSAD?

Agca well remembers the time immediately after his capture in St Peter's Square when two MOSSAD officers had arrived in his cell in Rome police headquarters. They had flown in from Tel Aviv. In their briefcases were detailed dossiers on his life and associates which had been carefully put together by the Israeli Legation in Ankara. The MOSSAD men spoke fluent Turkish. They told him who they were and that if he did not co-operate they would make him. There was such menace in their manner Agca believed they might even kill him. For three days, over five long separate interviews, he told them all he knew about the Bulgarian Connection and the role of the KGB. He has often wondered since why it took so long for the information he furnished to become public.

He has asked his recent visitors, but they ignore his questions and continue to press their own.

After an intelligence officer has finished and left the cell, a psychiatrist returns to assess Agca's mood. Had he been happy with the visit? Did the questions bother him? Why? Had he told the truth? Was he certain? To each answer the doctor listens sympathetically. Later the information is passed to Martella.

But still the days drag and the nights more so. They would be even lonelier but for Agca's hate list – the lengthy litany of persons and places he loathes.

He first composed and began to recite aloud the list in those teenage years when his mind was being formed – and disturbed – by the hostile atmosphere of Yesiltepe, the shockingly impoverished hamlet on the route the Crusaders travelled to and from the Holy Land. Here Agca grew up in debilitating summer heat and winter winds so bitingly cold they frequently turned his lips blue. When he was old enough he became a willing recruit to the village way of life: smuggling and drug peddling.[40] He saw that killing was a natural way to settle differences. It all helped to blunt him, to make Agca what he now is: a young man who has experienced and enjoyed more evil than most; a street-wise professional killer who is one of the most infamous political assassins of the century.

On this, the 600th day of his life sentence, Agca cannot always be certain of all the twists and turns in the long trail which brought him from Yesiltepe to St Peter's Square. He has forgotten the dates he was in the Syrian training camp and the names of some of those he met there. He is hazy on almost everything which happened to him in Bulgaria. But what he terms 'my big moments' are vividly clear: there was the time he first met his KGB paymasters, the time they opened a bank account for him, the time a fee of three million German DM was promised for shooting the pope, the time he first handled the Browning pistol he used; these moments he does remember – just as he never forgets to recite his hate list each night, much as a child says his prayers before going to sleep.

Agca no longer feels what he has called 'my inner devils' rising within him when he recites the list. Powerful drugs to treat his melancholia and stimulate his appetite have also controlled the all-consuming rages which previously gripped

71

him. Pharmacologists, not intelligence agents, now influence his mind.

He has made some striking additions and deletions to his list.

President Reagan is now at the top – the very first name which Agca ritually consigns to his idea of hell. He hates Reagan so much that he repeats the president's name five separate times, chanting each time, 'I hate Reagan'.

Next he expresses a similar feeling for ketchup, Levi's, American news magazines and the products of Hollywood. Everything he has read, heard or seen on television about the United States he hates: the Empire State building, Dodge trucks, freeways, toll booths, Fifth Avenue, the Golden Gate Bridge, Chicago, Arlington Cemetery, the Goodyear dirigible: he needs a full five minutes to rid himself every night of all he hates about America.

NATO is next. He hates its bases and its strike potential. He sees NATO as 'an instrument of the devil', a phrase he picked up in Syria and one which has remained locked in his memory. He cannot explain the meaning of the words precisely to his psychiatrist. Nor has the analyst pushed for one. He thinks it important for Agca to retain some of his past images. They may help him to feel he is not being manipulated.

After NATO Agca has added a newcomer to the list: his long-dead father.

When he was in Yesiltepe, and in deference to his mother, Agca kept his father off the hate list, though his recall of him was of a bullying brute, terrorizing the family right up to the moment he was killed in a road accident. His father's inclusion dates from the time Martella began to establish his parental substitute role with Agca. The psychiatrist is pleased that things are working so well; in the doctor's view Agca is developing the essential psychological *introjection* whereby affection for his father is being transferred to Martella. Freud calls it Psychic Positioning.

When he has recited his father's name, Agca chants out

his hatred for Saudi Arabia. He despises the kingdom because of its close links to the United States. The psychiatrist thinks this is a typical reaction for Agca's type of derangement.

The Russian Czars, introduced on to the list in Yesiltepe, remain – hated for their imperialism.

South Africa has been moved up to precede the Queen of England. Elizabeth II is included because, to Agca, she typifies the ruling classes he abhors; the republic is castigated for its ties with Israel. So far the psychiatrist has let this pass, even though Martella is pressing for any deeper insights into Agca's feelings towards Israel plus his continuing desire to sustain the class war.

Next on the list is another intriguing new entry – 'Major Frank'. The addition has interested not only the psychiatrists and Martella but also the intelligence officers. Each in his own way has tried to induce Agca to explain why he now feels as he does about Major Frank.

This is the name Agca still uses when referring to Frank Terpil, the American who helped train him. It was Terpil who coached Agca in the skills of assassination, car bombing and urban mayhem of all kinds. The two men had sat together for hours watching news footage on the murder of President Kennedy in Dallas and similar successful attacks on politicians in Spain and other countries. Afterwards Terpil had further instructed Agca on the techniques required to carry out a killing in a crowded public forum such as St Peter's Square.

Agca once implicitly believed what he gleaned about Terpil's background: Major Frank was both a fugitive from the CIA and American justice; he had been convicted of running US arms into Libya, trying to murder Libya's opponents, recruiting former US military pilots to fly Libyan aircraft.

Agca now believes Terpil was still in the CIA when they met; that Major Frank was performing his most dangerous mission yet for the agency – acting as a deep penetration agent, pretending to work for Libya while in reality acting in the service of the United States.

It is enough to gain Major Frank his place on the hate list.

Agca has no proof for his belief that when Terpil helped to prepare him to shoot the pope he was still with the CIA (for years Terpil had been a sabotage specialist with the agency). But, as he has scribbled in his diary, what other explanation can there be for all the questions he has been asked about his relationship with Terpil by those who come to see him?

Martella has not mentioned Major Frank's name. This, too, has been deliberate. The psychiatrists have suggested Agca might enjoy the feeling of concealing something, much as a child enjoys hiding some piece of news from a parent.

On to the hate list has come the name Colonel Arpaslan Turkes. He is the founder of Turkey's Grey Wolves, once the country's most powerful terrorist group. Agca had sworn his eternal allegiance to Turkes, howling, wolf-like, his oath of loyalty. But after his arrest in May 1981 Turkes denied that Agca was ever a Grey Wolf.

So the hate list continues: name after name, places and things, each one called out in regular order. President Reagan, Heinz baked beans, the KGB, NATO and the Bulgarian secret service – a diverse and bewildering catalogue.

For years Agca reserved the climax of his list for the most vehement of his outcries, the hatred which consumed him like a malignancy, hatred so powerful it had made him weep copiously: his loathing for all religions except his own. He believed them part of a worldwide campaign to weaken Islam, and that the conspiracy was controlled from the Vatican, master-minded personally by the pope. Ever since he could remember he had wanted to kill a pontiff. First it had been Paul VI, then John Paul I. They had both cheated him by dying of natural causes before he had the opportunity to strike them down. But he had almost succeeded with their successor.

In St Peter's Square, on that evening nineteen months

previously, he had been consumed by hatred for the papacy, the Church, the Virgin Mary, even St Peter's Basilica.

Now, after his talks with Martella, they have been removed from the list.

Agca still believes the details of his hate list are a secret from everyone. This is why he feels able to chant the list aloud as he prepares for bed – but not so loud the prison guards can hear. In recent weeks he has started to talk to himself quite a lot. He barely notices he is doing so, just as the psychiatrists hoped. They have quietly encouraged Agca to express aloud his deepest inner feelings whenever he is alone, explaining this will help him to cope better with the bouts of loneliness he will inevitably feel from time to time. Though no one mentions it, a further twenty-six years must pass before Agca will be considered for parole.

Tonight, as on every other, Agca works his way through his list to the end. He is unaware every word he utters is picked up by a microphone wired into the ceiling light fitting. The microphone is linked to voice-activated recording apparatus specially installed in a nearby room.

Each morning the spool of magnetic tape is removed and transcribed by a secretary in the prison governor's office. Then a copy is sent to Martella.

VATICAN CITY
Wednesday
Mid-morning

When Cibin opens the envelope brought by a papal messenger and scans the single sheet of paper, he knows a rumour racing up and down the Vatican's corridors is true.

John Paul is once more off on his travels. The memo from the pope's Secretariat states he will shortly visit eight Central American countries.

The political problems involved in making a trip to one of

the most turbulent and unstable areas in the world are not of immediate interest to Cibin. Others will have to walk that minefield.

When he has digested the memo his first call is to a Rome number – 4674. It connects him to the United States Embassy to Italy at 119 Via Veneto. He asks for an extension and is put through to the CIA station chief.

Cibin, for all his mistrust of the agency, wants its help in preparing a near as possible foolproof plan to stop the pope from being murdered in Central America.

4
Roman Responses

The question lies between us across the lunch table: what
sort of pope *is* John Paul?

Father Lambert Greenan is in no hurry to answer. He is
not against directness when it comes to choosing a good
wine or expressing his appreciation of a menu; during the
years we have known him, the editor of the Vatican's
English-language weekly has always shown a proper respect
for his taste buds. But when judging the papacy he prefers
the oblique approach. What he hints at and what he leaves
unsaid are equally important: a Gaelic shrug can suggest
volumes. He uses the gesture a good deal when talking to
us.

We are in the back room of Rasella's and Romaul, the
capocameriere, has served us *prosciutto* followed by *abbac-
chio,* baby lamb, garnished with tiny Roman artichokes,
young enough to be completely edible. There has been a
fine Tuscany white wine with the ham and generous
pourings of a Capri chianti with the lamb.

We tell him we hope he will make sense of the latest
rumours about the pope which are floating around the
Vatican corridors that Greenan prowls with such skill to
help him distinguish fact from something else – pure
fantasy, wishful thinking or half-truth.

On a dozen different fronts inside the Vatican we had
heard the persistent assertion that the pope is becoming
more of a prophet than a traditional pontiff, that he is a
better preacher than administrator, a formidable mystic but
a poor pragmatist. We ask Greenan again: what sort of
pontiff will he be?

Greenan begins by arguing that even well-informed
Catholics often fail to see that the Church is in a permanent

process of development whereby the relationship between pope and magisterium is being constantly redefined. While it still holds true that John Paul likes to make all the major decisions and continues to state his principles with firmness and total conviction, the real question is not whether the pope is in charge. That's 'the sort of absurdity the pop magazines of the religious world pose'. Greenan genuinely dislikes them. But today is not to be one where he sets about their wilder excesses. He sticks to his theme.

John Paul, he continues, is increasingly fitting into a role. He is doing all he can to implement his beliefs while accepting that not everything he does will be judged correct and proper by everyone. His pontificate is running on a dynamic seldom seen in previous reigns. Many issues are not being settled by papal fiat or on the order of the Congregations. Rather, they are being allowed to ferment throughout the Church, finding their own natural solutions. Certainly John Paul is responsible for integrating the teachings of the Church, but he is not the only one shaping its policies.

Greenan insists that the pope will continue to take a hard line against theological and liturgical dissenters, 'but only as part of a dialectic exchange within the Church'.

During the meal the talk has been general. The Italian press are speculating that Antonov will be released in a few days, bringing the *Pista Bulgara* to a certain dead stop.[1] The Polish government has set up 2,500 'small trade unions' – whatever that means – to replace Solidarity.[2] Another Soviet spy has been expelled from Sweden. There is a nasty little scandal brewing at the Rome offices of FAO, the UN Food and Agriculture Organization, about manipulating figures to match the funds advanced by major development banks.[3]

Greenan holds a distinctive view on each item. He is a tall, slim, grey-haired, ascetic Irish Dominican priest, with spectacles that rest on a nose with furrows running from the nostrils to the corners of his mouth. When he comments

78

with particular forcefulness, the furrows twitch and deepen. Today the lines above his mouth positively quiver as he deals with the issues.

He is certain Antonov will remain in prison. Martella is no fool. Besides, Henry Kissinger had just raised the temperature with his assertion that all the known facts about the attempt on John Paul's life pointed to the KGB.[4] That's good enough to keep Antonov behind bars for some time. It's Greenan at his crispest. He shrugs off Poland's mini unions as 'cosmetic Communism'; he likes the phrase and rolls it out a couple more times in his Newry brogue. The expulsion of another Russian agent from Sweden brings forth Greenan's waspish humour: 'the fellah's tailor-made for FAO; that place can't keep anything secret'.

He knows we will pick up on the word 'secret'; it's his signal he is ready to move to the main purpose of this lunch: an opportunity for him to play a role he relishes and for which he is well fitted.

He believes the pope will increasingly give the Church a more forceful voice in the world. The reformist spirit of Vatican II is flourishing, but had benefited from losing its rebelliousness by becoming more mature.

We asked another question: how does all this fit in with the papacy's role on the secular political stage?

Again an evocative shrug. He meanders back through John Paul's pontificate – Greenan offers a compelling mixture of fact and personal reminiscence, a reminder that the editor has remained close to the sources of Church power for a good many years – back to John Paul's first journey abroad, to Mexico, when he started a debate still alive today. It was over John Paul's insistence that priests stay out of politics. In the same speech the pope had demanded economic justice for the peasants: a blunt political statement. Some discerned a contradiction here. Not Greenan. Like the pope he can see the distinctions: the *first* duty of a priest is to attend to his pastoral, sacramental and teaching functions, leaving the laity to bring the Gospel to

79

bear on the social and political issues of the world. The key word, Greenan repeats, is *first*.

In other words, we press, once the spiritual side has been attended to, a priest, especially a pope, can involve himself elsewhere?

This time, Greenan's shrug is unrevealing. A final *digestivo*, a blessing, followed by an Irish 'good luck, lads', and he is off to say early evening Mass.

It had been a useful lunch. Later, back at the Albergo Santa Chiara, our unpretentious but accommodating base in Rome (the management don't mind us turning bedrooms into offices or using the phone on the reception desk to call New York or Warsaw), we compare impressions. As usual there are a number of matters which Greenan has either skirted, ignored, or thought not worth mentioning; these suggest that, contrary to what we have been told elsewhere, they were not considered problems in the Vatican circles the editor moves in.

We had tried to broach the Jesuit Question. The Society of Jesus, the largest and most élite of the Church's orders, was badly shaken when the pope, against the wishes of the Jesuit leadership, had appointed the Rev. Paolo Dezza as caretaker head of the order.

Dezza has the reputation of being a hard-line conservative, a priest with no compunction about dealing harshly with anyone who steps out of line. A number of our Vatican sources forecast there would be what one called, not altogether facetiously, 'holy fireworks' when Dezza set about the Society of Jesus. Greenan predicted there would be no real bloodletting. That, he said, John Paul would not allow. He forecast Dezza's vaunted toughness was only a threat, to be used if all else failed; Dezza would use his equally well-developed wits to bring 'order to the Order' (another of Greenan's quotable phrases).

The editor had been right. For the moment, as Greenan's lack of interest implied, the Jesuit Question was off the boil. Yet how, we wondered, should we interpret Greenan's pointed disinclination to discuss the present status of Opus Dei? The facts, such as they were, are not in dispute. Opus Dei is conservatively minded, highly secretive and fosters piety, obedience to the Church and is pledged to influencing those persons in government and private life who are loosely described as being in 'high places'. The organization has 72,000 members in eighty countries.

Liberal critics call it 'the Santa Mafia' because of the way, they say, it has infiltrated all strata of the Church. This view John Paul seemingly didn't share when he raised the status of Opus Dei from a 'secular institute' to a 'personal prelature'.[5]

The society's President General, Mgr Alvaro del Portillo, reports directly to the pope. That form of access is a sign of unusual power, suggesting, as *The New York Times* recently has, 'an important endorsement of a particular means of adopting and applying theology – with caution and with total loyalty'.[6]

We had hoped Greenan would indicate whether the comment echoed current thinking in papal circles. Had the *Times* overstated matters?[7] Could it be that John Paul did not want any internal rocking of the Church boat now that he is engaged upon such delicate manoeuvring on the secular stage? Greenan would not be drawn.[8]

For the remainder of the afternoon we mull over the names of the eighteen prelates John Paul has announced he will confirm as new cardinals early next month.[9] The choosing of cardinals is largely dictated by practical concerns. Popes may dispense red hats to climax outstanding clerical careers, rather like the giving of knighthoods, seats in the House of Lords or plum ambassadorial posts. Popes sometimes create a cardinal to recognize publicly the importance of a Third World hierarchy, or to support a politically beleaguered prelate, or to send what is described around the Vatican as 'a sign', a message of hope, to a persecuted flock. John Paul has managed to achieve all these aims by naming new members from five continents to the Sacred College.

The only American who will receive a red hat is Joseph

Bernardin, Archbishop of Chicago. We dig out a file. Bernardin is fifty-four and took over the archdiocese from the late and generally unlamented Cardinal John Cody. The file is filled with accusations that Cody was a racist, a procurer of Church funds for his personal use and with a way of life – violent rages, gargantuan appetite and at least one love affair – which had brought despair to the Vatican. During the five months he has been in Chicago, Bernardin has achieved wonders rebuilding morale and speaking out on social, if not doctrinal, issues.

We make a few telephone calls to Rome 6982, the Vatican switchboard, and ask for extensions in the Apostolic Palace. Our sources are puzzled. Bernardin has been outspoken in his criticism of the Reagan administration's hard-line nuclear arms policy. They are wondering whether, by honouring Bernardin, John Paul was giving a 'sign' that he shared similar views – and wanted to make that known to Washington?

Nobody knows – of course. But it is a fascinating piece of speculation. We turn back to the list of cardinals.

Bishop Paul Marcinkus is conspicuous by his absence from the list – a fact a number of Italian commentators have gleefully hit upon. They continue to heap calumny on the chief executive of the Institute for Religious Works, the Vatican Bank. The bank is undoubtedly caught up in some very peculiar financial deals, and Marcinkus has indeed had some unfortunate business friends. But on all the evidence we have obtained – including some plain speaking by two cardinals, Felici and Benelli, before they died – it appears Marcinkus is more sinned against than sinning. Gullible rather than criminal would be the best epitaph to apply to his association with Michele Sindona, now in an American gaol serving a lengthy sentence for wholesale fraud perpetrated with money obtained from Vatican Bank, and the late Roberto Calvi of Banco Ambrosiano. Calvi had been found dead in 1982 suspended from scaffolding under Blackfriars Bridge, London, hanging by the neck on a three-foot length of rope, his pockets filled with heavy stones, his passport, spectacles and £7,000 in cash. The circumstances seem too elaborate to suggest Calvi took his own life. But we cannot believe – evaluating the evidence so far – that Vatican Bank is implicated in Calvi's death. Yet who knows what will turn up in this extraordinary financial soap opera which one of our sources in the Bank now terms 'Holy Dallas'?[10]

By the time we have gone through the list, made our phone calls and written up our notes it is time for dinner with Henry McConnachie of Vatican Radio. We meet at the Excelsior on the Via Veneto. McConnachie is wearing a diplomat's dress cape and trousers so tight they might have been sewn on to his body. He sets the tone for the night by murmuring that a man seated in a lobby chair is with the CIA.

We let the comment pass. McConnachie loves spy dramas, whether in fiction or real life; at times he sounds like Le Carré's Smiley or Greene's Wormold. This makes it that much harder to be sure with the broadcaster when fact ends and teasing begins.

For thirteen years he has been broadcasting news in English for Vatican Radio. He knows a great deal of things which interest us. As usual he needs a little prompting to give a very personal but worthwhile view of what has been happening since we last met.

At the end of dinner, he mentions almost casually that the programmes of one of his colleagues are being recorded by the CIA and passed on to President Reagan's personal envoy to the Holy See, William Wilson. Wilson is apparently collecting the tapes as 'evidence' that Vatican Radio is anti-American in its broadcasts.

We ask McConnachie who is his colleague. He says Clarissa McNair. McConnachie cannot understand why the CIA is now taping McNair's broadcasts. Perhaps, he adds with a wicked smile, it is something we should look into.

Back at the Albergo Santa Chiara, McNair joins the list of

those destined for further enquiry. On the surface McConnachie's revelation makes little sense. Vatican Radio's reputation for impartiality is well founded; there would seem no way any broadcaster could continue to subvert the station's neutral position. Yet Reagan's envoy – who *ipso facto* has ambassadorial status – must have some cause for concern to be collecting this kind of evidence. And why would the CIA be involved gathering material on the broadcaster? If it sounds like overmatter from Watergate, this is also something we cannot ignore because it is another indication of the external pressures on the papacy.

5

VATICAN CITY
Friday
Late Afternoon

Shortly after five o'clock Severia Battistino, a nun of the Pious Disciples of the Divine Master, the order which operates the Vatican switchboard, receives yet another international telephone call. There have been hundreds all week, far more than usual, a clear indication to Sister Severia that 'things are really humming'.[1]

The Maltese-born nun is middle-aged, jolly and can mimic passably an Irish brogue, a reminder of her days in Co. Athlone before she had suddenly been transferred to the Vatican. Like the other nuns seated before the ultra-modern telecommunications console, Sister Severia is a religious, receiving no salary, only her board and lodgings. She lives a frugal existence within the Vatican walls. As well as her switchboard duties Sister Severia acts as the order's nurse in the Vatican and frequently finds herself having to tend to sick sisters. Twice already this week she has spent a night-long vigil at the bedside of a nun dying from cancer. While the combination of lack of sleep and the unusually heavy workload give her a wan-faced look, her cheerfulness has not diminished. If she recognizes the voice of a priest complaining that his calls are not being handled quickly enough, she invariably finds time to tell him he wouldn't get better service in Heaven.

The switchboard is behind the Apostolic Palace, sited in a featureless building near the Porta Sant'Anna; its door is always locked from the inside and under constant watch from a nearby *Vigilanza* guard post. Cibin knows the switchboard could be a prime target for a terrorist attack.

In her black habit relieved only by a gold cross, today Sister Severia has so far sat for several hours and helped to connect any one of the Vatican's 2,868 telephone extensions with the world.[2]

Just after five P.M. there is yet another voice in the headset which she wears perched on top of her coif, its plastic-covered microphone a few inches from her lips. Archbishop Pio Laghi calls at this time almost every weekday to speak to one of the civil servants in the Secretariat of State.

Laghi is the apostolic delegate in Washington, DC, a post he has held since 10 December 1980, the day he moved into the papacy's official residence on Massachusetts Avenue. Laghi acts, among other roles, as the link between the White House, State Department and the pope. He is iron-willed, unflappable, reticent, observant, ruthless should the need arise, an attentive host and a popular guest on Georgetown's cocktail party circuit. Above all he is a purveyor and keeper of secrets, big and small. Reagan's administration respects, if not always completely understands, this strongly independent diplomat.

It is an open secret in Washington that John Paul sent Laghi to the United States to help enforce his authority on the country's fifty-two million Catholics. Laghi had made it plain that the members of one of the largest of the Churches within the Holy Roman fief are duty bound to obey the pope's commands: American Catholics must end their preoccupation with materialism and permissiveness; they must take to heart the pope's appeal to cease their 'escape in sexual pleasures, escape in drugs, escape in violence, escape in indifference'.[3] Their priests must accept that celibacy is for ever; their nuns must stop their requests to be ordained. Laghi has also reminded the American cardinals and bishops that all priests and nuns must wear clerical garb. Nor should they continue to claim that homosexuality is not always 'morally wrong', or suggest that in certain cases abortion is permissible. Yet for all his efforts Laghi's crusade has largely failed. American Catholics continue to seek divorces, continue to use contraceptives, continue to enter into homosexual liaisons, continue to have abortions, continue to advocate euthanasia; priests and nuns continue to dress as they please, continue to experiment dangerously in theological areas the pope holds sacrosanct. And as if this was not enough there are dismaying signs for Laghi that the American hierarchy is becoming increasingly opposed to the administration's hard-line nuclear policies.

In their second draft of a pastoral letter – *The Challenge to Peace: God's Promise and Our Response* – the US bishops have bluntly taken issue with their government's position on when a nuclear first strike is admissible.[4] The letter condemns certain Reagan administration views as 'immoral'; it calls for a total nuclear arms freeze and describes the United States position on nuclear deterrence as 'unsatisfying from a moral point of view'.

Reagan's supporters have been outraged. A White House aide reportedly asked Laghi whether 'your bishops plan to oppose Russian nukes with their croziers'.[5]

After the draft was released the president urged his personal envoy to the Holy See, William Wilson, to use, in Wilson's words, 'every avenue open to get the pope to make the American bishops realize what they are doing – leaving our country naked'.[6] In support of Wilson, the president sent senior representatives to the Vatican. They were listened to politely but no firm promises had been given. Part of Wilson's frustration at not getting through 'to them' may have led him to start collecting Vatican Radio broadcasts. Laghi, who frequently listens in Washington to the station, has apparently not faulted its balance. But there is a growing mood of general apprehension about the Vatican within the Reagan administration. For reasons nobody in the White House or State Department quite understands – even allowing that the draft pastoral letter is as yet no more than a working paper, open for discussion – some officials there have come to the conclusion John Paul, in the words of one, 'carries no real clout with our hierarchy'. President Reagan's feeling about the American bishops' letter has prompted Laghi to make today's transatlantic call. He asks Sister Severia to connect him to Casaroli's office.

For the Secretary of State this has been another long and varied day. In the morning he studied a disturbing report from the pro-nuncio in Algeria, Gabriel Montalvo. For the past three years, from his fan-cooled office in the Rue de la Basilique in Algiers City, Montalvo has been monitoring the unpredictable behaviour of Libya's Colonel Gaddafi. Montalvo has the gift of being able to reduce hours of circumlocutory Arabic conversation into a series of pithy reports; they are among the shortest and most precise of all the papal diplomatic dispatches.[7]

Montalvo has worrying news. Gaddafi is planning a full-scale propaganda offensive against Chad which may be followed by direct Libyan intervention. This would inevitably bring a firm French response as France is pledged to defend Chad. Should this occur, another African trouble-spot will then have been well and truly ignited. Though Montalvo's responsibilities in North Africa include Libya, he has rarely been allowed into the country, effectively barred entry by Gaddafi's religious fanaticism; the colonel categorizes the nuncio as another representative of those hated Christian states which, he believes, have vowed to topple him. There is no way, then, that the Holy See can put directly to the Libyan leader its views about the dangers to peace any incursion into Chad would create. However, there might be, suggests Montalvo, another means of making Gaddafi pause over his plans.

Delegates are about to assemble in Algiers for the annual Palestinian National Council meeting. Among them will be Yasser Arafat, chairman of the PLO. While the relationship between Arafat and Gaddafi has been icy for some time – because of Libya's support for even more extremist groups than the PLO – Montalvo believes Gaddafi might, just might, listen if Arafat was persuaded to caution him over the consequences of invading Chad.[8]

The suggestion was raised when Casaroli lunched with the pope; the two men usually dine together twice a week when they are in the Apostolic Palace. As usual, there was a full table: among the guests were two bishops the pope had received during his morning audience. On these occasions John Paul is remarkably open about the subjects to be discussed – sometimes more so than Casaroli likes – and the question of involving Arafat had been taken up around the table. The general feeling was that Arafat would make little headway because Gaddafi is now effectively beyond reason.

After the meal in the papal apartment, Casaroli returned to his office to continue studying a current preoccupation, the Lebanon. John Paul wants the Holy See more involved. To help Casaroli make a recommendation on how best this may be done, the nuncio in Beirut, Luciano Angeloni, has sent a lengthy report which begins by stating that after months of delay, the Lebanese army is about to return into East Beirut to take formal control of the city from the right-wing militia of the Phalange Party. The Lebanese president, Amin Gemayel, is heralding the move as another sign that the years of civil war will soon be ended. But the nuncio does not share this optimism.[9]

Archbishop Angeloni has been in Beirut for less than a year. In that time he has established a string of reliable contacts throughout the Lebanon and extending into Damascus on one side and Jersualem and Tel Aviv on the other. All hours of the day or night Angeloni receives telephone calls and visitors at his nunciature on Rue Georges Picot. They include leaders of the communities which have fought bitter battles and turned Beirut into a capital battered into rubble, and Lebanon itself into a nation which faces the possibility of extinction from both the Israelis and Syrians who, for almost a decade, have used the country's airspace and land to fight their battles. Angeloni is outwardly an unemotional man, yet in recent months the distress he has felt over some particularly monstrous crime – an Israeli bomb which has killed scores of civilians, or the dynamiting by Muslim fanatics of an apartment block – has been obvious in his reports to the Secretariat. Casaroli does not like his diplomats to be involved emotionally in what they see, but he feels genuine sympathy for Angeloni's anguished verdict that 'Lebanon is hell on earth'.[10]

His latest report suggests that at best the strife will be only temporarily halted. Lebanon – created in 1926 and for almost fifty years a model of communal concord – could later in the year be the powder keg which rips apart the Middle East, perhaps in an explosion even greater than the one a decade earlier which paved the way for Arab oil embargoes and a world recession.

Angeloni argues that the present tinderbox situation must be seen in historic perspective.[11] It was King Hussein who drove the Palestinians out of Jordan into Lebanon. Overnight a series of refugee camps for a dispossessed people sprang up; they became power bases for a vengeful PLO. The PLO gave a new killing arm to the Muslim community which was already locked in rivalry with Lebanon's Christians. The national army could do nothing to keep the factions apart; it was neutered by ineffectual leadership and an almost equal composition of Christians and Muslims.

Civil war proper started in 1975. Three years later a Greek Orthodox Church deserter from the Lebanese army, Major Saad Haddad, created in the south a separate entity which he called Free Lebanon. Israel openly supported this mini-state because it both provided a buffer from Palestinian attacks on the Jewish state and allowed Israeli ground forces to use Free Lebanon as a springboard to launch fierce attacks against PLO targets in Lebanon. A MOSSAD agent had once explained to Angeloni that, for Israel, supporting Lebanon's Christians is an essential part of its own survival.[12]

But, continues the nuncio's review, there is now a reawakening in Israel of an old yearning: many Zionists are again reminding themselves that a sector of southern Lebanon belongs to ancient Eretz Israel, part of the Promised Land which they say must become part of modern Israel. The PLO threat has sharpened their craving to see Israel take personal permanent control over a sizable portion of Lebanese territory. Their vociferousness is influenced by what Angeloni calls 'a dangerous fallacy':[13] that, for all its posturing over Lebanon, the Soviet Union will not intervene directly; Russia will certainly keep the cauldron boiling with arms and financial aid, but will do no more.

Angeloni's view is that this is a dangerous miscalculation.[14] Russia, in the nuncio's opinion, is poised to exploit the Lebanese crucible, stirring it both economically and militarily. The situation is now more unstable than ever. Angeloni concludes with the mordant view that peace might then no longer rest in the hands of the local combatants but in the grasp of their armourers, the United States and the Soviet Union.

Nevertheless while the pitfalls are obvious, Casaroli thinks Lebanon could indeed benefit from a more vigorous Holy See involvement – one which in the long term would pave the way for the only permanent solution he sees for peace in the area: providing the Palestinians with a state of their own.

Laghi's telephone call from Washington ends Casaroli's deliberations. Laghi says the White House has just asked him whether the pope will receive in private audience Vice-President George Bush. He wants to explain the president's latest thoughts on what Reagan calls 'The Year of the Missile'; if no agreement is reached at the Geneva arms talks before the end of the year, NATO will deploy a new arsenal of nuclear weapons in Europe.[15]

Placing Laghi on hold, Casaroli calls John Paul on 'the internal hot line' between secretary and pontiff.[16]

The pope agrees to see Bush. Casaroli tells Laghi to inform the White House.

John Paul's decision puts further pressure on the Secretariat.

Its staff is already dealing with matters reflecting the far-reaching interest of the papacy in secular matters.

The Latin America Desk is evaluating a report from its observer in Managua that delegates to the summit of non-aligned nations, due to start in a few hours' time there, plan to denounce the role of the United States and Israel in Central America. Cuba and Nicaragua propose to accuse Israel of acting as proxy for the Reagan administration by arming neighbouring regimes opposed to the left-wing Sandinista government ruling Nicaragua. The observer wants to be given instructions. After discussion a response is drafted. He is informed he should make every effort to soften such condemnation by working through the delegation from Egypt and India, two of the more moderate of the ninety-six nations which belong to the Non-Aligned Movement.[17]

The observer does not need reminding that at no stage must the hand of the Holy See be detected. To openly support Israel – a nation it does not diplomatically recognize – could create problems in those countries opposed to the Jewish state with which the Holy See has formal links. Nor must the Holy See publicly condone the role of the United States in the region; this could damage the Church's reputation of impartiality, something that must be avoided at all costs with the pope's visit to Central America less than two months away.

The papal trip has caused analysts on the Latin America Desk to study even more carefully a sermon the nuncio in El Salvador, Lajos Kada, proposes to deliver in San Salvador's metropolitan cathedral. Its content marks a departure from the Holy See's public position on El Salvador.

For many months Kada has worked behind the scenes to try and end the country's civil war, one in which he has seen fellow priests tortured and even murdered by a regime which President Reagan supports. Kada has until now scrupulously avoided involving the Holy See in a confrontation with the authorities. But he believes he cannot any longer stay silent. He intends in his sermon to urge the government to start talking with the left-wing rebel forces. Mild though his words are, they would undoubtedly have an effect: they will be seen by the regime, and in washington, as evidence that the Holy See is taking an active political interest in El Salvador; this could well be unwelcome.

Every word of the sermon is scrutinized and weighed by the analysts. In the end they pass it without deletion. Kada is given the go-ahead to serve notice on President Magania that he must start to put his house in order before John Paul arrives.

The Middle East Desk, involved in preparing further briefing papers on the Lebanon for Casaroli, is trying to assess the real influence of four pro-Syrian Palestinian groups who are violently opposed to the United States' efforts to bring peace to the area.[18]

The North America Desk is absorbing the latest dispatch from an elegant New York address, 20 East 72nd Street, the office of the Holy See's Permanent Observer to the United Nations, Archbishop Giovanni Cheli. With his cable address – Vatobserv – and two telex machines – numbered 429502 and 425085, having the common answer-back VVOUN – Cheli is one of the best-equipped of all the papal nuncios to contact the Secretariat. His telexed report is deemed sufficiently important to be xeroxed and sent to Poggi, the pope's specialist on Soviet affairs. Cheli provides clear indication of how serious was the rift between President Reagan and the man he has just sacked, Eugene Rostow, director of the US Arms Control and Disarmament Agency. Rostow has gone because some of the administration's arch-conservatives accused him of 'being too soft with Moscow'.[19]

Cheli has learned Rostow's dismissal hinged on his support for a secret plan to decrease the number of Soviet missiles in Europe, while at the same time reducing the number of new weapons to be deployed by NATO. Rostow discussed the idea with a senior Soviet official at a confidential meeting in Vienna. Shortly afterwards Rostow was removed.

Analysts on the North America Desk feel that Bush will play down the episode on his trip to Europe. But the Desk requests that papal diplomats in each country Bush is to visit should include any official local response to Rostow's dismissal in their reports; these will form part of the final briefing the pope receives before he meets Bush. They are also alerted to seek reactions to a US Defense Department document, deliberately divulged in Washington, which details Pentagon strategy including contingency plans for fighting a nuclear war against the Soviet Union in outer space. The document, *Fiscal 1984–1988: Defense Guidance*, suggests a possibly significant shift in US military policy.[20]

Politically hyper-sensitive men like William Wilson, the president's personal representative, sometimes see in the Secretariat's interpretation of present US policies cause for both alarm and bafflement. Wilson is convinced John Paul is sympathetic to the Reagan administration's over-view of the world. Therefore he cannot understand why some of the pope's civil servants seem almost hostile in their attitude to America's conduct of her affairs.[21]

Wilson is not the only observer who finds it hard to comprehend that the response of these Secretariat staff towards the United States is partly governed by their desire to keep a professional distance between themselves and what they perceive as the increasingly uncritical position John Paul is assuming towards the Reagan administration.

These same civil servants point out that while it is true the pope is passionately opposed to ever seeing nuclear weapons unleashed, he has also said any discussion on their reduction calls for 'reciprocity: in the progressive reduction of armaments, nuclear or conventional, the parties must be equally involved and together travel the various stages of disarmament'.[22]

This attitude, they continue, is what lies behind the very careful stage managing now under way in the Vatican to deal with Cardinal Bernardin and Archbishop John Roach of Minneapolis-St Paul. They are shortly due in Rome to argue support for the US pastoral letter before a gathering of eminent European Catholic prelates. To try and ensure the outcome is as he wishes, John Paul has been holding some very late, and very confidential, meetings in the papal apartment.

THE PAPAL APARTMENT
Same Day: Close to Midnight

Fridays are the days the CIA station in Rome delivers its weekly intelligence summary to the pope. It is couriered late in the afternoon from the American Embassy on Via Veneto, past the Fountains of Trevi and across the Tiber to the Vatican. After the twenty-minute car journey the courier hands the report to one of the pope's aides who carries the sealed envelope to John Paul's private study adjoining his bedroom.

Tonight, as usual, the pope studies the report after dinner. If anything needs amplification, John Paul will instruct a secretary to find time for the Station Chief to be seen during Saturday in the pope's second-floor office, where he prefers to meet visitors, however secret their business might be.

Though the reports vary in length from one week to the next, they generally contain a number of highly classified documents from the agency's departments which deal with Soviet operations of all kinds; there are economic assessments, political evaluations and, occasionally, military predictions. Sometimes there are data provided by the National Security Agency, NSA, responsible for a portion of the electronic surveillance which the United States carries out in all parts of the world. NSA specializes in wire-tapping and radio monitoring; every day its staff pluck many millions of words from the air, capturing them on magnetic tape for translation and analysis. It is a routine precaution which the US takes to better defend itself and, if needs be, to alert friends.

The pope also sees the results of visual reconnaissance by space satellites which the CIA operates jointly with the US Air Force. John Paul has been known to gasp at the definition obtained from satellites orbiting the earth at 50,000 land miles an hour; in the presence of staff he has marvelled over technology which allows a camera from more than one hundred miles out in space to photograph the bolts on the deck of a Soviet warship.

Week after week the CIA reports have, more than any other source, revealed to John Paul the full, awesome might of the Soviet war machine. From them he has learned that the Russians are spending *half a million dollars a minute* on their capability to wage total war: forty-four per cent of the country's gross national product supports an attack system which could, in a surprise assault on the United States, kill 160 million people. British experts predict seventy-five per cent of their population might perish under a similar onslaught. The French, Italian and West German governments believe their casualty figures could be even higher.[23]

John Paul has admitted to aides he finds the sheer size of the Soviet fighting machines 'totally overwhelming'.[24] Within the Warsaw Pact there are an estimated 4,800,000 airmen, soldiers and sailors to operate some 8,000 Europe-based combat-aircraft, 200 major warships, nearly 300 operational submarines, 50,000 tanks and 5,000 missile-launching systems. No one in the West knows how many thousand nuclear warheads the Warsaw Pact has. What is known is that most are aimed at Western Europe, but many could hit America.[25]

The pope asked for, and received, comparative figures for the West. NATO has approximately 3,000,000 combatants, 3,000 aircraft, 300 major warships, 200 submarines, 13,000 tanks and 3,000 missile-launchers – many of which are situated in the US, incapable of dropping their nuclear missiles on Soviet territory.[26]

John Paul was horrified to hear there may now be close to 200,000 nuclear weapons ready to be launched from ground or underground sites, from submarines and from the air. He has repeatedly used the same word to his staff to describe the situation: 'Madness. Madness. Madness'.[27]

The pope has been assured by the CIA, and accepts the promise, that the United States will never launch a preemptive first strike, and that neither Britain nor France – whose forces are not committed to NATO – has the capability to do so without being destroyed by the Soviet nuclear response. No such assurance can be given by the agency about Soviet intentions. And the CIA weekly reports portray Russian actions as increasingly volatile and unpredictable.

When there are no outsiders present, the effect of all this information on John Paul is noticeable. More often than not his secretaries and 'members of the Polish Mafia' – an allusion to the evergrowing papal inner court of Eastern Europeans – accept that a working dinner with the pontiff can mean a lengthy discourse on the Soviet threat. John Paul will pick at his food and water down his wine as he expounds arguments which are largely based on what the CIA tell him reinforced by his own experience of living under Soviet domination.

Those around the table do not disagree with the pope – nor would they wish to do so. Many of them have also witnessed Communism in action. They see themselves as the core of an inner élite, an informal caucus of opinionmakers within, but separate from, the established Vatican government; a small group who deliberately cut themselves off from the attitudes of those civil servants in the Secretariat of State who so openly criticize the policies of President Reagan.

Never before has the CIA, and through it the White House, had such a powerful group close to the pope.

On any important issues John Paul takes the most careful note of these he has brought closest to him. The ultimate decision will still be his, but more often than not it will have been strongly influenced by what the group has told him.

This evening over dinner he outlined the speech he will deliver in the morning to all the foreign diplomats accredited to the Holy See. There was considerable discussion; suggestions have been made, talked through, new ones have surfaced. John Paul listened. Then he had gone to his study to peruse the latest CIA report. Close to midnight he sends for one of his secretaries and hands him revisions to the speech. The pope is going to reserve his sharpest criticisms for what is happening in Afghanistan, Iran and Iraq, all areas of current Soviet influence.[28] It is the ideal way, members of the group suggested, to let Bernardin and Roach know they had better look again at the pastoral letter they are hoping to gain support for in their forthcoming meeting in the Vatican.

THE HOLY OFFICE, OFF ST PETER'S SQUARE
Saturday
Early Morning

Shortly before seven A.M. Fr Fruno Fink resumes what he has been doing most of this week.

He is a tall bony figure with thick spectacles and large teeth so uniformly perfect that when he grins he looks like a final-year student playing the young priest in a college drama. He has indeed the mannerisms of a natural actor: expressive little shrugs, a quick lowering of the eyelids and an even faster chopping motion with his right hand when he wants to emphasize something.[29]

At this hour, apart from the *vigile* in the guardhouse at the entrance to the Holy Office, there is nobody else around. It will be a further two hours before this imposing building just beyond the Vatican perimeter will be filled with officials going about their special activity of stamping on all kinds of heresies. Between them they rule on the subtleties of teaching the Catholic faith, condemn those books containing what they call 'dangerous affirmations', and correct what they also insist are 'fundamental errors' in sex education for Catholics. There is no shortage of work for the bachelors who run the Holy Office.

During the years Fink has been here he has seen such eminent Catholic theologians as Jacques Pohier and Edward Schillebeeckx summoned to answer charges that they had transgressed what the Holy Office deems to be correct. And in the larger and altogether more splendidly appointed office adjoining Fink's he had witnessed the moment the decision was given that henceforth Hans Küng had lost the right to be formally designated a Catholic theologian. The enormity of what was happening sent a shiver through Fink: the ban was visible proof no one who professed to be a Catholic in good standing was beyond the reach of the Holy Office.[30]

It has always been so, from 1542 when the Inquisition was run from here and the command regularly given to burn some medieval heretic at the stake. Nowadays it is the occasional priest who is 'deleted' in Rome, defrocked for immoral teaching or behaviour. Renamed a few years ago the Sacred Congregation for the Doctrine of the Faith – the most senior Sacred Congregation in the Curia, ranking second only to Casaroli's Secretariat of State – the Holy Office is a forbidding place filled with its own kind of residual terror for those it has condemned – and also cold enough on this Saturday morning to make Fr Fink glad he is wearing a thick sweater under his cassock.

He is officially listed on the Holy Office staff as *addetto tecnico di 2a classe*, a relatively low civil service grade which in no way reflects his true position; in a rare moment of gallows humour he says he is 'rather like the Soviet Embassy chauffeur who is really the KGB Resident'.[31] The terms of employment for this 32-year-old German are carefully defined within the *Regolamento Generale della Curia Romana*, the General Rules of the Curia; forty-three pages, 130 clauses plus three appendices, all inscribed in the deadly prose of bureaucracy, each word personally approved by the pope. The rule-book is supposed to govern Fink's life. It sets out the physical, moral and scholastic requirements for his grade; it reminds him his duties include 'dispatching and delivering letters and packets, looking after the cleaning before superiors arrive and after they leave'. The rule-book specifies his holidays will include the anniversary of the pope's coronation, his patron saint's day and the commemoration day for the death of the last pontiff. It informs him he must be at work from nine A.M. until one-thirty P.M. at least.

Fink has been breaking the rules for as long as he can remember. He has no time to deliver mail around the Vatican, except those letters marked for the pope's personal attention. He has never been able to spare a minute to supervise the cleaning; he assumes the women can be trusted otherwise they would not be here. And Fink cannot recall when last he worked the official minimum time laid down; his week is often twice as long as the prescribed thirty-three hours.

He is in reality one of the most powerful private secretaries in Vatican service, the confidant of Cardinal Joseph Ratzinger, prefect of the Holy Office and probably the Curial cardinal closest to John Paul. Theologically Ratzinger shares the same outlook as the pope. He is also from the same mould: Ratzinger possesses a steel trap of a mind, as those who try to deviate from Catholic doctrine and behavioural standards swiftly discover.

John Paul has appointed Ratzinger to chair the two-day conference which will discuss the draft US pastoral letter. The conference is now only four days away. Fink has the job of assembling the material Ratzinger needs for his brief. For the past week the secretary has worked from early in the morning until late at night translating from English into

German for the Bavarian-born cardinal who, apart from Latin and grammatically imperfect Italian, has no other language. Much of the documentation has come from Laghi in Washington and from what Fink calls 'our friends in the American hierarchy'.[32] It is all being annotated, indexed and placed in folders that now form several piles on Fink's desk. Between them they chronicle how the American bishops came to their conclusions.

Fink finds the story behind their decisions both riveting and often bewildering. To his German way of thinking, it could only happen in the United States. He cannot imagine any Church hierarchy in Europe putting itself in such direct confrontation with the ruling government. More than once, as he reads the evidence, he has paused and asked himself where it will all end.[33]

He knows now how it began.

The secretary is a careful worker. His methods are well suited to the task in hand.[34] First he read everything, steadily working his way through perhaps a million words of submissions, arguments, aide-memoires, memorandums, documents and letters. He ticked salient paragraphs with one of the felt pens from a box on his desk. He uses a simple colour code: red is for most important, blue comes next, then green and finally black. Any material which was ticked is automatically placed in one pile, the balance put aside in another. The first pile is prime source material. No matter what the colour coding, Fink has decided it is essential data for Ratzinger to read. He sifted through the second pile once more, this time marking paragraphs with yellow or brown ticks as supportive evidence. The documentation that remains unmarked has been stacked in a corner; this contains some of the more nonsensical speculations of priests turned pop commentators on the nuclear issue.

Fink quickly isolated the crucial paragraph in the original pastoral letter which opened the peace offensive of the American bishops that had been brewing for some years. After declaring modern warfare so savage it can no longer be morally justified, the letter had stated: 'As possessors of a vast nuclear arsenal we must also be aware that not only is it wrong to attack civilian populations, but it is also wrong to threaten to attack them as part of a strategy of deterrence.'[35]

Fink detected the thoughts, if not the actual drafting hand, of Cardinal John Krol, Philadelphia's influential archbishop, behind the sentiment. He knows Krol is a conservative in doctrine and ecclesiastical discipline, but an avowed 'liberal' over disarmament, never swerving from the position he affirmed when testifying on behalf of his fellow bishops before the Senate Foreign Relations Committee.[36] Fink had marked in red Krol's brisk exchange with the committee members as the cardinal rejected any 'declared intent' to use nuclear weapons in certain circumstances on the grounds that 'masses of civilians would inevitably be involved'.

Fink cross-referenced Krol's testimony with a brief summary of Christianity's traditional position on war. Krol's views are in keeping with the Church's position, itself based upon St Augustine's original 'just war' theory which had been refined and developed by Thomas Aquinas and other theologians. The theory – one generally accepted by all faiths before the nuclear age arrived – is that a war can be 'just' when it is declared by a legitimate authority, when it is conducted for 'a righteous cause', when it is launched with 'good intentions', when it is 'a last resort', when it is waged with 'limited means'. The atomic bomb had dramatically affected two further criteria for a 'just' war: 'discrimination' – no indiscriminate killing of civilians; 'proportion' – a war's devastation cannot exceed the evil it seeks to overcome. Krol's argument was that nuclear warfare excludes these two factors and consequently could not be justified.

The secretary had also cross-referenced the cardinal's views to those of Pius XII. Nine years after Hiroshima, Pius had approved the use of atomic, bacteriological and chemical weapons only if 'they did not totally escape from the control of man' or produce 'annihilation of all human life within the radius of action'. Pius had also ruled that a war of 'righteous aggression', in order to punish a wrong-doing or to recover territory, was no longer justified because – and once more Fink's red pen had come into play – modern weaponry was so devastating. However, wars of 'natural self-defence' were still permissible.[37] This sentence had also been ticked in red by Fink.

Pius's views prompted a coalition of US and European bishops to draft a document which had been hesitantly approved by the Second Vatican Council. It promoted the idea of nuclear deterrence. Fink marked, with blue this time, the important paragraph in *The Pastoral Constitution on the Church in the Modern World* which was published in 1965: 'Since the defence strength of any nation is considered to be dependent upon its capacity for immediate retaliation, the accumulation of arms serves in a way heretofore unknown as a deterrent to possible enemy attack. Many regard this as the most effective way to which peace of a sort can be maintained between nations at the present time.'

But Vatican II had also promulgated a rider: 'Any act of war aimed indiscriminately at the destruction of entire cities or extensive areas along with their populations is a crime against God and man himself.'

Fink marked this declaration and attached appropriate references so that Ratzinger could consult them.

The evolution of 'peace theology' was taken a stage further with the formation of a drafting committee for the pastoral letter. Its five members span the spectrum of views held by the US hierarchy on nuclear arms.

Fink has collated the attitude of individual members. Each bishop has a separate folder, filled with all kinds of documentation that shows how wide is the gap between, for example, Bishop John O'Connor, who runs the American hierarchy's military ministry, and Bishop Thomas Gumbleton of Detroit. Gumbleton heads Pax Christi, a movement with strong pacifist leanings that has fifty-seven other bishops as members; he believes that even if the Soviet

Union is unwilling to disarm, the United States should begin to dismantle its arsenal of nuclear missiles. O'Connor argues that at minimum nuclear weapons can be used to destroy exclusively military targets.

The slimmest file is for the committee's chairman, Cardinal Bernardin. Fink thoroughly approves of the way the archbishop of Chicago has been careful to restrict his public comments to the minimum. He has marked with red Bernardin's balanced comment. 'We don't expect everyone to accept our conclusions but we believe we must think this thing through to the end.'[38]

Just as the committee itself was intentionally composed to assure that opposing points of view would be considered, so the evidence for and against present nuclear policies had been gathered from a wide range of witnesses, including important members of the Reagan administration. Many of them had been surprised to discover how well prepared were the bishops; the questions they posed revealed an informed understanding of the nuclear debate.

Yet the criticisms continued. Fink has assembled a sizable file of dissension. There have been arguments that the bishops' activism violates the constitutional principle of the separation of Church from State. Archbishop Roach, president of the US Bishops' Conference since 1980 and a member of the drafting committee, answered the accusation: 'We may never allow the separation of Church and State to be used to separate the Church from Sanity.'[39] Fink has marked the quotation in green, his way of indicating Roach's views are familiar, and can be found in similar form scattered among half a dozen of the files on his desk.

The most frequently repeated charge in recent months is that the committee has often consulted documents prepared in the offices of the controversial US Catholic Conference, a Washington-based organization which many Church conservatives regard as being well to the left of the political spectrum.

The activities of the organization are not unknown to the

Holy Office. On more than one occasion its tactics in trying to get amnesties for draft dodgers or its protests on human rights violations in Chile and South Korea have been carefully examined by staff at the Holy Office. Each time the decision had been made that there was no infringement of doctrine or ecclesiastical behaviour.

A part of Fink's brief for Ratzinger concentrates on the extraordinary attention focused by the media on the pastoral letter. It has been analysed, excoriated and extolled; it has made *Time* and *Newsweek* cover stories, peak-hour television, occupied editorials and columns in virtually every American and European newspaper. Fink has carefully assembled a selection of critical accounts.

Some of the reporting is obviously aimed at undermining the credibility of the bishops. There is also the problem that the media is overemphasizing the disagreement between the bishops and the Reagan administration. Finally there is the risk the media is over-simplifying the issues and failing to grasp what is the very essence of the pastoral letter: the bishops are courageously trying to formulate, within current Church doctrine, an attitude to nuclear arms for the millions of American Catholics – and others – who fear atomic Armageddon will come unless something is done, and soon.

Fink has gathered a cross-section of views, marked them in various colours and cross-referenced them. It is the kind of research the secretary thrives upon.

He has singled out the attempt by President Reagan's national security adviser, William P. Clark, to bring pressure on the bishops. Clark had delivered a stern letter to the conference, having leaked it to *The New York Times* beforehand. He maintained that the administration's nuclear policies were 'moral under the principles outlined in the pastoral letter. We believe that our weapons systems (which are not designed to be "first strike" systems), our deterrence posture (which is defensive), and our arms control initiative (which calls for deep and verifiable reductions), do conform to those objectives.'

Fink noted that Bernardin was careful not to respond publicly to Clark's claims. But the secretary also has no doubt the cardinal will not remain silent before his peers at the Vatican forum.

Most of the US bishops had shown no difficulty in presenting their views as a reflection of the pope's words to the United Nations. Only Philadelphia's Archbishop Krol had gone so far as to correct John Paul, 'with due deference to our Holy Father'. Krol argued the pontiff should have said deterrence was '"morally tolerable" not "morally acceptable". I suggest that the word "tolerable" is more precise than the word "acceptable". Toleration is a passive living with something that is less than satisfactory, and doing so only for a greater good.'[40]

Fink suspects Krol's words will be repeated at the Vatican debate as those present try and go beyond the verdicts which have so far surfaced on the pastoral letter.

Fink is one of the few priest-officials in the Holy Office who is fully aware how formidable is the opposition. Every day the Secretariat of State sends him copies of messages from London, Bonn and Paris reflecting concern over the pastoral letter. Foreign ambassadors accredited to the Holy See have called at the Secretariat to reinforce the views of their governments. There have been separate submissions from European hierarchies and from influential private individuals. All have been tabulated by Fink.

By nine o'clock on this Saturday morning, when Holy Office staff are beginning to occupy themselves with the day's problems – doctrinal posers, sacerdotal issues raised by a priest's wish to leave holy orders, a couple's request to have exercised the petrine privilege to annul their marriage – Fink may be forgiven for thinking that, important as such problems are, they are insignificant when compared to the burden he now shares with his cardinal.

From all he has read the secretary is convinced that, however well intentioned, the American bishops could have gone too far in the challenge to their government. Just as they must have been conditioned in their responses by their backgrounds and mores, so Fink concedes his own thinking is also influenced by his upbringing.[41] His home in Bavaria is only a minute's flying time from the nearest Soviet nuclear silo in East Germany.

Fink is thankful it is his cardinal who has the task of removing any unnecessary emotion from the forthcoming debate. Nobody will do it better.

SECRETARIAT OF STATE
Monday
Late Afternoon

The first position papers detailing reactions to Bush's forthcoming European trip have arrived in the Secretariat and are distributed on a strictly need-to-know basis.

Casaroli is top of the list. Copies go to Mgr Audrys Backis, the Lithuanian-born permanent under-secretary at the Council for the Public Affairs of the Church. This department normally deals with foreign affairs which have strong political overtones, such as the appointment of nuncios to countries whose governments are particularly sensitive about the relationship between Church and State; the Council also deals with concordats and agreements.[42] A separate set of papers has gone to the Council's secretary, Mgr Achille Silvestrini. On such a critically important matter as the Bush visit, the opinions of both Backis and Silvestrini will be solicited.

Luigi Poggi has received a set because of his deepening involvement in the Holy See's commitment to help avert nuclear conflict. A further set has been sent to the pope's office.

Each recipient brings his own special knowledge to bear on the documents.

This is Casaroli's forty-third year in the papal diplomatic

service. He has witnessed all the pivotal events of the past half-century: Hitler and the Holocaust, the aftermath of World War II, the Cold War, Korea, Vietnam, the emergence of the Third World as a force, the decline of the British Empire, the Suez Crisis, the Arab oil embargo; these and many more events have occupied Casaroli. They have helped make him what he is: indisputably one of the greatest diplomats the Holy See has ever had. A specialist in canon law, his skills as a negotiator allowed him to force an unprecedented series of 'understandings' and agreements with Communist bloc countries. It is this background which enables the sharp-eyed Casaroli to skim-read the position papers, knowing he is missing nothing of importance as he flips through the pages.

Casaroli's main interest is focused on the report from Archbishop Del Mestri, his nuncio in Bonn. Del Mestri's excellent connections have once more paid off. Chancellor Helmut Kohl is going to make plain to Bush that the United States must be more flexible in its negotiations in Geneva.

Del Mestri fears that the entire Bush trip could be stillborn before the vice-president leaves Bonn unless Kohl is convinced the United States will be more malleable.

Mgr Backis at the Public Affairs Council has special responsibility for British and Irish affairs. The nuncio in Dublin, Archbishop Gaetano Alibrandi, has sent a report indicating that once more pressures are mounting to end Ireland's neutrality.[43] In the event of a European or world war, control of the north and east Atlantic areas adjacent to Ireland would be vital.

There are powerful voices in Ireland's Defence Forces who envisage Shannon Airport acting as part of an Atlantic airbridge, carrying American reinforcements to Europe. Some even say missiles could be sited on Irish soil.

Further afield, supported by often highly sensitive material garnered by M16, British and American diplomats continue to wage a ceaseless battle in Washington to win the hearts and minds of strong Irish voices on Capitol Hill, such

108

as Senator Edward Kennedy and Tip O'Neill, speaker of the House of Representatives. It is an open secret that both Britain and the US believe Ireland could become an effective member of NATO only after urban terrorism is eliminated in Ulster. No NATO member, runs the argument, would be happy to have part of its defence shield against Soviet attack placed in a country riven by internal unrest. Consequently, Britain's Secret Intelligence Service and its lethal arm, the SAS, have been given what amounts to a blank cheque – both in money and methods – to wage total war against those they consider 'subversive'.

Backis knows instinctively this will be yet another year when the situation in Ireland causes constant anxiety. He also knows he will need great skill in handling the repeated demands of influential members of the Vatican's 'Irish Mafia' for the Holy See to become more aggressively involved in Ulster.[44] It won't be easy to resist their demands. The Irish, Backis has found, are both persistent and persuasive.

He turns from Alibrandi's report to one from London. There, pro-nuncio Bruno Heim keeps a watchful eye on the activities of both Church and State. He has surprising news. Mrs Thatcher may be feeling a little less resolute about the deployment of missiles at Greenham Common. A group of women have set up a 'peace camp' nearby which has helped focus worldwide attention on the proposed rocket site. Heim reports that the views of the anti-nuclear campaigners, led by Mgr Bruce Kent, are being increasingly heard as rumours grow of a possible general election. Greenham Common could highlight the opposing positions of Mrs Thatcher and the Labour Party, who are pledged at all costs to stop the weapons being placed on British soil.

On a wider front there is developing a serious rift between the Prime Minister and her Foreign Office over how Britain's foreign policy should be managed.

Heim argues that there are now two decision-making centres: Downing Street and the Foreign Office. This is already having an important effect on Britain's attitude towards arms control. Mrs Thatcher had recently shown her scepticism for the latest Soviet proposal to pull back some of its SS20 missiles aimed at the West. She rejected the Russian suggestion on the grounds that it still did not allow 'the essential balance which is required for our security'.

Her Foreign Secretary, Francis Pym, took a different position. He announced that the Soviet proposal was of great significance, made at a critical time. Pym's views, in fact, persuaded Mrs Thatcher to move from her initial dismissal to a slightly more moderate view. But even Heim is uncertain whether this means she is taking a new direction or whether it is a shrewd piece of politicking in the run-up to an expected election.

Reading nuncio Felici's position paper from Paris, Silvestrini learns that the French have, if anything, hardened their position on missile deployment: the government now totally supports it. Felici predicts that in a few days the world will see the unusual spectacle of François Mitterand, France's Socialist president, delivering a speech to the West German Bundestag urging its members to support the siting of the new missiles.[45] And many French military analysts are indicating that at the very least a partial deployment is essential to show the Soviet Union any attack will meet with positive retaliation. Bush is going to find himself in an unusual position when he visits France: an American in Paris who is genuinely welcome.

Poggi is studying the situation 'down the road'. Beyond the Vatican walls, and across the Tiber, a mere couple of miles away, the Italian government of Prime Minister Amintore Fanfani is struggling for its political life, and coming to realize that to survive means modifying its support for the placing of 112 Cruise missiles at Comiso.[46] The Italian Communist Party, which can now count on thirty per cent of the national vote, has asked the government to postpone any decision on the Comiso site. The Party is supporting its argument by quoting from the US pastoral letter.

The nuncio concludes that the mood of the position papers suggests the United States should take heed of the Soviet proposals Poggi had been given in Geneva. Since then he has prepared a detailed analysis of the Soviet position. Copies have been circulated and this time the need-to-know prelates included Laghi in Washington and Cheli at the United Nations. Both men have made good use of Poggi's arguments to promote in the US the Secretariat's view that the Soviet position merits serious consideration.

Poggi also sent a copy of his analysis to the pope. He is waiting for a response.

6
Roman Responses

This is the sort of situation on which Vatican moles thrive. They have up for sale the supposedly secret deliberation of the two-day meeting in the Synod Hall to discuss the US pastoral letter. It is still going on. But already on offer to competing wire services and the gaggle of other media who are in Rome for the occasion – including us – is who-is-saying-what, who responded this way and then that way, who lost his temper, who made a particularly biting remark, who riposted, who was cut off in mid-flow, who remained silent and why. It's always: why. That's a mole speciality, explaining not only what supposedly occurred but giving the reasons – putting them always in the context of what they loftily call 'the Vatican position'. This allows the moles to make the unlikely and even the outlandish appear acceptable. The art is to decide who is going too far – and never mind why.

The ploy is as old as those long-ago days – certainly before we came to Rome – when priests discovered they could personally profit from what they know, or say they know. Their price varies from a good dinner to hard cash. It's surprising how bare-faced some of the staff of the Apostolic Palace have become over money. They have dropped the pretence of passing it on to some charity. Nowadays it's simply made clear that the normal asking price of 50,000 lire is acceptable. For this meeting, though, we have heard that 100,000 lire, about sixty US dollars, is being solicited for an especially intriguing exchange of views within the Synod Hall.

It has always been our policy never to buy. But it is fun, and sometimes rewarding, to hang around this Vatican market-place.

The meeting is now in the final day. Officially the

participants are saying nothing. They flit in and out of the Synod Hall, often familiar faces, most with little smiles for the cameras and polite refusals to speak to reporters. There must be a score of news persons waiting for each appearance of the delegates. These journalists are the media foot-sloggers, eternal optimists hoping a bishop will drop even a hint of what is going on. The more wily reporters have set up contact points with the moles to try for an inside track on what Vatican Radio blandly bills 'Vatican consultations on peace and disarmament', and the Italian tabloids banner as Europe's bishops locking horns with the United States hierarchy while Ratzinger plays his favourite role – the tough referee. Without investing a lire we know *that's* nonsense. The three cardinals, thirteen bishops, and their retinues from the episcopates of the United States, France, West Germany, England, Scotland, Wales, Belgium, Italy and the Netherlands are not the sort to indulge in argy-bargy.

Nevertheless, what they might be up to is rather more than the faces of Bernardin and Roach suggest. The Americans have nursed the pastoral letter this far. The strain shows: a certain tiredness around the eyes, the refusals to comment a little sharper than usual. They had posed for a picture in St Peter's Square on the day Soviet Foreign Minister Andrei Gromyko ruled out – again – President Reagan's zero option, and the CIA confirmed the arrival of long-range Soviet anti-aircraft missiles in Syria.[1] The cardinal and the bishop have nothing to say about Gromyko or what is happening in Syria.[2]

In the fourth floor *Quattrovoci* studio of Vatican Radio, Clarissa McNair reads both items in her noon newscast, placing them next to a mention that the bishops are continuing with their deliberations.[3] In down-town Rome The Mad Mentor diligently noted what she had done and sent the transcription along to the US envoy to the Holy See.[4] It joined the growing pile of what William Wilson would call 'McNair's anti-American transgressions'.[5]

Her colleague, Henry McConnachie, has just suffered a

setback.[6] One of the delegates, Cardinal Gordon Gray of Scotland who leads the British team to the conference, has vetoed McConnachie's plan to interview Archbishop Thomas Winning of Glasgow about the Scottish hierarchy's view on disarmament. With Polaris submarines berthed in Holy Loch and NATO looking at the possibility of siting missiles amid the heather and along the high road to Loch Lomond, McConnachie thought Winning would be a useful interviewee. But after agreeing to do the broadcast, Winning had a word with Gray.

McConnachie thinks Gray's involvement a significant pointer to what is happening in the Synod Hall. The broadcaster deduced 'the heat was on to beef up the pastoral letter and they didn't want Vatican Radio rocking the boat'.[7] We find it hard to imagine the station ever doing that: the daily output of religious music, masses, sermons interlaced with carefully worded newscasts and mini-documentaries is surely fodder for only the really dedicated among the faithful.

It's a ten-minute stroll from the station's headquarters in Piazza Pia to Porta Sant'Anna; time enough for us to ponder again a story that has got the bite of a bullet stamped on it. Three sources – a cardinal's secretary and two other members of the Curia – insist the story is true. It comes down to this. The pope prayed a great deal before elevating Bernardin to the Sacred College of Cardinals. Further: he took most careful soundings in advance of deciding the Chicago archbishop should get a red hat. So what, we say. Well, say our informants, the pope's doubts about Bernardin spring from the American's private feeling that unilateral disarmament is acceptable.

We raised the issue with Greenan when we reach his office. The editor has just taken his blood pressure; he keeps the cuff in his desk. It helps him decide whether he can pay a call on his cupboard of the holy spirit – the well-stocked bar in a filing cabinet which makes his office such a convivial place to visit.

Greenan admits he has indeed heard of the way Bernardin is being pilloried. The editor does not like the idea we are even discussing the matter. We remind him it's part of our job to verify or deny such rumours. He shrugs. 'Look at it like this, lads. The tale says the Holy Father prayed a great deal. Well now, isn't it a fact he decided to give Bernardin his hat? And well then, doesn't that show the power of prayer to give the right answer?'

He smiles – a signal not to press further. We ask how the meeting in the Synod Hall is going.

'It's going very well, lads, very well. There's no blood-letting and the Germans are the surprise. But remember they always are.'

A clue to pursue.

We walk over to the Apostolic Palace to meet the monsignor who had telephoned us late one night at our hotel. We have met him twice since then. He is more relaxed and has volunteered that he's helping us because he's decided so much of Vatican secrecy nowadays is counter-productive; he'd gone so far as to say over dinner one night in his apartment that what the Vatican needs is a White House-style spokesman, with full access to the pope and to what is going on. We agreed the present Vatican Press Officer appears ill-equipped to deal with the demands of the modern media: he lacks charisma and seems uncom-fortable in the presence of tough-headed secular journalists. Our monsignor predicted that before the year is out the man could be working as a parish priest in some Church outpost. If so, he won't be missed.[8]

Our monsignor suggests we walk in the Vatican gardens. It is a clear mild day and there are a number of priests strolling the paths. They don't give us a second glance. We climb towards the pad from which the pope flies in a gleaming white helicopter to avoid the risk of being kidnap-ped, a precaution introduced during the closing months of Paul VI's pontificate when a plot was discovered whereby West German terrorists planned to snatch the aged pontiff and take him to Libya. There he would have been held hostage against Israel freeing all the terrorists it held.[9]

We stand in the lee of the helipad looking out over Rome while we hear of a very different kind of German attitude – that of Cardinal Joseph Hoeffner of Cologne, leading the German delegation to the conference.

Our monsignor is marvellously to the point – and his own connections are clearly impeccable.[10] They include Casaroli, Silvestrini and Backis, along with three experts from the Council of Public Affairs who between them represent the Holy See in the Synod Hall. After the first full session Casaroli had assembled his team in the Secretariat and reviewed the first day's developments.

The proceedings had been dominated by Hoeffner; elderly and scratchy in so many ways, the cardinal must be the surprise to which Greenan alluded. Hoeffner has softened his position on nuclear arms. He is not quite so dogmatic about rejecting the latest Soviet proposals as he had been towards previous Russian ones. Our monsignor says the feeling in the Holy See team is that Hoeffner is becoming more realistic in old age. He has made it clear he is not opposed to the tone of the US pastoral letter.

The French have said little, made a lot of notes and murmured a great deal among themselves. The British are cautiously firm: they think the letter is a valuable document – but one which still needs work done on it. The chief opponent has turned out to be the auxiliary bishop of Rotterdam and chaplain to the Dutch armed forces.

We ask how Ratzinger is managing the conference.

Our monsignor smiles. 'Just like Ratzinger. He knows how to play the rules within the rules. And he's got a well-prepared brief. Things will go exactly the way he – and His Holiness – wish them to go.'

We wonder about the final outcome. He surprises us: 'Oh, they'll all go home, hold "discussions" with each other in the coming weeks and offer suggestions for how the next draft can come closer to what Reagan and the Holy Father want.'

The next day we find his forecast was roughly accurate. The conference is hardly over when Roach is speaking about the 'very broad-based consultations' which have taken place. He says they will be 'useful' in helping to complete the final draft of the document to be unveiled in Chicago. Gazing into his crystal ball, the archbishop added, 'Obviously there are going to be differences in perspective, but that is to be welcomed to help us with the final document.'[11]

It's journalistic whistling in the dark to report that the Italian delegates severely criticized the pastoral letter, that the French finally came out and said it needed revision, that the British were vaguely unhappy, that the Belgians gave cautious support along with Hoeffner. But that's the way it seems to many reporters on this damp Roman night.

All in all it's not been a very inspiring meeting. But a good one for the moles. In the coming days they will pop up as guests of the media in all sorts of fancy Rome restaurants, singing for their suppers. They really won't carry much of a tune.

7
THE PAPAL SECRETARIAT
Monday
Morning

There is no let-up, and Kabongo would not want it any other way. He thrives on the demands put on his judgement and stamina. The more intense the pace the more relaxed and smiling he appears. His demeanour works wonders on those around him; they too become imbued with good humour and his attitude that everything is under control.

This morning there are no signs of pressure in the papal secretariat on the third floor of the Apostolic Palace. The loudest noise is the ticking of clocks, sixteenth- and seventeenth-century pieces, collector's items, like the baroque furniture, carpets and paintings. The superbly appointed suite of offices is equipped with the latest devices to record and transcribe. Since the moment Kabongo and Dziwisz arrived at their desks the lights on their cream multi-line telephones have been flashing.[1]

Officially Kabongo is an *Uditore di 2ª classe* in the diplomatic section of the Council for the Public Affairs the Church – in effect the Church's Ministry for Foreign Affairs; Dziwisz is attached to the diplomatic section of the Secretariat of State as one of the many *Ufficiali Minori di II Grado*. The comparatively low ranks of both men do not indicate their real power and authority. Each works and lives close to the pope: they know his whims and dislikes; they understand as well as anyone and better than most the many facets of his character. They know how to anticipate his occasional anger and try to divert it; they can sense when he wants to be alone, when he wants to hear their opinions, when he is in a mood to relax and reminisce.

So far this morning the impatient side of the pontiff has dominated their routine. John Paul is anxious to fill this day even more than others. His secretaries sensed the feeling when they joined him for the first mass of the day in the pope's own chapel, a coldly austere place completely walled in white marble, relieved only by the Stations of the Cross and light percolating through stained-glass windows.[2]

Over breakfast, as is their custom, the two secretaries went over the pope's appointments.[3]

Cardinal Pietro Palazzini, Prefect of the Sacred Congregation for the Causes of Saints, is due to spend ten minutes making one of his infrequent reports. Since 1588 the Congregation has handled such pleasurable matters for the pope as canonizations and the preservation of holy relics. Afterwards Cardinal Laszlo Lekai will have a full fifteen minutes to bring John Paul up to date on the constant struggle between Church and State in Hungary. Then Cardinal Michael Kitbunchu of Thailand will have ten minutes with the pontiff. He will be followed, at five-minute intervals, by the archbishops of Bombay and Evora in Portugal.

Finally George Bush will be received for a full thirty minutes. It is this visit that has made John Paul impatient; he cannot wait to sit down with the vice-president.[4]

Since eight o'clock the two secretaries and their assistants have been finalizing the paperwork involved in the meetings.

A *minutante* is going through the minutes of Palazzini's last visit.

Dziwisz is checking the brief he has prepared on the situation in Hungary now that Brezhnev is dead. One of the central changes introduced by the Soviet leader had been a cautious acceptance of the concept of détente; to gild the idea Brezhnev allowed in Hungary a slight loosening of the leash on the local hierarchy. But even before Brezhnev died there had been serious questioning in the Politburo about the wisdom of easing the position of the Hungarian Church. Dziwisz suggests in his paper that the pope try and elicit from the Hungarian archbishop something of the new leader's attitudes.

119

Lekai in Budapest has watched Soviet foreign policy switch and change during his seven years as a cardinal; in the Vatican he is as much respected for his outspoken sermons as for his skill in dealing with Communism on the ground. Consequently Dziwisz has prepared a number of specific questions for the pope to ask Lekai. Are there any signs in Hungary that the new Soviet leadership will embark on a reorientation of foreign policy which will be significantly different from that which dominated the final years of Brezhnev? How does the Hungarian regime see the lack of progress in the strategic arms limitation talks? How deep is the sense in Hungary of being caught up in the adversarial relationship between the United States and Russia?

There are supplementary questions to be asked on Hungary's view of Soviet involvement in Afghanistan, and on the Hungarian attitude to Russia's wish to make its frontier with China a 'border of friendship'. There may not be time for the pope to ask all these questions, nor is he likely to pose them in the order or form that Dziwisz indicates. But the secretary is satisfied his brief will help to continue the endless process of keeping John Paul abreast of events.[5]

An equally detailed document has been prepared for Archbishop Kitbunchu of Bangkok. The newly elevated Thai cardinal who received his red hat with the seventeen others at the consistory held five days ago will be expected to answer some searching questions on how he perceives China's obsession with Vietnam. He will also be asked to comment on Vietnam's attempt to dominate Indo-China, a move which has both brought it into deepening dispute with China and attracted the unwelcome and menacing presence of Russia into the area.

The five minutes reserved for the Archbishop of Bombay will be devoted solely to the Indian hierarchy's financial problems.

The visitor from Portugal will, thanks to Kabongo's research, find John Paul well briefed on the earthquake which has just jolted Lisbon, and the Portuguese president's sudden decision to dissolve parliament. This has ended months of petty squabbling within the right-wing alliance. The archbishop will be required to indicate what preparations his Church is making against the possibility of a Socialist-Marxist coalition being elected in Portugal.

Then it will be time for the pope to take a last-minute look at the most important brief of this morning, the one provided for his meeting with Bush.

The preparation of this brief began after John Paul received in audience a group of US congressmen. He told them to rededicate themselves 'to those sound moral principles formulated by your founding fathers', and to remember their 'duty to respect the wishes of the entire international community'. Afterwards, mixing with the politicians, papal staff took soundings on the congressmen's views of the forthcoming Bush trip. The next day the pope had explored the Reagan administration's reservations about the pastoral letter when he met Bernardin, Laghi and Hehir.[6] Their replies were passed on for analysis.

Kabongo, who has been spending as much time as possible planning for the Bush visit – frequently calling in on the Secretariat of State to study the steady flow of material coming into the North America and Western Europe Desks – found himself caught up in the on-going row between Czechoslovakia and the Vatican. The secretary had helped co-ordinate the Holy See response – a coolly worded rejection – to Czech accusations that the Church was trying to introduce a 'clerical-fascist' regime in the country.[7]

The announcement that the pope was to visit Switzerland later in the year had brought a few good-natured groans from his staff; shortly afterwards they were told John Paul's Polish trip was definitely on. This time there were no groans, only fear for what could happen to the pontiff.

The political implications of that trip, Kabongo realized, might very well be raised by Bush. The secretary had begun to gather data on the current US attitude towards Poland.

* * *

At ten-fifteen a squad of blue-overalled *sampietrini*, the Vatican maintenance men, unroll a red carpet which runs from the Door of John XXIII out over the cobbles of San Damaso Courtyard. Their action is the first item on the Vatican's detailed printed protocol for the Bush visit.

Seven minutes later, as per the protocol, there assembles here in full splendour a group led by Mgr Jacques Martin, Prefect of Casa Pontificia, the papal household. It includes the pope's Almoner, the Vicar-General of Vatican City, the Prelates of the Antechamber, the Assistant at the Throne, the Special Delegate of the Pontifical Commission for the Vatican City State, the State's Consultor, the Commandant of the Swiss Guard, the Gentlemen of the Pope, the Attendants of the Antechamber, the Dean of the Hall and the Guard of Honour of the Swiss Guard. The Pontifical Band is not present. It plays only for visiting heads of state. Otherwise this is the splendidly robed and ruffled retinue which greets any important guest.[8]

Standing to one side are those described on the Vatican protocol sheet under 'special arrangements'.

Among the tallest is William Wilson, Ronald Reagan's special envoy. He could, in the indistinct morning light, almost pass as the president's double. Wilson has the same Californian tan, twinkle in his eye, ready smile and folksy manner. His dark business suit is English worsted but the cut is comfortably West Coast. In his custom-made shoes, Brooks Brothers socks and Pierre Cardin silk tie, in the way that he speaks and occasionally gestures, Wilson nearly out-Reagans Reagan.

Sixty-eight years of age, this former captain in the US Army Ordnance Corps 'is still active in real estate development and cattle interests in the United States and Mexico' – a piece of State Department public relations flummery which gives no inkling of his immense wealth. Wilson is on a hospital board and a regent of the University of California. He is a devout Catholic. But above all he is proud to say, 'Ronnie Reagan is my friend.'[9]

The president chose Wilson as his first foreign political appointment, a decision which has brought Wilson to this historic courtyard. He has been here many times since he was appointed to the Holy See in 1981; he likes the job even though there is no salary, only living and entertainment expenses. He returns to the United States frequently. When in Rome he is known as 'Mr Gaffe' among the more disrespectful members of the media. He shrugs them aside as 'just a bunch of pinko journalists trying to make a living'.[10]

Wilson has had no formal diplomatic training. Foreign Service professionalism is in the hands of the two aides who flank him. Michael Hornblow, highly intelligent, fortyish and filled with inner tension, is someone who sometimes gives the appearance of suspecting a hidden motive in the simplest of greetings. He is sad he is due to relinquish his post shortly but nevertheless admits the workload in Rome is gruelling.[11] The man due to take over from Hornblow, Don Planty, is, in contrast, totally relaxed. He has a smile which would grace a toothpaste advertisement, a suit which probably cost almost as much as Wilson's, and a diplomatic track record which placed him in Chile during the time the CIA attempted to block Allende's elevation to president.[12]

Punctually at ten twenty-six, the Bush motorcade enters the courtyard. As the vice-president's car stops before the red carpet – protocol item twenty-four – the Swiss Guards present arms with their halberds. Bush steps out and acknowledges the salute, just as the schedule prescribes he should. Martin leads his prelates forward.

Wilson and his men converge on Bush – item twenty-eight – and the envoy has a few words with the vice-president. His secret service detail bunches around him, edging some of the priests away – an action the protocol sheet did not describe.[13]

Martin leads Bush into the Apostolic Palace. Behind them ecclesiastics in red-trimmed cassocks and sashes and dark-suited secret servicemen eye each other as they follow.

Bush has a politician's gift for small talk. He plies Martin with questions which a US embassy official in Rome has prepared. Martin is the Vatican's resident specialist on its history.[14] He knows who painted the wall frescoes they are passing, the religious scenes on ceilings, which pope placed a particular cherub or satyr on their route, which supervised the hanging of a triptych in oils. The prefect delivers his facts with a hint of the sardonic wit which has made him famous.

The journey from the courtyard is completed in precisely the time itemized on the protocol paper. At ten twenty-nine Martin and Bush arrive in a small salon. There is a door facing them. Beyond is the pope's library.

Wilson and his aides, Martin's staff and the secret servicemen remain here while the prefect takes Bush in to see the pope at exactly ten-thirty.

The waiting group glimpse the pontiff seated on a chair. Behind him is a painting by Perugino and two sixteenth-century bookcases.

Martin makes the formal introduction and then leaves the two men alone, closing the door behind him.

For most of the next forty-five minutes the pope and the politician examine the US attitude to nuclear arms and disarmament.

Bush emphasizes America's 'moral position', one which includes favouring a total ban on intermediate-range nuclear missiles in Europe.[15]

The pope expresses a similar desire.

Bush reviews the results of his trip through Europe. The Dutch had been helpful, the Belgians and the West Germans realistic, the British totally supportive, the Italians a pleasant surprise in their enthusiasm.[16]

The vice-president's answers to questions then put to him by the pope closely reflect the responses predicted in the final briefing paper John Paul had studied.[17]

The pope enquires whether the United States might agree to move from its zero option negotiating position – while still aiming for the administration's well publicized objective of 'banishing once and for all from the face of the earth land-based intermediate-range nuclear weapons'.[18]

Bush repeats what he has said in Bonn, explaining the United States would do nothing dramatic before the forthcoming West German elections, just a month away, in case this damaged Chancellor Kohl's chances of re-election.

The pope's brief contains some pertinent questions concerning scenarios depicting various potential crises for NATO, until now one of the most successful military alliances in history. What would the US response be if one or more of the European members refused to accept the new missiles on their soil? What would America do if a decision was taken by, say the Socialist government of Greece or Spain, that US naval and air bases must be vacated? What would be the response in Washington if any NATO country decided out of economic necessity to make a significant reduction in defence expenditure? How would the Reagan administration respond to the refusal by a NATO member to allow US military planes to land on or even overfly its territory in the event of a new Middle East war which threatened Persian Gulf oil?

All these questions are based on precedent or growing possibilities.

France had demanded in 1966 that the United States withdrew her land forces. In the current political climate in Spain, it could be possible for the new Socialist government to go beyond questioning membership of NATO and order the closure of all US bases on Spanish soil. Britain's Labour Party, if returned to power, might well remove the nation's nuclear shield, including scrapping its own system.

Present NATO governments are committed to increasing their defence budgets by three per cent a year, *after inflation*, and most are making real efforts to achieve that target. But if one – possibly Spain or Turkey – finds the financial burden too great to meet on defence, then serious questions would be asked by other NATO members about whether a defaulting country should expect to continue to benefit from the alliance's protection; in the United States this could lead to a groundswell of public opinion demanding the removal of all US forces from Europe – also for economic reasons.

During the 1973 Arab-Israeli war, the US air force was refused landing permission and overflight rights by certain NATO members which seriously slowed supplies to Israel, to the point where the Jewish state barely survived against Egypt and Syria.

The discussion moves to the pope's concern over the possibility of Western Europe being no longer unanimously willing to accept US leadership of the alliance – particularly if both the Soviet Union and the United States continue to pursue their committed and uncompromising line on disarmament and the struggle to win the Third World.

John Paul wants to know whether the Reagan administration fears – even remotely – the prospect that West Germany, Greece and Denmark, and perhaps other European nations, could distance themselves from NATO to join the growing non-alignment movement.

When Bush leaves the library at eleven-fifteen A.M. – a full fifteen minutes later than anticipated on the protocol schedule – he takes with him the pope's personal view of the US pastoral letter plus an impression which allows the vice-president to conclude that on all the important points in the administration's disarmament policy, Pope John Paul and President Reagan are in accord.

Before the Bush motorcade sweeps out of the San Damaso Courtyard, the vice-president can truthfully say to Wilson that 'it was really very, very worthwhile. Very worthwhile.'[19]

REBIBBIA PRISON, ROME
Wednesday
Mid-Morning

Sirens wailing and blue roof-lights flashing, the three vehicles force their way through the heavy suburban traffic.

The leading Fiat contains four *carabinieri*. The pair in the back have machine-pistols on their knees, cocked and ready to be fired. They sit slumped in their seats to offer less conspicuous targets. They constantly scan the ugly apartment buildings either side for any indication of trouble. Their eyes smart from the rush of wind coming through the open car window in the front; the *carabiniere* in the passenger seat has his right hand out of the window, clutching a red disc on a short pole. It is an additional warning for all other traffic and pedestrians to remain well clear of the convoy. The two policemen in the front have pistols in waist holsters.

The second car, an unmarked saloon, has special armour plating. A sheet of thick steel protects the underside of the chassis against a bomb being detonated in the road. The bodywork has been reinforced to withstand the spray of a machine-gun from quite close range. The windows are bullet-proof and the tyres shielded by metal guards. It would require an anti-tank weapon to stop this car continuing to race pell-mell behind the first Fiat.

Sitting in the front of the saloon are two armed policemen. The one in the passenger seat is in constant contact by radio with Rome city police traffic control. There, the saloon's progress is continuously monitored as it speeds eastwards across the city. At the first call for help, a dozen other police cars will be immediately diverted to the rescue.

Seated in the back of the saloon is magistrate Martella and an aide.

Behind them is a third Fiat, also carrying four *carabinieri*. They are equipped exactly like the men in the first car.

This is the road to Rebibbia, the prison which is named after one of Rome's seediest districts. From the cheap construction housing on either side of the convoy's route have come many members of the Red Brigades. These buildings are always among the first to be searched for kidnap victims. A mere hour by road from St Peter's, the neighbourhood is the city's Hell's Kitchen, a breeding ground for every kind of violence and vice. Outsiders whose business brings them here rush through the area, fearing they will get pelted with bricks or even shot at.

Martella has covered this route many times to interrogate convicted terrorists, drug peddlers and supergrasses, criminals who turn informers for reduced sentences or to be released from behind the high cement walls which appear on the left side of the speeding cars.

The traffic has thinned. Only those who have to, travel on this empty stretch of road. The *carabinieri* relax; the houses on their right are for prison staff.

The convoy roars past the first checkpoint but stops at the second, near the main prison gate. Nobody, not even those in these official cars, is allowed beyond here without careful scrutiny. There have been attempts by terrorists posing as policemen to enter other Italian gaols; it would be impossible to do so at Rebibbia. That is what makes the prison so formidable.[20]

The three cars are allowed to proceed. Beyond the gate are beds of shrubs bordering a maze of roads.

From a distance the prison looks like an impoverished college or hospital in need of repair. By the time the convoy parks in front of the entrance, there is no mistaking the real purpose of this place.

Beside the main door is a metal box where briefcases and bags must be deposited. The box is then drawn into the building and its contents examined by the soldiers on duty in the guardhouse.

They unlock the door for Martella and his companion and waive inspecting their briefcases. The two men pass into a maximum security keep of armoured doors, jangling keys, cement floors and staircases.

Martella and his aide take a caged elevator to the first-floor administrative block. The judge has an office here.

It is bare but for the furniture. Placed in the middle of the room are two cheap desks, positioned at right angles, each with a wooden chair behind.[21]

In front of Martella's desk is a third chair. Standing behind it are two soldiers, hands ready to restrain the seated man if he makes any move.

The judge and his assistant ignore the prisoner and his escort. Sitting down, they open their briefcases and remove files and writing blocks. The aide produces a pen and then waits.

Only after he is satisfied his files are open at the correct place and he has taken his gold-plated fountain pen from his pocket and tested it, does prosecutor Martella look at Sergei Antonov.

The Bulgarian airline official has been held in this prison since November 1982, since the day he was arrested by a DIGOS squad on suspicion of helping Agca to try and assassinate the pope. His three months in Rebibbia have physically and mentally changed Antonov. He is thinner and less aggressive: he has given up protesting about the food, that he is not allowed to receive newspapers, that he is denied a radio, that, like any other prisoner here, he is allowed visitors only once a week. They have usually been his wife or members of the Bulgarian Embassy.

Just as the judge has a special way of dealing with Agca, so Martella has developed one with Antonov which is more in keeping with the traditional relationship between prosecutor and prisoner. Martella can be alternately harsh and disdainful, disbelieving and distant: when Antonov prevaricates, the judge cuts him off; when he attempts to remain silent, Martella bombards him with questions. The judge's behaviour is kept within the strictly defined rules of obtaining evidence, but his tactics have contributed to the pensive and crestfallen attitude Antonov has developed these past weeks.

This is what makes the change in him now more marked. Martella would undoubtedly have been surprised by Antonov's new-found confidence this morning had the judge not already known the reason for it.

Pista Bulgara has gone reeling off in a direction that has badly rocked even the normally unflappable Martella. In Washington the CIA is orchestrating a press campaign in which the agency is claiming neither the Bulgarians nor the Soviet Union instigated the attack on the pope. The CIA is saying that while there is a '99 per cent certainty' officials of the Bulgarian government had advance knowledge of what was planned, there is no 'smoking gun' absolute proof which ties Agca either to the Bulgarian Secret Service or the KGB. While Agca was determined to kill the pope, he acted totally on his own initiative.[22]

The agency's version sounds remarkably similar to the one Vassil Dimitrov, the Bulgarian diplomat in Rome, has been trying so hard to promote.

Not for the first time in his career does Martella realize his search for truth and justice has become entangled with pragmatic international politics.

Martella came to his conclusion a few days ago following a meeting with the controversial Republican senator of New York, Alfonse D'Amato.[23] The senator is a member of the Helsinki Commission on Security and Co-operation in Europe and a specialist on US intelligence matters. D'Amato had planned to bring with him to Rome a member of the Senate Select Committee on Intelligence. But the move, the senator told Martella, had been blocked by the CIA. D'Amato warned the judge the CIA Station in Rome had been ordered to deny him additional assistance and that from now on the agency's efforts would be aimed at discouraging any further investigation into a possible

Bulgarian or Soviet involvement in the plot to kill the pope.

The judge quickly deduced what lay behind the CIA's actions. The agency was almost certainly responding to a discreet but direct intervention by the White House; Martella has heard that the Reagan administration regards his investigation as a case 'where the pursuit of truth, while necessary, could put an enormous strain on Moscow's relations with the West'.[24]

The view in Washington is that even by East European standards Bulgaria is an unusually slavish satellite of the Soviet Union; if the Bulgarian secret service is linked to the attack, the consensus is it could not conceivably have acted without the foreknowledge and active complicity of the KGB. *Ipso facto*, if the Bulgarian connection is established beyond doubt, it would then become virtually impossible for President Reagan or any other important Western leader to meet Andropov. And in the atmosphere of anger and hostility which would follow, it would also be very much harder to negotiate new arms control agreements, or to have them ratified if they were negotiated.[25]

For the White House – and for the Kremlin – this would be an unsatisfactory, even dangerous, state of affairs.

Martella can easily understand the reality behind the thinking. He has suspected that President Reagan's public hard-line towards the Russians is often for domestic consumption, an attempt to win Republican votes in the next election. Martella's own visits to Washington have convinced him that the president, or at least his advisers, would stamp hard on his investigation – as they are now doing – if it threatened wider considerations. And the prosecutor can well appreciate that it might become politically desirable for Reagan to meet Andropov personally to discuss arms control negotiations and world peace. Martella would not be surprised to be told that when Bush spoke to the pope the vice-president tactfully suggested that John Paul should not pursue quite so energetically his own interest in the plot. Nothing would astonish Martella: he has spent too many years straddling the worlds of politics and justice not to know they are frequently indivisible.

But he is also determined about one thing. No one – the US president, the pope, the Italian government and least of all the CIA – is going to stand in the way of his pursuit of the truth.

That is why he has come to Rebibbia this morning. He knows Antonov believes he might soon be freed, partly because he steadfastly denies he ever met Agca.

Martella proposes to test the truth of this in a striking way.

The judge looks at his aide. The clerk gets to his feet and leaves the office. Martella resumes questioning Antonov about Agca.

The Bulgarian again stolidly denies they have ever met.

Martella presses: why is Antonov lying?

Antonov denies the accusation.

The clerk returns to the office and takes his place at his desk.

The judge and his aide stare at Antonov. He looks as defiant as when they arrived.

Outside the office there is the sound of approaching footsteps.

Martella orders Antonov to stand and face the doors. His arms are gripped by his escort. He is confronted with the man he claims never to have met – Agca.

Martella turns to Agca and indicates Antonov. 'Ali, do you know this person?'

'It's Sergei. Sergei Antonov. He helped me.'

Antonov screams that Agca is a liar.

Martella ignores the interruption and motions for Agca's escort to take him away.

Agca has been moved from Ascoli Piceno prison for a confrontation which has lasted less than a minute. But Martella believes these crucial sixty seconds have sent his investigation leaping forward.

Later he will tell his staff that the CIA or anyone else can spread as much disinformation as they like, but he is satisfied that Agca is telling the truth about knowing Antonov. It was there in his eyes, Martella will say, a clear look of recognition. And what about Antonov, an aide will ask, how did he appear?

'Guilty. Now all we need is more proof.'

THE VATICAN
Saturday
Early Morning – Late Evening

On a wall of Cibin's office is a calendar which has one date he has ringed in red. It is the date by which he must have completed all the security preparations for the papal trip to Central America. Cibin is one of those making the trip, the seventeenth he will have made with John Paul in the past four and a half years. None of them has filled the security chief with such dread.

At every public moment during the 18,000-mile journey John Paul will face a potential assassin. The killer could be waiting in the relative calm of Costa Rica, or in Nicaragua, run by a Marxist-dominated government in which several priests hold high office in defiance of the pontiff. John Paul could be struck down in Panama, or even more likely in El Salvador, itself gripped in all-out civil war. He might be attacked in Guatemala, whose regime is both anti-Catholic and has a deserved reputation for murdering those who give it offence. Honduras and Belize and finally Haiti are all places where John Paul might come face to face with a terrorist. Already twenty-four bishops, priests and nuns have been murdered during his pontificate in the region; most have been the victims of right-wing death squads.

In each of the countries on his itinerary the CIA has prepared appraisals of security arrangements for the pope's visit. The reports do nothing to lessen Cibin's worries.

These have increased after the Archbishop of Managua, Miguel Obando Bravo, arrived in Rome for urgent talks about the possibility of cancelling at this late stage the visit to Nicaragua. The monsignor painted a grim picture of increasing harassment of those priests and nuns who do not totally support the Sandinista regime. Ironically the removal of the previous right-wing dictatorship was the first popular revolution in the area to have been openly endorsed by the local hierarchy. Since then a growing number of the clergy, despite Obando Bravo's warnings, had become involved working with the Christian-Marxist fusion of the liberation theologians.

Cibin was among those this morning who assembled in the pope's library to hear the archbishop describe the latest situation as one which presents John Paul not only with complex diplomatic challenges, but deepens the risk to his life.[26]

When Obando Bravo finished his presentation the pope had not hesitated. He would go to Nicaragua: 'There will be no cancellations. No shortening of the schedule.'

It was another way for him to state his determination to make all Catholics – whatever their social outlook – feel united in one great family, whether they represent the traditionalist right wing, the reforming centre, or the radical and often revolutionary left.

Cibin returned to his office to grapple with the problem of protecting the pontiff.

The security chief knows he must depend entirely on local help to ensure the pope's safety. Apart from a ceremonial platoon of Swiss Guards, Cibin will have only two *vigili* with him. Each of the Central American regimes has vetoed a Vatican request to have present its usual squad of sharp-shooting guards. A number of excuses have been offered. They all have one thing in common so far as Cibin is concerned. He does not believe any of them. That, too, heightens his anxiety.

★ ★ ★

Kabongo has thrown all his energies into preparing for the Central American trip.

In practice this means keeping constant contact with the tour's co-ordinator, Fr Roberto Tucci, and the Latin America Desk in the Secretariat of State. Literally hundreds of requests, suggestions and advisories have been arriving from the eight countries to be visited. Many have found their way on to Kabongo's desk.[27] Will the pope be able to spend an extra two minutes on the tarmac at Costa Rica airport so that he can personally greet more junior members of the government? When he reaches Guatemala could John Paul make some reference to the two-storey steel cross which will remain 'for ever' in the Campo de Marte Stadium, where he is to celebrate one of the dozen masses scheduled on the eight-day journey? Will he be able to respond 'in some way' to the Honduran jingle which is the local theme song for the visit?

There are scores of such questions which need to be pondered and carefully answered so as not to give offence when a request must be refused. Part of Kabongo's task is to balance the festive mood the tour is already generating among the faithful against practical considerations.

The secretary knows that a couple of extra minutes at Costa Rica's international airport on arrival could have a knock-on effect: junior ministers are, in Kabongo's experience, renowned for engaging the pope in small talk. Those two minutes might easily stretch to ten. Equally, Costa Rica is particularly well-disposed towards the trip: there could be further goodwill for the local hierarchy in allowing a few more politicians to be added to the receiving line. Kabongo makes a note on the Costa Rica schedule. The airport ceremonies should be extended by 120 seconds, with the proviso that those two extra minutes must not under any circumstances be allowed to last longer than five.

It's easier for him to settle the requested reference to the Guatemala stadium cross; a suitable mention can be written into the pope's address. Kabongo makes another note.

But there will be no papal endorsement of the Honduran jingle; for the British visit the Vatican had approved the hiring of a talent-promoting organization, which normally handles golfers and show business personalities, to take care of the profitable spin-off in 'authorized' books and souvenirs, a move which caused sniping afterwards over the Church's commercialism. Kabongo drafts a polite reply to Honduras that the theme song, like the local bumper stickers and lapel buttons, cannot be officially blessed.

There are still other matters to consider: the climate and health precautions. It will be hot and humid all the way, and malarial tablets will be needed: in several countries the drinking water is not safe. There is a warning from Nicaragua that it is forbidden to import matches. From El Salvador have come details of currency exchange rates, electricity voltages and a reminder that only two bottles of alcohol for each member of the papal entourage will be allowed in.

Kabongo knows paying proper attention to these small details can make or mar the trip for the pope and his staff.

The high point of the tour will be the quadriennial assembly of the Latin American Bishops' Conference (CELAM). The protocol for the occasion requires a separate booklet. Dziwisz is working on that.

As well as coping with other aspects, Kabongo is also concerned to have an over-view of the potential areas of maximum danger on the trip.

Like Cibin the secretary believes the visit to El Salvador is the one most fraught with risk. On Kabongo's desk is a bluntly worded refusal by the country's government to Casaroli's appeal for a cease-fire while John Paul is there.[28] And among the pile of paper the secretary has before him is a report which accurately portrays the schism within the Salvadoran Church. The document has been prepared by Bishop Rivera Damas of Santiago de Maria. Couched elegantly and filled with circumspection and personal reminders of the prelate's own unquestioning loyalty to the pope, the report describes the growing conflict among his clergy over the forthcoming visit.[29]

Following a recent appeal by Nuncio Lajos Kada for the government to start talking to the rebels, conservative priests who support the government have told the bishop they fear the pope will also lend his authority by calling for a dialogue between the guerrillas and the regime. If that happened the Salvadoran Church could be split even deeper, perhaps irrevocably.

Equally, the proponents of liberation theology fear John Paul may indicate his support for the ruling oligarchy.

Kabongo knows the pope would never do that – especially after he reads the summary on El Salvador assembled by the Secretariat of State.

A draft has been sent to Kabongo. It is a sobering document. Devoid of emotion, rhetoric or bias, the brief merely recites the facts. It begins by explaining how part of the Salvadoran hierarchy had dramatically switched from supporting the minority élite to identifying with the country's impoverished majority. These priests had organized what they called 'base communities' which quickly evolved into political camps where the doctrine of liberation theology was preached.

Kabongo can, if asked, list the tenets of a movement that now has over 100,000 *comunidades eclesiales de base* throughout Latin America. They work in 'the spirit of the Gospels', and draw many ideas directly from Marxism: some of its theologians go so far as to identify the Gospel poor with Marx's proletariat; their sermons contain regular references to winning victory in the class war, approving the classic Marxist defence that violence *is* acceptable when used against the inbuilt violence of oppressive regimes. The movement endorses the Marxist view of capitalism, and believes revolution alone can purge what they see as an unjust society. Only when that is successful will there be reconciliation – but only on the terms the movement has fought to establish.

Kabongo is not alone in thinking the sole visible difference between the movement's aims and Communist doctrine is that liberation theology does actually reject atheism.

The pope has repeatedly criticized the movement's teachings.

Yet in El Salvador he has been asked to pray at the tomb of Archbishop Oscar Romero. Assassinated because of his outspoken opposition to the government, Romero has become an authentic martyr for the poor and the rebellious left.

The Secretariat document dispassionately lays out the government's view – endorsed by some local clerics – that the guerrillas have made a mockery of what Romero really stood for: non-violence and non-partisan social reform. The government has made plain it strongly disapproves of the pope praying at the murdered archbishop's tomb on the basis that if John Paul does so, he will be giving succour to the insurgents.

The matter is so sensitive the final decision has been left to the pope. And Kabongo knows that with only fifteen days to go before John Paul actually sets foot on Salvadoran soil, the solution continues to torment the pontiff.

What Fr Roberto Tucci calls 'the nuts and bolts' of the forthcoming trip are being assembled in his office in the Palace of Leo XIII inside the Vatican. Hour after hour, day in and day out a stream of people have sat across from the dark-skinned Jesuit and explained their problems and plans. Tucci is invariably relaxed and friendly. Visitors say it is easy to understand why he has made an impression as director-general of Vatican Radio. He has been seconded from that post to organize the tour. The man now seated opposite Tucci says, again, that the priest is doing a good job.

Adriano Botta, an Alitalia executive, has come to explain the airline's role in the pilgrimage.

Alitalia have evolved a master plan for papal flights that

includes reconnoitring in advance all the airports to be used and examining their security precautions. Diversionary airfields are similarly checked. The papal aircraft carries its own armed security detail which remains continuously on board while the plane is on the ground. Additionally the aircraft is equipped with certain other 'proper preventive measures', sufficient for Botta to insist 'we offer more security than do the host countries'.[30]

He continues to explain the plan. The normal internal configuration has been drastically altered. The First Class section has been moved back to accommodate the pope's suite and galley. There will be thirty-four First Class seats behind the galley reserved for the papal retinue and, behind them, economy class seating for the press.

Not all of the reporters who want to go on the flight have yet been approved; more have applied than will be taken, many of them doubtless wishing to be present in case the unthinkable happens – another attempt on the pope's life.

One broadcaster who knows exactly what he will do if there is an attack on the pope is Sean MacCarthy. 'I'll announce it on the air as fast as possible – and then I'll say a prayer that the pope will survive.'[31]

For nearly fifteen years MacCarthy has been one of Vatican Radio's most celebrated voices, a position which virtually guarantees him a place on the trip. His soft Irish brogue attracts more fanmail than almost any of the station's other broadcasters. He is sixty-three years old, a compact man with a Celt's mournful smile and a voice devotees claim is crystal clear on the short-wave bands the station uses to transmit the Sacred Word.

MacCarthy will be covering part of the pope's trip to Central America. Typically he is immersing himself in background, absorbing all he can on the political and religious differences of the region. His office on the third floor of Vatican Radio is filling with research; he is a steady and methodical worker, not a skim-reader but one who knows instinctively what is important to read. As he works he shapes tentative phrases which he will later polish and then deliver with skill from his special vantage points during the tour. Standing on a podium only feet from where John Paul will be speaking, MacCarthy realizes he could be directly in the line of fire should violence break out in the volcanic atmosphere he detects building up in Central America. The broadcaster tries hard to put such thoughts from his mind.

Late in the afternoon Casaroli learns that war in Europe is scheduled to start in four days' time.

The Holy See's permanent observer to the United Nations in Geneva, Archbishop Edoardo Rovida, has sent Casaroli a NATO release which explains the Soviet Union believes it must go to war to survive. Since the middle of this month some two and a half million NATO troops have moved from 'military vigilance' alert – no home leave and command posts constantly manned – to 'reinforced alert', a state of readiness throughout the alliance in which reserves have been mobilized, warships and submarines sent to secret destinations and bombers at bases from Turkey to Britain armed with live, though conventional, weapons. Wives and children of Allied servicemen will be evacuated. Each family has received a booklet telling them what they must do: leave their car where it will not cause an obstruction and with the key in the starter switch; destroy all family pets 'as humanely as possible'; take a change of underwear as well as a torch, a first-aid kit, a spoon for each family member and suitable high-calorie food for twenty-four hours, such as candy bars, Coca-Cola, apples and oranges. The booklet contains instructions on how to ask for the nearest police station or friendly consulate in German, French, Italian and Spanish. On reaching a Channel port, each family will receive a sum of 500 US dollars to help them relocate. They are warned to expect congestion on the French coast as 100,000 British reserve troops head for

West Germany. From Fort Bragg in the United States, the vaunted 'Screaming Eagles' will be flown to the Rhine. Diplomatically not even the Holy See is allowed to offer its offices for mediation. The hot line between Washington and Moscow is cold.

The Soviet bloc forces are moving equally swiftly. Hungary and Yugoslavia are completely mobilized. Neutral Finland has already fallen. Two Soviet divisions have landed in Norway to attack NATO bases there and open a safe sea route for the Russian navy to roam the Atlantic.

Now there is to be further escalation. Just as two previous world wars started in Europe, so now World War III is about to begin.

The one redeeming feature of this nightmarish scenario – as Casaroli thankfully knows – is that it is all pretence, a gigantic military exercise, in which NATO is testing its readiness to meet just the kind of Soviet invasion its planners believe might one day come. The Secretary of State can reflect that the two-week war games will cost more to run than the Holy See actually spends in a year on its entire foreign service.

Casaroli is among those who work on the third floor of the Apostolic Palace who believe exercises like WINTEX reflect a common attitude among western leaders that the driving force behind the nuclear arms race is Russia's wish to maintain superiority, and that if the Soviet Union could commit itself to genuine parity, the weapons race would be halted.

Priest-diplomats like Casaroli tend to view matters in a somewhat different light. They see no essential difference between the fears in Washington and Moscow; the United States and the Soviet Union each harbour a genuine concern that the other side will always jockey for nuclear supremacy.

Having listened on more than one occasion to the Reagan administration envoy, William Wilson, Casaroli is in no doubt the president believes the Soviet Union already has a superiority of nuclear forces in Europe.[32] Equally, the Secretary of State knows from Luigi Poggi's reports after

141

his visits to Moscow that the Soviet leaders insist equality now exists in medium-range nuclear weapons in Europe, and that the United States is trying to break existing 'understandings' by deploying new systems.

Casaroli believes there is an urgent need to develop an agreed means of measuring nuclear potential so parity can be clearly defined.[33] Even now, as the laborious arms control talks resume in Geneva, both sides continue to differ about the categories of weapons to be discussed. And there have been sharp differences over what should be reduced or limited. The United States remains committed to limiting warheads; Russia is more concerned to reduce launchers. Washington would like to see restrictions on Soviet medium-range systems east of the Urals, warheads pointing into the Pacific at Japan and perhaps ultimately the West Coast of America. Moscow is bent on confining agreement to Europe; it wants to remain unrestricted in its military policy for the Far East.

There are those on Casaroli's staff who have long argued the Soviet leaders see military power as not only guardian of Soviet security but also the best way to fulfil the dream of 'catching and overtaking' capitalism. Military power is also the fuel which ignites Moscow's ambition to try and create a new world order. For months now Casaroli's staff have been showing him evidence that Soviet globalists think the present order created in the wake of World War II is collapsing and that the time is ripe for a new international order – in economic, political and military terms – in which the Soviet Union can cast itself as the champion of peace which stepped into a void left by the diminishing authority of the United States.

Casaroli personally finds such theorizing as disturbing as the NATO war games. Though he will not go so far as the pope's implacable suspicion about Soviet intentions, Casaroli does believe it would be intellectually naïve and politically disastrous to ignore Soviet military power and the wider ambitions it cloaks.

Equally, there are some who work in offices only a few yards from Casaroli who believe Russia is misunderstood, and that the growing anxiety over the possibility of nuclear war should be directed against NATO governments, in particular the United States.

It is this kind of attitude which has made Envoy Wilson finally act. All his doubts, concerns, worries and unease over the way the Vatican at times seems to regard the Reagan administration are about to boil over. He has reduced the reasons for his *angst* to one ideograph. It is that of Clarissa McNair seated before a microphone on the fourth floor of Vatican Radio and in her distinctive accent broadcasting six days a week to the world the sort of 'slanted news' that in these dire times no patriotic American should be doing. Wilson has never met McNair; he tries not to listen to her every day – 'she is just too much to take'.[34] But The Mad Mentor has furnished the envoy with the evidence he needs. As the president's man, Wilson feels he must act. And this is no time for diplomatic niceties. This is an occasion to behave like Ronald Reagan did in his movies – go hell-for-leather to the source of the trouble.

ROME CITY POLICE HEADQUARTERS
Friday
Morning

At ten thirty-five one of the police operators receives a telephone call. The man says the pope will be shot this coming Sunday as he delivers the noon Angelus from an Apostolic Palace window to the crowd in St Peter's Square. The operator tries to keep the man talking while colleagues trace the call. It is a waste of time: the man rings off. The call is logged and sent on to DIGOS. The anti-terrorist squad has received at least twenty such calls already this year. Threatening to kill John Paul has become a game for

143

Rome's lunatic fringe. DIGOS still have to act. An officer calls Cibin. He informs Kabongo. The secretary tells the pope. John Paul says nothing. On Sunday DIGOS will post extra men in the square. Nobody is prepared to take a chance after Agca.

VATICAN RADIO
Saturday
Early Afternoon

Shortly after one o'clock Clarissa McNair arrives in the office of the station's vice-director of programmes, Fr Sesto Quercetti. She has been on duty since six forty-five A.M.; she looks pale and tense.

There has been yet another anonymous postcard to the station, this one accusing her of being anti-Soviet in her broadcasts.

Quercetti tells her he has more bad news – far more serious than the postcard.[35]

He explains Wilson has been to see the director of programmes, Fr Pasquale Borgomeo, to complain about her broadcasts.

'What disturbs us is that he should not have come to us . . . he should have gone through channels . . . he should have used the diplomatic route . . . he should have gone to see Casaroli.'

McNair blanches. She feels 'a vein the size of a garden hose has taken over in my neck'. She keeps thinking: *Casaroli. He is higher to me and scarier than George Schultz or George Bush or anybody. I'd be less intimidated by Henry Kissinger.*

She becomes aware Quercetti is still talking.

'. . . I explained you did not make radio policy. That I go over your reports first . . .'

She begins to recover, asking questions about her work.

144

He reassures her that in his view neither her writing of the news nor the way she delivers it is slanted.

After calling on Borgomeo and being told he was 'out of channels', the enraged envoy tried another tac. He has just had delivered to the station a pile of excerpts of McNair's alleged transgressions. They are compiled from the transcripts The Mad Mentor has made. On the outside of the envelope is written Wilson's name.[36]

McNair is genuinely stunned as she begins to study the compilation. It goes back to her documentary on Haiti in which she had questioned some of the Reagan administration policies towards the island. Another cause for Wilson's wrath was her coverage of El Salvador, and her reporting of the abortion and sterilization issues in India. He even objected to the way she used the words 'Reagan administration' in her broadcasts. For page after page the accusations follow each other.

McNair tells Quercetti: 'I feel frightened. I didn't think I was so important.'

'You are important.'

'What will happen?'

The news director replies: 'Don't worry. We know how to handle such matters.'

Suddenly she began to tremble. 'Wilson didn't do this by himself. Somebody else is behind it. And I know who that is.'

The broadcaster explains about The Mad Mentor.

She shrugs and points at Wilson's complaints. 'It has to be the CIA who did this . . .'

Quercetti watches her carefully. 'This will have to be reported to Casaroli. He may recommend Wilson be recalled. We can't have this going on.'

He tells McNair to go home.

Only when McNair is back in her apartment does she begin to laugh uncontrollably. She realizes how badly frightened she really is.

The Mad Mentor had once told her he was quite capable of murder if the situation required it.

She wondered now whether he might harm her because of what she planned to do. She will continue with her broadcasts, not altering her attitude by one syllable. But, thanks to what The Mad Mentor had told her, McNair thinks she knows enough about the CIA and its methods to believe he could still actually arrange for her to die. Equally, in her present frame of mind, she feels she would rather risk even that happening than give up her sense of integrity.

8

ON BOARD PAPAL FLIGHT
'DANTE ALIGHIERI'
Wednesday
Mid-Afternoon – GMT Minus Six Hours

The third officer adjusts the cockpit's VHF radio frequency to reduce atmospherics. This allows a clearer reception of the latest weather forecast from Costa Rica's Juan Santamaria airport. In the past hour the possibility of turbulence has receded. For even the experienced Alitalia flight deck crew both conditions are potentially difficult to handle.

The co-pilot checks the heading: latitude nine degrees, fifty-nine minutes north; longitude eighty-four degrees, twelve minutes west. At 32,590 feet, with a present cruising speed of 820 kilometres an hour, *Dante Alighieri* is exactly on course and on time to land at San Jose's airport in just twenty-nine minutes – three-thirty in the afternoon, Costa Rica time.[1]

The captain uses the intercom to inform the pope, his entourage and the fifty-one journalists seated in the rear of the plane.

A few correspondents give a weary cheer. Nearly fourteen hours out of Rome – there was a one-hour stopover in Lisbon for John Paul to greet the local hierarchy at the airport – they are now tired and bored.

Nancy Frazier of the US National Catholic News Service is among those who are veterans of such trips. This is her seventh, and it follows a familiar pattern. Her economy seat has cost almost as much as First Class, helping the Vatican to reduce the expense of chartering the aircraft. There has been an excellent main meal and an old cowboy film; most of her colleagues ignored the movie and speculated on the outcome of the trip.

During the flight the pope visited the press section. Frazier and many fellow reporters inwardly groaned when they saw Fr Romeo Panciroli accompanying him. The Vatican press officer was his wintry self as he introduced each journalist individually to John Paul. The brasher reporters tried to ask the pontiff about his expectations for this pilgrimage. John Paul ignored them. Panciroli looked furious, hissing there must be no questions.

Frazier thinks the press officer's performance 'zilch in terms of news and even lower in public relations. It's a bit like the head-keeper coming to greet the monkeys.'[2]

Some of the journalists wonder whether the pope is riled, or perhaps even worried, about the way the journey is being regarded both inside and outside the Church.

Only hours before he boarded *Dante Alighieri* John Paul finally made up his mind about the most contentious part of his visit to El Salvador. Defying the US-backed government's wishes, he has decided he will after all pray at the tomb of Oscar Romero, the archbishop who was murdered while saying mass three years ago, presumably by government supporters. The pope has further angered the regime by appointing the apostolic administrator in El Salvador, Rivera Damas, as Romero's successor. Rivera Damas immediately urged the government to negotiate with the left-wing guerrillas. Capitalizing on this support from the newly promoted archbishop, the rebels have announced a cease-fire during John Paul's planned ten-hour visit to El Salvador.[3]

As *Dante Alighieri* begins a gradual descent towards Costa Rica, there is debate among the reporters over whether Damas has been too politically outspoken, and whether the pope's Salvadoran decisions may affect the entire tour. Some argue John Paul's action will make it that much harder for him to order priests out of the hills and back into their pulpits: others suggest his moves herald a dramatic reversal of John Paul's hard line against the theology of liberation activists.

Nancy Frazier remains unconvinced. She thinks Central America an area where economic injustice, political violence and ideological competition have combined to create a profound moral and geopolitical crisis – and the chances are neither the conservatives nor the radicals will get much comfort from the pope's visit. Frazier has come to see John Paul as someone who, after sixteen demanding foreign trips and over thirty very public pilgrimages inside Italy, is now as skilful as any secular politician in remaining welded to the briefs his civil servants prepare for him. She feels John Paul will be traditional in matters of Church discipline; that he will deliver his quota of memorable phrases; that for many his very presence will be sufficient indication of how concerned he is about their grinding poverty, while during the next eight days he will also constantly be confronted first-hand with the political oppression they face. But Frazier fears the trip could ultimately end up as a 'glorious failure – pomp without lasting substance'.[4]

She believes a fundamental reason for this is because the pontificate has become increasingly 'easternized: too many Poles, Hungarians and Rumanians who are out of touch with western Catholic attitudes on birth control, divorce and priests marrying'.[5]

As *Dante Alighieri* continues its descent, the reporter has no high expectation of lasting impact from the tour.

In First Class seat 2A – one that offers a view through the window of blue ocean and, out over the port wingtip, a hazy outline of Costa Rica – Mgr John Magee is convinced foreign papal journeys are important both for spreading and strengthening the faith as well as serving to promote human dignity and world peace.[6]

It is just a year since Magee was appointed Master of Ceremonies, a position which effectively makes him the priest who is always at the pope's elbow in public. Outwardly he looks the same as during those years he was English-language secretary to John Paul and, before that, his two predecessors. Magee has the same open face and keen searching eyes, the same muscular frame, the same soft lilt to his Irish voice that marks him down as a man from Newry. He is forty-six years old but looks younger. With his fund of Irish stories and jokes, his fluen̄ Italian and Celtic charm, he remains one of the most popular men in papal service. He makes his work look easy. But those around him today – Casaroli in an adjoining aisle seat, Kabongo and Dziwisz partnered together in seats E and F, Prefect Martin and Casaroli's deputy, Eduardo Martinez Somalo in Seats G and H – know how hard Magee works. For weeks he has spent ten full hours a day preparing for this trip.

Magee, too, has sensed the criticism. He believes much of it is rooted in the endless preoccupation of some to define and explain every action the pope takes. The Master of Ceremonies still finds it astounding how so many people dwell upon the fact the pontiff is Polish, an irrelevancy Magee considers gets in the way of understanding 'what the real man is about. His intellectual consistency; the way he leads from the front, his charisma and rare understanding with all sorts of conditions of men'.[7]

The Irishman knows these qualities will be tested during the coming eight days, just as he realizes even if the trip turns out to be less sensational than many are predicting – or perhaps because of that – the question will be asked: was it worth while?

Magee is one of the few on board who has read the speeches the pope will deliver. He knows that each gesture and sentence John Paul produces will be scrutinized. Shortly after he has kissed the soil of Costa Rica – a tradition begun by Paul VI which Magee urged John Paul to continue – the pontiff will speak of 'a clamour that rises from these lands . . . a sorrowful clamour that I would like to give voice to with my visit'.

But, ponders Magee, would the world understand this is John Paul's way of saying he has *really* heard the voices of the voiceless, the pleas of the dispossessed, the anguish of those who are immersed in Central America's passiontide?[8]

Or will people see it as 'political' when the pope denounces murder, kidnapping and torture in Guatemala, when he adds his voice to Archbishop Damas by advocating 'dialogue' between the government and the insurgents in El Salvador, when he preaches in Nicaragua of a need for the Church to be unified and the hierarchy to be more authoritative? And when the pope calls for social justice, warns about the dangers of ideological manipulation and commands the priests in the region to avoid partisan politics: can this be viewed as other than 'political'?

Magee knows how he sees it. It is John Paul making a positive attempt to bring the local Church to a new awareness of its mission: to make it realize it must avoid entering into any accommodation with oligarchies or with Marxist-Leninists; it must oppose what the pope will attack as 'pure economic capitalism' while rejecting the collectivism of one-party systems.

The Master of Ceremonies hopes the huge crowds expected to turn out will do so because they wish to demonstrate fidelity to the Gospel and show the pope they passionately believe that he, and he alone, can respond to their plight and give them at least an inkling of hope. That, feels Magee, will be the best answer to any criticism.

He has concluded that the doubts already raised show a deplorable lack of understanding of John Paul's character. Magee 'simply knows' there will be no way to baulk the pope.[9] Local politicians may well attempt to distort his pronouncements through their controlled media, but it will be impossible for them to stifle word of mouth reaction to the pope's message, let alone diminish the attention the pontiff will get on the international stage. Again, while it is true to say the tour schedule is extraordinarily gruelling – which has allowed some critics to say the pace is an affront to the pope's health – Magee knows John Paul personally approved every move on his itinerary.[10]

But as the giant airliner descends towards the runway and the captain lifts its nose slightly to reduce speed, even the perceptive Magee cannot foresee the full extent of the strains the pope is about to face in the coming week to maintain his energizing vision of what the Church should be.

ALDBROOK FIELDS AIRPORT, PANAMA
Saturday
Mid-Morning

A little before eleven o'clock, Fr Sean MacCarthy coughs, a professional broadcaster's clearing of his throat just before going on the air.[11] He is positioned on a platform fifty feet from the raised altar from which John Paul will concelebrate mass. MacCarthy's vantage point is crammed with a television camera and technicians huddled over equipment. MacCarthy suspects he looks an odd sight seated beneath a parasol clutching his microphone; as further protection against the sun he is wearing a white floppy beach hat. His clerical suit is festooned with official badges: one identifies him as Vatican Radio, another is from the Panamanian government, a third from the local hierarchy, a fourth from the apostolic nuncio. Ever since arriving in Panama Mac-Carthy has been assiduously collecting insignia; it seems the only way to impress the legions of troops and police who have turned this former World War II bomber base into an armed citadel in which over 300,000 people are crowded.

For hours they have been singing hymns in broiling heat while MacCarthy remained perched above them, absorbing the atmosphere, preparing to put it in the context of the trip so far. He has no doubt that John Paul set the tone in Costa Rica when he said, 'one should be with those who suffer'. The words now allow MacCarthy to remind his scattered audience – the live broadcast is being heard in Europe and Africa and on into Asia – that 'it is very difficult to separate religion from politics – but for those who are in pain, the

Holy Father is bringing a message of hope, peace and unity'. MacCarthy also stresses this is a purely pastoral visit, yet one in which the pope is fully prepared to give firm guidance and even to correct the wayward.

MacCarthy's soft brogue quietly conveys to listeners his deeply felt sense of shock at yesterday's confrontation between the pontiff and the Sandinista revolutionary regime in Nicaragua. Although he was not there himself – Vatican Radio have a team of broadcasters leapfrogging each other to cover the tour – what MacCarthy heard about the event has left him visibly shaken.

John Paul had spent only twelve hours in Nicaragua, returning to sleep in Costa Rica. When *Dante Alighieri* had spirited the papal party in and out of Nicaragua, it carried extra passengers in the First Class section. The badges on their dark business suits identified them merely as members of the papal entourage. The men were security agents provided by the CIA as part of the agency's promise to Cibin to help protect the pope.[12] Working closely with the Vatican team the operatives formed a shield around John Paul, one which was further strengthened by the constant presence of Magee, Dziwisz and Tucci. Cibin felt that in the potentially dangerous circumstances existing, the pope would not complain he was being over-protected.[13]

Immediately John Paul had arrived at Managua's Cesar Agosto Sandino airport – a ramshackle place in spite of its imposing name – he was plunged into crude politics. He had been forced to stand grim-faced while a member of the junta launched a bitter attack on the United States, warning his listeners that 'the footsteps of interventionist boots echo threateningly in the White House and the Pentagon'. The spokesman harangued John Paul, telling him the people of Nicaragua were being 'martyred and crucified every day', and that 'Christian patriots and revolutionaries are an integral part of the popular Sandinista revolution'.

Then came the first direct confrontation. Moving down the official receiving line, the pope had stopped before the country's Minister of Culture, Ernesto Cardenal, one of the priests who continue to hold office in a government which is dedicated to melding Marxist ideology with Christianity. Cardenal wore a white rustic shirt, blue denims and a black beret, the typical uniform of senior Sandinista revolutionaries. When the pope reached him Cardenal removed his beret and dropped on bended knee to kiss John Paul's ring. The pontiff quickly pulled back his hand – and coldly rebuked the priest for his defiance in holding political office against the pope's expressed wish. When Cardenal tried to speak, John Paul sharply wagged a finger at the kneeling figure, further admonishing him to 'straighten out your position with the Church'.[14]

The crestfallen priest was left genuflecting as the pope continued down the line, teeth clenched and chin resolute.

During the following twelve hours John Paul had hammered the country's revolutionary heroes and those priests involved in the 'popular church', a grassroots religious movement committed to radical change. In strident voice he delivered an uncompromising message to Nicaragua's liberation theologians: they were following an absurd and dangerous course.

The backlash, when it came, was all the more alarming because of its setting – the papal mass in Managua's largest plaza. Scores of revolutionaries shattered John Paul's homily with chants of 'Power to the people!' and 'We want peace!'

The outraged pope had shouted back, 'Silence!'

But the disruptive heckling increased, amplified over the loudspeakers. For the first time in his pontificate John Paul came close to losing his temper in public. He was still furious when he returned to Costa Rica.

Now, at Aldbrook Fields in Panama, high above the vast crowd that stretches as far as he can see, during a break in his broadcast MacCarthy makes his own assessment of what happened in Nicaragua. Clearly the pope sounded the death knell for the Sandinista slogan which claims Christianity and revolution are not in contradiction. He went further: even more than on his last visit to Latin America John Paul was showing himself willing to become embroiled in local issues that impinge upon his view of the Church. Before leaving Nicaragua he went out of his way to champion the cause of the Miskito Indians, one of the country's minority groups. He publicly declared, 'I love the Miskitos because they are human beings!' and he called for more 'Miskito power!'

Some of the lay reporters in the press centre branded this papal politicking, but MacCarthy believes the pope's behaviour in Nicaragua was 'really just the Holy Father preaching the Gospel of Christ'.

As the radio producer's voice in his headphones informs him there are just two minutes to go before the mass begins, MacCarthy switches his thoughts from Nicaragua to the scene below.

He begins to paint a vivid portrait of the vast crowd sweltering in ninety-degree heat, silent now as the pope approaches the altar, Magee at his elbow gently motioning him towards the papal throne. MacCarthy sketches word-pictures of the co-celebrants for the mass: Casaroli, Martinez Somalo and Prefect Martin. He does not mention Cibin hovering at the edge of the platform or the wall of security men peering into the crowd.

THE APOSTOLIC NUNCIATURE, SAN SALVADOR
Sunday
Early Afternoon

In the apostolic nunciature on Avenida Norte, the telephone specially reserved for this call now rings.

Nearly six thousand miles away in Bonn, West Germany, where it is nine o'clock in the evening, Guido Del Mestri, the nuncio to the Federal Republic, asks to speak to His Holiness.

The nuncio to El Salvador, Lajos Kada, leads John Paul into the library of the nunciature, a room of tropical-wood shelving stocked with rare books. Others follow, among them Casaroli, Somalo, Dziwisz and Kabongo. They stand in silence, watching the pope who is concentrating on what Del Mestri is saying.

The visit to El Salvador has so far been overshadowed by what this telephone call could presage. The pope has indicated the news Del Mestri conveys concerns nothing less than the fate of Europe.[15]

The nuncio is calling with the first computer prediction of the outcome of West Germany's election. The last of the nation's 43.4 million voters have this Sunday cast their ballots in what does indeed have the dimensions of a genuine pivotal event. Not since the days of Hitler has a German electorate been so threatened (by Moscow) and exhorted (by Washington) to do their 'duty' over the issue of whether a new generation of NATO missiles can be sited on German soil.

Many Germans feel they are pawns in a 'superpower election'.[16] The entire campaign has been personalized around the two main candidates: the incumbent Chancellor Helmut Kohl who favours the installation of the missiles, and Hans-Jochen Vogel of the Social-Democrats who opposes the idea.

Not even Del Mestri in previous reports to the Secretariat of State was clearly able to assess the effect of these bald attempts by foreign governments to influence the electorate, epitomized by the Russians extending a heavy-handed embrace to Vogel, and Reagan receiving Kohl in the White House.

John Paul has followed the campaign attentively.[17] He noted its overtones of prickly nationalism; Kohl's efforts to distance himself from Reagan during the closing stages in an attempt to win support from Vogel; the constant public opinion testing which showed even some of the chancellor's most committed supporters wanted him to postpone the installation of the missiles. While it had also been an election riven by fears about a drooping economy and rising unemployment, the nuclear question provided the real *angst*.

The pope remains convinced the undertow of pacifism and neutralism evident during the campaign will persist. John Paul is certain – and on this he and Casaroli share common ground – that the West European peace movement, particularly strong in Germany and Britain, is not the creation of Moscow: indeed, apart from rhetorical support, the Soviet Union has offered the movement no comfort in practical terms by limiting or reducing the deployment of Russian weapons. Equally, the movement challenges the pope's own carefully enunciated view on nuclear arms – that unilateral disarmament is simply not possible, let alone desirable, at least by the United States.

During the election, the West German hierarchy has, wherever possible and with the pope's blessing, quietly fostered the idea that while everybody wishes disarmament, it must be on a realistic basis.[18]

Del Mestri's call will settle the question which has preoccupied John Paul as he has gone about his business in San Salvador: how have the West Germans finally made up their minds?

The nuncio's answer is unequivocal. The computer predictions all tally. Kohl will be returned to office by an impressive majority.[19]

It is the best news John Paul has had since coming to this bitterly fragmented country. During his few hours in San Salvador he has come to realize the position is even worse than his briefing paper indicated. There is a bitterness and a feeling of hopelessness throughout the hierarchy which no words prepared in the Secretariat of State have been able to encapsulate. Priests are deeply divided between those who support the government and those who favour the insurgents. While the great majority hover somewhere in between – often sadly confused and uncertain which way to move – the opposing clerical factions are more entrenched than ever. At a mass earlier in the day, John Paul urged the warring sides to come together and talk. But he warned: 'The dialogue which the Church wants is not to be used as a tactical truce to fortify positions as part of a plan to continue the fighting, but as a sincere effort to answer the search for an accord.'

Just as Del Mestri's telephone call reassures the pope that the position on nuclear disarmament of the West German electorate is in accord with his own, so he is convinced his words in El Salvador will help pave the way for a reconciliation within the local hierarchy – and also lead to the government and guerrillas agreeing to meet around the conference table.

Precisely at six-fifteen this afternoon – item fifteen on Magee's detailed timetable – the pope leaves the nunciature. He boards a specially constructed bullet-proof 'popemobile' for a three-kilometre journey through cheering crowds to the city's Metropolitan Cathedral. There he kneels and prays at the tomb of Archbishop Romero. Then he rises and expresses the hope Romero's memory will always be respected, and that 'no ideological interest will try to exploit his sacrifice as a pastor leading his flock'.

The pope's plea, like so many others he utters in Central America, will prove to be in vain.

CAMPO DE MARTE STADIUM, GUATEMALA CITY
Monday
Morning

MacCarthy's mellifluous voice continues to weave a tapestry of impressions for his radio listeners. Out there, in the enormous crowd – 'there must be half a million, perhaps more, all here to testify to their faith' – he says he can see a gigantic banner which sums up one view of the pontiff's visit: DONDE ESTA EL PAPA ESTA CRISTO – 'Wherever the Pope is, Christ is'.

MacCarthy talks expertly about the problems of erecting the huge steel cross towering over the stadium – and about the fact many of those standing beneath it no doubt thought this mass, and indeed the whole visit to Guatemala, might have been cancelled. He does not dwell on the reason. By now the whole world knows.

The broadcaster cannot quite believe any government could be so crass, so inept at protecting its image, that it would behave in the way President Rios Montt's has over the papal visit.

Montt is a born-again Christian who leads a form of firebrand Protestant evangelicism which is eroding Catholicism's traditional supremacy in Guatemala. In the time he has been in the country MacCarthy has sometimes been uncomfortably reminded of the bigotry of Northern Ireland. On the one side there have been protests that the Protestants are 'dangerous to the traditional culture here, to the unity of the family, also to the spiritual stability of the people'; on the other hand Montt's followers have used the visit as an excuse to remind their followers that the country's seven hundred priests – barely enough to minister Guatemala's six million Catholics – have a long history of siding with oppressive regimes. Montt has personally displayed pettiness by refusing to authorize $32,000 for a 'popemobile', suggesting instead that John Paul should ride in a regular sedan the government would lend him. A wealthy local Catholic arranged to import a used popemobile from Europe for the papal motorcade. Montt had gone further. In a move guaranteed to offend Guatemala's fervent Catholics, the president decided he 'personally cannot receive the pope as head of the church'.

But these have been comparatively minor infractions of normal diplomatic courtesies compared to the incredible insult Montt delivered on the eve of the papal visit. The president rejected an official Holy See appeal not to execute six men condemned to death for terrorist offences. They had all died just five days ago before a firing squad not far from where MacCarthy now stands.

The commentator knows the papal entourage still seethes with anger over the timing of the executions. He can gauge it in the faces of many of its members, now approaching the altar in procession.

The local nuncio's public condemnation of the executions has been the most scorching MacCarthy can ever remember.

MacCarthy can only guess what agony and humiliation the affront has caused John Paul. From many of the pope's entourage he has received the same reaction: the executions were no more than a cynical and sickening attempt at what Kabongo would describe as 'trying to rub our noses in their dirt'.[20]

As the massed choirs sing a haunting Spanish anthem, MacCarthy ponders how the pope will respond to the Guatemalan government.

Avoiding any direct reference to the executions, John Paul launches a challenge to Montt's 'born-again' sermonizing – an attack not in his prepared text.

The pope virtually orders the huge gathering, and the world, to heed what he says: 'Men of all positions and ideologies, listen to me.'

He then delivers a stunning assault on abuses of human rights. The very words, he thunders, are meaningless unless embodied within the framework of political systems. Religion alone cannot protect human rights: only properly functioning political institutions can do that.

MacCarthy sums up a peroration which has obviously moved him.

'The pope has just told us to let religion be religion, and politics be politics. But above all we must, through the workings of both, respect human beings as human beings. For each of us here who have heard this appeal it has made this pilgrimage worthwhile. I doubt the Holy Father can say anything more meaningful during the remainder of his stay in this troubled area of the world.'

In Honduras John Paul will again appeal for an end to 'all fighting', in Belize for Christian unity, in Haiti for 'concord and peace'.

Finally, on the way home, he will insist the entire journey has been 'a great experience for me – I would return to Central America with pleasure'.[21]

Nobody doubted his sincerity. Some wondered if this is the predictable response of a pope who, in Kabongo's words, 'has just glimpsed the meaning of hell on earth'.

ASCOLI PICENO PRISON
Wednesday
Morning

Three months after making his request, Agca receives permission from Martella to write to the pope. At the psychiatrist's suggestion, he has been left alone this morning in cell 47 to compose his thoughts. The evidence of Agca's labour is scattered on the floor: sheet after sheet of crumpled cheap notepaper testify to the problem he is having in finding the right words.[22]

Later the discarded sheets will be studied by the psychiatrist in the hope they will provide further insights into his patient's mental state. The doctor thinks the words could help him establish the extent of schizophrenia existing in Agca. He has already discovered a great deal about the prisoner's disorders of the emotions, of the will, of bodily movement, and the presence of delusions and sometimes hallucinations. But a deeper understanding of Agca's illness is crucial to the advice the psychiatrist continues to give Martella on how much reliability the judge should place on the prisoner's statements.

Agca has great difficulty even beginning his letter, not knowing how he should actually address the pope. Among the thoughts he tries and discards are: 'Dear Pope'; 'Holy Pope'; 'Holy Man'; 'Your Excellency'; 'Great Father'; and, mixing Turkish and Italian, *'Bay Papa'*.

In the end he chooses to address John Paul as 'Father of Your People'.

That hurdle negotiated, Agca is confronted with a bigger problem: how to start his letter. He has made several attempts at an opening: 'This is Mehmet Ali Agca writing to you'; 'This is your prisoner, Mehmet Ali Agca who is writing'; 'You will know who I am by the address'; 'I hope this letter will not surprise you'.

None of these phrases satisfies Agca. The sheets of paper on which he has scrawled them lie on the cell floor around his chair.

He is also not happy with his pen. He asks for, and is given, a fountain pen, but the nib leaks ink blobs and he finally discards it for his usual felt-tip.

Agca still finds the words hard to come by. For a while he paces his cell, trying to express his ideas aloud. He is unaware he is being recorded; the psychiatrist will later listen to the tape looking for symptoms of *thought blocking*, a condition in which gaps appear in what should be an orderly sequence of thoughts.

Finally, Agca returns to his chair and begins to write again.

The letter, written in Italian, is in the end short and well ordered enough. Agca eventually decides to come straight to the point, telling the pope he is writing to ask forgiveness. 'I know now that you are a true Holy Man and that it was wrong of me to have done what I have done.' He goes on to wish John Paul, 'the best for your Holy Year, for your occupation and life'. He signs the letter: 'with great respect, Mehmet Ali Agca'.

He places it in an unsealed envelope which he addresses: 'His Excellency the Pope, Father of His People'.

Agca summons a guard who collects the letter and all the discarded notepaper.

They are taken first to the psychiatrist. He makes a copy of each sheet of paper and the envelope. The originals are given to Martella in Rome. The judge places the discarded paper in a file. He orders a photocopy made of the letter and envelope. These are then placed inside a Ministry of Justice envelope which is sealed and addressed to Kabongo. A *carabiniere* dispatch rider carries the envelope to the Vatican. Kabongo opens it, reads the contents and takes Agca's envelope and letter in to the pope. John Paul studies it. The secretary is instructed to convey the pope's feelings 'by a suitable sign'.[23]

Agca will eventually learn his letter has been favourably received.

SECRETARIAT OF STATE
Friday
Mid-Afternoon

A Vatican limousine drops Poggi in San Damasco Courtyard. The nuncio barely pauses to sniff the air before hurrying to his office. He is back – again – from 'my listening post'[24] in Warsaw.

Poggi's sources in Warsaw include high-ranking Soviet officials who have close links to Andropov. The nuncio keeps their identities secret; it is doubtful even Casaroli knows who they all are. Some Secretariat officials speculate that one of Poggi's contacts is Georgi Arbatov, director of the Moscow-based institute for US and Canadian Studies, who is an old friend of the Russian leader. Arbatov and Andropov holiday together.

Whoever they are, his sources have alerted Poggi that contrary to some well-timed leaks in London, Paris and Bonn this past week, Andropov does not believe Kohl's victory in the West German elections will produce a hardening of the Reagan administration's position towards the Soviet Union.[25] This is in spite of the president's natural inclination for anti-Soviet rhetoric to which he has given full vent since Kohl returned to power. Poggi has been told the Soviet leadership views this as no more than Reagan trying to please the hardliners around him.

Poggi's sources have indicated future Soviet strategy hinges in part on what is almost certainly a KGB appraisal of a split within the Reagan cabinet. Secretary of Defense Casper Weinberger is opposed to any compromise over siting further missiles in Europe.[26] But Secretary of State George Schultz is becoming increasingly sensitive to the unease in some European capitals.

At this stage Poggi is unwilling to suggest what position the Holy See might adopt, because he is uncertain of the relative strengths of Weinberger and Schultz in the Reagan administration. That will be a matter for Laghi to establish. But Poggi's long experience of 'reading the signs'[27] suggests the Russians now believe they can put the United States on the defensive.

If this does happen, the nuncio can be certain of one outcome. It will not please the pope.

THE PAPAL SECRETARIAT
Monday
Morning

It is once more, in Kabongo's cheerful words, 'business as usual'.[28]

This morning the Spanish ambassador to the Holy See has an audience with the pope to discuss the forthcoming visit of King Juan Carlos. Then the under-secretary of the Sacred Congregation for Catholic Education will see John

Paul to discuss financial support for seminary students from the Lebanon who are destitute through the fighting.

During these meetings the papal secretariat will continue its regular processing of promotions, resignations and appointments to Church posts all over the world. The huge amount of paperwork involved must all come through here on the way in and out of the pope's own office; often only he can stamp and sign a document.

And there are other matters to occupy his personal staff. This morning John Paul's latest prayer to Our Lady of Jasna Gora, which he will say in his native tongue at the next general audience in two days, must be translated from Polish into other languages. The task will occupy a couple of *scrittori* for the rest of the morning.

A *minutante* has the job of summarizing the latest report from the Secretariat for Non-Believers. It is a complex document dealing with problems of secularization which will require careful editing. After the *minutante* has made his appraisal it will be checked by Kabongo or Dziwisz; they may send the summary back to the *minutante* for further work or rewrite his conclusions in the light of what they know the pope will want to read.

An *addettore* is checking the paperwork on three decrees from the Sacred Congregation for the Cause of Saints.

Kabongo is preoccupied reading the text of Reagan's latest speech to the nation on national security, and the Soviet response. Both documents arrived in the papal Secretariat this morning with Casaroli's evaluation attached to them. The Secretary of State concludes neither side has changed its basic position.

The president announced a new programme to improve the United States' defences against attack: the Soviet leader saw this as an 'extremely perilous path – all attempts at achieving military supremacy over the USSR are futile'.[29]

Casaroli thinks such responses are only to be expected during the current missile-rattling between the super-powers.

9

Roman Responses

Campo di Fiori is where the Holy Office ordered heretics to be burnt. There's a statue on the site of the stake. And the *campo* itself, its flowers and grass long replaced by cobbles, is now a Roman market-place. Dr Rudi explains the fish is often frozen and the grapefruit come all the way from South Africa. It's his hobby to know such things.

He continues to display his knowledge as we cross the large plaza. He also mentions – casually slipping it in after saying the market traders like to pretend the Israeli-grown avocados come from Greece – that here, in 1978, he kept a *treff* with a member of the Red Brigades to discuss terms for the release of Pope Paul VI's great friend, Aldo Moro. Had the plan worked it would have been 'quite a triumph' for his security service. Instead it turned out to be another of those fruitless exercises Rudi long ago accepted as normal in his work. Weeks of careful preparation wasted, sighs Rudi, just as he suspects the contents of the bulky envelope he is carrying will turn out to have been a waste of time.

The envelope contains a xerox of the latest draft of the US pastoral letter. Two copies have just been flown across the Atlantic. One has gone to the pope, the other to Ratzinger at the Holy Office. But before either actually saw the document it had been secretly and quite illegally photocopied for Rudi.

He knows that his counterpart in Washington has almost certainly also got his hands on the draft and sent a copy on to West Germany; that in a few days the world will learn of this latest official communiqué on the American bishops' thinking. But no matter: Rudi knows he is the first in Rome to see the draft. That's important to him. In part it is what makes him such a good professional intelligence officer, this ability to stay ahead of others in his business.

We first met Rudi a year ago in Vienna through a mutual contact, Simon Wiesenthal, the Nazi-hunter. We never did learn what precisely Rudi was doing in the Austrian capital. What he does in Rome is work under diplomatic cover – he refuses to be more specific – for the BND, the West German secret service. Nor can we go further in describing him than to say he is a clever, foxy man and that his doctorate is in law. He clearly knows a great deal about what he still calls *italienische Kultur* and the sexual failings of some of the more influential Romans. He is not fond of *shekel* Jews, or the Communists who inhabit the part of Rome we are in on this early spring evening. When aroused, Rudi has a driving urgency which allows him to pass on his own pressures to colleagues. In many ways his approach to work is little different from that of The Mad Mentor or most of the others whom we have met in the intelligence community here – except that Rudi is probably better than most.

He claims he gets a kick out of helping us from time to time. Whether that is true or not, he has proved a reliable source on Agca and his ongoing Bulgarian Connection information seems to stand up. We have also used him as a sounding-board for some of the things we hear in the Vatican, but until now we had no evidence of how well placed his sources are there. Anyone who can snaffle a photocopy of a document intended for the pope and a very senior cardinal has the sort of contacts only time and money well spent can buy.

Rudi has chosen a side-street restaurant for our *treff* (like many BND men he uses the old Abwehr word for a meeting). He is known here and we are shown to a table at the back, screened off from other diners. We order German beer and antipasti. Rudi tells the owner he'll send for him when we want to reorder.

He opens the envelope and takes out the pastoral letter. Rudi grins and points at the word stamped on the cover: EMBARGO. He rifles through the document, 150 pages plus appendices and footnotes. He says he's been through it

167

and that we have to take his word the letter is going to make many people think they have 'won'. The tragedy, insists Rudi, is that it will do little to appease those who badly need what he calls 'defusing' – the extremists at either end of the spectrum of the nuclear-arms debate.

'Here,' he says, pointing to a page. 'Here they say they are against the first-use of nuclear weapons, and to deliberate attacks against non-combatants under any circumstances. Fine.' He skips to another page. 'And here they say deterrence is "acceptable" as part of the process towards progressive disarmament. But what about the *threat* of first-use as a deterrent? And how much value as a deterrent is a threat without the willingness to follow through?'

We tell him what we have heard around the Apostolic Palace about the 'small print', about the debate over whether to use the word 'halt' or 'curb' when applied to the production and deployment of nuclear weapons.

'*Mensch!*' he says, sipping his beer. 'In the first two drafts they spoke about "halt". Now they have softened it to "curb", probably from pressure by the European bishops and Reagan's people. Maybe they'll change it back for the final draft. What difference will it make?'

He continues to leaf through the document, commenting that such 'fine writing' has produced 'such a little result'.

Our attention is caught by a paragraph which expresses the bishops' 'profound skepticism' about the prospects of limiting any nuclear war. We suggest that sounds pretty unequivocal, and certainly not aimed at pleasing the militarists.

Rudi shrugs. 'Two and a half years' work is a lot to produce something which has been said so often.'

Over dinner – thick Florentine steaks and red Sardinian wine – we turn to another matter.

A couple of weeks ago we asked Rudi if he could try and establish whether the repercussions following a minor motor mishap on a lonely road in the Irish Republic were genuinely connected with Agca's attempt on the pope's life.

Not for the first time we have been caught up in events we merely wished to observe. This particular experience has proved to have unforeseen and nasty implications about the way intelligence organizations operate.[1]

The facts are deceptively simple. A British-registered BMW crossed the Irish Sea to Rosslare. At the wheel was a Dutchman named Gerrit Kusters; his passenger was his Irish girl-friend, Marie McCarthy. Apart from their physical attraction for each other they shared a more unusual bond: in Beirut they had both been close friends of Frank Terpil up until the time he disappeared in November 1981, eight months after Agca shot the pope.

It was Terpil, insists Agca, who helped to prepare him for his assassination mission. This is what the Rome intelligence community now call the Terpil Connection. The words carry the shattering implication that at some level the CIA might have been involved in the papal plot.

The BMW Kusters was driving belonged to Terpil's wife, Marilyn. After Terpil disappeared from their Beirut apartment – accompanied by three men some Rome intelligence agents say (but not Rudi) were from the CIA – Marilyn Terpil had moved to England and stayed with Kusters and Marie McCarthy in their London apartment.

Mrs Terpil suddenly decided to fly to New York, telling Kusters to sell her BMW while she was gone. She gave her hosts no reason for her decision to leave, but shortly after arriving at Kennedy Airport she was charged with gun-running to Uganda during the reign of Idi Amin. She was released on bail.

Next day Kusters and Marie McCarthy drove to Ireland. In her luggage was a green-covered folder containing a collection of telexes, a copy of Terpil's will, some aircargo manifests and the address book of another close associate of Terpil who had also worked for the CIA, Gary Korkola. He was then being held in Madrid's Central Gaol, a fugitive, like Terpil, from American justice: Korkola had

169

previously been convicted in New York of arms-smuggling charges.

Before selling the BMW, Kusters decided to take his girl-friend home to see her family. They had only driven some fifty miles from Rosslare when the BMW went out of control, ran up a bank, and suffered about 500 dollars' worth of damage. The couple decided to return at once to London. Shortly afterwards Kusters flew to Saudi Arabia – where coincidentally Idi Amin lives. Marie McCarthy was left alone in London with her folder and its intriguing documents.

Four days before Agca wrote his letter of atonement to the pope, FBI agents spirited Korkola out of his Madrid cell. They had a Spanish judge's warrant ordering Korkola to be extradited to New York. Two days later he appeared in a Manhattan District Court charged with 'taking part in a scheme with a former US intelligence officer to sell weapons illegally to Uganda'. Korkola's co-defendant was Marilyn Terpil.

Back in London Marie McCarthy became increasingly alarmed. She was convinced either the SIS, the CIA, or some other foreign intelligence organization was trying to intimidate her. She believed her telephone was tapped, that she was being followed and that her life might even be in danger. She finally flew to Ireland to be with the only person she felt she could trust in this very unpleasant situation: her brother, John, a Dublin advertising man.

He contacted us.

While we normally work in tandem, from time to time we do divide forces. On this occasion one of us remained in Rome while the other travelled to Ireland to pursue matters.

John McCarthy had an incredible tale to tell, which he agreed to put on tape. He claimed London's Heathrow Airport had been used by Terpil to ship arms to the Middle East; he named a senior Scotland Yard officer who had been involved with Terpil, seemingly under the belief Terpil was still with the CIA. McCarthy reeled off dates and names, all

170

of which he said his sister Marie had provided him. During his tape recording he repeatedly said he had told Marie her best chance of 'survival' was 'to go public'.[2] She had agreed, hence his original call to us.

Next day Marie spent twelve full hours making a lengthy statement about the stack of documents in her green folder.[3] It included the address book Korkola had given her before his arrest in Spain. The book listed secret service telephone numbers in London, New York, Washington, Mexico City, Damascus, Beirut, Paris and other European cities. Other documentation did indeed identify a senior Scotland Yard officer, listing his home and office numbers. Marie agreed for photographic copies to be made of all the material.

Then, as she had in London, she panicked. She feared that by taking her brother's advice 'to go public', she had only increased the danger to herself. She described what had happened to an old friend, Kevin Mulcahy, who had similarly spoken out. Mulcahy had been in the CIA with Terpil. They had met again in Beirut. The two men had fallen out. Mulcahy returned to Washington publicly vowing he would 'get even' with Terpil. Shortly afterwards he had been found dead. Marie McCarthy is convinced he was murdered – as she would be if 'they' knew she had talked. Filled with such forebodings she disappeared as quickly as she had entered our lives.

Shortly afterwards a man, claiming he was an Irish Special Branch detective, made a telephone call to one of us stating we were about to be arrested under some unspecified offence against the Irish state.[4] We felt it prudent to check with the uniformed branch of the Irish *garda*, and retained a Dublin solicitor. Both quickly established we were in no danger of arrest. When the *garda* studied all the evidence Marie and John McCarthy had provided, they came to regard the bogus call as posing a threat sufficiently serious for them to provide a twenty-four-hour armed guard in case the fake detective, or his friends, made more physical moves.

The Irish police, however, were unable to provide answers

to some very pertinent questions. Were the McCarthys to be believed when they independently insisted Terpil was still in the CIA when he trained Agca? Was Marie McCarthy's interpretation of the documentation in her folder accurate when she claimed that 'Frank was, and remains, in the CIA'?[5] Was John McCarthy to be trusted when he recounted details of a telephone conversation Marilyn Terpil had with her husband in December 1982, one in which Terpil had reportedly indicated he was 'strapped for cash because the Company was squeezing him'?[6] Finally, could either of the McCarthys be taken seriously when they claimed Terpil continues to perform that most dangerous of all roles – a CIA 'deep penetration double agent' in the Middle East?[7]

We gave Rudi John McCarthy's tape along with copies of all the data his sister provided to see what he could discover.

Tonight over coffee and *grappa* the BND agent is more forthcoming than his counterparts in Irish security.

He has no doubt the telephone threat by the man claiming to be an Irish detective was a crude – if not totally unsuccessful – attempt by a member of Dublin's foreign intelligence community to frighten us. It indicates, continues Rudi, that we may have 'disturbed something of significance'.

The intelligence officer begins to explain that the BND has begun seriously to question what lies behind the CIA's attempt to denigrate Martella's investigation into the Bulgarian Connection and to present Agca as 'a loner'. Rudi describes how in Pullach – his service's headquarters on the outskirts of Munich – analysts had produced a hypothesis that depends on the possibility of a common link between the CIA and the Bulgarians. This would not, Rudi hastens to add, be one either agency connived at; it could have arisen purely through circumstances. Such situations had happened before: rival agencies unwittingly sharing a common source or double agent. If – and again Rudi stresses this is only a hypothesis – Terpil had been 'working double', then it would have been essential for him to continue to train Agca to maintain his own cover.

We all look quizzically at each other. Rudi orders another round of *grappa*. Then he proceeds to put, and answer, a number of questions.

Given that Terpil *was* still working for the CIA, would he have told the agency he was training Agca? Almost certainly not. There would have been no need to do so. Agca at that stage was just another terrorist. True he was wanted in Turkey for murder and was on an Interpol Red Alert. But in that Lebanese training camp this would hardly have made him stand out. He was at the time just one of perhaps a hundred hard-bitten young men passing through Terpil's hands.

Would Terpil have known in advance about Agca's mission? Doubtful. On Agca's own admission he had only been finally briefed on killing the pope shortly beforehand.

After the assassination attempt would Terpil have informed his CIA superiors of his involvement?

'*Mensch!*' says Rudi. 'That's the second big question. The one that comes immediately after the first: could Terpil have been working double with the Company's knowledge and approval? This we don't know.'

He proceeds to raise and settle other questions. Does the CIA know where Terpil is today? If he is alive, yes. It would be a matter of pride for the agency to have the information, even if Terpil is on the run, a fugitive from American justice.

Rudi asks and answers yet another question: why hadn't the CIA picked him up? That, he says, is the most intriguing part of the entire scenario. The CIA has unmatched facilities for 'recovering' somebody like Terpil – if that is what it wanted to do. But supposing he has become too great an embarrassment. Though it may well have been part of his cover, his behaviour in the year before he disappeared in Beirut had indeed been quite extraordinary. Among other things he appeared in a television film of his life, *The Most Dangerous Man in the World*. In it he spoke about working with Amin's killer squads in Uganda and creating general mayhem in the Middle East.

Throughout the film Rudi had detected the tantalizing suggestion that Terpil still had, at minimum, strong CIA links. Appearing in such a film, he need not remind us, is hardly normal procedure for an intelligence officer. Rudi is certain if Terpil was knowingly 'working double' he would have received clearance from the CIA to appear in the film. If, on the other hand, he was in fact on the run from the CIA, then the film should have acted as a trigger for the agency finally to 'recover' him.

Yet Terpil back in custody could be a constant worry about what he might say: the film had shown something of his capability to compromise all sorts of people. This then raised two other possibilities. First, Terpil has not been 'recovered' because he is dead – killed to avoid him talking, either directly by the CIA or through one of its surrogates. Secondly, the agency is still running Terpil in some under-cover capacity in the Middle East. That alone would be sufficient reason for the CIA to present Agca as a solitary and unbalanced fanatic motivated only by religious passions to murder the pope.

Rudi savours his *grappa*. 'You want my gut feeling? Terpil's alive and working double. That's why the CIA is worried about Martella. If the judge believes Agca, then the Terpil Connection is going to turn up on the *Pista Bulgara*. And nobody in the CIA will be happy about that. Martella might find himself in for a very nasty time.'

'Poor Martella,' one of us says.

'Amen,' sighs Rudi.

There is one final matter we have asked Rudi to help us with. Clarissa McNair.

Rudi says the agency has an active file on the broadcaster. We ask how he can be so certain. He replies rather sharply it is his business to know.

Well past midnight we return to the Albergo Santa Chiara. As always we write up our notes, adding to those we made at the time, trying to recall Rudi's mood when he spoke. When we have finished and read them back to each other – checking we neither overlooked nor misreported anything – we begin to formulate further questions and possible follow-up interviews.

Rudi has persuaded us of one thing: we were right to let Kabongo borrow a set of the McCarthy tapes and documentation.

This is not the first time we have provided the Vatican with information. During our investigation into Agca's background we had lent Kabongo copies of Agca's schoolbooks, medical records and prison reports, all of which we had obtained in Turkey.[8] The secretary had said, somewhat to our surprise, that none of this material had previously been seen in the Vatican. He explained it would be placed before the pope, 'as the Holy Father has an understandable interest in all there is to know about Agca'.[9]

We realize that providing this information might perhaps give us an advantage over others working in our field, but we are careful not to exploit the situation. Only data we believe to be of prime interest to the pope have been delivered to Kabongo, and never have we attempted to use such material to barter for anything in exchange.

In the case of the McCarthy documentation, the secretary asked whether he could keep it for a few days so the material could be copied. Kabongo subsequently told us that it has been studied in the Secretariat of State. John Paul himself had listened to excerpts from the John McCarthy recording. Cibin had also examined our evidence.

Kabongo was at his most diplomatically evasive when we enquired about reactions to the material.

Rudi had reinforced our feeling that Kabongo's unusual reticence was because the documentation did go some way towards supporting what Cibin and certain of the people in the Secretariat of State are saying. The CIA, through

175

Terpil, could have had 'an involvement' in the assassination plot. But how? And at what level? Above all what are the chances now of ever proving the CIA is, or is not, implicated?

The business of the CIA having an active file on McNair is not surprising. It would be remarkable if it did not. The real question is: is she an exception? Or does the agency have a number of Vatican employees on its computers?

And how does it use such information?

10

SECRETARIAT OF STATE
Monday
Morning

What is known for brevity's sake as the China Question – actually a number of individual yet interrelated questions – is back on the desk of Secretary of State Casaroli. The file is there along with an estimate of PLO strategy in the near future; an analysis of the present role of the Italian Communist Party; an assessment of Ireland's abortion controversy; an update on Andropov's health; a guide to the latest twist along the *Pista Bulgara;* and a report on the behaviour of William Wilson and The Mad Mentor.

There is also a score of other matters travelling through the parallel pipelines of the Secretariat of State and the Council for the Public Affairs of the Church. Staff are assessing the latest fragile peace in the Lebanon; the likely effect of the Reagan administration's decision to transfer to El Salvador $60 million in military funds previously destined for Morocco; the decision of France to devalue its franc for the third time in under two years; the outcome of Finland's general election; the latest extent of the fighting in Nicaragua; the tensions in Canada over the United States' request to test its Cruise missiles in Alberta before they are installed in Europe. The files on these and other subjects move from one office tray to another, acquiring recommendations for additional action and, eventually, the ultimate symbol of priest-diplomat power, an initialled tick indicating a document requires no further marginal notes.

As in any other foreign ministry, paperwork is the backbone of the papal civil service. Every morning its staff – some thirty departmental heads, senior counsellors and secretaries, each highly experienced, plus their full-time supporting staff of over one hundred – sort through the dispatches. This is the first sifting in a process which grinds

177

and refines information in a diplomatic policy-making mill whose professed ideological purpose is to 'further the cause of international peace and the creation of conditions which foster the full development of the human personality'.[1] In practice those on the third floor regard it as a mandate to protect the continued independence and influence of the Holy See: almost everything that comes before them is viewed from the perspective of existing and future relationships between the local Church and State. These overriding considerations extend from the cubbyhole of a *scrittore* to Casaroli's office. They are implicit in all the paperwork.

The documents on the Secretary of State's desk this morning are embellished with sets of initials indicating at once to Casaroli their course through the hierarchy he controls with a benign but firm hand. The flexible cast of his mind makes him an ideal administrator. He is a good listener, skilled in balancing evidence against opinions, in timing his interventions, in the way he redirects someone who has proposed a course of action which is mined with potential pitfalls for the Holy See.[2]

Even before he turns to the vexing China Question, there is another issue that must, at the pope's request, take precedence. John Paul wants Casaroli's view on whether the latest move involving the outlawed Solidarity trade union in Poland is the harbinger of a campaign which could force the Polish government to cancel the papal trip again.

Some 2,000 Solidarity members had gathered outside the Lenin shipyard in Gdansk – birthplace of the union – and sung hymns in front of a monument dedicated to workers killed during clashes with government forces. Riot police had quickly dispersed the shipyard demonstrators.

The Polish Desk reports that an old Solidarity slogan of defiance – 'The winter is yours, the spring will be ours' – is again being daubed on walls all over the country. However, the position adopted by Lech Walesa in this ominous situation remains unclear. On the one hand he has just called publicly for Solidarity to display 'more effective means of protest'.[3] Yet in the aftermath of Gdansk, his only comment was that the demonstration had gone ahead without official union support and the entire episode was a cleverly staged 'provocation' by the authorities. The Polish Desk's view is that the protest was a genuine expression of frustration.

The trade unionist's behaviour over the Gdansk protest suggests he is increasingly under pressure. Many of his fellow union leaders are still in prison or facing trial. Without the benefit of their guidance and support, Walesa seems uncertain what strategy the union should pursue against a regime sufficiently confident of its own position to introduce further price increases for such staples as petrol, cigarettes and coffee.

The concern in the Secretariat is that Walesa might in the coming weeks become yet more unpredictable, raising tensions in Poland to the point where the Polish government would cancel the pope's visit.

Casaroli's report to John Paul firmly reflects the thought that the Church's interests in Poland will best be served by reminding Walesa what cancellation will mean.

Poland out of the way – if only briefly – allows Casaroli to turn to the China Question. Broadly speaking it falls into two parts: how best to achieve what Casaroli wants, full diplomatic relations with the People's Republic, and what the Secretary attaches somewhat less importance to, the pope's desire to visit Peking. John Paul wishes to go not only as a head of state but also as the universal pastor come to reclaim a flock isolated since 1957 when the Chinese Catholic Patriotic Association was established by the government to take full and complete responsibility for the spiritual needs of believers in China – refusing Rome any further role in the direction of the Church or the appointment of bishops. There were then some four million Christians in the country, most of them Catholics.[4]

In the past three years two senior cardinals, Roger Etchegaray of Marseilles and Franz Koenig of Vienna, have made official visits to Peking. They both reported the Chinese leadership implacable on one point: the Holy See must sever diplomatic ties with the Nationalist government in Taiwan before there can be any formal relations with the People's Republic.[5]

But the Catholic Church continues to flourish in Taiwan. Currently there are well over 200,000 baptized Chinese nationals on the island. They have an enviable educational system which includes the world's only Chinese Catholic University. Just as the United States so far refuses to turn its back in a secular sense on Taiwan, so the Holy See is committed to maintaining its religious support.[6]

In 1981 matters were not helped when the pope announced he was appointing as Archbishop of Canton a Jesuit who had just been freed after twenty-two years spent in a Chinese prison because he refused to join the Catholic Patriotic Association.

The Secretariat's then specialist on China had suggested that the release of the Jesuit was an olive branch, Peking's way of indicating it was prepared to accept that the Holy See could play a direct role in the affairs of the Chinese Catholic Church, as it had before 1957.

The specialist was woefully wrong. The Patriotic Association condemned the appointment and the government issued a strong denunciation of the Holy See, accusing the pope of interfering in the internal affairs of the Chinese Church.

Casaroli was reportedly mortified. It has taken him almost two years – with the help of a new adviser – to regain lost ground. In the past few months there have been encouraging reports that more Catholic churches have been reopened in cities, that in the countryside party officials now tolerate religious gatherings: it all suggests a definite move towards greater freedom of worship.[7]

This morning Casaroli is once more trying to interpret these moves within the framework of the enduring economic and demographic problems facing the People's Republic.

Cardinals Etchegaray and Koenig have set up lines of

communication – through Hong Kong, Singapore and Manila, where Cardinal Jaime Sin has his own separate source for gauging the situation in China. Between them they provide Casaroli with a surprisingly detailed view of the contemporary scene there.

The country's system of agricultural collectives still cannot provide enough food: grain imports have trebled.[8] China's commitment to self-sufficiency is daily falling by those quaysides where a wide range of essential foreign goods are unloaded. Nor is the government's rigorous campaign of birth control having any real effect: by the end of the century China's population will have grown to an estimated 200 million – roughly equal to the present population of the United States.[9]

Militarily, China continues to give defence a relatively low priority. The current budget shows virtually no increase in arms spending over the previous year. Casaroli has told his staff that China's present inability to protect herself with the latest weapons and technologies goes some way towards explaining the country's cautious détente with the Soviet Union during the closing years of Brezhnev's leadership. In those days there had been no hostile response from Moscow about the Holy See's overtures to Peking. But will this attitude continue? Or will part of the Sino-Soviet flirtation in the future include another of those 'understandings' in which the Holy See must remain out in the diplomatic cold?[10]

And Taiwan has raised yet another perplexing question, one which places the Holy See squarely between China and the United States. The vigilant Laghi in Washington is reporting that some influential Republican Congressmen are saying to Reagan that the way he behaves towards Taiwan could be crucial to their future support. These politicians argue that Taiwan provides striking proof of America's commitment to remain loyal to small but faithful friends.

If not actually to muddy the waters further, then at least

to ripple their surface, the Secretary knows consideration must be given to China's role in Europe. For years the People's Republic, even during the height of its détente with Russia, has been trying to gain support for its anti-Soviet campaigning.[11] Much of this effort has been directed at West Germany and France, countries where Catholic influence, although on the wane, remains powerful. Previous Paris and Bonn administrations conducted foreign policies in which a good working relationship with Moscow was a prerequisite; this had virtually strangled Peking's hope of success. Consequently, China welcomed the arrival of Mitterand and Kohl. But the French president has authorized economic aid to Vietnam and the sale of Mirage jets to India, while the German chancellor shows no inclination to be ready even covertly to side with the People's Republic against the Russians. These attitudes have not pleased Peking.

There has been a suggestion around the Secretariat that the Holy See might use its influence to discreetly prod Kohl and Mitterand into taking a more malleable line. Casaroli has rejected the idea: it could upset relations with Bonn and Paris and also arouse well-seated suspicions in Peking about the ways of papal diplomacy.

This morning there is yet another suggestion designed to try and win over the People's Republic to the point where it will consider opening realistic talks with the Holy See on diplomatic links – without the Chinese moving negotiations from the realm of pragmatic discussion to one dominated by principle and national honour.

The proposal is attractive. It is that Vatican Radio should focus on the issue not only in its Chinese dialect programmes but also transmit a full account of the Holy See's position in English, with translations into other languages. The broadcast should minimize the Holy See's connection with Taiwan and stress the Vatican's pleasure at recent religious developments in mainland China. Nobody is suggesting that Holy See foreign policy is dependent upon the outcome of a radio programme: only that such a broadcast might be seen in Peking as a further indication of the Holy See's willingness to make a commitment before the world of its wish to enjoy full formal relations with China.

The idea arises from a visit Fr Sesto Quercetti, Vatican Radio's vice-director of programmes, recently made to Hong Kong. He was there to attend a conference on broadcasting. But some of his staff are openly talking about Quercetti also having had confidential talks with representatives of the Patriotic Association.[12]

Partly because of the unduly sensitive nature of the entire China Question and partly because the proposal to use Vatican Radio has merit, it has been laid before Casaroli.

He approves the idea.

The Secretary can now turn to the next matter requiring his attention: a report on the future of the Palestinian Liberation Organization.

The PLO has been a factor in the cautious moves Casaroli continues making for the Holy See to become involved in attempts to bring peace to the Lebanon. During the past month papal representatives in Algeria, Cyprus, Greece, Iraq, Sudan and Lebanon itself provided assessments of the PLO's likely future actions.

These reports have gone through the Secretariat's normal processing: one of the priests on the Middle East Desk prepared the first distillation; this was passed to the head of his section, and returned with a request for elucidation on certain points. There followed a general rewriting, which produced more queries. Gradually the paper was refined and whittled down until it assumed the form of all the others which come before Casaroli: concise, clear and balanced.

Like other Secretariat documents it is divided by a number of sub-headings. The same stylized clarity of thought runs through Problem, Background, Argument and Conclusion.

The Problem is neatly defined at the start. Israel continues totally to reject the organization's claim to be a valid voice, as does the United States. No Arab country will fight for the movement and the PLO cannot wage war on its own. With all means of negotiation blocked, what options are open for an organization which remains passionately convinced of its cause?

The Background argues that not only has there been little forward movement in PLO strategies during the past decade, but that after the loss of its power base in Beirut, the PLO is now more deeply divided than ever before. The movement is characterized as being both *immobiliste* and *attentiste*.

Its militant members appear to be gaining ground. While the conference made clear the policy is no longer to launch attacks against Jewish targets abroad,[13] every effort would be made to escalate the civil war in Lebanon – with the support, it was hoped, of the Soviet Union. The Background concludes with a review of Russian involvement in the area, including the presence of more anti-aircraft missiles around Baghdad and an increase in the number of Soviet military advisers in Syria.

The Argument is concerned with possibilities which could unlock the PLO's present paralysis. There seem to be none.

The PLO, ends the Argument, is in the classically unfortunate position of being totally dependent for its future activities on developments over which it has no control. These are: the end of the Iraq-Iran war; Egypt returning to the Arab camp; a Soviet-American détente.

The Conclusion asks Casaroli to consider one course of action.

Arafat has said he is prepared to 'talk peace without preconditions' if the Reagan administration would make 'overtures'.[14] So far these have not been forthcoming. Given the Holy See's position – that the only permanent solution is to provide the Palestinians with their own homeland – the

Secretary of State should consider intervening to discover what 'overtures' Arafat requires, and whether Washington is willing to provide them.

When the paper makes its way back to the Middle East Desk, it contains Casaroli's scribbled decision. There will be no Holy See intervention. No reason is given.

An assessment of the sixteenth congress of the Italian Communist Party (PCI) does not require action from the Secretary. It is a briefing paper intended to update him on *lo strappo* – the break – between the PCI and Moscow. Over a year ago the PCI leadership announced that the 'evolutionary force' of Soviet Communism was spent. This year's conference in Milan reconfirmed the evaluation by a thumping majority. *Lo strappo* remains as total as ever.[15]

There is, nevertheless, a sobering factor for Casaroli to consider. In a bid to win a larger portion of the national vote than the thirty per cent it presently has, the PCI is about to launch a determined attempt to move from being a party of protest to one capable of governing. The PCI plans to do this by aligning itself with the Church in those areas where there is a common interest: in campaigns against drugs, sexual abuse, municipal corruption and pollution.

Casaroli marks the assessment for distribution throughout the upper echelons of his Secretariat, with a copy to be sent to the pope's office.

Even if the paper on Ireland's abortion controversy did not carry his initials in the top right-hand corner, there could be little doubt the analysis was prepared by Mgr Audrys Backis, whose speciality includes Irish affairs. The submission is short: Backis is a man of few words either in conversation or on paper; those he uses are elegantly framed and very much to the point.

He begins with a brief reminder that although abortion is already illegal in the Republic, for months the country's anti-abortion pressure groups have been waging a vociferous campaign to reinforce the prohibition by inserting into the Irish Constitution a clause which protects specifically the unborn child. The issue has uneasily united the country's two main political parties, while Protestant Churches have joined women's groups and trade unions in opposing any addition as divisive.

The Irish Catholic Church tacitly supports those who wish to see the clause inserted.

Backis's paper is concerned with warning that the present government, led by Dr Garret Fitzgerald, is having serious second thoughts about the amendment. Fitzgerald has been crusading to have removed from the Constitution clauses which offend Protestant feelings in Northern Ireland; he hopes this will help bring reconciliation between the two sides. If the amendment is carried it could compromise this laudable desire. And in the Republic itself, increasingly the wording of the proposed amendment is being described as sectarian, allowing as it does only the two exceptions to the prohibition of abortion which the Catholic Church accepts: namely, when the mother's life is in jeopardy through an ectopic pregnancy – resulting in dangerous internal ruptur- ing – or if there is an early diagnosis of cancer in the uterus.

In the final terse paragraph Backis predicts the amend- ment will be carried because there is in Ireland a general antipathy to abortion. Its population maintains strong rural roots and attaches considerable importance to children and the family. But support for the amendment must not be seen as indicating any reversal of the growing secularization of Irish society. What should be watched is not the size of the vote in favour, but the percentages of those against. Even among the mainly Catholic populace this could be as high as thirty per cent.

Casaroli asks to be kept closely informed on the Irish government's position and suggests that the papal nuncio in Dublin, Archbishop Alibrandi, should assess Northern Ireland Protestant reaction more fully.[16]

* * *

Luigi Poggi has authored a short report on Andropov's health. This is partly based on information originally provided by the CIA; almost certainly Poggi will have confirmed it with his own well-tried and very secret contacts which seemingly reach all the way into the Kremlin.

Even so, Poggi is careful. Despite years of experience monitoring events in Moscow, he knows it is virtually impossible to be absolutely certain about the health of a Soviet leader.[17]

Nevertheless, the clues and intelligence whispers suggest Andropov could be seriously ill. During his first months in office he has obviously lost weight. For weeks he was seldom seen in public. When he did emerge he seemed to be more gaunt-faced than western diplomats could remember. 'He looks like someone who has just come out of hospital,' Poggi quotes one of his sources. Another suggests Andropov might be suffering from chronic nephritis, a disease of the kidneys. A third wonders whether Andropov's appearance is linked to heart trouble.

There are other indications that all might not be well with the Soviet leader. Recently TASS failed to publish a summary of the Politburo's weekly gathering: this is interpreted as suggesting the meeting was cancelled. Then Russia's Defence Minister suddenly cut short a visit to Budapest; such curtailing has previously signalled an impending crisis in the Kremlin. Finally Andrei Gromyko, Soviet Foreign Minister for a record twenty-six years, has been suddenly given the further responsibilities of First Deputy Premier.

Poggi's sources agree this is not only surprising but a significant move. It means Gromyko will have even greater control over Soviet foreign policy. Could this be a further indication that Andropov is physically, and perhaps even mentally, finding the strain of office too great?

Luigi Poggi does not know – and he is practised enough to say so. He is merely sounding a warning. Implicit in it is the thought that an ailing Andropov could turn out to be even more dangerous.

Casaroli flags the memo for the attention of John Paul.

The Secretary may well suspect the pope has already seen a copy of the next report. It is yet another twist in the *Pista Bulgara*. John Paul's interest in the affair remains as keen as ever.

This particular report originates from Archbishop Felici, the nuncio in Paris. It is an attempt to bring order to what might be called the Mantarov Mystery.

Isordan Mantarov was a technician attached to the Bulgarian Embassy in Paris when he defected on 11 April 1981 – only a month before the assassination bid in St Peter's Square. Mantarov has just been revealed as the source who told the French Intelligence Service shortly after defecting that an attempt on the pope's life was in the offing. The then head of the service, Alexandre de Marenches, took the information sufficiently seriously to send two senior aides to the Vatican to advise about the threat.

They had been seen by, among others, Cibin and John Magee, at the time the pope's secretary. They reported directly to the pope. Casaroli was informed. Shortly afterwards the French claim had been referred to CIA Rome, almost certainly at the suggestion of John Paul. The Station had been unable to verify the French information. It was reportedly described as 'vague'.[18] Magee suggested that, as a precaution, the Gemelli Hospital – the medical centre in Rome designated by the Vatican to deal with a papal emergency – should be put on some sort of alert. This had been deemed unnecessary by others on the pope's personal staff.[19]

A month later Agca struck – and Casaroli's fury at the CIA failure boiled over.

Now snippets of what Mantarov told French Intelligence have surfaced. The Bulgarian is claiming the papal plot originated from a KGB fear in 1979 that Zbigniew Brzezinski, then President Carter's Polish-born National Security Adviser, had influenced the election of John Paul – and that the pope was being guided by the CIA on how best he could foment unrest within the Soviet empire; the order therefore had finally been given to kill him.

Nonsensical though Casaroli knows the KGB's alleged anxieties to be, the remainder of Mantarov's story does support reports which the Secretary believes have much truth in them. Mantarov has outlined a conspiracy which fits the known facts; the French Intelligence Service are insisting that what he has told them does bring the *Pista Bulgara* that much closer to Moscow.

With a commendable show of restraint, Felici has refrained from any comment. But Casaroli could be forgiven if he senses his nuncio arching his eyebrows as he appends the latest twist to the story. His sources in French intelligence are saying that the person photographed running from St Peter's Square with a gun in his hand after Agca had fired at the pope had not been there to help his accomplice, but to assassinate Agca once he had completed his mission. There is, writes Felici, no proof that this gunman is still alive or what his intentions were.

Casaroli merely initials a curious story. What he personally thinks of it he will not reveal – at least publicly. He is equally careful not to comment on what many in the Secretariat see as John Paul's fixation with those who tried to murder him.

A clue to the Secretary's view on the next item marked for his attention is in the way he draws sharp lines in the margin beside certain paragraphs: it is a sign of his irritation over what he is reading.

This particular report has taken several weeks to reach him, first moving from Fr Pasquale Borgomeo, the director of programmes at Vatican Radio, on to Mgr Sepe in the Secretariat of State. From there it travelled to Silvestrini in the Public Affairs Ministry. Finally it has been sent in to Casaroli.

It is a full account of how envoy William Wilson and The

Mad Mentor acted over Clarissa McNair. The question Silvestrini has posed is: what further action, if any, should be taken?

Casaroli's decision is final: no further action is called for at this time.

The report will go back down the third-floor pipeline. Silvestrini will file a copy of the Secretary's decision. So will Sepe. Borgomeo will keep one copy under lock and key in his second-floor office in Piazza Pia. The last copy will be placed in McNair's file. Later, when she asks, she will not be allowed to see the documentation. Her superior, Fr Quercetti, will gently explain there is no point in her upsetting herself all over again.[20]

Meanwhile, having spent only moments on the matter, Casaroli turns to more important questions.

THE PAPAL SECRETARIAT/THE POPE'S OFFICE
Same Day: Noon Onwards

The morning portion of the protocol sheet distributed to papal secretariat staff shows that six bishops from Zaire had been received by John Paul on their annual visit to Rome. The bishops spent twenty-eight minutes with the pope: the protocol allowed a further minute at each end of the meeting for introductions and leave-taking. It is a neat thirty-minute time-block, fifteen minutes shorter than the one reserved for King Juan Carlos and Queen Sofia of Spain when they visited the previous day.

The African bishops spoke about the possibilities of John Paul making a visit to southern Africa; the king came to thank him for visiting Spain.[21]

Both sets of visitors had their pictures taken with the pope. He assumed his favourite pose for such occasions: hands clasped before him and a faint, quizzical smile on his lips. The bishops can buy copies at $15 a photo. The royal visitors will receive, free, a white leather-bound album of colour prints commemorating their visit.

Brief details of the audiences, like every other official one, have been sent to *L'Osservatore Romano* and will be published as a public record of whom the pope sees during his long working day.

The protocol seldom tells the full story. There are almost always deliberately designed gaps in the daily sechedule – sometimes a mere five minutes, more often fifteen, occasionally a half-hour and, once in a while, a full hour. Into these slots are quietly fitted certain visitors whose presence it has been decided should not be revealed.

Cardinal Glemp is frequently one such person, bringing sensitive news from Poland. Luigi Poggi is another. Sometimes on a Saturday it can be the station chief of CIA Rome.

This morning it is Mgr Edoardo Rovida, the apostolic nuncio and permanent Holy See observer to the United Nations in Geneva. He has brought with him his *uditore*, Mgr Giuseppe Bertello.

They arrive punctually in the papal secretariat as a sixteenth-century French clock begins to strike noon. The two men – clerically garbed, Roman collars gleaming, a whiff of expensive aftershave about them – carry slim briefcases. On past form they will not need to open them in the pope's presence; only when they leave will they deposit with secretariat staff the contents of their cases – copies of briefs they know by heart.

Rovida and Bertello have, as usual, worked right up until leaving their mission headquarters in Geneva and catching the flight to Rome. They travelled First Class, sitting together for the seventy-minute journey, quietly reviewing the facts they will shortly place before the pope. They continued their discussion in the back of the Vatican Fiat during the thirty-five-minute drive from Rome's Fiumicino airport to San Damaso Courtyard.

By the time Kabongo shows them into the pope's office,

the nuncio and his principal assistant are as prepared as anyone can be to tell John Paul what is happening behind the closed doors at the nuclear arms reduction talks in Geneva.

It is a story which not only can surprise John Paul but also is unlikely to please him.

The two chief negotiators – for the United States, Paul Nitze, the 76-year-old ex-merchant banker millionaire with a distinguished record of public service behind him; for the Soviet Union, Yuli Kvitsinsky, a 46-year-old career diplomat, protégé of Andrei Gromyko, with a glittering future ahead if he succeeds at the talks – have kept unusually high profiles through Geneva's early springtime. They dined together at lakeside restaurants; they took drives into the mountains; in a dozen different and very obvious ways they have fostered the notion that though the going is tough, there is a willingness to talk on, that a break could be just around the corner.

Living up to their own considerable reputations for not missing a nuance, both Rovida and Bertello know a great deal about what actually transpired in private between the two negotiators and their separate teams of military advisers, statisticians and scientists. Knowing the truth, both priests tell the pope that the likelihood of agreement appears more remote than ever.

The reasons are many.

Rovida and Bertello have come to the conclusion that a degree of cynicism permeates the present sessions which exceeds even that of previous rounds. The Soviet side remains convinced the United States will ultimately realize that in terms of pure superpower relations, the Reagan administration must – if only at the last moment – abandon its commitment to the new NATO missiles as a countermeasure against Russia's weapons. The reasoning behind this Soviet attitude is extraordinary. Kvitsinsky has argued – supporting his claim with a wealth of data about range, capacity and even siting, information not entirely believed by the Americans – that the Soviet missiles are not 'strategic', insofar as they do not have the capability to strike directly at the United States; but the proposed siting of the Pershing and Cruise missiles in NATO countries in Europe does make them 'strategic' – because they will have the range to strike directly at the Soviet Union.

The fact that the Russian SS-20s have a capacity for decimating any, or all, of Europe's sixteen NATO nations – who cannot, without the new American weapons, counter with equivalent nuclear strength – does not appear to be a consideration in Kvitsinsky's case. He has on more than one occasion made it very clear to Nitze that, in the realities of superpower plays, the fate of allies should not be of prime concern.

The Reagan administration, for its part, has advanced its arguments in some very dubious ways. Nitze and his team spent long hours trying to distance themselves from what that powerful voice, *Time*, describes as 'the simplistic charts and selective statistics' the president himself has used to portray the extent of the Soviet threat.[22]

Rovida and Bertello both know this has not helped Nitze's attempts to reach what the nuncio has termed 'the beginning of a beginning of a compromise'.[23]

Behind all the talk of 'build-up' and 'build-down', 'bilateral bargaining' and other nuclear gobbledegook bandied around Geneva, barring some extraordinary break-through, the Vatican's observers believe that the talks are doomed to fail: because the ideological, political and military gaps in the thinking between the superpowers are too great; because the delicate balance has been lost between idealism and the essential desire to find a just solution through hard bargaining; because self-interest and suspicion have almost totally dominated the last round of talks.

Moving between the two camps, Nuncio Rovida and *Uditore* Bertello established how wide is the gulf separating the negotiators; it is a far broader and deeper chasm than even they originally thought. They have come to see it is not a question of what Bertello had earlier referred to in Geneva as 'numbers and locations'.[24] The real issue, they tell the pope, is far more profound – and depressing. Europe is the buffer zone. If all else fails a limited war there would be infinitely more acceptable to the two superpowers than direct action against the United States or the Soviet Union.

It is not hard to imagine how the very Polish John Paul receives this disturbing thought.

VATICAN RADIO
Tuesday
Early Morning

Precisely at six-thirty A.M. Clarissa McNair strides through St Peter's Square, head characteristically tilted to one side, shoes clattering across the cobbles. Every other week, when she is on the early shift, she crosses the piazza at this time. The patrolling policemen still watch her with interest. They know who she is. Their contacts in the Vatican have told them all sorts of intriguing details about McNair; that she lives alone in an expensive apartment, that her salary is rather higher than her other lay colleagues receive, that outside her work she seems to lead a solitary life after her encounter with The Mad Mentor.

The residue from what he has done continues to dog McNair.[25] This morning *Newsweek* has published its version of how her broadcasts came to be taped.

The story will be drawn to Casaroli's attention. He will ponder whether, after all, the Holy See should make some official representation to Washington about this clumsy attempt to pressurize the papacy. In the end Casaroli will stick to his original decision and take no action.

In the White House and State Department the story will be seen as a crude attempt to embarrass the administration. In Washington and Rome a decision will also be taken to watch

194

McNair's work more carefully: the Secretariat of State will continue to regard her with quiet approval; the Reagan administration with suspicion.

In the particularly sensitive area in which she works – presenting to the world Vatican Radio's view of current events – both her employers and foreign governments are mindful of the influence she possesses. The station continues to give her unusual freedom. McNair selects and edits her own news to broadcast and chooses almost all the subjects for her more in-depth documentary treatment. Apart from the guiding hand of Sesto Quercetti she has virtually no editorial restrictions on what she transmits.

Her immediate concern is that the *Newsweek* story will continue to be an embarrassment. Other reporters are calling her for comment. Quercetti has told her to say nothing.

McNair knows that her documentary on South Africa, which had been transmitted four days ago, has also been taped. A diplomat at their Rome Embassy, named Darrell, had warned her the programme would be recorded off-air and sent to Pretoria for evaluation. The documentary dealt with the delicate issue of voting rights for coloureds and Asians in South Africa. The final script bore all the signs of thorough research and careful writing. In it, McNair had mentioned the Reagan administration gave 'tacit approval to South Africa's brand of segregation'.[26]

She is unaware that in the Secretariat of State and the papal secretariat, her documentary had been listened to with unusual attention. Staff there have all wondered what effect the broadcast may have on a plan for the pope to visit South Africa before the end of the year. Like many trips to what are deemed sensitive areas, the projected visit to South Africa is being discussed in the utmost secrecy. Cardinal Owen McCann of Cape Town and the papal nuncio in Pretoria, Edward Cassidy, have made tentative approaches to the South African government. The response in Pretoria has been non-committal. Nuncios in countries neighbouring South Africa have quietly sought from their host governments reactions to the proposed visit. Again, there have been no firm responses. The feeling in the Apostolic Palace is that those who have been approached are taking stock, assessing the implications – including the potential benefits – before reacting.

In many ways a papal visit to South Africa could be as politically explosive as the forthcoming trip to Poland. This is why McNair's broadcast was studied so carefully. No attempt has been made in the Vatican to modify her own firmly held belief that the South African regime needs urgently to change its ways. She visited the country, and the criticisms of what she saw there have given an additional edge to the programme.

At ten o'clock this morning – breakfasting on pizza and Coca Cola in the station's library – she is interrupted by a telephone call from Darrell. The diplomat is livid, and abusive. McNair crisply cuts him off, telling Darrell to call Quercetti.

She has no doubt her boss will back her. After all, her next assignment is preparing the programme on the Holy See's attitude towards the People's Republic of China.

The South African government's response to the broadcast is carefully assessed in the Secretariat of State. The calculated risk of allowing McNair's spiky broadcast to be aired had been worth while. Weighing the volume of the protest against the programme content, staff are able to judge more clearly the parameters in which the pope could speak on controversial issues in South Africa.

The episode also demonstrates how McNair herself is sometimes a pawn in the covert and constantly shifting moves of papal diplomacy.

11

Roman Responses

It's a Sunday afternoon, and even by Roman standards our driver is reckless. We are not so much being driven as hurtled across the city ahead of the main papal convoy.

On most alternate Sundays – when he is in residence and not in some foreign land – the pontiff appears in one of the city's parishes. He is going to San Filippo Apostolo less as pope than as Bishop of Rome. His staff say he enjoys these excursions just as much as the full-blown overseas trips.[1]

The outing, John Magee told us, is another chance for John Paul to step back, if only briefly, to that time in Poland when he was 'fundamentally a parish priest'. Emery Kabongo sees this afternoon's visit as a further opportunity 'for the Holy Father, for us all, to get back to the real grass roots of the Church'.[2]

The secretary had suggested we should come along to get a further perspective on this remarkable pontiff.

At high speed we continue careening through Rome's suburbia. Unlike the road to Rebibbia, this one takes us past the condominiums and houses of the middle classes. Along the route, coming closer to San Filippo Apostolo, we see clusters of well-dressed children being shepherded by nuns and priests, and adults in their Sunday best. But the turnout is smaller than we had expected. Perhaps what some of our contacts have told us is true: many Romans are bored, even annoyed, by the forays the pope insists on making around the city.

If this trip is anything to go by, one possible reason is not hard to see. It is causing further unwelcome chaos to Rome's already serious traffic problems.

The entire fifteen-mile route from the Vatican has been sealed off as a security precaution; traffic is backed up for miles and diversions are sending irritated Romans far out of their way.

They most certainly don't know what we have been told by Kabongo. Shortly before the pope left the Vatican there had been yet another warning that he will be attacked at some point during the journey. This is now the twenty-sixth such threat this year, the secretary informed us; 'thankfully all so far have turned out to be bogus'.

Cibin and the Rome police *capo* jointly responsible for security think this is probably another hoax, but it still means a maximum alert is in force.

All roads intersecting the papal route are blocked off; there have been spot checks on houses which could provide a position for a sniper. The whole area is teeming with *carabinieri* and DIGOS patrols. At regular intervals are stationed communication vans linked to city police head-quarters, ready to activate *Pope Alert* at the first sign of trouble.

An ambulance and medical team is keeping pace with the papal cavalcade. On board are two doctors, one a surgeon, a couple of nurses and sufficient emergency equipment to deal with serious gunshot wounds. The ambulance is in contact with the Gemelli Hospital where the pope will be taken if he is injured.

Every effort has been made to minimize the effect of any assault. John Paul's Fiat is an impressive compromise between his own wish to be seen and security considerations.

The pope is seated alone in the rear of the limousine on a throne-like chair with buttons in the armrests which allow him to swivel the seat from side to side. The underside of the beige-upholstered chair is reinforced with heavy-gauge steel. So is the car's chassis. Only a powerful landmine could penetrate this shield – and the entire route has been swept by detectors for such a possibility.

The car's windows are extra large to allow a better view of the pontiff. Not only is the glass bullet-proof, it would very likely withstand a hand-grenade.

The pope's chauffeur travels in his own protective capsule to eliminate the risk of an attempt to hi-jack the car. Cibin is satisfied there is virtually no way intruders could overpower the driver and take control of the Fiat.

The entire convoy is further protected by police and motor cyclists and carloads of accompanying DIGOS and *carabinieri*.

We cannot help but reflect the scene is more reminiscent of a Central American dictator going about his business than the Supreme Pastor out for a quiet afternoon among the faithful. It is a very sad sign of the times.

As our car passes another *carabinieri* checkpoint – half a dozen paramilitary figures cradling Uzis – we agree this kind of intensive protection goes a long way towards confirming what we have been hearing for weeks. As the year goes on, the number of personal threats on the pope's life will grow.

The probability that there are plenty of people wishing to harm John Paul is in itself hardly surprising: the papacy has always been a high-risk occupation. Each of the first eighteen pontiffs was a victim of violence – either crucified, strangled, poisoned, beheaded or smothered to death. Popes have been skinned, their bodies hauled through the streets of Rome, or imprisoned, exiled and deposed; one was even disinterred months after burial, his bones robed in vestments and strapped to a chair to face trial before an ecclesiastical court presided over by his successor. Many have been confronted by rival claimants, faced intense secular interference, heresies, mass defections and schisms.

But none we can recall has, in recent history, faced such a constant threat as nowadays confronts John Paul.

The thought that, even on a weekend afternoon like this one in Rome, the pope is in danger whenever he appears in public, is not easy to accept were it not for sane and balanced prelates like Magee and Kabongo who insist this is so.

Only the other morning we sat with Kabongo in an

ante-room adjoining John Paul's private chapel in the papal apartment and discussed with the secretary the reality of the situation.

Now, as our car approached San Filippo Apostolo, we remember Kabongo suggested that following the Central American visit, the physical risks have increased for the pope. The secretary also admitted frankly, 'Sometimes we think it too easy to say they all come from the East or from Leftists. The threats could also be from the Right.'[3]

If nothing else this makes the spectrum of potential assassins a wide one.

Yet any attacker would have a difficult time at San Filippo Apostolo.

The first person we recognize when we get near the open air altar is Cibin. He has positioned himself exactly in front of the high-backed chair on which the pope will sit.

Nobody, unless invited, approaches Cibin – not even the pushy young prelate on the dais who is whipping up the crowd before John Paul arrives; bossily rehearsing children who will present the pope with flowers and gifts, and church elders who will be introduced to the Holy Father, or local priests who will co-celebrate the mass. The prelate appears to enjoy his power. He upbraids a child who misses her cue, berates a local dignitary who takes too long to reach the papal chair, rebukes a priest who stumbles over his words.

Cibin, from time to time, beckons to one of his *vigili*. There is a whispered conversation and the guard hurries off. Occasionally the Rome police *capo* lumbers over to Cibin. The *capo* waves his hands a great deal. Cibin remains impassive. The *capo* stalks away.

The entire area for a square mile around the playing field is under heavy surveillance. There are police with carbines on the roof of each apartment building in sight of the dais. There are more *carabinieri* on the ground. And, we have been told, moving through the crowd – about 5,000 we estimate – are DIGOS squads, posing as some of the blue-jeaned teenagers and middle-aged men waiting patiently for John Paul.

Women and children predominate in this gathering. They pray and finger their rosaries and at the command of the overbearing prelate sing again and again the hymns for the mass.

The eventual approach of the papal entourage is signalled by a number of unexpected and almost simultaneous actions.

Cibin abruptly leaves his place and walks to the right-hand side of the altar.

The *capo* goes to the other.

They are now in position to direct their forces in the event of trouble.

The policemen on the rooftops turn to cover John Paul and his retinue, the marksmen slowly pivoting in time with the movement of the procession.

Vigili and *caribinieri* and some rather scruffy-looking young men we take to be DIGOS face the crowd lining the cleared path leading to the altar.

The priest on the dais is brusquely motioned away by a bishop who suddenly appears from nowhere.

Important guests hurry to their armchairs.

The choir breaks into an anthem praising the Virgin.

The crew of the ambulance which has shadowed the convoy station themselves just behind the altar.

Various policemen start to whisper into their walkie-talkies.

The bishop shouts into a microphone that the pope will be here in one minute.

The crowd begins to clap, the children to cheer. But the applause is surprisingly brief, ending as soon as the pope appears, walking slowly between the avenue of parishioners; perhaps they cannot quite believe he is actually among them. It is a very moving moment, this reverential hush which comes over the crowd.

John Paul looks older than he did before going to Central America. These first four months of the year do seem to have taken their toll. Since New Year's Day when he stood in St Peter's and delivered his uncompromising warning about the nuclear peril facing the world, John Paul has definitely aged.

Even allowing for what Magee told us[4] – that the pope has a bad cold and is full of antibiotics – this John Paul somehow seems a shrunken version of the pontiff of even a few weeks ago. Today he is moving almost listlessly, not so much walking as shambling. He appears to be bowed down not only by his regalia – Kabongo says the pope's heavy silk and brocade vestments and mitre weigh close to twenty pounds – but with something else. It could be he is a man now feeling his years. It could also be he's a spiritual leader who increasingly wonders whether his political voice is being heard.

Publicly the pope's speeches continue to follow the same theme: evil is afoot and the world has never been in greater danger. But his dire warnings are no longer automatically reported except for the obligatory coverage in *L'Osservatore Romano* and on Vatican Radio.

Standing close to him, able to look in to those deep-set blue-grey eyes as he approaches, it is easier for us to believe John Paul has been deeply affected by all sorts of recent happenings.

We have been told the growth of world terrorism continues to preoccupy him.

The pope is still distressed by the news that Pakistan may be close to possessing a nuclear device; that Brazil is refining its own plutonium without international inspection; that both Israel and South Africa are reported to be adding to their nuclear arsenals.

Closer to home he has been dismayed by the success of Italy's Planned Parenthood Association, which has dramatically cut the country's birth-rate. John Paul has ordered ways must be found to combat the Association's newest campaign – using popular actors in picture books to urge that people use contraceptives.

We have also been told the pontiff is irked by the ruling of the Court of Cassation, one of Italy's highest tribunals, which now allows topless sunbathing on public beaches. The court solemnly pronounced that bare breasts should no longer be considered offensive, but 'exposure of genital areas remains forbidden because certain intimate parts of the body are bound by atavistic custom as being set apart for the coupling of physiological functions'.

A memo has been circulated among the handful of lay families living in the Vatican to remind them that not only is topless sunbathing forbidden, but so is the wearing of bikinis and 'certain kinds of male trunks'.

Here at San Filippo Apostolo, everyone is suitably attired: there is not a hint of a bosom in sight.

As we watch the pope working his way down the avenue of people, we have to admit he has lost none of his natural skills in handling an audience. He has an unerring instinct for spotting a child to be lifted out of its mother's arms, kissed and returned; for blessing an old woman, a nun or a priest. It is a genuine and tremendous performance.

Magee is there at his elbow, constantly leaning forward to whisper into John Paul's ear the name of some local notable who has been placed at this spot just so the pope can greet him; the Master of Ceremonies is marvellously skilled at his job and keeps the pope moving forward all the time.

Preceded by priests and flanked by security men, John Paul, crozier firmly held, makes his way to the altar dais.

As he climbs the red-carpeted steps he pauses on each tread. Perhaps it is no more than his cold which slows him down; perhaps he is pacing himself for the mass. Perhaps, too, all the unseen pressures have combined to make him what he now appears: a tired man who is driving himself too hard.

We know that back at the Secretariat of State, matters are being processed which will, before the day is out, require the pope's attention.

West Germany's Catholic bishops have produced a pastoral letter, *Justice Creates Peace*, which falls short of totally condemning nuclear weapons. Secretariat staff are preparing a brief on the likely effect – both short and long term – of the document.

From El Salvador Nuncio Kada has sent a long and complex report indicating that the Reagan administration is deepening its involvement in the country, causing a further rift in the local Church. From neighbouring Nicaragua the nuncio in Managua has sent a report that the CIA has increased its secret funding of the country's right-wing insurgents.

These reports form part of a continuous check the Secretariat is making on the after-effects of the Central America trip. No matter how carefully the words are couched, the plain truth is that while the pope may well, as Kabongo indicated, have 'disturbed' a lot of things in the region, he seems to have had little success in changing the overall situation.

The Middle East Desk continues to monitor the position in Lebanon. We have been told – but cannot confirm – that the PLO office in Rome has begun to brief the Desk on moves to have the organization officially recognized by both the European Community and the United States. Eventually, if not tonight, the pope must decide whether the Holy See will support such a move.

Watching John Paul celebrating the mass it is difficult for us to believe that any one man can possibly carry the burden of being both full-time spiritual leader of a billion Catholics and a world statesman capable of constant involvement in the political arena.

Equally, we have to concede, John Paul does continue to do just that. But at what personal cost?

This afternoon, when he prays for the hungry of the Third World, he is also reminding the essentially middle-class and comfortably well-off gathering around us that they – and for that matter, us, and indeed the pope himself – all belong to what might be termed the 'Haves', those with the where-withal to live well above the poverty line, as opposed to the multiplying number in the world who could accurately be described as the 'Have Nots'.

Kabongo, increasingly the social conscience closest to the pope, has told us that, on top of all his other concerns, John Paul is deeply troubled over the possibility of a future conflict between the two groupings.[5] The pope seemingly visualizes not so much a war between East and West as between North and South, between the entrenched older industrial nations and the increasingly deprived of the Third World.

This is the deeper message behind his homily at San Filippo Apostolo.

Having delivered it, John Paul returns to his Fiat and is driven at high speed back to the Vatican.

We make our way to the Cavalieri-Hilton where Henry Kissinger is about to host a press conference on behalf of the Trilateral Commission, a sort of superior private think-tank whose members seem to be a marriage of the intellectual and the influential.

The conference is a shambles. There are only eighty seats for some two hundred correspondents, each eager to interrogate the former Secretary of State. Kissinger is at his most stonewalling. He flicks away questions with the same bored gesture: a curious hand movement which starts as a karate chop and ends with him apparently taking a peek at his watch.

We plan to ask him how, following his own findings of a KGB involvement in the papal assassination plot, he now assesses the role of the CIA in the affair.

There are, as he must surely know, strange developments going on. The CIA continues cleverly to pour cold water on Martella's investigation. The agency portrays Agca as an authentic member of terrorism's lunatic fringe.

But this is the point: if Agca is so crazy and untrustworthy, why is the CIA bothering to traduce Martella in such a heavy-handed way? The Mad Mentor is going around Rome telling anybody who will listen 'this little wop judge has got it all wrong; there was no conspiracy'.

Martella, we know, is not stupid. Laboriously meticulous, painstakingly thorough, cranky about the slightest misrepresentation of evidence: he is each of these things. But dumb he is not. Certainly he would not doggedly question Agca if it was as futile as the CIA says.

So what *is* going on? It would have been helpful to have had Kissinger try and answer this question.

But it is not to be. Twenty-nine minutes after the press conference opens, it closes. Kissinger disappears back into a Hilton suite. None of us will actually know when he leaves Rome. Now that *is* security.

President Reagan's personal envoy to the Holy See, William Wilson, is clear about what bothers him.[6]

'Poland,' he said, 'kinda dominates my thinking. It's right up there. Up front.'

We are seated in his office at Number One Piazza Della Citta Leonina, a square almost adjoining the Vatican walls. Geographically Wilson is the closest foreign emissary to the Holy See.

The US mission is on the first floor of the sixteenth-century building. Wilson's office has been recently painted and smells faintly of turpentine. There are spotless white ashtrays and over-stuffed beige cushions on the modern sofas and chairs. The entire effect would not go amiss in a Bloomingdale window.

Wilson, as always, is a splendid advertisement for the Good Life. He may well not intend to, but he does give the impression that money is something he rarely thinks about. Here, in his own domain – dominated by a large Stars and Stripes behind his desk – he is utterly relaxed.

Across from him, strategically seated to catch the envoy's eye, is Michael Hornblow. He looks even tenser than usual. His smile seems more fixed, his eyelids move like shutters on a high speed camera: flicker, flicker, flicker. He somehow radiates suspicion.

We decide to proceed slowly. We are interested not only in why the personal representative of the most powerful leader in the western world should have concerned himself with Clarissa McNair's broadcasts, but also in discovering just how Wilson is shaping up as the president's man in a key listening post.

Hornblow's presence is a clue. Before Wilson answers a question he almost always turns to the young career diplomat, studies Hornblow's expression, and only then responds.

How exactly is Poland dominating Wilson's thinking?

'Is he gonna go, or not go? That's the key question. I see it like this . . .'

Wilson looks at Hornblow, perhaps to be certain *both* see it like this.

Hornblow blinks.

Apparently reassured, Wilson launches into his personal assessment.

'The pope wants to go. He won't cancel. That's my reading. It will be up to them.'

Them?

Wilson looks at Hornblow. Flicker, flicker – like morse-code. If it is, it signals Wilson should continue.

'Them . . . the Poles. The regime. It will be up to the Polish authorities to decide. Up to them . . . the regime to make the move.'

Hornblow sits coiled and wary: should there be a condition known as 'tensely relaxed', Hornblow has it.

Wilson is speaking again. 'If the Polish regime cancels then it will have a shattering effect on the Church within the Soviet bloc. But remember this. The Poles are a strong people. They are used to oppression. They rise above adversity. That's what makes them so special to . . . to us.'

Us?

Hornblow uncoils himself. 'Mr Wilson is referring to our

government. The people of the United States. We are very close to Poland. We always have been.'

The professional diplomat sits back, more relaxed now.

We turn to Wilson. We remind him he is physically much closer to the pope than the people in Washington: what advice does he give the State Department on not just the Polish visit but more general matters?

'Well . . . I try to explain . . . the problems. The whole situation is fraught with problems right up until the pope goes . . . if he goes . . . and comes back again. . . .and maybe even afterwards . . .'

What specific problems?

'Oh . . . well . . .' He turns to Hornblow.

He is firm. 'We can't give you specifics.'

'Right,' says Wilson.

The envoy sounds relieved. He continues. 'You know, when history comes to assess all this, it will only be a little footnote . . .'

We look quizzical.

Hornblow takes over. 'Don't misunderstand Mr Wilson. Of course we are all concerned. We want the pope to go to Poland. And the Polish government should have no doubts about the benefit to them. The pope's presence will be taken as evidence of an on-going dialogue.'

It seems neither man has more than this to say on the Polish trip.

There is silence in the room. We sit back and reflect on which way to continue. Wilson is clutching his right knee, crossed over his left leg: it does not look nearly so ungainly as it sounds. Hornblow's eyes are fast flickering again.

We decide the time has come to introduce *Newsweek*: we have interviewed Clarissa McNair, spoken to her superiors at Vatican Radio, in the Secretariat of State and to people in various intelligence services. Now we want to hear Wilson's version.

He shrugs. 'I can live with it. It's just rough on my wife.'

We sympathize. But why did he lend the authority of his

office to such a matter? Surely it isn't edifying for the American president's personal envoy to be party to taping broadcasts – '

We never finish. Hornblow cuts in. 'Mr Wilson doesn't have any real problems in this area. It is just at this time some reporters are looking for targets.'

Wilson adds: 'Just pinko journalists trying to make a living.'

It's our turn to blink. We haven't heard the term 'pinko journalists' since the late Senator McCarthy stormed through Washington when Ronald Reagan was still an actor and William Wilson was amassing his fortune from real estate.

Hornblow steps in again. 'Let's get back to the real issues.'

He has made it pointedly clear he will not welcome any attempt to pursue the activities of The Mad Mentor in this office.

'The real issues,' echoes Wilson. 'Yeah, let's talk about them. You know, the trouble spots.'

He begins to enumerate them, unclasping his knee, counting the crisis areas off on his fingers.

'There's El Salvador' – he touches his little finger. 'There's the Lebanon' – he touches his index finger. 'Anywhere in Asia you care to mention' – this time it's his middle finger. He continues to reel off a daunting list.

We are confused; surely his fief does not extend to these areas.

He smiles. 'No, but the Holy See's does.'

We nod, understanding. Then where does he detect differences in these areas between the policies of his government and that of the Holy See?

There is sudden silence. Hornblow's eyes dart from us to Wilson and back again. He is clearly thinking hard. His reply has an edge.

'We don't see any lasting conflicts.' It is flat and unequivocal.

Wilson's right foot starts to tap the carpet, a curious reflex action.

'No conflict at all,' he insists.

Well then: perhaps misunderstandings?

Wilson's foot taps harder. 'None at all. We talk a lot to them. We explain our position very carefully. They listen very carefully.'

Who do they talk to in the Vatican?

Hornblow is cautious. 'It depends.'

On what?

'On what we have to say.'

'Exactly,' chimes Wilson. 'On what we have to say.'

We let that pass for the moment. We ask how he actually got the job, what took him from selling property in California to peddling policies around the Vatican? We naturally frame the question rather more politely.

Wilson is immediately smiling and relaxed. He is like a man who has come through his own mine-field.

Hornblow settles back. This is straightforward.

The envoy clearly relishes recounting the story. It is one which seals his undeniably special relationship with Reagan. It also offers an insight into how the president chooses an envoy for such a sensitive post as the Holy See.

Wilson begins. 'I was sitting at home, back in California, just after the president was elected, thinking it was just wonderful he was there in the White House. The phone rang. It was Ronnie, sorry, the president' (there is no coyness in his self-correction, just a reminder to himself that Reagan is now always 'the president' to all but intimates like Wilson). 'It was the president on the line. "Bill," he said, "how'd you like the Holy See? I sure would like you to go there for me." I was just stunned. I said, "Hold on a moment while I get the wife on the phone." I called out to her to pick up the extension. She was in the bedroom. I think I was in the den. She came on the line and I said, "Mr President, would you just repeat what you told me?" He did. And I said, "You bet I'll take it." That was it. I was on my way here in no time.'

The story has been well worth the telling. But it does raise a question. Good friend though he is of Reagan, Wilson has no diplomatic training: if he had, did he now think it might

210

have helped him avert the sort of incidents he seems prone to get involved in?

Hornblow is once more alert.

'No,' he says, flatly. 'No, no, no. No amount of formal training would have stopped the Soviet Embassy here in Rome accusing Mr Wilson and the president of being behind the assassination attempt on Pope John Paul.'

It is delivered as a calculated throwaway; afterwards we wonder whether they teach the technique nowadays at the State Department. Hornblow knows he has a trump and plays it to the full.

Can we hear more?

'Sure,' says Hornblow. 'It was like this. The Soviet Embassy put out a release that made these accusations. TASS carried it. We made a formal protest, to the Italian government. Their appropriate minister hauled in the Soviet appropriate attaché and gave him hell.'

What happened then?

'It died a death,' says Hornblow. 'We killed it.'

The words seem unfortunate in the context of the question.

Do they often protest?

'Well . . .' Wilson hesitates. 'It . . . depends.'

On what?

The envoy and his assistant exchange looks.

Impulsively, and in spite of Hornblow's previous cut-off, we try once more to introduce the *Newsweek* item: had they made a formal protest over the report?

'Not worth it,' snaps Wilson, irritated.

Had he himself received any criticism as a result of the item?

'From whom?' Hornblow is back at the ramparts.

From the State Department? Maybe the Vatican?

'No. Nothing at all.' Hornblow is clearly anxious to end such questions.

We prod away: *had they any idea how* Newsweek *got the story?*

'Vatican Radio leaked it.' It is Wilson, and he is emphatic.

Hornblow is less certain. 'That's our assumption. But it is a fair one to make.'

Wilson interrupts. 'You ever hear their broadcasts? You ever actually hear their tone? The way they slant things?'

Can he be more specific?

Hornblow bulldozes his way back into the conversation. 'It's pretty wild the way they sometimes report things. But we are not making a blanket criticism. Don't think that. It's just that some people seem to have a lot of freedom there.'

Wilson will not be contained. 'Yeah. You might call it "pinko freedom". You get some of those voices on that morning show spouting what they like. Too much of a free hand. No strong control.'

Had he ever taped any broadcasts he found offensive?

'Well . . . no. But I listen.'

Newsweek had clearly stated that an unnamed American citizen complained to Wilson about McNair's broadcasts.

Hornblow is snappish. 'We did have a protest. Yes.'

Can he name the person?

'Well . . . no.' Hornblow's voice seems to come from pack ice.

Had the person who taped the broadcasts done so in a private capacity – or officially on behalf of the CIA?

Hornblow is emphatic. 'No, no, no. Mr Wilson absolutely is not going to discuss this matter further. Now, any more questions?'

We ask Wilson about his role in the US bishops' pastoral letter. We have heard he met Bernardin –

'Sure, when he came here as cardinal-elect. I listened to his views. I arranged for him to be briefed by the appropriate personnel in State. I encouraged him to be exposed to all points of view. In turn, I exposed Bernardin and his colleagues to this administration's point of view. There is nothing wrong in that.'

We assure him we are not suggesting there is.

The envoy nods, mollified. 'Bishops cannot speak on military matters without full cognizance of the facts.'

Indeed not. How had he briefed them?

'I hope thoroughly . . .'

We remind him anything he cares to say will not see the light of day for perhaps a year; that by then his thoughts would be well along that footnote-in-history road he has alluded to. He seems reassured.

'Okay. The bishops began with one stance. We in the administration have another. Part of my job here, on the ground, is to bring them together to reconcile all that is good in both positions, good firstly for the United States as a whole, good for the defence of the entire West. Does that sound clear enough?'

Absolutely clear, we assure him.

'Well, there was some straight talking. That Bishop Roach and at times Bernardin, they had to be told what the position really is. And that fellah Gumbleton . . . out in Detroit. What can you do with a fellah like that? Where does he get those ideas from?'

Hornblow will not be denied his qualification. 'But there was no acrimony. Nothing like that. It is just that we had to get our points across. They were big enough to listen. It all requires a measure of understanding. That is why we go along to the Vatican together.'

Hornblow is moving the question of Wilson's involvement with the American bishops off in another direction, and at top speed. 'Yes, we always go to the Vatican together. It helps to keep things moving, having us both there.'

Who do they get on with best?

'It depends,' repeats Hornblow.

On what?

'On what we have to say.'

It's time for us to go.

It is late afternoon when we enter the Vatican through the Porta Sant'Anna, and go into the Apostolic Palace. This seems the best possible place from which to observe the growing tensions over the Polish visit.

12

THE PAPAL APARTMENT
Sunday
Early Morning

The day begins with a sense of foreboding.[1]

It is present in the pope's private chapel where John Paul says mass shortly after dawn; his voice is filled with feeling as he offers a special prayer for Poland during what he is already calling 'this day of trial'.[2]

There are a dozen co-celebrants around him. Some, like Dziwisz, Kabongo and the Polish nuns who run the papal apartment, regularly join the pope in early morning prayer. For them the first mass of the day is what Kabongo calls 'a family gathering' – an opportunity to rededicate themselves to the service of God in the presence of their pontiff.

This morning the papal 'family' has been augmented by Casaroli, Silvestrini, Somalo and Poggi. They kneel together in one row, murmuring their responses and quietly reciting their prayers. When the mass ends, they follow John Paul to his office.

There they review the overnight situation report from Poland which the Polish Desk prepared. Normally the report would have been included in the buff-coloured Summary file, but because of what is happening in his homeland, the pope has asked that a special separate briefing be submitted.

The news is grim.

All the signs point towards bloody confrontation between the Polish government and the outlawed Solidarity movement. During the night vans filled with thousands of riot police have been dispersed around Warsaw and in at least twenty other Polish cities; in many cases they are supported by armoured vehicles and water cannon. Poland's army is on full alert: the sounds of tanks and half-tracks manoeuvring has been heard in the outskirts of many towns.

Undaunted, Solidarity members have, under cover of

darkness, distributed leaflets calling on people to use this Sunday's morning mass as a convenient way to assemble for the demonstrations the union proposes to stage throughout Poland.

Solidarity's clandestine radio transmitters – scattered across the country and operating in a similar manner to those used in Occupied Europe during World War II – have somehow managed to avoid being jammed long enough to warn listeners to ignore a mysterious radio broadcast. Claiming to be 'the voice of the underground', the station has repeatedly announced the planned demonstrations have been called off.

During the night the indefatigable Josef Glemp, Primate of All Poland, has telephoned from his palace in Warsaw. Despite knowing his call was certainly being monitored by the Polish secret police, the cardinal told the ranking night-duty monsignor on the Polish Desk that the broadcast was a last-minute attempt by the authorities to disrupt Solidarity's plans.

Glemp had actually noted down snatches of the bogus broadcast and dictated them to the monsignor. The transmission claimed that already there had been mass arrests, and went on to remind Poles the riot police could be exceptionally violent: 'The only way to avoid injury is to heed the latest instructions from Solidarity and stay at home. Let us consider our absence from the streets the best form of protest. Do not take part in any rally.'

The pope repeats the words to the prelates in his office, adding that such knavery must be expected.

He turns to Casaroli and asks what is the very latest news. The Secretary of State replies that two hours ago, at five A.M. – thirty minutes before he usually wakes – his bedside telephone rang.

Glemp was on the line once more. The embattled cardinal – tanks were by then patrolling back and forth in front of his residence – stated that the country's deputy prime minister had just telephoned to make what he called 'a final desperate appeal' for the Polish hierarchy to cancel morning mass throughout the country.[3]

John Paul asks how Glemp had responded.

'Very firmly,' says Casaroli. 'Our brother cardinal pointed out that even at the height of the Nazi occupation morning mass had never been cancelled. He saw no reason to do so now.'[4]

The pope nods his satisfaction. He explains he expected the regime to act like this; it is all part of the relentless campaign the authorities are waging to crush Solidarity further.

He turns to the briefing and again reads aloud: Warsaw is decked out with Party banners and slogans; there have been more television programmes and newspaper articles attacking Lech Walesa and other Solidarity leaders. Ought anything be done about these attacks?

The question is answered by Poggi: the attacks should continue to be ignored by the Polish hierarchy. Glemp has only recently reminded his priests that, tempted though they might be, they must not preach against the regime – not with the pope's visit less than six weeks away.

John Paul alights on another item in the Polish Desk report. It is an account by Glemp of Walesa's latest brush with the authorities. A few days ago the union activist was given back his old job at the Lenin Shipyard. But almost immediately militiamen had forcibly taken him away for interrogation about what he knew of Solidarity's plans.

Glemp, in recounting the matter – he now has a standing request from the pope to report anything involving Walesa – describes the incident as 'crude intimidation'.

John Paul says such tactics will never intimidate Walesa. He reminds the senior diplomats gathered around him that Walesa has a 'difficult role'. The regime is badgering him in the hope he will make a mistake sufficiently serious for Walesa to be rearrested, a move which just might be planned as a pretext to cancel the pope's visit. Equally, while Walesa remains free he will continue to act as the catalyst for all Solidarity's aspirations.

The Secretary of State and his aides listen without interruption as the pope explains he has lately advised Walesa that, though he should not sign any of the actual communiqués concerning today's planned demonstrations, it would be right for him to associate himself with them.[5] John Paul then expounds a familiar theme: Solidarity can still be a potent force in Polish affairs, able not only to offer progressive programmes but, in doing so, to expose the inherent weakness of Communism; his own visit to Poland will force the government there – and beyond it, Moscow – to recognize a fundamental truth: nothing can now extinguish completely the beacon Solidarity has lit.

Jabbing with a forefinger at the Polish Desk briefing – those around him know the action betrays deeply felt emotion – the pope declares the Polish government's campaign agaisnt Solidarity will ultimately fail.

Silvestrini poses a question: granted that the regime has been unsuccessful in halting Solidarity's plans to demonstrate during the day throughout Poland, how is bloodshed to be averted?

Casaroli reports that, even as they are sitting here, Glemp has planned to issue an appeal for the authorities and the demonstrators to avoid clashing with each other.

John Paul is emphatic. It will not work: the regime wants confrontation. He turns to Casaroli. Should a direct approach be made to General Jaruzelski at this late stage to see whether there is any way at all his government might allow some form of Solidarity demonstration which would not be disrupted?

The Secretary of State deflects the question to his aides; he wants a consensus of opinion on such a crucial matter.

Silvestrini, Somalo and Poggi are of one view: it would be a mistake to approach Jaruzelski; doing so would only reinforce the general's belief that he had been right to declare a 'state of war' exists in Poland. Any form of papal intervention would be exploited by the regime.

The pope leads the senior prelates into breakfast. If he is disappointed, he hides his feelings.

Dziwisz and Kabongo are waiting in the papal dining-room. The table is covered with plates of Polish ham and sausages, baskets of *chleb*, Polish bread, platters stacked with buckwheat *blinzes*, pancakes served with sour cream.

The Polish secretary is unusually jovial. In the early hours of this morning Dziwisz had been awakened by a call from Copenhagen.[6] The telephoner was the pro-nuncio in Scandinavia. He had just indicated Lech Walesa could be a candidate for the Nobel Peace Prize.

Dziwisz breaks the news over breakfast. For the first time this morning John Paul smiles.

CENTRAL SECURITY OFFICE OF THE VATICAN
Same Day: Same Time

At eight o'clock – around the time the nuns begin to clear the pope's breakfast table – Camillo Cibin approaches his office near the impressive Palazzo San Carlo, itself over-shadowed by the towering back of the basilica.

Apart from patrolling *vigili* there is no one about in this quarter of the Vatican at this hour. Raincoat collar turned up against another squall of rain, Cibin continues his measured stride. Ignoring the downpour, every now and then he pauses to survey the surrounding buildings. It is an instinctive action, a throwback to those days he was a Rome detective hunting criminals in the Trastevere quarter. He knows that the only thieves he is likely to catch in the Vatican are those priests and nuns who filch stationery. He walks on, picking his way around the larger of the puddles.

The security chief has already completed his morning circle of St Peter's Square, checked the guardhouse at the Bronze Door and inspected the devices on the roof of the papal apartment – those sophisticated detectors the CIA trusts to provide sufficient advance warning of any terrorist attack on the Apostolic Palace from the air.

Some of his staff say Cibin sees the presence of the detectors as yet another example of the entangled relationship between the intelligence agency and the present papacy; one in which John Paul keeps the kingdom and the glory while the CIA clings to its power inside the Vatican.

This morning Cibin is going to proceed with his review of a more immediate question: how much does the CIA know about the facts surrounding the attack on John Paul? In just twelve days it will be the second anniversary of the shooting which for very different reasons obsesses the pope and his security chief.

Cibin does not know what continues to motivate the pope's interest in the matter. He knows what drives himself on – a professional determination to get to the bottom of an increasingly complex story which has blurred the boundaries between international politics and the search for justice and truth.

In spite of excellent contacts among the Italian security forces, equally reliable sources in foreign intelligence agencies and his well-developed sixth-sense which separates merely a good policeman from the born detective, Cibin has been unable to obtain answers to some very nagging issues.

He reaches his headquarters, goes to his office, unlocks its door, hangs up his sodden raincoat, and settles down at his desk. From a locked bottom drawer he removes his bulky dossier on the papal shooting. Cibin knows even before studying it that political expediency is denying him the answers he seeks.

It is the only explanation for the polite, but firm, brush-off he receives whenever he raises the possibility of seeing the full transcript of the interrogation of Agca by members of West Germany's BKA – the country's equivalent to the FBI. In May 1981, the day after Agca was arrested, a BKA team from Wiesbaden had flown secretly to Rome and put 192 questions to him. He answered fewer than half.

But his responses are still deemed so sensitive that one of the first things Chancellor Helmut Kohl did when he took office in March was personally to reconfirm a decision that the complete BKA report could only be seen by directors of the BKA and the West German secret service, BND.

A copy of an Austrian Intelligence file which has come into Cibin's hands goes some way towards explaining why Kohl is so anxious to keep the full BKA report confidential.[7] The Austrian dossier shows that one of the key men in the human chain which guided Agca to St Peter's Square is Horst Grillmeir. He had bought in Austria the Belgian-made Browning 9-mm semi-automatic pistol and bullets which Agca had used. Immediately after the assassination attempt, Grillmeir, like so many others involved with Agca, disappeared – almost certainly to Bulgaria.

Grillmeir has now been arrested at an Austrian frontier check-point bordering Czechoslovakia. His pick-up truck was loaded with arms. Grillmeir produced documents showing he was licensed to import the guns into West Germany. He gave the Austrian police the name of an associate living in Munich called Paul Saalbach. Grillmeir urged his captors to telephone Saalbach, 'so that we can end this nonsense'.

Instead a senior member of Austrian Intelligence had contacted West Germany's BND and BKA – only to be told by both agencies that Saalbach was a BND officer based at the service's headquarters at Pullach, near Munich.

The notion that the BND had been using Grillmeir as a gun runner – in all the truck contained over 700 weapons and 15,000 rounds of ammunition – not only infuriated the Austrians, but also made them speculate whether, when they had badly wanted to interrogate Grillmeir about his dealings with Agca, Grillmeir may have been sheltered by the BND. Clearly, by expecting to drive through Austria to West Germany with such an arsenal, he must have been brazenly confident of his connections.

Cibin knows the entire Austrian episode raises more serious questions. Was Grillmeir involved with the BND when he bought the gun for Agca? Who had told him to buy the weapon? Why did he purchase it in Austria? Had the pistol travelled to Rome through West Germany? Did Agca tell his BKA interrogators that he had an affiliation – however remote – with West German intelligence in addition to his proven contact with Grillmeir? And could the answers to these, and undoubtedly other embarrassing questions, be in the full BKA report?

The Vatican security chief thinks it likely; his gut instinct tells him that just as recent CIA actions seem to muddy the trial, there may be every reason for one of Western Europe's most powerful police agencies to do the same. The Austrian file indicates that both the BKA and its sister service, the BND, know a great deal more about the papal plot than either have chosen to reveal.

He has spent hours studying the emasculated version of the BKA report which the West German government circulated in late 1981 to, among others, the Vatican. While Cibin cannot be positive -- being the sort of old-fashioned investigator who accepts nothing he has not personally examined – he suspects the full BKA document also contains evidence which could implicate the KGB in the papal assassination plot, and therefore the Soviet leader, far more definitely than has emerged so far.[8]

Cibin is not, he likes to tell friends, 'unduly political'. But he has not needed his BND contacts to tell him that for West Germany publicly to accuse the Soviet leader of trying to murder a fellow head of state would create a political maelstrom.

Spurred on solely by dogged determination, Cibin had tried to get a copy of the unedited BKA report through CIA Rome. The Station Chief claimed not to know if its existence.

Thoroughly aroused, his detective's nose sniffing international intrigue, Cibin turned to MOSSAD. Like most western intelligence agencies, the Israeli service is usually co-operative when presented with requests from the Vatican. This time the Israelis were brusque. There was no way they could help.

Now, as he has in the past, Cibin applies techniques to assist him which he learned when in Rome's police academy a quarter of a century earlier. He begins to put on paper what he knows for certain. From this he will extrapolate what is probable, what is possible, what is impossible. It is a time-consuming exercise. Even before he is finished he again faces a fact which has troubled him for weeks: the BND and BKA do not have close ties to MOSSAD; but all three agencies have strong links to the CIA.

From this Cibin is able to deduce that the clamp on the information he so badly desires has been made by the American intelligence agency. The constraint may also, in part, be related to how MOSSAD itself became involved in investigating the attempt on the pope's life.

On Good Friday, 17 April 1981 – a full month before Agca shot the pope – he had been spotted in Perugia, an university town north of Rome, by a Turkish Intelligence (MIT) 'casual', parlance for one of the informers MIT maintains in Western Europe's Turkish ghettos. Agca was with two other men.

News of their presence was telephoned to MIT headquarters in Ankara. There, a senior officer informed Colonel Istahak Cahani, defence attaché at the Israeli Legation. Cahani was also the MOSSAD resident in Turkey. He had assembled his own dossier on Agca, identifying him as one of the more dangerous terrorists Turkey had produced. Cahani feared, understandably, that one day Agca might strike against Israel.[9]

The description of the two men with Agca in Perugia alarmed Cahani. MOSSAD computers listed them as KGB operatives Teslin Tore and Maurizio Folini. Cahani teleprinted to Tel Aviv late Good Friday night the news that the three men were in Perugia.

On Easter Saturday, 18 April, the DIGOS office on the third floor of Rome police headquarters received a telex from MOSSAD, Tel Aviv. The message stated that 'almost certainly' Agca was travelling under his latest alias, Faruk Ozgun. Included in the MOSSAD teletype was a copy of the Interpol alert and descriptions of Tore and Folini.[10]

The telex was – by all later accounts – not received with any great enthusiasm by the senior DIGOS officer on duty. Possibly he was one more policeman who believes the Israeli agency has a penchant for sending out too many fliers. This attitude may account for what happened.[11]

The officer called the DIGOS office in Perugia. Their enquiries were seemingly perfunctory. Rome was quickly told there was no trace of the trio in Perugia. The news was telexed to Tel Aviv. Perhaps the most active persons in the entire incident, at least as far as the Italians went, were the police teletype operators. In Tel Aviv the telex traffic was stored on MOSSAD computers.

Within hours of the pope being shot MOSSAD asked permission to interrogate Agca. The request was refused by a senior civil servant in the Italian Ministry of Justice.

A telephone call was made by a MOSSAD officer in Tel Aviv to the ministry official. The Israeli carefully pointed out that MOSSAD had previously alerted DIGOS of Agca's presence in Italy; in the clamour following the shooting the Israelis wanted the world to be clear about their role. Might not the best way to ensure this be for MOSSAD to make public the telex traffic it held? On the other hand, if the official could sanction MOSSAD's request, there would surely be no need for those embarrassing telexes to surface.

The civil servant immediately agreed MOSSAD could send two fluent Turkish speakers to interrogate Agca. The officers had spent three days with Agca, questioning him alone.[12]

Assessing all the information available to him, Cibin can see a plausible chain of events.

Having blackmailed its way on to the case, MOSSAD turned to the CIA for support. The American agency smoothed ruffled Italian feelings. In turn MOSSAD handed over a copy of its lengthy interrogation of Agca to the CIA – an example of how the machinations of intelligence agencies transcend national boundaries.

With a compliant MOSSAD, BND and BKA – and perhaps even other Western European security services – the CIA can move forward with newfound confidence in its attempt to impede Judge Martella's own trek along the *Pista Bulgara*. The agency is about to call on two formidable names to downgrade further Martella's investigation. President Reagan's National Security Adviser, William P. Clark, and William J. Casey, director of the CIA, will shortly tell selected journalists the *Pista Bulgara* has reached a dead end, and that Antonov could be freed soon.[13] Already CIA Rome has begun carefully to plant doubting questions. Why, if Antonov is a full-blown Bulgarian intelligence officer, did he remain in Rome so long after Agca failed to kill the pope? Surely the risk was great that Agca would betray him? And why had Agca taken so long to name Antonov? In a dozen different ways scorn is being poured on *Pista Bulgara* by the CIA.

Why?

Having finally reviewed the evidence in his file, Cibin is convinced the CIA is going to extraordinary lengths – if the agency itself has nothing to hide in the matter.

THE PAPAL SECRETARIAT
Same Day: Later in the Morning

Shortly before nine o'clock papal messenger Ercole Orlandi reports for duty. Sundays are usually uneventful. There are few visitors for the messenger to usher either to the pope's apartment or his Secretariat; nor are there normally many sealed envelopes for him to fetch and return to the Secretariat of State. Sunday provides a chance for Orlandi to read the newspapers, or to do what he prefers even more, talking about his children to the pope's staff.[14]

After twenty-five years of rearing them, Orlandi still manages to convey genuine enthusiasm about his sons and daughters. Of late, though, that excitement has been tempered by his concern over their future in an increasingly uncertain world. His eldest daughter recently lost her job with a Rome cosmetic firm, another statistic to add to the rising number of unemployed in the city. Like thousands of other Romans she is now finding it almost impossible to get work. Living at home she has become a sudden and unexpected drain on her father's modest salary. His eldest son is coming to the end of his studies and is also finding employment prospects discouraging. Another daughter has just announced she plans to marry. Both she and her future husband have no savings, and Orlandi is wondering whether he should economize on the cost of a traditional and expensive wedding, and give the money to the young couple.

Orlandi's favourite daughter, Emanuela, is against the idea. She wants her sister to have a splashy wedding: it will be a chance, she thinks, to display her natural good looks before the photographers who are bound to cover the marriage of a member of a family with such close ties to the pope. Her father had gently reminded Emanuela that he's just a messenger, and that the press is not likely to turn up for the wedding. He did not pursue the real reason Emanuela hopes the photographers will be there – that their pictures could help launch her on a career as a model. Orlandi is specially careful nowadays to make sure Emanuela has no idea how troubled he is over her wish to pursue such a career.

It is Kabongo who suggested such a tactic.[15] The astute secretary told Orlandi the worst thing he can do is to engage in confrontation with his vivacious young daughter: that will only make her more determined to go her own way.

This morning Orlandi hopes to discuss the matter further with Kabongo. Yet the moment the messenger enters the papal secretariat he knows this will be impossible.

The entire staff is totally engaged with events in Poland. They are making and receiving calls to and from Warsaw and other Polish cities. The news is sombre. Hundreds of thousands of demonstrators have defied the authorities and are now out on the streets. There have been clashes with riot police. Priests continue to make appeals for calm, but nobody is listening.

Orlandi watches as a grim-faced Kabongo continues to cradle the telephone to his ear while with the other hand he steadily writes down the latest description from Warsaw from a tired-voiced Cardinal Glemp: 'The situation is growing worse all the time.'[16]

The secretary tells Orlandi to place the report in the special tray reserved for communications which are most urgent for the pope to see.

For the messenger this is going to be one of the busiest days of the year. He will lose count of how many times he hurries from the papal secretariat to the Secretariat of State and back again.

Since breakfast John Paul has been alone in his office, working on the final draft of his Angelus address. He writes slowly, frequently pausing to reflect in mid-sentence before continuing. It is part of his intellectual make-up, part of his scholastic discipline. He works on a large lined pad. His penmanship is bold and distinctive; there are no flourishes, no wasted whirls.

The theme of his address is a commemoration of St Joseph the Worker. He will deliver it at noon to a crowd of some hundred thousand in St Peter's Square, and a radio and television audience of millions around the world. Primarily, though, his phrases are directed at his fellow countrymen. The pope's writing pad is punctuated with such emotive words as 'solidarity', 'fraternity' and 'freedom'.[17]

John Paul intends to leave no Pole in any doubt as to where his pontificate stands – firmly behind the workers in his homeland.

He writes on, amending a phrase, sharpening a sentence; adding a word here, deleting one there, reading it back.

Late morning Dziwisz arrives in the office with Magee. The Master of Ceremonies carries a red velvet cloth edged in gold.

The pope ignores the pair as they move quietly to the middle of the office's three windows.

The secretary opens the window. From the square below come cheers and applause. Dziwisz helps Magee drape the velvet cloth over the window ledge. Then they position and secure to the ledge a heavy glass lectern. Finally Magee fixes a microphone to the lectern.

The two priests stare down for a moment longer at the piazza, providing the rows of television cameramen and still photographers with a chance to check focus and the exposure of their lenses. Behind, Magee and Dziwisz can hear the pope rehearsing his address.[18]

Shortly before noon they turn back into the room. John Paul continues reading aloud. He has underlined key words which he wishes to emphasize, indicated places where he will pause. It is the scoring of a natural actor determined to give of his best.

Sixty seconds before noon the pontiff walks purposefully to the open window. Even before he reaches it there is an anticipatory swell of sound from the square.

CLARISSA McNAIR'S APARTMENT
Same Day: Noon Onwards

Less than half a mile from St Peter's Square, the amplified voice of the pope booming out over the piazza's loudspeaker system goes unnoticed by the broadcaster. She is totally immersed preparing her script on the Holy See's developing relationship with the People's Republic of China.[19]

Her worktable is covered with documents about China's

own view of its relations with the superpowers. There are also articles from the Peking *People's Daily* and *Pravda*. Spread before her, too, are the recent utterances of the American and Russian leaders relating to the People's Republic. There are also McNair's own notes on a highly confidential briefing she has received from the pope's chief adviser on China. Her superior, Fr Quercetti, was surprised the priest-mandarin agreed to meet her; even those bishops with an interest in Chinese affairs do not always find it easy to see the prelate.

Because of the sensitive nature of the material, McNair has decided to prepare her broadcast in the solitude of her fifth-floor apartment in one of Rome's more exclusive residential streets. Via San Telesforo stands close to the Leonine Walls. From her balcony McNair can see into the Vatican gardens where John Paul used to walk at dusk before he was persuaded by the CIA that there he provided an easy target for a sniper.

The apartment reflects McNair's restless lifestyle. Its walls are covered with Haitian paintings, prints from Afghanistan, African ju-ju beads and safari hats she has worn on her travels around the world. Pride of place is given to the rows of tape recorded broadcasts McNair has made for Vatican Radio.

Over the past months she has turned the apartment's balcony into her own, very private, cemetery. Here she has buried Nero, Julius Caesar, Hadrian, Barberini, Claudio and Constantine in geranium pots. McNair does not expect others to understand how affected she was by the death of her miniature turtles.

Nor, she suspects, would colleagues understand why she has chosen to give up her free day to continue preparing her documentary on China. The broadcaster was so impressed by what the pope's adviser told her about the way Chinese Catholic priests cling to their faith that she is devoting every spare moment she has to preparing the documentary.

228

She has pored over the joint communiqué establishing full diplomatic relations between the United States and the People's Republic, noting that Washington acknowledged 'the Chinese position that there is but one China and Taiwan is a part of China', but that equally the US would continue to maintain cultural, commercial and other 'unofficial relations' with Taiwan.

Both sides she discovered had expressed themselves satisfied with these diplomatic niceties. Beside the communiqué McNair has pencilled a note to herself: 'Can I suggest perhaps Holy See may find similar expression?'

In August 1982 President Reagan felt it necessary to issue a further statement 'on the historical question of US arms sales to Taiwan'. He went on to remind Peking that 'the Taiwan question is a matter for the Chinese people, on both sides of the Taiwan Strait, to resolve. We will not interfere, or prejudice the free decision of, or put pressure on, the people of Taiwan in this regard.'

McNair sees this as the president wanting to show the American electorate he is still a politician who supports small but loyal friends. She wonders whether Reagan might yet decide the geostrategic benefits from China's support against the Soviet Union are hardly worth all the US diplomatic and domestic posturing.

Clearly, China is concerned to avoid establishing a 'special relationship' with the United States; to do so would run counter to the Republic's plan to become leader of the Third World – an arena where it is directing the major thrust of its foreign policy.

The Third World is also where the Holy See is increasingly focusing its attention.

Could this lead to confrontation there as both the Church and China vie to assume the role of spiritual guide? McNair does not know, but instinctively she realizes that her documentary, intended to be placatory to Peking, should eschew such areas. Equally, difficult decisions remain for the broadcaster, providing a constant worry about balancing them within the Holy See policy of seeking a genuine rapprochement.

Should she even hint that the Vatican might be prepared to give up its long-held hope of starting a new missionary period in China, and of seeing surviving displaced missionaries return to the missions from which they had been expelled? Ought she to raise the question of Chinese Christians living abroad; would they ever be allowed to return home and freely practise their faith? Might she mention the fact that today in China, religion faces a society which has known secularization for centuries? How far dare she reflect the view of those priests in China who think Rome should abandon its insistence on a close union with the local Chinese Catholic Church? Many outside China, she knows, would see this proposal as a betrayal of all the foreign missionaries who were deported following the cultural revolution, and a reneging on support for the Chinese priests who stayed at home, remaining faithful to Rome at such great cost to themselves. Perhaps she could allude to their position as being similar to that of the elder son who was scandalized by the feast given to the prodigal?

McNair is certain of one thing. There is a growing awareness in the Secretariat of State that the present Chinese government appears far more committed to a foreign policy similar to the Holy See's in one essential area: each outspokenly argues a peaceful solution must be sought for all international disputes. China has taken a neutral stand in the war between Iran and Iraq, urging both sides to stop fighting and negotiate. It adopted the same attitude over the Falklands War. Possibly most dramatically of all, the People's Republic has said it would even recognize the existence of Israel, if this will help bring peace to the Middle East. And recently, China's premier, Zhao Ziyang, during a tour of ten African states, said the People's Republic was probably the only major power equally acceptable in countries with such diverse political and economic systems.

230

The pope himself could hardly have defined more accurately his hopes for his own mission.

Perhaps, after all, concludes Clarissa McNair, she too can hope: that her documentary will be a positive influence in the grand design of Holy See politics.

The thought is heady enough to drive her on – searching for a balanced way of describing for a worldwide radio audience the very complex issues behind the Holy See's desire to exchange ambassadors with Peking.

THE PAPAL APARTMENT
Same Day: Early Evening

Polish riot police charge, wielding their batons and firing tear-gas guns. Troops direct water cannon. Solidarity workers turn and hurl a fusillade of rocks at police vehicles. Suddenly, there is Lech Walesa.

John Paul reaches forward and raises the sound on the television set in his study.

Dziwisz presses the recording button on the video system.

The camera team outside the Lenin Shipyard in Gdansk are jostled by militiamen as they try to film Walesa. A second crew is filming the incident.

The group in the pope's study are transfixed by the unfolding drama on the screen. The militiamen harassing the first film crew are roughly elbowed aside by burly shipyard workers who form a protective cordon around Walesa. He stares defiantly into the camera and delivers a challenge to the Jaruzelski regime.

'Negotiate with us. You have already seen our power.'

The clip of film is replaced by more footage showing how widespread the demonstrations have been. In all an estimated seven million members of Solidarity, their families and sympathizers have taken to the streets of every large

Polish city and town. The government's official May Day parades have attracted fewer than 200,000 marchers.

John Paul does not bother to hide his satisfaction. He rises to his feet and briefly addresses his personal staff. 'It will be hard for the authorities to cancel our trip after this.'[20]

THE SECRETARIAT OF STATE
Friday
Early Evening

Emery Kabongo cannot quite believe it – but things are 'back to normal'.[21] There are accounts of a dozen separate international issues moving through the Secretariat of State. Many are existing, or potential, world flashpoints. Each requires fine judgement by the Secretariat's diplomats.

But for the first time this week Poland and Lech Walesa no longer overshadow everything else. This evening the Polish Desk has not circulated its daily assessment to colleagues in other departments; nor do those reports automatically precede all others Casaroli must read before the end of the day. Busy though it still is, the Polish Desk, at least for the moment, is just another department going about its specialized business. Everybody in the Secretariat is pleased this is so.

They are equally relieved that neither the Polish regime nor Solidarity have wished to provoke a full-scale showdown, with its potentially calamitous consequences – one of which would almost certainly have been the cancellation of the papal trip. The clashes of last Sunday, which augured the worst, petered out during the week into a series of skirmishes.

Predictably, Walesa had been detained following his statement on television. But he was soon released and in a well-publicized move went off on a fishing trip.

Poggi received a late-night telephone call from a senior member of the Polish Communist Politburo insisting the authorities wanted the pope's visit to go ahead. In minuting the call, the nuncio added his opinion that Jaruzelski hopes to use the visit to show that 'normalization' has returned to Poland.

In the light of Poggi's assessment, John Paul authorized Glemp to reinforce in Warsaw the pope's own appeal for an amnesty for all political prisoners, the lifting of martial law, the restoration of full civil rights, 'and the re-employment of people dismissed because of their views'.[22]

The regime's religious-affairs minister has promised his government will do everything possible to 'further improve relations between the Church and State'.[23] Yet at the same time, the government's official spokesman, Jerzy Urban, is saying 'it's out of the question' for John Paul to meet Walesa during the visit; further, the pope will not be allowed to move freely through 'dissident strongholds' like those in Gdansk.[24]

To the experienced Kabongo the regime's responses are 'just more posturing'.[25] The secretary is certain Poggi is right: Jaruzelski thinks the pope's presence will give the regime badly needed respectability in the eyes of the world.

Making his nightly visit to the Secretariat of State, Kabongo can also reflect how little the Polish leader seemingly understands about the mentality of a very Polish pope. The secretary knows John Paul is giving careful consideration to how best he can avoid giving the slightest comfort to General Jaruzelski. Just how he will do this will remain a closely guarded secret until the pope actually bends down and kisses his native soil – when it will be too late for the regime to cancel the visit or make any meaningful move to forestall what John Paul has in mind.

To maximize the eventual effect of those plans, the pope has ordered everyone involved in preparing for the trip to let it be known, in any communication with members of Solidarity, that they should do nothing to upset the regime – no matter what the provocation.

As he moves from one Desk to another, Kabongo is reminded again how disparate are the secular issues Secretariat staff deal with as a matter of regular course, constantly evaluating them in the context of the Holy See's policies.

For the past month Casaroli has been closely involved in an initiative over El Salvador. He has had almost daily contact with Nuncio Lajos Kada. Even at the height of the latest Polish crisis, the Secretary of State has found time to speak to Kada and the other papal representative most directly involved in the initiative, Pio Laghi in Washington. He has counselled them both on how to respond to the view that the Reagan administration now holds on what is undoubtedly an increasingly dirty and complicated guerrilla war, whose outcome the president has once more made clear is vital to the long-range security interests of the United States.

Reagan has just told Congress that his strategy in Central America is identical to the one adopted by President Truman to keep post-war Western Europe from turning Communist. El Salvador, Reagan claims, is a proving ground for Soviet and Cuban supported subversion; another he has identified as Nicaragua. Unless checked, this subversion will infect the rest of Central America, spread to Mexico, and swiftly end up on the very doorstep of the United States.

The Holy See does not dispute that if this did happen it would indeed be a serious situation. But the policy view, formulated by Casaroli and quietly expressed through Kada and Laghi to their respective host governments, is that, on the present evidence available to the Holy See, the Reagan administration is over-reacting to the situation.

Casaroli's assessment has now gained credence in Congress. There, the momentum against the administration's policy is steadily mounting. Reagan recently called for a further $100 million in military aid for El Salvador; the request was rejected by the House Foreign Affairs Committee. The Intelligence committees of both houses of Congress are poised to stop funding the secret war against Nicaragua. Further military aid to Guatemala has been vetoed.

The president is fighting back, and has taken his case before a joint session of Congress; it is the first time a president has made such an appeal on a major foreign policy issue since Jimmy Carter went to Capitol Hill to talk about nuclear arms in 1979. Reagan has not only asked again for his $100 million to be approved for El Salvador, but also that an additional $250 million be earmarked for military and econimic aid in 1984 for this smallest nation on the Latin American mainland which, until the United States showed an interest, was considered a strategically unimportant country.

While the president has repeatedly insisted in public that he will never commit US forces in Central America, Laghi, in some very confidential talks with administration officials – so secret he reputedly encoded his reports in Latin – has learned that the president is exploring with his Joint Chiefs of Staff the viability of American military intervention in the area.

It is this possibility which has caught the attention of Casaroli. He is appalled by the prospect of another Vietnam, and particularly by what an offensive would do to an already divided church in El Salvador.

Further, Kada has reported the CIA presence in both El Salvador and Nicaragua is being stepped up. American diplomats have told the sceptical nuncio that, in the case of El Salvador, the CIA presence is part of a 'shield' behind which the country's shaky democracy can be given time to establish itself.

The careful thrust of Casaroli's response is to try and convince the Reagan administration that, well motivated though it undoubtedly is – the Holy See's view is that a violent Communist take-over in El Salvador would be an unmitigated disaster – the US government is in essence supporting what Kada has called a 'strongly established and corrupt social order'.[26]

His judgement is that while many of the rebels fighting to overthrow the Salvadoran government are certainly ha.d-line Marxists, there are also a growing number of political moderates taking up arms. In Kada's opinion they have been forced to do so because they have given up all hope for peaceful change through the ballot box in the face of the repressive measures of the government.

Casaroli has entrusted Kada with the difficult task of persuading these moderates to lay down their weapons and resume their opposition within the framework of what is possible during the admittedly difficult conditions prevailing.[27]

In Washington Laghi is involved in an equally delicate mission the Secretary has authorized. The apostolic delegate is hoping to convince the administration to support negotiations between the Salvadoran government and the rebels as the only humane way to end the bloodshed. Laghi continues to find that the consensus in Washington is that such talks would give the guerrillas power they do not deserve.[28]

Yet, in the wake of Reagan's bellicose rhetoric before Congress – the president resurrected memories of the Nazi threat to Caribbean shipping during World War II when speaking of what could happen if Central America now 'fell' – Laghi has detected a glimmer of hope.

He transmitted it to the Secretariat's Latin America Desk late this afternoon. A monsignor is now assessing the news. Laghi has spoken to senior officials in both the State Department and the White House. They confirmed the American administration 'would be willing' to discuss the idea of guerrilla candidates taking part in Salvadoran elections.

The monsignor knows there is still a long way to go before, in this instance, Holy See views coincide with presidential policy.

But the information is promising – sufficiently so for the secretariat priest-diplomat to prepare a telegram for Laghi. He is asked to explore with his Washington contacts the question of whether, if all sides freely agree to stop fighting and participate in properly held elections, the United States would use its influence to organize a neutral peacekeeping force, drawn from other Latin American nations, to protect candidates.[29]

A second telegram is drafted to Kada. This summarizes what Laghi has reported and the instructions he has been sent. In addition Kada is asked to remind the Salvadoran government that if it supports such an initiative, the onus for continuing the fighting will be placed on its opponents. The Holy See's view is, given proper protection, rebel candidates will find it difficult not to participate in the elections without losing the considerable backing they now have in Latin America, Asia, Western Europe and also among a growing body of Americans.

Another monsignor on the Latin America Desk is dealing with a report from Nicaragua which describes how the Marxist regime is maintaining pressure on the local hierarchy to confer moral legitimacy on its politics. The nuncio in Managua writes with undisguised bitterness that the government 'is insisting the Church links the New Testament with Marxist ideology, the Messiah with the vanguardia, and the Kingdom of God with the country's "socialist paradise"'.[30]

A separate communication from Managua's new archbishop, Obando Bravo, is equally disturbing. There are still five Catholic priests in government posts – in direct defiance of John Paul's request that they resign.

Bravo wants to know whether their behaviour should be referred to the Holy Office.

The nuncio and archbishop receive similar responses: every effort must be made to resist government pressures on the local hierarchy; the question of the future of the five priests will be referred to Cardinal Ratzinger.[31]

A third priest on the desk is absorbed with a report from Archbishop Ubaldo Calabresi, the nuncio in Buenos Aires.

For months Calabresi has been the very low-key spearhead of yet another Holy See endeavour which is committed to trying to solve an Argentine dilemma that has no easy answer.

It is the passionate question of how to return the country to democracy after seven years of harsh military rule – the elections are due in five months – while still producing a proper accounting for the fate of at least six thousand Argentinians, known as The Disappeared, who vanished at the height of the military's anti-terrorist campaign.

Calabresi, supported by the country's cardinals and bishops, has been advocating a policy he calls 'truth and forgiveness'; the slogan has formed the theme of countless sermons for the nation's priests.

The campaign appeared to be enjoying a marked success. But suddenly, in the past few days, the military rulers have demanded guarantees that neither they nor their predecessors will face investigation over The Disappeared once democracy is established.

Some opposition parties – for so long suppressed, now sensing their time is coming – refuse to give such pledges.

Both sides are trying to gain the approbation of the Argentine hierarchy.

Calabresi has so far managed successfully to avoid accepting the junta's claim that The Disappeared were regrettable casualties 'in a war to save the nation'.

Now, reports the nuncio, the regime has asked him to support yet another attempt to exonerate them from any future investigation into their culpability.

The latest plan is what Calabresi witheringly calls 'a self-amnesty law', a stroke of doubtful legislation which will make it almost impossible to bring to trial any soldier or policeman for the disappearance, torture or any other 'actions aimed at preventing terrorist activity or plotting, regardless of the judicial dispositions infringed'.[32]

Despite his own dislike of the proposal, the nuncio has learned it has found favour among some of the country's leading civilian politicians. They are concerned that any incoming democratic government will face enough problems without creating a crisis with the military – who, if driven far enough, could ultimately stage another coup and return themselves to power. Several opposition leaders have indicated that once they are in office they would quietly forget the question of The Disappeared.

The nuncio considers this wishful thinking. Separate human rights groups, often led by committed priests, are uniting as a powerful lobby specifically to urge prosecution of those they think responsible for the fate of the missing.

The Radical Party – whom Calabresi believes could surprise everybody by winning the forthcoming election – is also trying to get the Argentine hierarchy to approve the idea of bringing the matter to the courts. The nuncio's concern is that, given the inefficiency of the country's legal system and the undoubted problem of providing hard evidence in most cases, few of those suspected of being responsible for The Disappeared will ever be convicted.

Archbishop Calabresi has come to the conclusion that perhaps the best solution is for the Argentine hierarchy to support a national plebiscite on whether to pardon the military – after a civilian government has been elected. He thinks with the arrival of democracy, the population would very likely vote for a pardon, if only to stabilize the new government. It could be an acceptable answer to a very real dilemma.

The monsignor on the Latin America Desk, having made his assessment of the nuncio's report, refers it to his section head. By nightfall Calabresi's proposal will be one more question for Agostino Casaroli to ponder. And in this case, having made his own recommendation, he will almost certainly refer the matter to the pope.[33]

The pope will assuredly see a briefing paper being prepared by staff in the office of Eduardo Martinez Somalo, Casaroli's brilliant Spanish-born deputy. The paper is a detailed review of the first six months of Socialism in Spain under the leadership of Felipe Gonzalez Marquez, a forty-year-old lawyer from Seville – the first Socialist Prime Minister since the Civil War, the first leader of a democratic party to have achieved an absolute majority in the Cortes, the first Spanish left-winger to be sworn-in by a Spanish king. Gonzalez is also the first Spanish political figure since the death of Franco to have encountered implacable opposition from the country's hierarchy. Spanish bishops had even tendered 'advice' during the November 1982 election suggesting that voters who wished to remain 'good Catholics' should not cast their ballots for Gonzalez's Social Democrats because the party supported legalizing abortion.

The 'advice' was given with the 'full approval of the pope'.[34] But by a massive majority the Spanish electorate judged it was time *Por el Cambio,* for change, which had been the Socialist election slogan. Ten million Spaniards, out of a 26.5 million electorate, supported Gonzalez. More significantly, eighty per cent of them were baptized Catholics.

The Spanish bishops were at first collectively stunned into silence, then they had taken a second look at what was happening.

Gonzalez has not flinched from taking tough measures. He devalued the peseta, increased the price of such essentials as petrol and on non-essentials like cigarettes. He also continued to confront the Church: his attitude is velvet-gloved and polite, but nevertheless a direct challenge in those areas where the Spanish Church has always maintained control.

Opus Dei, with 22,000 members in Spain, expressed a fear that the new emphasis on secular State education will seriously diminish the Church's traditional hold over the schooling system.

Several right-wing Catholic lay pressure groups have suggested to the hierarchy it might be sensible to have Gonzalez invited to Rome for a private audience with the

Holy Father. The proposal was forwarded to the Secretariat of State and has now reached Somalo's office.

He has asked his staff to prepare a briefing paper which could persuade John Paul that he should indeed receive Gonzalez and explain that while the pope fully endorsed King Juan Carlos's view that the arrival of Socialism in Spain was the essence of democracy, it must not be forgotten there are millions of Spanish Catholics who might feel threatened by new and permissive policies.

Somalo hopes there will be no need for the pope to say more. Gonzalez would certainly, after his hard-fought campaign, be only too aware of how dangerous, when aroused, Spanish Catholic pressure groups can become.

The papal pro-nuncio in Havana, Giulio Einaudi, who for months has been patiently collecting articles from Cuban newspapers claiming that the CIA trained Agca – cuttings which eventually are translated and shown to John Paul – has now found a more worthwhile outlet for his diplomatic skills.

President Reagan has said that the tiny Caribbean island of Grenada posed a potential threat to the security of the United States. He personally authorized the Pentagon to declassify satellite photographs of a new international airport being constructed on the island. The president insisted the airport could be capable of handling Soviet bombers equipped with nuclear warheads to attack the United States.

As a matter of routine Einaudi has submitted to the Secretariat of State his own appraisal of why the airport is being built.

The report bears all the hallmarks of a professional diplomat going about his business. Einaudi has spoken to the Cuban authorities, his fellow ambassadors in Havana, newspapermen and other sources. It is a thorough trawl, one very much in keeping with Einaudi's years of training at the pontifical academy for diplomats in Rome.

The nuncio's report is reassuring. The airport might

indeed cost more than the estimated $70 million before its two-mile-long runway is completed. But everything he has heard suggests the enterprise is little more than Grenada's People's Revolutionary Government trying to improve its image and prestige. Having seized power in 1979, the Marxist regime is determined to live up to its promise to better the lot of the island's workers. Many of them are migrants, employed in other parts of the Caribbean. For them to travel beyond Grenada means making lengthy stopovers in Trinidad or Barbados. The new airport will make it easier for them to earn a living. Further, the island's exports – and economy – would be vastly improved if larger planes could land on the island.

Grenadians have been asking for over twenty-five years for just such an airport. In spite of the fact it is financed by Cuba and the Soviet Union, and being built largely by Cuban workers, to suggest the airport could be a military threat to the United States is perhaps an overstatement, concludes Einaudi.

His report is filed in the Secretariat. The priest who does so doubts it will ever need to be referred to again.[35]

The North America Desk is busy assessing the continuing reaction to the US bishops' pastoral letter. At their meeting in Chicago to ratify the document, the American bishops, predictably, reinstated the verb 'halt' for 'curb' when used as a declaration against the testing, production and deployment of nuclear weapons.

The final version of the letter now not only opposes the controversial concept of 'first use' of nuclear weapons, but also condemns retaliatory nuclear attacks on an enemy's cities after US population centres have been struck by nuclear arms.

All in all, the letter flies in the face of much current administration policy.

To encourage 'awareness' of their position, the bishops have agreed to once more go without meat on Fridays as 'a peace penance'. They hope all good American Catholics will follow their example.

Staff on the European Desk are evaluating the effect the US pastoral letter may have on the latest round of arms talks due to resume shortly in Geneva. The priests on this desk are tiredly familiar with the alphanumeric codes and geopolitical euphemisms which continue to hedge in the talks. They believe the next session will continue to be dominated by discussions on how to limit INF, the acronym for intermediate-range nuclear forces in Europe. The European Desk estimates that amidst the endless shuttle of proposals and counterproposals between the United States and Soviet delegations, it could yet be possible for a deal to emerge.

The desk's judgement is based on a number of factors.

Having initially resisted the idea, Russia has now indicated it is willing to include in the calculations the actual number of nuclear warheads mounted on missiles which the Warsaw Pact has targeted on Europe – as opposed to counting only the individual launchers. Since it is believed the Soviet Union has many more warheads than NATO, this may be a significant step forward.[36]

The proposal for a renewed American nuclear freeze has finally won approval in the US House of Representatives. The European Desk sees the vote as an important gesture, part of a groundswell of concern on Capitol Hill over the need to settle the arms reduction issue.

The desk thinks the US pastoral letter will lend considerable weight to those voices which are critical of the Reagan administration's present nuclear policies. This judgement goes somewhat further than the one prevailing on the North America Desk.

Both views will make their separate way to Casaroli's in-tray. The Secretary of State will consider them, then extract what he sees as the essentials needed for him to prepare his own briefing for the pope on the matter.

After Emery Kabongo completes his nightly visit to the Secretariat – leaving with, among other papers, the latest batch of papal plot clippings for the pope to peruse – its staff continue with their varied tasks: between them they analyse a copy of an agreement which will, it is hoped, see Israel withdraw from the Lebanon; assess the likely impact on the Italian Church of the national elections to be held a full year earlier than expected; consider the implications of a protest from the Irish government that Britain is trying to subvert its neutrality; evaluate the depressed state of the French economy. In all there are a score of such matters being worked over. Much of this labour will never go beyond those who man the various desks. It does not appear to bother them.[37]

13

THE BULGARIAN EMBASSY, ROME
Friday
Morning

A month ago, Vassil Dimitrov had dreaded this day, marking another anniversary of the papal assassination attempt.[1] Then he had every reason to fear the media would 'whip up an orgy of hate against Bulgaria. Life would not be worth living.'[2]

Nowadays, this dedicated Communist likes to tell colleagues that, thanks to the CIA, he feels as if he has been born again. He has even joked he is thinking of sending the agency's Rome Station a bouquet of flowers – 'red, naturally' – with a suitable note of gratitude from a fellow traveller on the *Pista Bulgara*. Jesting aside, Dimitrov does find it incredible the way his fortunes have improved.[3]

Only three months ago the gangling First Secretary had been physically and mentally exhausted and cast into the diplomatic doldrums. Dimitrov's expectations were few – other than the anticipation of being recalled in disgrace to Sofia as a scapegoat over the way the Bulgarian Connection had seriously damaged his country's, and his own, reputation.

Though he had always believed himself blameless, Dimitrov was sufficiently realistic to recognize that in those dark winter days in Sofia his future was being weighed by some very senior Foreign Ministry officials. The Kremlin had forcibly expressed its own anger at the way *Pista Bulgara* was leading towards Moscow; there were demands from the Soviet Foreign Ministry that Bulgarian heads must roll.[4] Colleagues in Sofia suddenly found it prudent to distance themselves from Dimitrov; when they had to communicate with him, their telexes were coldly brief and their telephone calls even icier.

The hapless diplomat had spent the Roman winter and

245

spring slumped at his desk, endlessly compiling press clippings about the *Pista Bulgara*. He had read, perhaps, a million words: accusatory, angry, bitter and critical words which often made his watery brown eyes blink in disbelief. It had been the blackest period of his career. There seemed no end to it.[5]

Then everything changed – literally overnight.

In his desk diary Dimitrov has ringed the key dates, and scribbled his own account of what he calls 'the miracle'. Reinforcing his version is independent analysis promulgated by the western media he has so often deprecated. The diplomat's confidential account and the published material are almost identical – and do indeed provide grounds for Dimitrov's new-found exuberance. It is there in his eyes, sparklingly clear once more; in his posture, alert and aggressive; in his speech, confident and crisp. It is even evident in the bold flourish he used to make those diary entries.

They, and the newspaper commentaries, tell an intriguing story.

Less than a month ago, word reached Dimitrov – and the press – that Judge Martella was going to interrogate two key witnesses, Donka and Kosta Krustev.[6] They are a Bulgarian couple who reportedly drove Antonov's wife, Rossitsa, from Rome to Sofia on 8 May 1981. Agca has repeatedly insisted that on 10 May 1981 – two days later – Rossitsa was present in the Antonovs' Rome apartment when her husband, according to Agca, had briefed him on his mission to kill the pope.

The Krustevs were questioned for twelve hours by Martella and his assistants. The Bulgarians could not be shaken in their claim to have driven Rossitsa out of Rome a full forty-eight hours before Agca says he met her.

Martella made exhaustive checks to see whether it was possible for Rossitsa somehow to have returned to Rome during those crucial two days. There appeared no plausible way she could have been smuggled back into Italy.

The judge warned the Krustevs not to speak to the press. But details of their interrogation soon leaked on to the front page of reputable Italian newspapers. *La Repubblica, Il Tempo and Il Giornale* bluntly asserted that not only was Agca lying but *Pista Bulgara* had suffered a serious blow.

Further damage to its credibility soon emerged. Three Italian frontier policemen who were on duty at the Trieste border crossing on 8 May 1981 were brought to Rome to confront the Krustevs. One of them stated he recognized the couple and a photograph of Rossitsa as having been three persons who passed through the checkpoint during his shift.

More responsible Italian newspapers – *La Stampa, Il Messaggero* and *Il Corriere della Sera* – began to question the validity of the Bulgarian Connection, and Martella's dogged determination to pursue it. There was a spate of editorials suggesting *Pista Bulgara* was about to collapse, freeing Antonov.

The predictions and the sheer force of the attacks on Martella both cheered and intrigued Dimitrov. The media coverage has a familiar ring. Essentially it is no different from concerted attacks he has seen in the Soviet bloc press against a person or circumstance. The assaults on *Pista Bulgara* have the same clear hallmark: a similar central theme, even often identical phrases, obviously suggesting a common origin. Dimitrov absolutely knows for certain that there is no way Bulgaria, or even the Soviet Union, could be behind this particular campaign; he is pragmatic enough to accept the limitations of Communist propaganda.[7]

Using his contacts, ones he will not discuss (though almost inevitably they include sources in the Italian security services), Dimitrov has become convinced – as have Martella and Cibin – that the press onslaught displays every symptom of being the work of the CIA. In the diplomat's view no other western intelligence agency has the resources to have co-ordinated it so effectively.

Dimitrov has noted that the London *Guardian* reported that Agca had been promised 'lenient treatment' so long as he continued to shore up *Pista Bulgara*. The report was followed up by leading newspapers in Western Europe.

Ever since Antonov was arrested, Dimitrov has been trying to encourage newspapers to publish sympathetic commentaries about his rigorous prison conditions, his poor health, his anguished wife and family waiting at home; he has attempted, and failed, to have Antonov portrayed as the victim of cruel circumstances.

Suddenly, without making so much as a single telephone call to a journalistic contact, Vassil Dimitrov has been dumbfounded to see any number of articles appearing in newspapers normally hostile to Bulgaria – all making the very points he was previously unable to get into print.

The First Secretary is in no doubt at all now: this has to be the machinations of the CIA. He is equally sure he knows why the agency is doing this. 'The CIA is anxious to avoid any embarrassing revelations emerging about its own role in the papal plot. There is, for a start, the question of Frank Terpil.'[8]

Like many others, the Bulgarian diplomat remains unsure of Terpil's status at the time he trained Agca. But, eagerly accepting the CIA was behind the extraordinary media campaign, it is that much easier for Dimitrov to believe Terpil was still associated with the CIA when he helped to turn Agca into a sophisticated assassin.

The diplomat's first reaction – a natural and instinctive one for someone trained in such methods – was to try to turn the Bulgarian Connection into the CIA Connection. Dimitrov has enough press contacts in Rome to plant some very troublesome questions about the American agency's role. But before doing so, he prudently sought the approval of his superiors in Sofia.

He had been firmly told to do nothing: the only important objective was that *Pista Bulgara* should be destroyed by Sergei Antonov being released from Rebibbia prison. Whatever its motives, the CIA must be allowed to continue manoeuvring without hindrance.

Dimitrov thought this the most inexplicable instruction he has ever received from a superior.

This morning he can see its wisdom. On his desk is a heap of press clippings calling for Antonov's freedom. He has never known anything like it: newspapers he always considered 'lackeys of capitalism' are vociferous in their calls for the airline official to be released. In his diary entries, Dimitrov adds the phrase, 'it is quite bizarre what is happening'.

His sense of bafflement is further increased by what he learns has occurred across the Atlantic.

NBC Television – whose earlier documentaries on *Pista Bulgara* made Dimitrov 'shake with fury' – has reported that CIA Director William Casey is suggesting Martella may not yet have a shred of proof to substantiate Agca's allegations which implicate both the Bulgarian secret service and ultimately the KGB. NBC appears to accept this.[9]

Hard on the heels of this astounding switch of attitude, NBC's rival, ABC Television, has networked across the United States the results of its own investigation into the papal shooting.[10] For four months ABC reporters had scoured twelve countries for evidence.

Dimitrov now has a copy of the text of the broadcast. The programme had been recorded off-air in New York, transcribed and then telexed overnight to the Bulgarian Embassy in Rome. Similar telexes have been sent to other Bulgarian embassies in Europe.

The ABC telecast raises additional questions about the reality of the Bulgarian Connection.

One of the programme's researchers discovered that Agca's description of the Antonovs' Rome apartment – where he claims he was briefed about the papal plot – contains a serious mistake. Agca reportedly told Martella that the apartment's living-room had wooden sliding doors. There are similar doors in other apartments in the same building. But Sergei Antonov had removed his doors and replaced them with a cloth curtain – three months before the time Agca was claiming he had been in the apartment.

As well as insisting he met Antonov several times in the week preceding the assassination attempt, Agca vows he saw two Bulgarian Embassy officials on two key dates, 11 May and 12 May, 1981, the eve of the attempt on the pope's life.

ABC said it had established that on the evening of 11 May – when Agca claimed the two Bulgarians had taken him to St Peter's Square to reconnoitre the area – one of his accomplices was actually at Rome airport supervising the despatch of a cargo of bicycles to Sofia.

Three Rome policemen, on duty outside the Bulgarian Embassy, testified to ABC that on 12 May – when Agca said he had gone to Antonov's apartment for a noon meeting – they saw Antonov enter the embassy in the late morning and he had not left the building for several hours.

On the actual day of the assassination attempt – 13 May 1981 – Agca insisted he had been accompanied to St Peter's Square by three Bulgarians, one of whom was Antonov. Nine Bulgarians and an Italian have sworn to ABC that Antonov was in his office at Balkanair at the time.

ABC unearthed more damning evidence. Agca claims he spoke to Antonov and the other Bulgarians in English. The television team established that Antonov speaks no English, and that in May 1981 Agca only had a smattering.

Finally, like NBC, ABC concludes that the CIA totally discounts Antonov's alleged connection with the shooting.

Vassil Dimitrov, after 'so many months of darkness', still finds it hard to accept the idea of 'the CIA riding to our rescue on a white charger'.

Yet, he says, there seems no other explanation. Granted ABC's investigative expertise, the diplomat is cynical enough to believe some of the information must have come from inside Martella's own team; he further believes the only organization with the capability and the desire to plant a mole in the prosecutor's office is the CIA.

This morning the BBC and the principal radio stations of Western Europe have broadcast lengthy summaries of

ABC's findings. The CIA may not, concedes Dimitrov, have had a direct hand in this.

But he is not so certain about the Vatican. There have been leaks emanating from the Apostolic Palace that the CIA's latest guidance to the pope includes the suggestion he should distance himself from *Pista Bulgara* by receiving, with suitable publicity, a Bulgarian delegation at the end of May. Officially the occasion would be to commemorate both Bulgarian Culture Day and the Day of Saints Cyril and Methodius, creators of the Slav-Bulgarian script. This would also be an occasion for John Paul to reinforce by his own words and actions the stated Vatican position on the Martella investigation: that it is taking place in Italy, and is as a consequence an entirely Italian affair.

Dimitrov has not paid much attention to the leaks. He felt that the pope's 'obsession with *Pista Bulgara*' would over-rule all other considerations.[11] He has therefore been astonished, and delighted, to learn today that John Paul will receive the delegation.

Even more gratifying is the unusual step the Vatican Press Office has taken. It has just reissued its well-known statement denying John Paul ever wrote that fateful letter to Brezhnev in August 1981, in which the pope allegedly threatened to return to his homeland if the Russians intervened in Poland.[12]

All these moves, when taken together, can only reassure Dimitrov that the CIA is going to do what the combined resources of the Soviet bloc have spectacularly failed to achieve: wreck the Bulgarian Connection.

His only concern now is whether this will happen in time to save Antonov's sanity, and perhaps even his life.

Three Italian experts, each a physician and one a psychiatrist, have followed up an earlier examination of Antonov by Bulgarian Professor Ivan Temkov, a member of the secretariat of the World Organization of Psychiatrists. Temkov diagnosed that Antonov was suffering from 'a vegetative dystonia and nervous depression'.[13] He expressed the opinion that Antonov might have been given drugs which not only affected his mental stability but also made him more malleable for interrogation.

Temkov's Italian colleagues have concluded that Antonov's condition is steadily deteriorating. Physically he is in poor shape; mentally he is suffering, in their view, from 'maniacal phobia and depression caused by his solitary confinement'.[14] The inference is Antonov could be a potential suicide.

Dimitrov fears Antonov may try and kill himself soon unless he can be convinced he will be freed. Yet Dimitrov also believes the only hope of this happening is for a successful conclusion to the campaign he is persuaded is master-minded by the CIA.

This, thinks the First Secretary of the Bulgarian Embassy, must be the most ironic twist so far in the *Pista Bulgara*.

He will do everything within his power to ensure the CIA succeeds; there will not be the slightest accusation coming from him or any other Bulgarian Embassy employee about the American agency and the reasons it can have for wanting to see the Bulgarian Connection destroyed.

But after Sergei Antonov is released things will be different.

THE PAPAL SECRETARIAT
Same Day: Same Time

Kabongo watches Mgr Jacques Martin run a bony finger down the list of forthcoming papal audiences. The elderly, beak-nosed prefect of the pope's household, Casa Pontifica, gives another disapproving head-shake. There are, he repeats, too many people for the blocks of time available.

The secretary smiles. He cannot remember when Martin has not made such a protest. Friday mornings, when they review the audiences scheduled for the coming week, and often beyond, would not be the same without the prefect's acerbic comments.

Separated by some thirty years in age, and backgrounds which are totally dissimilar – most of Martin's life in the Church has been spent around the Apostolic Palace while Kabongo has seen service in far-flung outposts – they have a common self-effacing manner, a passion for detail and an astonishing capacity for hard, unremitting work.

Today, as usual, both have been up well before dawn; in between their devotions they briefed themselves on the news by listening to Clarissa McNair's breakfast summary of world events. Kabongo was relieved she did not mention this is the anniversary of the attempt on John Paul's life.[15] The secretary fears the continuous publicity in the secular press can only increase the possibility of some fanatic making a new attempt to kill the pope. It is a view Kabongo shares with Martin.

The audience roster is another matter; the list remains a subject of friendly disagreement between them. As one of the pope's secretaries, Kabongo helps to prepare it. But Martin can veto a name; it is one of the many privileges of his office. Nor, unless personally requested by the pope, does the prefect have to give a reason.

When Kabongo was appointed to his post, he had been warned Martin would frequently find some fault with the list. It is either too long, or too much time would have been allotted for somebody Martin does not think important; more often the prefect will complain there are insufficient gaps between audiences for what he obliquely refers to as 'secret visitors' – those able to insist at very short notice that they must see the pope. It can be a nuncio, a foreign ambassador, the CIA Rome Station Chief or even one of the Curial cardinals who wants to tell John Paul some piece of news which he feels cannot be conveyed via the Vatican's internal telephone system.

Unexpected though they are, these visitors normally

make their appointments to see the pontiff through Martin. Usually he does not question them about their reasons. It is sufficient for a caller judiciously to use the words *urgente* and *importante*. But if a prelate or secular diplomat turns out not to have had a genuinely urgent or important reason to see John Paul – afterwards the pope makes no bones about telling the prefect if this was the case – then that person will never again get past Martin so simply.

The audience list is prepared well in advance and is almost totally filled with the names of senior members of the Church, cardinals, bishops and nuncios. Some could have flown 12,000 miles, as an Australian bishop did before arriving this morning; he had spent ten minutes with the pope.

South Korea's Minister of Culture was allotted fifteen minutes. He used most of it to urge again that the pontiff should come to Seoul, a trip which is under active consideration. John Paul had been smilingly non-committal. Most of his visitors make similar pleas.

It is Martin's job to find suitable words to fob off a too-persistent request. Over the years he has developed an unerring instinct for spotting anyone likely to go beyond the strict rules of papal protocol and even pressure the pontiff to agree to a visit at once. On these occasions Martin is never far away, ready to step in and cut short an audience.

His finger continues to move down the list of forthcoming engagements. He repeats: there are just too many names.

Kabongo, well versed in what is expected of him, agrees, but says he cannot see where cuts can be made.

The prefect continues to study the list. For the second time in a matter of weeks His Eminence, Cardinal Pietro Palazzini, Prefect of the Sacred Congregation for the Causes of Saints, is tomorrow to see the Holy Father. Why?

Kabongo explains the pope is about to appoint a new Consultor to the Congregation and wants to discuss his nominee with Palazzini.

Martin does not pursue the matter. After over four years

serving John Paul, the feisty prefect knows better than to intervene in such areas. While he will fight fiercely to retain the privileges of his office – they include the ancient right to enter the papal presence without being summoned – he has learned to temper his autocratic ways. When in the service of Paul VI, the prefect would sometimes behave imperiously towards the frail old pope, brusquely ordering him to curtail a meeting or even cancel an audience previously approved.[16]

From the outset John Paul made clear he would not tolerate such behaviour. For the strong-willed Martin it has not been easy to change. This may be the reason he is so fussy over the audience list; perhaps he sees his behaviour as proof that he still has power.

He wants to know why the apostolic delegate in Angola, Fortunato Baldelli, has been given a full thirty minutes with John Paul.

Kabongo reminds Martin that Baldelli is new to his post, having recently moved from Strasbourg where he was Holy See Observer to the European Council, and the pope is particularly anxious to hear the delegate's views on the attitude of the Black African Church towards the possibility of a papal visit to South Africa. Kabongo knows John Paul remains keen to go there in an attempt to change what Kabongo calls 'mentalities from within'.[17] The pope hopes he can help remove the fears which underpin the country's ideology, buttressing an illusion of white supremacy and immunizing minds against objective argument.

John Paul also wants to hear from Baldelli his ideas on what more the African bishops can do to combat secularism, and what is the present grassroots relationship in the region between Christians and Muslims. Kabongo has just prepared a brief for the pope which confirms there is no real sign of an Islamic revival in southern Africa, and that the Moslem faith continues to face a crisis which started some thirty years ago. Then Islam, unlike Catholicism, had done little to promote schooling, and particularly neglected the education of girls at a time when Black Africa was entering the modern era.

Thirty minutes, says Kabongo very firmly, is the very least Baldelli needs to explain matters.

Nor, he continues, can he see how a minute can be cut from the allotted forty-five reserved immediately afterwards for Archbishop Obando Bravo of Managua and four of his senior priests. Between them they will no doubt brief the pope about the reality behind President Reagan's latest statement on the Nicaraguan regime: 'We do not seek its overthrow but we will not protect the Nicaraguan government from the anger of its own people.'

His friends on the Latin America Desk have given Kabongo a shrewd idea of what the Nicaraguan Church delegation is likely to say – that the Reagan administration *is* doing everything possible to remove the present regime; CIA-sponsored operations have increased dramatically in the wake of the pope's own visit when he attacked the 'people's Church' as 'absurd and dangerous', a condemnation with which the agency doubtless agreed.

If anything, sighs Kabongo, three-quarters of an hour might not be long enough for the delegation to explain the latest ramifications in Nicaragua.

Martin next turns to the crowded schedule for the coming Monday morning. The pope is to receive prelates from Ecuador, Ethiopia, Brazil, Lebanon and four more from Nicaragua on their *ad limina* visit. Between them they have ninety minutes of the Holy Father's time.

The prefect proposes this might be reduced to seventy.

Kabongo agrees – so long as no one is slighted.

They start to go through the names. The Ethiopian archbishop has five minutes cut from his audience. So does the bishop from Brazil. And, they agree, forty minutes is unnecessarily long for the Nicaraguans; thirty should be sufficient. The Lebanese slot remains unchanged. So is the time allocated for the Ecuadoran cardinal.

On the following day the entire morning has been given

over for the pope to confer with Cardinal Glemp and a large delegation of Polish bishops who will be travelling to Rome to discuss the forthcoming papal trip.

Martin swiftly agrees not a minute can be cut from the scheduled three hours reserved for this audience.

Nevertheless he continues to fret over the list. In part this is a manifestation of the prefect's genuine concern about the pope's welfare. Like many others close to the pontiff, Martin is troubled that John Paul is doing too much. The prefect knows his predecessors found audiences a definite strain. They do require considerable preparation and deft handling during the actual meetings: bishops are not above trying to get an unwary pope to commit himself to a particular cause they espouse. In the early days of this pontificate the prefect had tried to warn John Paul of the pitfalls. Martin had been firmly rebuked for his pains. John Paul made clear he does not want to be coddled.

Martin comes to Thursday. 'The Holy Father will receive in audience Their Excellencies: Most Rev. Pio Laghi, titular Archbishop of Mauriana, Apostolic Delegate in the United States of America; Most Rev. Luciano Angeloni, titular Archbishop of Vibo, Apostolic Nuncio in Lebanon; Most Rev. Vartan Tekeyan, Bishop of Ispahan of the Armenians (Iran); Most Rev. Jean Vilnet, Bishop of Saint-Dié, President of the French Episcopal Conference.'

Eighty minutes have been set aside for the two papal representatives and the bishops.

A long time, says Martin. Kabongo replies that he cannot see how it can be altered. He has reviewed the correspondence relating to the audiences.

Laghi wants to discuss among other things the implications of a matter which has even overshadowed in America the discussion about the pastoral letter on nuclear arms.

The case is that of a Detroit nun, Agnes Mary Mansour, a member of the Sisters of Mary and the Union, and a director of Michigan's social services – an agency which has been spending over $5 million a year providing abortion-on-demand. Detroit's archbishop, Edmund Szoka, asked Mansour to protest publicly against the agency providing the service. She refused. He reminded her that with her vows went the pledge to follow Church doctrine which regards abortion as an 'unspeakable crime'.

Although she personally opposes abortion, Sister Mansour declined to condemn the agency's willingness to offer it on the ground that abortion is legal in the United States and women who cannot afford to pay for termination should have the operation done at public expense.

Szoka advised Mansour either to resign her post or leave her religious order. She was unwilling to do either. The archbishop reported her to the Holy Office. Ratzinger recommended that the pope issue an order for a canon-law expert, a bishop, to call on the nun and inform her she should withdraw from the social services.

The bishop failed to persuade Sister Mansour. Instead she asked whether the Church would grant her leave of absence from her order so that she might continue to keep her state position. The request has been refused.

The case is now a fiercely debated issue among American Catholics. Laghi will tell John Paul how he thinks the controversy can be ended: as Sister Mansour feels so strongly, she must be persuaded to leave her order; no longer a nun, she will soon fade from public interest.[18]

The pope wishes to hear from Nuncio Angeloni the latest position in the Middle East. During the past few weeks, the Soviet Union has tightened its hold on Syria, adding a new dimension by insisting that its missiles now be completely manned by Soviet troops and technicians. Effectively, this gives the Russians autonomous bases in Syria, a factor guaranteed to alarm Israel as well as further increase the danger of the superpower confrontation which Angeloni predicted was not impossible in his earlier reports to Casaroli.

The Iranian bishop will bring the pope up to date on the situation of the country's 28,000 baptized Catholics under the increasingly unstable regime of Ayatollah Khomeini.

The Bishop of Saint-Dié plans to brief John Paul on a subject which is sending shudders through the French Church. It is the disturbing decline in the number of men and women entering diocesan seminaries and convents. If the present trend continues, by early next century there will be almost no newcomers taking up religious vocations in France; by the year 2050 this once-staunch bastion of the faith could be left with only a handful of priests and nuns.

Martin agrees with Kabongo it is going to require every one of the allotted eighty minutes for the pope to receive the reports of these four prelates.

Nor, he reluctantly concedes, is there any way to cut corners with another pair of audiences scheduled for the same day. The ambassadors to the Holy See of Honduras and Portugal will expect, and receive, full ceremonial treatment when they call on the pope. Each of these visits, from greeting to final farewell, will take twenty minutes. The protocol for such occasions has been reviewed and honed at John Paul's request. Martin now agrees it has been pared to the bone. There are some things the prefect prefers not to skimp – and ceremony is one.

So it goes on: Martin questioning and calling for cuts, Kabongo resisting and explaining why they are not possible.

Finally, they reach Thursday: 'The Holy Father will receive in audience a delegation of the People's Republic of Bulgaria.'

There are thirty minutes allotted. The prefect wonders whether this might be trimmed.

Kabongo is emphatic. John Paul himself indicated he would like a full half-hour with the Bulgarians. This time the secretary does not explain why.

SECRETARIAT OF STATE
Same Day: Early Afternoon

What is known around the Apostolic Palace as the *Affare Inglese* is once more on the desk of Mgr Audrys Backis. In the past month its ever widening ramifications have frequently been on his mind. During all his years of experience, Backis has told colleagues, he cannot easily recall a more deplorable diplomatic shambles. Certainly he has encountered nothing quite like it in his four years with the Council for the Public Affairs of the Church. *L'Affare Inglese* has grown to the point where many of the Council's senior diplomats, and several of their colleagues in the Secretariat of State, have been asked to suggest how best to end the embarrassment.

Their recommendations are now on Backis's desk: one favoured solution is to remove a central figure in the drama, Archbishop Bruno Heim, the pro-nuncio in Britain.

Backis accepts this could diffuse a situation which is damaging both to the Holy See and the English Church. He also realizes there are grounds to recommend that Heim should either be recalled to the Vatican or sent to some outpost where he could serve out his time. The archbishop is seventy-two and in three years will have reached the Holy See's mandatory retirement age for papal representatives.

Equally, Backis realizes recalling Heim would be a particularly cruel blow for a diplomat who has served the Holy See with distinction. Nor indeed, as Backis well knows, is there any guarantee that removing Heim from the scene will put an end to the matter; there would remain on stage the two other protagonists: Mgr Bruce Kent and Cardinal George Basil Hume, Archbishop of Westminster and Primate of All England and Wales.

Heim, Kent and Hume are at the very core of the *Affare Inglese*.[19]

The entire business has burgeoned around an astonishingly candid personal letter the pro-nuncio wrote and which was passed to the press. In it, Heim accuses Kent – the general secretary of Britain's Campaign for Nuclear Disarmament, CND, a powerful pressure group opposed, among other issues, to plans to install Cruise missiles on British soil – and his fellow unilateralists of being either Soviet sympathizers, 'useful idiots' or 'blinkered idealists'.

To compound matters, Heim had attached to the letter an excerpt from John Paul's address to the United Nations in June 1982: 'In current conditions "deterrence" based on balance, certainly not as an end in itself, but as a step on the way towards progressive disarmament, may still be judged morally acceptable.'

By juxtapositioning the pope's words and his own swingeing attack on Kent and CND, the pro-nuncio committed a major diplomatic gaffe.

Backis cannot imagine what made Heim behave with such uncharacteristic foolhardiness. But he has. And the fallout continues.

At the very minimum, by quoting John Paul, Heim implied that the pope supported his attack on Kent. Far graver, the pro-nuncio's intervention has raised the spectre of the Holy See blatantly dabbling in the internal affairs of another country – and on an issue which deeply divides the British public. Heim is being portrayed as acting for the pope in castigating Kent – and supporting Mrs Thatcher's policies.

Following the disclosure of Heim's letter, Cardinal Hume is being quickly sucked into the controversy. He had already warned Kent that 'recent developments' caused him 'serious misgivings' and the general secretary might have to give up his CND position if the movement's activities become predominantly political. It has also been reported that Hume himself supports the Thatcher view that Britain must retain its nuclear weapons unless the Russians scrap theirs.[20]

The cardinal has felt compelled to issue a statement. 'I have had no direct contact with Conservative politicians. I know what they think. One reads that in the press. But they have not been in contact with me. I react rather badly if I feel I'm being pressurized by any group.'[21]

Only Kent has chosen to remain silent.[22] But the furore surrounding him continues.

From his hospital bed in West Germany, where he is recovering from surgery, Heim stubbornly refuses to retract his attack on the CND leader.

The question Backis now faces is: what should be done with the pro-nuncio?

Clearly some form of punishment seems called for. To have dragged the pope into such a damaging controversy cannot be allowed to pass. One suggestion that Backis has been asked to consider is for the Vatican to take the unusual step of publicly stating that Heim's letter was a 'strictly personal' initiative which had no official authorization. Backis agrees this should be done and has already drafted a statement. But will this be sufficient? Should Heim be removed?

Both in London and in the Vatican there are influential Church voices saying Heim's intervention is too serious to be dealt with by anything other than the severest of measures. It is axiomatic that a papal representative should present the views of the pope; this Heim had done by attaching John Paul's words to his letter – yet by so doing he had also embroiled the pontiff in the political affairs of another nation, something the Holy See is committed not to do.

Hume, in what will be seen as something of a *volte-face* around the Secretariat, has decided after all to renew his permission for Kent to continue leading CND.[23] It also seems likely that, of the two, the cardinal finds Heim the more embarrassing.

And yet Backis still hesitates to recommend the nuncio be removed from Great Britain.

One possible reason is potentially far more controversial than anything Heim has written about Kent and CND.

For the past four years the papal envoy has played a crucially important role in a secret Holy See move to try and bring peace to Northern Ireland.[24]

Apart from Backis and Casaroli, few people in the Vatican know all the ramifications of this initiative. Because of his own specialist knowledge, John Magee is one. Born in Ulster, Magee, the secretary to three popes before he became Master of Ceremonies, spearheaded a previous, unsuccessful, attempt to save the lives of IRA hunger strikers in the province. Now, his experience of Irish attitudes has been called upon to help carefully push this new initiative along.

In Dublin, Nuncio Alibrandi is deeply involved in gauging responses.

But the linchpin is Heim.

Working independently of Hume, the pro-nuncio has been having informal meetings with senior members of the government and opposition. Some of them have been dinner-party guests at Heim's grand residence overlooking Wimbledon Common in south-west London. There, in the privacy of his dining room – Heim likes not only to arrange the flowers and mix the cocktails but even cook the food for these very special occasions – the pro-nuncio has listened a great deal and then carefully advanced the idea that the time may be coming for Britain to withdraw her forces from Ulster, and allow a United Nations peacekeeping army to take over.

At first his guests had been shocked at the very mention of foreign troops ever being based on what is after all British soil; such action could precipitate serious political repercussions. But would they be as grim as what the future for the stricken province appears to be – a land wasted by fear and bigotry? Surely, argues Heim, almost anything is worth considering which could end the killing. He has to concede the idea of a UN peacekeeping force is not new and, when mooted before, it was scathingly rejected.

But now, it may be different: the pope has given signs of support for the proposal as a possible step towards bringing peace to Northern Ireland.

Right up until he left England for that West German clinic, Bruno Heim continued discreetly to mention the notion. He has reportedly indicated to the Secretariat of State – shortly before he unleashed his attack on Kent – that he was getting a sympathetic response.

This may well be the main reason Audrys Backis has hesitated about urging Heim be removed. Highly embarrassing though the pro-nuncio's gaffe over Kent continues to be, his withdrawal from London could be even more damaging to one of John Paul's great hopes – to be the pope who helped stop the killing in Ulster.

Heim, decides Backis, should be allowed to stay on in London.

THE SECRETARIAT OF STATE
Friday
Morning

The day begins badly.

The Southern Africa Desk has two overnight telegrams conveying the same discouraging news. Both Cardinal McCann in Cape Town and Archbishop Cassidy in Pretoria report that the South African government is not prepared in the foreseeable future to welcome a papal visit.

The prelates offer an identical reason for the government's attitude. White South Africa has become suddenly, and bitterly, divided over a controversial proposal to modify the apartheid laws by giving voting rights to Asians and persons of 'mixed race' who are officially categorized as 'coloured'. The proposal has government approval, but white extremists are outraged: there have been ugly demonstrations and talk of *broerertwis*, Afrikaans for a fight to the end between brothers. The once closely knit tribe of mainly Dutch-descended whites who control the country's politics are locked in an increasingly nasty feud.

The mere possibility of the pope making even an oblique comment on the matter, let alone that he might go further and actually condemn apartheid, is now seen as too big a risk for the government in Pretoria to accept.

The Middle East Desk has independent confirmation of what the nuncio in Beirut, Luciano Angeloni, told the pope. Not only had he briefed John Paul on the continuing Soviet military build-up in the region, but Angeloni also revealed that his own attempts have so far failed to get Israel, Syria, Lebanon and Jordan to support a papal visit to the region.

This morning perhaps the most unusual priest in the Middle East telephoned the desk from his spartan hospice in Beirut to say all his sources are insisting it is Israel which most strongly opposes the idea of John Paul coming to Lebanon and the Holy Land.

The caller is Fr Ibrahim Ayad, for the past decade a familiar frail figure in Beirut as he hurries through the city's Muslim quarter, frayed cassock trailing in the dust, padre's hat planted squarely above his pinched face. But the wraithlike Ayad – he is barely five feet tall and weighs less than a hundred pounds – is no ordinary priest.[25] He serves with equal devotion both the pope and the Palestinian Liberation Organization. His bedroom walls in Beirut are decorated with a large photograph of John Paul and a slightly larger portrait of Yasser Arafat. The room contains a shortwave receiver which Ayad tunes regularly to Clarissa McNair on Vatican Radio; he believes the broadcaster's visits to the Middle East give her a sense of balance about conditions there which is frequently lacking in other western commentaries.[26]

With the PLO driven out of Lebanon, Ayad has continued his lonely and dangerous role, acting as an important link between the warring factions in the area and the Vatican.

Ayad's contacts have now told him that Israel remains opposed to John Paul visiting the region – because, behind all the reasons offered, Ayad detects Israeli suspicion that either the pope or, more likely, the PLO would exploit the situation and call again for the creation of a Palestinian state.

The Israeli fears are not new, nor, insist the five Jewish 'observers' attached to the Holy See, are they without foundation, largely due to the efforts of Fr Ayad.

It was Ayad who cemented the first ties, in 1979, between the PLO and the Holy See; who had helped Arafat draft a letter in 1980 to the pope which, in the PLO chairman's flowery, evocative language, conveyed imagery which John Paul could not but be moved by: 'Please permit me to dream that I am seeing you going to Palestine and Jerusalem, surrounded by returning Palestinian refugees, carrying olive branches and spreading them at your feet.' It was Ayad who suggested guerrilla leader and pontiff exchange courtesies on holy days: Arafat sends John Paul a Christmas card, the pope conveys his greetings on the Prophet Mohammed's birthday. It was Ayad who arranged for the PLO Foreign Minister to meet Casaroli, to the undisguised fury of Israel.

In a score of other ways since, Ibrahim Ayad has continued to anger the State of Israel.

The nation's officials have coldly told him Israel's refusal to support a papal visit is based on a familiar fear: that Israel will find it impossible to guarantee John Paul's safety in one of the most turbulent areas on earth; if the pope was harmed – let alone killed – in any of the holy places over which Israel has jurisdiction, then anti-Semitism throughout the world would reach unprecedented levels.

Ayad believes there is yet another reason behind Israel's refusal. Many of its leaders still harbour a deep-seated grudge against the papacy which is largely rooted in the belief that Pope Pius XII did little to stop Jews from going to the Nazi death camps of World War II.[27]

Fr Ayad is convinced, too, that until the Jews put such feelings behind them, Israel will never achieve the special status he has helped to gain for the PLO at the Vatican.

He ended his telephone call this morning to the Middle East Desk with a pious hope – that one day soon John Paul will kneel at Christ's tomb in Jerusalem's Church of the Holy Sepulchre.

The monsignor on the desk has a wider Holy See view of the current situation in the Middle East, one in which the PLO may no longer have such an important role to play. The feeling on the Middle East Desk is that while Ayad has a function as an important and unique 'listening post', the PLO is becoming so riven internally it is in danger of losing support from the Vatican for what both the Holy See and the Palestinian movement wants – a permanent homeland for the PLO.

The Latin America Desk also has disappointing news.

During his pastoral visit to Guatemala, John Paul had been promised by the country's born-again-Christian military president, Rios Montt, that there would soon be democratic elections.

Now the local nuncio has sent a report that Montt is reneging on this promise; it appears almost certain there will be no elections until the president has created a new electoral roll – which could take years.

The nuncio is concerned that the delay may lead to an increase in political restlessness throughout the country – a situation which may, in turn, exacerbate further the lot of the country's six million Catholics, some of whom Montt suspects of being behind at least four recent coup-plots against his regime.

The priest-diplomat who handles Guatemalan affairs realizes the news must be referred to Casaroli. The monsignor will spend the rest of the day preparing a briefing paper.

Another monsignor on this desk is preoccupied with a report from the nuncio in Chile. This deals with the country's Day of Protest. The monsignor has already received several accounts of the demonstrations which had swept Chile. One came from Chile's ambassador to the Holy See, Hector Riesle Contreras, who played down the entire matter; he had insisted that accounts of police brutality were part of 'a Communist plot against Chile'. The monsignor had listened to Contreras without comment. Later, he weighed the ambassador's views against other reports – newspaper accounts and eyewitness descriptions from some of the Chilean priests who were involved in the protests. These views do not tally with those of the ambassador.

The nuncio's report confirms the monsignor's worst suspicions. The demonstrations have been far more violent than Contreras indicated. It reveals that the Chilean Church failed to ensure that the demonstrations, called to protest the country's economic plight, would be peaceful. Pleas from the hierarchy to avoid violence had gone unheeded. Hundreds of thousands of Catholics – almost ninety per cent of the Chilean population are members of the Church – took to the streets. Waiting for them were the forces of the military regime of Augusto Pinochet, who seized power almost ten years ago, overthrowing the Allende government with the blessing of the CIA. The Day of Protest had produced the worst clashes since Pinochet took over. Thousands of demonstrators have either been injured or arrested.

The account ends with a question which will preoccupy the monsignor for much of this day: how far should the Chilean Church go in both protesting to Pinochet over what has happened, and admonishing the demonstrators who so openly disobeyed the orders of their priests to avoid confrontation?

The Polish Desk has also received a blow.

Shortly before leaving Rome the previous day, Cardinal Glemp felt optimistic enough to tell reporters he was going to try once more to arrange for Lech Walesa to meet the pope in Poland next month.[28]

Not everyone on the Polish Desk had felt it wise of Glemp to make such an announcement publicly. Some of the staff detected the hand of John Paul behind the statement: they saw it as the pope once more pushing too hard to get what he wants. These priest-diplomats feared there could be a backlash.

This morning it came. Glemp telephoned from Warsaw to say the regime remains firmly opposed to a meeting between Walesa and John Paul.

The cardinal also has more salutary news. Even during the few days he was away in Rome, the regime has become more flint-like in its attitude. Glemp warns that the Polish government is adopting a very tough line: this is simply not the time to seek concessions. Driven too far, Glemp believes General Jaruzelski might yet cancel the trip.

The mood of cautious optimism about the visit which had taken root in the Apostolic Palace earlier in the month begins to evaporate when the Polish Desk quickly circulates Cardinal Glemp's views.

The staff on the third floor cannot recall a morning of such unrelieved gloom. One of them, a monsignor with a decade of diplomacy behind him, says rather colourfully that this 'is a morning when the Holy See is running against the tide'.[29]

THE HALL OF THE THRONE, THE APOSTOLIC PALACE
Thursday
Mid-Morning

John Paul watches from his throne on a raised dais as the twelve members of the delegation from the People's Republic of Bulgaria file into the audience hall, one of four in the palace.

The pope looks tired. He has just returned from a three-day visit to Milan. There, in spite of all security precautions, a young man had hurled a petrol bomb at the altar where John Paul was due to say mass; the bomber escaped, and the pope had gone ahead with the celebration. But John Paul was shaken by the attack. He has told Kabongo that 'the forces of evil are as virulent as ever'.[30]

Prefect Martin motions the delegation to sit on gilt chairs set out in a single row before the throne. Some of the Bulgarians glance at the frescoed ceiling and religious paintings on the wall.

Ushers close the double doors of the audience chamber.

The delegation's leader rises to make the formal address of introduction.

A good deal of thought has been given both by the pope and the Bulgarians over what to say to each other at this first formal contact between them since Agca shot John Paul and the *Pista Bulgara* was born.

14

Roman Responses

The official line on what the Bulgarians said to the pope and what he told them is about as revealing as any other communiqué for such occasions: a 'helpful exchange' of views on matters of 'mutual interest', 'meaningful dialogue', a 'deeper understanding' being reached. The phrases are culled from the directory of clichés spokesmen the world over consult when composing their bland brush-offs.

The delegates sped from the Vatican in the black limousines the Bulgarian Embassy in Rome uses for its formal business – cars which somehow suggest a cortège travelling at high speed.

In their Bulgarian-cut suits and fedoras, at least from what we glimpsed as they came through the Arch of the Bells, they did not look exactly overjoyed at meeting the pope. They seemed more like undertakers who haven't been paid for a particularly difficult funeral.

So: what had happened?

Half a dozen calls to the Apostolic Palace have resulted in unusual disagreement. Sources who normally can be counted upon to support each other have this time been flatly contradictory. One monsignor, usually rock-solid in his recounting, said the delegation leader, Bulgaria's vice foreign minister, had warned the pope that *Pista Bulgara* was not exactly helping the religious life of the country's handful of Catholics – and that John Paul had roundly condemned any nation involved in trying to kill him. A second monsignor, equally sound in the past, insisted neither side even mentioned the Bulgarian Connection. A third priest, a man we have also always found truthful, is emphatic that the 'meat and bones' of the audience was devoted to another kind of Bulgarian Connection: the steady flow of heroin through this Balkan country into lucrative western markets.

This priest says that the pope wanted to know what Bulgaria is doing to close one of the great natural pathways in the world's drug trafficking. The country is the most direct overland route between Asian opium growers and West European markets; seventy-five per cent of all the illicit drug movement to these markets crosses Bulgaria's frontiers.

A fourth priest is equally adamant; there had been no discussion about drugs. He will not say what was discussed, but drugs were not on the agenda.

The Bulgarians are playing the subject the same way. Vassil Dimitrov, so forthcoming on other matters, is close-mouthed. He has positively nothing to say about the audience.

We have visited Vatican Radio. On this occasion there has not been a peep – at least as far as Henry McConnachie is concerned.[1] Neither of us have seen him for some weeks and we are quite surprised how keyed-up McConnachie is, chain-smoking and with a nervous habit of impulsively moving his head. The pressure, he says, is intense: the entire station is gearing up for the papal trip to Poland.

We trot along to see Fr Lambert Greenan. The editor also looks exhausted. He consistently produces with the help of a priest-assistant a twelve-page weekly of respectable standard. Greenan has the not always easy job of translating the pope's words into acceptable English. We hope Greenan has a clear idea of what happened between the pope and the Bulgarians.

He shakes his head. 'Lads, I don't. Anyway, what does it matter? It's just another audience.'[2]

We remind him of the implications of the Bulgarian Connection, with the KGB and Andropov in the background. Wars have started over less.

The editor remains resolute. So far as he is concerned, the audience is only going to get a couple of lines in his paper's

Vatican Bulletin column. He is not overly worried that he might be missing a good story in the pope's audience with the Bulgarians.

We still are. That's why we pay another call to some of the ambassadors accredited to the Holy See.

Sir Mark Heath, since April 1982 Britain's full ambassador, has his chancellery among the boutiques on Via Condotti, near the Spanish Steps. He is a strikingly towering diplomat – Heath must be close to eight feet tall when he's wearing his plumed ceremonial cocked hat – with that languidly incisive manner which only the Foreign Office seems to breed. He has served in Bulgaria. What he has to say about that, and most everything else, is strictly, he insists, off the record. It's what we call in our business 'background guidance'. It's highly useful.

Canada's ambassador, Yvon Beaulne, is a little plumper than when he served his country in Brazil, Venezuela and at the United Nations. He relishes his present posting. 'It's politics on the grand scale. What is at stake is the future of the world. The pope is literally the only world leader with moral authority.' A rewarding hour is spent with Beaulne.

Sweden's ambassador, Gunnar Ljungdahl, is balding and sixtyish, good with small talk and detail. He points out that the internal doors of Swedish embassies around the world are all protected by similar push-button systems. Only senior members of staff know the secret sixteen-number sequence to press which opens a door – a combination of digits that, for reasons of security, is frequently changed. Ljungdahl, who arrived in Rome a mere couple of months ago to initiate the first formal diplomatic ties the Swedes have had with the papacy for over 350 years, says his ambassadorial role at the Holy See is confined to 'only political work'. He, too has served in Bulgaria: another well-worthwhile hour.

Argentina's ambassador, José Maria Alvarez de Toledo, is almost as tall and aristocratically imposing as Sir Mark. He has been two years in Rome, during which he had put his country's position over the Falklands to the Holy See. He was not as successful as Heath in getting his government's point of view accepted, but de Toledo has done a creditable job in other areas. He tells us, again, that the post places him 'at the centre where the great issues of the world are discussed'.

Another ambassador, after insisting we must not name him, said he'd heard the pope was at his Polish toughest, 'preparing for his return match in Poland'.

John Paul, suggested another envoy, is far too 'shrewd and dignified' to become personally involved in the 'nitty gritty' of the plot to kill him.

We think of that monsignor on the third floor of the Apostolic Palace patiently collecting press clips from all over the world, and Kabongo explaining the pope understandably has an interest in why he became a target for assassination. We wonder where the 'nitty gritty' might stop.

Yet another ambassador offered the most intriguing possibility. He thought the pope would 'merely have made clear that he knows Bulgaria has been "read out" by Russia. That would be enough.'

This particular minister we know almost certainly has official access to CIA material; his nation is deemed as 'friendly and favoured' by the agency. The opinions he advances closely mirror what is currently happening: the CIA continues to promote the idea in Washington, Rome, London, Bonn – that there is no proof whatsoever to connect the Kremlin with the assassination attempt on the pope.

This campaign – which amounts to the CIA exculpating Yuri Andropov – is growing in intensity. We are now being told that Moscow 'has demonstrated unusually visible anger with Bulgaria' at being snared on the *Pista Bulgara*.[3] Andropov, says the CIA, 'read out' Bulgaria's leader, Todor Zhivkov, in the Kremlin, and that shortly afterwards the new head of the KGB, Viktor Chebrikov, travelled to Sofia to give the luckless Zhivkov a second drubbing.

How, we wonder, does the CIA know such details: such

minute, specific details as where in the Kremlin Zhivkov received his dressing down, how angry Andropov was, what happened in Sofia?

We put the question to Rudi, our BND source, over dinner at Rasella's.[4] He responds by choosing the finest chianti in the house and vintage *spumante* to follow. He is settling in for a long night.

The CIA *knows*, he says, returning to our question with a confidence which brooks no argument; we should take his word for it: the CIA really *does* know what happened. By way of explanation he adds that if the KGB can penetrate western intelligence services, so can 'our side' get into Dzerzhinsky Square in Moscow, where the KGB has its headquarters in the infamous Lubianka.

For appetizers Rudi has ordered thin slices of smoked ham roled into coronets and stuffed with alternate layers of melon slivers and caviare. We are consuming them with iced vodka.

The coronets gone, the vodka diminishing by the glass, Rudi says he has learned what actually happened at the audience.

'The Bulgarian leader got up and read a lot of platitudes about fraternal greetings and respect for the Holy Father and Mother Church. The pope began to tap his thumbs on the arms of the throne' – a wolfish grin from Rudi and a quick wave of the hand – 'don't ask me how I know. I *know*. OK? So he sits there, twiddling his thumbs, a sure sign he is not accepting all this nonsense about "a long history between Church and state" in Bulgaria. That sort of stuff. I gather the Bulgarian spoke for five minutes. Then it was the pope's turn.'

Rudi pours himself more vodka; he has a capacity for alcohol that we have not seen surpassed.

'The pope just sat there, on his big throne, and told them off. He began by reminding them what he'd told their foreign minister, I can't remember his name but I think it was four or maybe five months ago.[5] Anyway, the date

275

doesn't matter. It's what John Paul said now that's important. OK? He came straight out and said he wasn't seeking any special privileges for the Catholics in Bulgaria, but that he did want proper living space for them. And he wanted the delegation to go home and tell their government that. It was all very low key. But he left no doubt what he meant. Living space, he kept on saying, living space was what he wanted for the Catholics in Bulgaria.'[6]

Rudi breaks off to accept the main course: a sirloin of beef, rare, garnished with sliced truffles, button onions and potato puffs dipped in a mustard *roux* and deep-fried. He orders a second bottle of chianti to wash this down. Then he continues with his account.

The pope, he says, reminded the Bulgarians that the papal tradition of 'thinking in centuries' has lost none of its value; that the Holy See makes no claim in this to infallibility, but does feel entitled to be believed when it says it weighs everything with Christian charity, judging all things from that standpoint, including deciding what it finds bearable and unbearable, even what it is prepared to give up and what it will not relinquish.

'In other words,' says Rudi, pushing aside his plate, 'the pope was telling the Bulgars he is not going to give up protecting not only that handful of Catholics they have but also the great mass in the Soviet bloc. The message, you see, wasn't just for Sofia. It was for Moscow. And especially for Warsaw. The pope knows the drill as well as anybody. He tells the Bulgars. They go home, and Sofia tells Moscow. Moscow passes the word to Warsaw. It's a way for the pope to bring pressure on Jaruzelski. He gets a call from Moscow saying the pope in Rome is talking tough. Jaruzelski won't have heard a word from Rome about this. So he thinks, "My God," or whatever good Communists say, "how come the pope is getting Moscow to put the squeeze on?" If you are as nervous as Jaruzelski is right now, that can only make you more nervous. What the pope did to the Bulgars is the pope at his political best. It's papal politics as of today. The pope doesn't need those divisions Stalin talked about. He's got this access which allows him all sorts of moves that aren't possible if you're Reagan, or Kohl or Mrs Thatcher.'

We eat for a while, silent, digesting not only the food but what Rudi has said. We can't expect him to furnish proof for any of this. But it makes sense, if only because it seems very much in line with John Paul's style. Perhaps this is why such pains have been taken to keep secret what happened in the audience.

Later, we realize we have both been mentally counting who, apart from the pope and the delegation, had been present. It comes to six persons. One of them must have told Rudi, or told someone who told Rudi. If that is what happened, it does indeed give him extraordinarily good sources within this pontificate. We have also both been wondering, while we eat – we discover later – why he is telling us what amounts to a papal state secret. We find no answer for that.

But now, as he finishes the last of his beef, Rudi is ready to answer other questions.

Had John Paul mentioned *Pista Bulgara*?

No.

Not even alluded to it?

No.

What about drug trafficking; had he mentioned this other Bulgarian Connection?

No.

How had the delegation taken what he said?

'Stoically. The pope was hitting them about human rights. They didn't like that.'

Rudi pauses to give fresh orders on the way he wants dessert prepared. The crêpes are to be soaked in Kirsch, flambéd in a sauce of freshly squeezed oranges and lemons added to which is a spoonful of grenadine, and then filled with cinnamon-flavoured ice cream.

'If Russia and America don't have their summit to settle the nuclear issue, the Bulgarian trail will get hot again.

277

Martella will get all sorts of help. There'll suddenly be a lot of publicity. Agca could be wheeled out. You mark my words. If there's no summit, the whole business will be up and running again.'

Did he actually believe the CIA had that much influence, and besides, wouldn't Martella know what has been going on? He is, by every account, a very straight investigator –

'*Mensch!* That's nothing to do with it! You think Martella can take on the CIA? You take my word. He hasn't a hope. They've already cut him off from a lot of evidence. And it will stay like that until the CIA are ready to turn on the tap. And that will only happen if a summit doesn't get off the ground.'

When did he think that could be?

He spreads his hands. 'My bet is they'll meet in Vienna late in the year. Maybe December. Maybe even in Geneva.'

He adds that only two things could stop a summit. If the rumours about Andropov's failing health are true, this would precipitate a political struggle in the Kremlin which will force the Reagan administration to sit back and await the outcome. The second possibility is that one of the superpowers does something 'stupid'.

The crêpes arrive. Rudi pours the *spumante*, says *prost* again and answers our question.

'By stupid? *Mensch!* I mean the Americans invading Nicaragua or Cuba. Or the Russians invading Poland or maybe Czechoslovakia. All on the cards, you know. Look what Weinberger said the other day. He's scared World War III could begin by accident. Just by somebody doing something stupid.'

And the pope: how is he trying to avert this happening?

'For a start by not pushing the Bulgarian Connection. Anyway, for him to do that would be another act of stupidity, now the CIA are saying it probably doesn't exist. The pope knows what's good for the Church.'

He finishes his crêpes and looks at us carefully. 'It must have occurred to you the last thing the pope wants is to have the good old Company starting to spread stories about his Vatican Bank. That could really cause him problems. It's one thing to have the Italians snapping at his heels. It would be another if the CIA got into the business of spreading poison about the bank.'

It is a provocative note on which to end dinner. If Rudi is to be believed, the influence the CIA has on this pontificate is firmer than we had thought.

We drop Rudi off at his embassy; he says he has to call Pullach on a secure line about the latest scam involving *Stern* magazine and the forged Hitler diaries, a hoax which has seriously undermined faith in investigative journalism.[7] We decide to walk back to the Albergo Santa Chiara. Rome at this hour, close to midnight, is at its most haunting. It is easy to see why people are seduced into staying on here: the city seems full of writers and painters who are somehow sustained by the fantasy that the eternal city will forever support them.

The problem we face, we agree, is avoiding another form of seduction. Tempting though it is – the saga is manna for any social historian – we do not wish to get caught up in the daily shenanigans of the Bulgarian Connection and inter-intelligence services intrigue. While we don't doubt Rudi's sincerity, he is nowadays clearly embarked upon something of an anti-CIA crusade. It may be a personal vendetta, he may be working to orders; we are not much interested in such in-fighting. As far as we are concerned, the role of the CIA is worth exploring only in the wider context of relations between the secular powers and the Vatican.

Nor, to be fair, is it solely the American agency which continues to batten upon the Vatican. Cardinal Franz Koenig of Vienna informed us he is sure the KGB has its hooks into the Apostolic Palace.[8] Cibin knows that the five Soviet-manufactured bugging devices he found in the Vatican in 1978 are almost certainly not the last to have been planted there – either by the Russians or one of their allies.

We have been told both the British and French agencies also have moles inside the Leonine Walls. And Rudi seems able to learn anything the BND wants to know. MOSSAD, we strongly suspect, has at least one pipe-line into the Secretariat of State, a monsignor fluent in several Middle East languages. The list of intelligence services appears to be depressingly long.

For centuries the Vatican has been a prime target for secular intelligence agencies. Today it remains one of the world's richest repositories of genuine secrets, acting as a magnet for spies of all colours and creeds wanting to get their hands on the kind of highly sensitive political, economic and ecclesiastical information which the network of over one hundred nuncios, pro-nuncios and apostolic delegates send in to the Secretariat of State.

Again, it is not idle mischief to say that of the hundred-plus representatives accredited to the Holy See, a substantial number are engaged in the business of attempting to wean secrets from the Vatican. John Magee, when a papal secretary, found himself bombarded by invitations to dine with ambassadors; he once told Sir Mark Heath that he refused almost all of them because 'people are just trying to pump me'.[9] Kabongo feels the same way.

The foreign emissaries are not always interested in obtaining information only for themselves. A striking number of the nations accredited are Islamic or from black republics of Africa;[10] they are often countries with insignificant Catholic populations, but they do have close ties with either the Soviet Union or the United States. Several Communist countries, notably Cuba, Nicaragua and Yugoslavia, maintain full diplomatic relations with the Holy See. It's an open secret around the Secretariat of State that sensitive material has found its way into the hands of their diplomats.

But it is the CIA which dominates the intelligence knowledge of the Vatican.

From that day, almost forty years ago, when one of the founder members of the CIA, General William 'Wild Bill'

Donovan, was received in audience by Pius XII and decorated with the Grand Cross of the Order of Saint Sylvester, the oldest and most prestigious of papal knighthoods, an award given to only one hundred other men in history, who 'by feat of arms, or writings, or outstanding deeds, have spread the Faith, and have safeguarded and championed the Church': from that day Donovan bowed his head before the pope, the CIA has remained ensconced, virtually without interruption, as the prime intelligence adviser to successive pontiffs.[11]

Back at the hotel we decide to spend time appraising the current role of the CIA within this pontificate. Putting aside everything Rudi said about the Bulgarian Connection, and what we ourselves know – the agency's weekly briefing for John Paul, the behaviour of The Mad Mentor, the recent further staff increase at CIA Rome, the newly set-up task force in Washington to 'study' the papal assassination attempt, a curious decision in view of the CIA's presumption that Agca was 'a loner', or at most a surrogate of Muslim religious fanatics – putting all this aside, we begin to try and evaluate what deeper influence the CIA has on the Holy See, the Roman Catholic Church and its pontiff.

We review the material we have accumulated. It has come from many sources: Cardinal Koenig; Major Otto Kormek of Austrian Intelligence; Kriminalhauptkommissar Hans-Georg Fuchs of the BKA in Wiesbaden; Rudi, of course; Archbishop Alibrandi in Dublin; a number of people working in the Vatican. There is also the published documentation our researchers have collected. And there is our own special data, marked 'highly confidential', which no one sees but us, obtained from ambassadors accredited either to Italy or the Holy See. Together, this wealth of material produces a comprehensive response to our question: where stands the CIA today?

The short answer, we conclude, is that the CIA is as close to the pope as the telephone which is never far from the reach of its present director, William J. Casey. He has, if anything, advanced the long-standing and intimate relationship which 'Wild Bill' Donovan formed with the papacy.

Casey, more than any other director since then, has systematically developed the CIA's ties with the Vatican. Apart from the distressing and short-lived period following the assassination attempt, the CIA has retained its position as John Paul's main guide through the murky world of secret intelligence.

It is the CIA which keeps him continuously informed on the situation in Central America, provides him with accurate evidence of the spread of liberation theology, reports the latest behaviour of left-wing clerics in Nicaragua, El Salvador and the many other troublespots where the interests of the Holy See and the United States intersect. While John Paul receives similar information from his own cardinals, bishops and nuncios, it is still comforting to have the CIA's confirmation.

At the height of the recent riots in Poland, Casey reportedly telephoned John Paul to reassure him the violence was not the precursor of something worse.

We remind ourselves Casey is a member of the Sovereign Military Order of Malta, a vaunted Vatican order which dates from the Crusades when 'warrior monks' served as the fighting arm of the Catholic Church.

Today, far from being simply a historical anachronism, the order has the status of a nation-state. Like the Vatican, it issues coins and stamps, and has a diplomatic corps which is accredited in forty-one countries as well as to the Holy See. The Church ranks its grand master the equivalent of a cardinal. The order's eight-pointed Maltese cross is a reminder of its original Hospitaller tradition: it still helps to care for the sick and supports international relief organizations.[12]

A large proportion of the order's 10,000 members are scions of Europe's oldest and richest Catholic families. With its ban on Jews, Protestants, Muslims and separated or divorced Catholics from becoming knights; its secrecy and rituals, its scarlet and black ceremonial uniforms; its annual formal visit to the Vatican to renew its allegiance to Holy Mother Church: if this was all, the order would nevertheless be little more than an organization steeped in tradition, its ranks filled with powerful men and women devoted to charitable causes.

But although it certainly is in many ways a caring and considerate society, it is also a convenient channel of communication between the CIA, under Casey, and the pope.

While CIA Rome remains 'the working level' at which the agency relates to the papacy, the Sovereign Military Order of Malta forms the ideal cover for Casey to operate under. Both the CIA and the Vatican know that now, more than ever before, it is essential for the Holy See never openly to be seen to ally itself with the political aims of the CIA and the Reagan administration. Working through the order – an honorific society of, in the case of the United States, the country's leading Catholics – the CIA can more safely engage in wider and longer-term contacts with the papacy than its Rome Station could ever achieve.

We ponder the proposition put to us by two European ambassadors: it is one thing for CIA Rome to send a weekly briefing to John Paul; it would be quite another, and unacceptable, if the Station Chief was 'popping in and out of the pope's office every day'.

Using the order, Casey has opened a sophisticated conduit which allows the CIA, on an indirect and informal basis, to exchange ideas and opinions with the pope.

Gone are the days when the then Director of the CIA, John McCone, himself a member of the society, found himself having to fly to Rome and then struggle to persuade a pope, John XXIII, to accept the CIA line.

Nowadays, Casey need not even make the flight – or even telephone the pope. There are powerful emissaries in the order who can convey the CIA's views to John Paul, in that essential 'informal' way which distances the agency from the papacy.

Casey has a wide choice of potential messengers among the thousand or so members of the American branch of the order. The names of the knights are supposedly secret. But some of them have become known, including Lee Iacocca, the car magnate; Spyros Skouras, the shipping millionaire; Robert Abplanalp, the aerosol tycoon; Barron Hilton, the hotelier; William Simon, one-time treasury secretary; Robert Wagner, the former mayor of New York and presidential envoy to the Holy See.[13] There is also Clare Boothe Luce who, after a distinguished career in American diplomacy, is now the *grande dame* of President Reagan's Foreign Intelligence Advisory Board, which supervises the CIA's covert operations – though presumably such an august body is ignorant of The Mad Mentor's taping of Vatican Radio.

All these persons have one common bond: the ability to call the Vatican switchboard and ask to be connected to extension 3101, the ivory-white telephone on the pope's desk.

And, if none of them is going to Rome, then Casey has a Knight on the spot. He is William Wilson.

Members of the order have continued to reinforce to the pope the CIA view that liberation theology is what Wilson has told us: 'the greatest danger the Church faces in Latin America'.[14]

The CIA has also explained – both in its weekly briefings and through those 'informal' talks John Paul sometimes has with visiting Knights of Malta – how it is updating the strategy formulated by a predecessor, Richard Helms, to combat clerical dissidents. Casey, we have been told, has personally stressed to John Paul that he has only the 'good' of the Church in mind.

We cannot be certain, but it would be difficult to believe in view of what has occurred, if the pope has not pondered on just how good 'good' is. There is ample evidence that the

CIA in Latin America has trained and financed police forces which have tortured and murdered bishops, priests and nuns.

And surely John Paul – through the watchful Pio Laghi in Washington – must know that the US Institute for Religion and Democracy (IRD), established in 1981, has received funds from other American institutions which had previously acted as CIA monetary outlets? The IRD is currently engaged in a powerful propaganda campaign against those it sees as 'Church activists' who do not agree with the Reagan administration's role in El Salvador or its support for similarly repressive regimes in Latin America.[15]

Again, it is difficult to us to accept that the pope is totally unaware of the developing links between the CIA and one of his favourite secret societies, Opus Dei. In Chile, where the order has the tacit support of many bishops, Opus Dei receives indirect financial support from the CIA. The agency has also reportedly provided Opus Dei with evidence of Jesuits who challenge papal pronouncements and who are involved in political causes the CIA opposes. Further, we have been told it was the CIA who suggested to John Paul that he should encourage Opus Dei to begin working in Poland.[16]

Reviewing all our material, we are left with the astonishing probability that it no longer matters whether John Paul wants to separate his pontificate from the CIA. He can cancel the weekly briefing they provide. He can prohibit all Curial contact with the agency. He could circulate his priests, warning them to have nothing to do with anybody remotely resembling a Company man. In the end it would almost certainly make no difference.

The Central Intelligence Agency could still reach Pope John Paul through both the Knights of the Sovereign Military Order of Malta and members of Opus Dei.

He could, of course, choose not to listen.

But from just that possibility springs an even more disturbing future prospect. The CIA, in common with other serious students of religious affairs, is aware that the Holy Roman Catholic Church is no longer a unified monolith. It has become divided on a number of issues. John Paul finds himself increasingly the focal point for converging and competing ideologies. So far he has managed to deal successfully with them all, a balancing act which must constantly challenge his considerable intellect.

Yet the day may come – and perhaps sooner than we think – when the pope is unable to do so. He may then decide that, with half of the world's Catholics living in the Third World by the end of the century, he is forced to denounce far more strongly than he has so far, those very dictatorships which the CIA is presently committed to supporting.

What then?

Will the CIA do what now seems unthinkable? Will it set out deliberately to destabilize a papacy it now supports so ardently? Will it give credence to a current Latin American maxim: 'When the Company goes to church, it doesn't go to pray'? Will the CIA treat one of the most revered figures in the Christian world as though he is another puppet on the Langley lanyard?

There are, for the moment, no answers to these questions.

But we can expect an answer to a more immediate one: how will the pope fare in Poland?

In the days leading up to his departure, the mood in the Vatican is consistent. Our daily rounds produce the same grimly sombre feelings. John Magee quietly repeats, 'we are all praying'.[17] Emery Kabongo speaks of 'this testing time for the Holy Father'.[18] Lambert Greenan sees it as 'a war of nerves, the Polish regime is trying to string us out'.[19] Crescenzio Sepe in the Secretariat of State simply feels 'too nervous to speak'.[20] The staff on the Polish Desk have no time to talk; they are working around the clock finalizing arrangements. Camillo Cibin is anxiously checking that he has overlooked nothing. At Vatican Radio Fr Sesto Quercetti is preparing for 'what is the most momentous event of my life'.[21]

Beyond the Vatican walls, a hundred or so ambassadors to the Holy See are constantly evaluating the mood. So are hundreds of reporters. They spend hours listening to Vatican Radio hoping to pick up a hint of what is happening. At the station itself Fr Felix Juan Cabasés prepares a list of home telephone numbers of all the broadcasters. He explains why to Clarissa McNair.

'I want you all to stay in Rome. I want to be able to call on any of you fast. I'm worried in case something happens on the tour. I'm worried in case somebody takes a shot at the pope.'[22]

VATICAN CITY
Thursday
Early Afternoon

Shortly after one-thirty John Paul kneels in prayer in the private chapel of the papal apartment. Kneeling, the exposed heels and soles of his black leather shoes show signs of wear. But it is the footwear he always likes to use for flying; the leather is soft and pliable. His valet has also chosen the pope's favourite wardrobe for travelling. John Paul is wearing a white cotton clerical shirt under a creamy-white cassock made from silk and linen.

The garments have been hand-sewn at Rome's House of Gammarelli, papal tailors for almost 200 years.[1] The cassock differs from those they have made for previous pontiffs. This one is cleverly cut so that John Paul can wear, undetected, a custom-made bullet-proof vest beneath the robe.[2] In the front the vest protects him from below the neck to the groin; it also completely covers his back. The CIA helped design the garment. It is packed in one of the seven suitcases of clothes the pope will need for the eight-day Polish pilgrimage. There are changes of vestments, cassocks, stoles, rochets, rozzettas and *zucchetti* (skull-caps). There is a small case filled with woollen socks and cotton underwear.

Carefully wrapped and stowed in one case is a very special sash. It has a bullet hole in it, and the crimson cloth remains stained by the pope's dried blood. John Paul was wearing the sash on the day Agca's bullet penetrated his abdomen. He intends to donate the belt to the monastery at Jasna Gora, Poland's holiest religious shrine. It will be, he has told his staff, a visible reminder that the Virgin Mary saved his life – and that she will continue to protect Poland.[3]

As well as his travelling cassock, the pope is wearing a skull-cap. A solid gold cross suspended by an eighteen-carat gold chain hangs from his neck.

Gold cufflinks can be glimpsed at his shirt cuffs. They are a gift from priests in his old Cracow diocese.

Flanked by Dziwisz and Kabongo, John Paul leaves the chapel. He is serious-faced. Members of the papal secretariat will speak of a 'resolute look' in his eye and a 'determined thrust' to his chin.[4]

The timetable for this jam-packed day allows John Paul just enough time to go to his office and deal with last-minute matters of state.

Since early morning he has been preoccupied with such affairs.

After breakfast he read the Secretariat of State's assessment of the economic summit – the ninth so far – between the leaders of the seven most powerful western nations. They have met in Williamsburg, in the United States. The Secretariat report says that by far the most important decision taken at the summit has not been concerned with economic strategy, but with the defence of the West. The presidents and prime ministers resolutely agreed to support NATO's intention to deploy more nuclear weapons in Western Europe.

The report is now in Dziwisz's briefcase, ready for the pope to discuss with Casaroli during the flight to Warsaw.

The briefcase also contains a report which John Paul has speed-read (like the late President Kennedy, the pope has the technique of swiftly reading a document and absorbing its essentials). This report was prepared by Luigi Poggi. Once more the nuncio has drawn upon his sources within the Soviet bloc to produce an authoritative interpretation of two significant events which occurred in Moscow less than two hours earlier.

Andrei Gromyko has told the Supreme Soviet, the country's parliament, that Russia is resolved to resist any attempt by the West to intervene in Poland. Gromyko spoke of Russia's 'legitimate interests' in Poland and its determination to take all necessary steps to maintain Communist rule there. Before Gromyko spoke, Yuri Andropov had accepted the position as chairman of the Presidium of the Supreme Soviet, making him the equivalent of head of state.

Working at top speed, Poggi has produced a comprehensive evaluation of what both Gromyko's words and Andropov's new title could mean.

While the nuncio regards Gromyko's warning on Poland as an obvious attempt to intimidate John Paul,[5] Poggi also believes it should be seen in a wider context. The warning is a mandatory growl, an unnecessary indication that, in the end, it has been the Kremlin which sanctioned the pope's visit. Gromyko's rhetoric about the Warsaw Pact ready to defend its interests was not, this time, aimed at the West, or even the pope, but at China as a reminder of the realities of superpower politics.

When addressing the Supreme Soviet, Gromyko had not been entirely successful in disguising Russian anxiety over its eastern neighbour. He was unusually frank: Moscow wants nothing more than to patch up its quarrel with Peking and see relations restored to 'a normal basis', one where the Soviet Union could develop its links and contacts with the People's Republic.

In many ways Gromyko's plea echoes that of Clarissa McNair's broadcast on the Holy See's own aspirations, so far as its relations with Communist China are concerned. Her documentary had been broadcast by Vatican Radio the previous morning. There was an unusually swift response from the Chinese. In Dublin, Madame Gong, the People's Republic ambassador to Ireland, has passed on the word she received directly from Peking to papal nuncio Alibrandi: the programme had been 'noted' in the Chinese capital. In the diplomatic world they both inhabit, Gong's word has meaning – 'noted' indicates the broadcast was considered of significance and did not cause offence. Alibrandi at once informed Backis in Rome. By then the under-secretary at the Public Affairs Council had also received the views of the Taiwan government's ambassador to the Holy See, Chow

Shu-Kai. He, too, appeared satisfied that McNair's report was fair.[6] A transcript copy of her broadcast is now in the Secretariat of State. Poggi had an opportunity to see it before preparing his paper for the pope.

The nuncio does not think that there is any way Gromyko would have been influenced by the Holy See's stated position on the People's Republic – though no doubt the broadcast will have been 'noted' in Moscow as well.

Poggi, however, does feel that it is not only a wish to mend fences with China which lies behind Gromyko's bellicosity over Poland. The Soviet Union, Poggi estimates, is once more evincing what amounts to political schizophrenia: trying to appear a peacemaker and yet unable to disguise its role as aggressor. Gromyko has floated, again, a long-standing Russian proposal for a Middle East peace conference, implying that if it does not come soon, Russia will have to take its own measures in the region. He has demanded, once more, an immediate freeze on nuclear arsenals on terms already rejected in Washington. Poggi is convinced there is nothing new in anything Gromyko has said. He concludes the Foreign Minister's words about Poland are almost obligatory posturing on the day the pope is going to Poland. The nuncio would have been far more surprised if the Russians had said nothing.

He sees Andropov's election to head of state as a move to end the persistent rumours that for health – and perhaps other – reasons, Andropov is losing support in the Politburo and among the 750 deputies of the Supreme Soviet.

One of Poggi's sources informed him Andropov appeared wan-faced and unsteady on his feet; that his voice, when accepting his new office, was weak.

The nuncio still believes Yuri Andropov could be a very sick world leader.

Poggi will have an opportunity to expand on this possibility with John Paul during their 825-mile flight from Rome to Warsaw.

There had been yet other reports for the pope to study during the morning.

From Honduras had come an urgent dispatch from the nuncio, saying the country's fragile democracy was about to be swept away, sucked up into Central America's vortex of violence; the fighting in neighbouring El Salvador and Nicaragua has become worse. The report – even on this hectic day for John Paul – is deemed of sufficient importance to have moved with unusual speed through the Secretariat of State pipeline on to his desk. He immediately authorized the Honduran hierarchy to convey to the country's military leaders John Paul's personal concern for the future of the poorest Catholic nation in the region.

Now, shortly before he leaves the papal apartment, there are new briefings the pope has asked to see.

The first concerns the Peruvian hierarchy's role in supporting the state of emergency which has just been declared in Peru: all civil liberties have been suspended and the police given wide powers of arrest. Thousands of persons have been detained. The pope is concerned that the country's fledgling democracy may never recover. He wants his fear conveyed to the Peruvian government.[7]

For the second time in less than a month events in Chile have forced themselves on to the pope's desk. The country's bishops have tried, and failed, to walk a middle line between the Pinochet regime's actions and a second national protest against its politics. There has been widespread violence, even greater than in May. Chile has a huge foreign debt and is seeking a further $1.3 billion from overseas to pay present interest charges on outstanding loans. Vatican Bank is involved in some of the transactions. If the rioting continues, the international financial community could become sufficiently nervous to reconsider its position. The Latin America Desk, supported by Casaroli, is advising that the Chilean hierarchy should take a firmer line; it should warn the regime of the consequences for the country's stability.

John Paul accepts the recommendation.

But now at long last, after weeks of agonizing, it is time to set off on what the Vatican press office describes as a pastoral visit to celebrate the 600th anniversary of the enshrinement of Poland's national symbol, the Black Madonna of Czestochowa.

Nobody doubts, least of all Dziwisz and Kabongo as they accompany John Paul out of the papal apartment, that behind all the forthcoming pageantry and symbolism, which will fuse national history and religious faith, the pope will use his extraordinary ability to pinpoint the one great contradiction at the official heart of his homeland: its regime claims to head a workers' state yet continues to try and break the will of the workers with crude force.

Lech Walesa is going to help John Paul dramatize this dichotomy.

At one fifty-three P.M. precisely – exactly on schedule, his every movement now being checked off against the detailed protocol Prefect Martin and John Magee, among others, have prepared for the entire trip[8] – John Paul reaches San Damaso courtyard.

Waiting there, in full ceremonial regalia, is the Dean of the Sacred College of Cardinals, Carlo Confalonieri. He is over ninety years of age, a venerated wizened walnut of a man with luminous eyes. He rarely appears in public nowadays. His presence in the courtyard is another pointer of the importance being attached to this trip.

Beside Confalonieri stands Cardinal Paolo Bertoli, the *Camerlengo*, who in the absence of the pope abroad is responsible for administering the Church. Bertoli is a sprightly 75-year-old, passionately concerned to help find a peaceful solution to the Middle East; he spent a spell as a nuncio in Beirut and makes regular visits to the Lebanon to maintain contacts with the warring factions.

The pope and the *Camerlengo* briefly discuss the latest news from the region. The uneasy peace appears to be holding, but Yasser Arafat seems to be under mounting pressure from within the PLO.

It must be hard for John Paul to equate this news with the image of Arafat as he last saw him: standing in this very courtyard at the end of their meeting, dressed in desert boots and wearing a *kaffiyeh*, his distinctive flowing Arab headdress. On that day he had personally promised John Paul the time would come when he, Arafat, would accompany the pope into Jerusalem. Then, the PLO leader had added, John Paul would receive a Palestinian welcome equal even to the one he received in Poland in 1979.

John Paul had smiled. Nothing, he had quietly explained to Arafat, could ever equal for him the fervour of a Polish homecoming.[9]

Now, almost four years later to the day, John Paul senses he is about to be engulfed in even greater rapture. Perhaps he also suspects the danger will be greater than last time. This can possibly account for his preoccupied look as he climbs into the papal limousine for the first leg of his odyssey.

The car drives out of the cobbled courtyard and swings round the right side of St Peter's, passing a small locked door. It leads down to the tombs of almost all his predecessors, lying in no special order around the monument to the Apostle Peter. It is here John Paul's body will eventually be laid to rest.

The route takes the car on past the Vatican mosaic factory and the rather overpowering *governatorato* building. From here Archbishop Marcinkus, as well as running Vatican Bank, administers this tiny city-state for the pope. The relationship between the two men has deteriorated. No longer does Marcinkus drop in to the papal apartment. The 'Polish Mafia' have effectively cut him off from all but the most formal of contacts with the pope. Marcinkus is now in the equivalent of the Vatican's limbo-land: he retains his positions but his prospects for further promotion during this pontificate are small.[10]

Three minutes after leaving the courtyard, the pope arrives at the helicopter pad, the car coming to a stop precisely where a red carpet starts opposite the rear door and runs on up to the entry hatch of the helicopter.

Four Swiss Guards, standing at each corner of the helipad, drop to one knee as the pontiff alights. They remain in that position as the gleaming white helicopter lifts off with John Paul on board. Only when it has reached its cruising height of 3,000 feet do the guards rise.

The flying time to Fiumicino Airport is ten minutes. Every yard of the flight is screened by Italian air force radar from a base near the civilian airport. At the military airfield a squadron of fighters stands poised to take-off at the first indication of an attempt to intercept the helicopter. On the ground police cars are stationed along the thirteen-mile flight path. An ambulance is on standby at Fiumicino and another at Rome's Gemelli Hospital. Both are equipped with a wide range of medical equipment which the ambulance crews have told themselves will almost certainly be useless if the helicopter crashes.

The machine lands at Fiumicino without incident.

One of the *vigili* already on board the Alitalia 727 which is the papal flagship for the trip turns to Cibin and says, as the helicopter arrives, 'One hurdle safely over.'[11]

The security chief grimaces. Better than virtually anyone Cibin knows the risks which lie ahead. He has been living with them for weeks. The knowledge has given him an ever present dull ache in his stomach. He wonders whether it could be the start of an ulcer. He would not be surprised: not after what he has gone through.

For the past weeks members of the Polish Mission to the Holy See have been endlessly calling Cibin with details of how the pope is to be protected in Poland.[12]

The stage was reached recently when all four telephones on Cibin's desk – Vatican extensions 3004, 3023, 3217 and 4612 – rang. The calls were not only from the Polish

Mission but also from CIA Rome and Cardinal Glemp in Warsaw.

Cibin has lost track of the number of calls he has made and received about the Polish trip. He thinks they probably run into 'hundreds'.

Yet, if anything does go wrong, Cibin has to admit it will not be for want of precautions on the part of the Polish authorities.

All told, over 100,000 troops, uniformed and plain-clothed police and marshals will be on duty wherever the pope appears in public.[13]

The Polish Mission in Rome has bluntly told Cibin the function of this huge force – perhaps one of the largest ever deployed to protect a single person, let alone a pope on a pastoral visit – is twofold: to safeguard John Paul and to prevent the huge crowds he will undoubtedly attract from holding demonstrations in support of Solidarity.

During several telephone calls to Glemp in Poland – in themselves difficult, for the cardinal's number, Warsaw 389251, has been besieged by other Vatican callers – Cibin had come to the same conclusion as the Polish primate: heavy-handed police tactics might spark just the kind of trouble both the Church and the regime want to avoid.

The flashpoint could turn out to be the hub of the Polish security plan.[14] It is called the Zero Zone. No one will be allowed within this area, a circle of fifty yards' radius around the pontiff, unless he or she has passed rigorous security checks. Even Cibin and his *vigili* will need permits to enter the Zero Zone. Additionally, no one will be allowed into the public viewing areas bordering Zero Zone without special passes. These are going to be issued only to persons who have been screened both by the Church and Polish security. Each of the primary spectator sections for the outdoor masses – referred to collectively as Zone One, part of vast areas capable of holding more than one million persons – will themselves be further divided into sectors. Even then, only those with tickets and accompanied by a priest will be admitted; they will often be over a hundred yards from the pope.

Cibin fears trouble could arise if a crowd becomes resentful for being kept at such a distance, and attempts to force its way closer to John Paul.

The security chief suggested, and Glemp immediately agreed, that since the regime is so nervous, the hierarchy should issue a formal request for the faithful not to throw flowers in the path of the papal motorcade, as they did in 1979; rather they should hold their bouquets above their heads, or lay them in the road well beforehand. Cibin also advised that people should be told to empty their pockets and purses of anything metallic, because all spectators in the areas closest to the pope will be checked by metal detectors. He is convinced that those carrying such objects will be ordered to leave – creating more potential for trouble.

Cibin had felt unable to resist one demand of the regime: that the Vatican arrange to send the popemobile originally built for the pope's Spanish visit. It is heavily armoured with a bullet-proof bubble top, in sharp contrast to the open, converted flatbed which John Paul used in Poland in 1979. After he left the authorities had ordered this vehicle destroyed – even though a Polish exile organization in the United States and a monastery in Poland wanted to buy it.

During a frosty conversation with a member of the Interior Ministry in Warsaw, Cibin was told the popemobile is now essential, 'because extremists in the Solidarity underground might provoke violence against the pope to embarrass the government'.[15]

Dealing with the regime, Cibin has the uneasy feeling that, for all its insistence on wanting to avoid confrontation, in some ways it is behaving in a less than sensible manner. He was shocked to discover the Poles insisted on approving the design of all the altars for the outdoor masses. In Poznan, Party officials rejected one plan because they said the cross was too tall.

Only this morning, before leaving for Fiumicino, Cibin

received a telex – Vatican prefix 2024 DIRGENTAL VA – from Glemp – Warsaw 816550 SEPOL PL – with more disturbing news. The Interior Ministry, despite all the precautions taken, has issued a provocative statement. It claims it has information that unidentified groups 'intend to disturb public order, sow unrest and turmoil and, as a result, belittle the importance of the visit'.[16]

Cibin has a copy of the message in his pocket. He planned to show it to John Paul during the flight, but watching the pope board the aircraft, the security chief decides otherwise.

Il Papa, he tells himself, *è gia abbastanza preoccupato*.

John Paul is even more worried than Cibin suspects. Just before boarding the Alitalia jet he was told that, by the time it reaches Warsaw, Lech Walesa will have been placed under virtual house arrest.

ON BOARD THE PAPAL FLIGHT TO WARSAW
Same Day: Mid-Afternoon

At two-forty P.M. – item three on the itinerary – the Alitalia jet climbs into a cloudless sky and begins its two-hour, twenty-minute flight to Warsaw. The papal party of fifty-seven is augmented by sixty-one journalists; over a thousand more are waiting in Poland.

John Paul divides his time on board between praying in his private cabin behind the flight deck – it has a prie-dieu bolted to the floor near a couch – and having discussions with Casaroli and Poggi on their reports on the Williams-burg summit and the morning's events in Moscow. Later Martin and Somalo join them for a more general discussion on Poland.

Among the subjects raised is the critical financial state of the country. Western economic sanctions since martial law was imposed in December 1981 have cost Poland a further $12 billion, making its foreign borrowings more than $25 billion. No one in the papal party thinks it coincidental that the regime has just announced it is going to ask for an eight-year 'grace period' before beginning to repay its debts over twenty years.[17] Half of the money is owed to financial institutions, many of which have dealings with Vatican Bank.[18] The remainder is owed to western governments. However, at Williamsburg, it was decided to postpone review of the Polish debt situation until after the papal trip.

The implicit message to the regime is clear: if the pope's visit goes well, a more sympathetic attitude to Poland's financial plight will be taken by the West. This is a strategy Casaroli carefully encouraged through prior meetings with ambassadors to the Holy See of nations which assembled at Williamsburg.[19]

Poggi can confirm the Polish government has made no secret of its desire for the pope's visit to end Poland's international isolation and induce western countries to drop their sanctions.[20]

For the remainder of the flight John Paul and his advisers discuss other likely goals the regime wants to realize. The consensus is that the authorities hope the pope's presence will act as a safety valve for people's frustrations; that the regime will try and use the visit to undercut its more outspoken critics. Most important of all – and this Casaroli emphasizes – the regime will use the visit to reinforce an argument it has been stressing to the Polish hierarchy and also abroad: the only alternative to the Jaruzelski government is a more repressive one. Casaroli thinks the point is well made and needs to be given most careful consideration.

Ironically, the Church in Poland is the main beneficiary from the political turmoil. Institutionally, it has made unprecedented gains. Circulation of Catholic publications has nearly doubled since 1979. The number of young men entering the priesthood is up by a quarter on this time last year. New churches and chapels are being built at several times the rate of the 1970s. But even so there are not enough to hold all those who wish to worship. On the latest figures the Polish Church is claiming that a staggering ninety per cent of the population are active Catholic worshippers.[21]

Yet the rise and fall of Solidarity continues to drive the Church into largely uncharted political waters, and often open conflict with the authorities.

It is this, more than anything else, which separates Casaroli and his Secretariat of State from John Paul and his entrenched 'Polish Mafia'.

There is, of course, no sign of open discord on the flight. That would be unthinkable. But it is there all the same – as it has been for weeks. It can be seen in silences that stretch a little longer than would be normal; in the carefully restrained language.[22] There is not a prelate in the papal entourage who is not aware that in many ways the diversity between the two groups is epitomized by the way Josef Glemp has switched camps.

The 53-year-old expert on canon law was created primate after the death of Cardinal Stefan Wyszynski, whose stewardship of Poland's thirty-two million Catholics far exceeded spiritual matters. For almost thirty-three years – three of them spent in Communist prisons – Wyszynski had been what John Paul has called 'the primate of the millenium'.[23]

Glemp, with his bland style and diffident pulpit manner, was at first openly criticized by his priests for failing properly to defend the gains made by Solidarity. He argued that while the Church can uphold democratic ideas, it does not have a function in changing political systems.

The pope had invited the primate to the Vatican. They spoke for an entire afternoon in the spring of 1982.

From then on Glemp noticeably hardened his attitude. There are some priests on the Boeing 727 who say the primate is now an authentic member of the 'Polish Mafia', lost for ever, in an apocryphal sense of the word, to the Secretary of State's policy of moderation.

None of them for a moment believes that John Paul will do anything to endanger the difficult position of all Christians in the rest of the Soviet bloc by being too outspoken in Poland. Equally, they hope that he will be conciliatory, edging rather than thrusting the regime towards a greater respect for human rights; that he will stress that the Polish Church, while remaining necessarily watchful, must operate within the framework of the revolution, but not be part of it; that he will bolster the original values of Solidarity, but only so that they might re-emerge at some later date.

These priests – sitting in their First Class chairs, sipping choice wines with their steak or lobster – once felt John Paul would fulfil their wishes. Now they cannot be so certain. They know John Paul intends to take an unprecedented line. As the aircraft descends towards Warsaw's Okecie Airport, they can visualize him – alone again in his cabin – going over every word of his first speech on Polish soil, a speech which will set the tone for the rest of the tour.

They sense that now nothing can stop him – short of this aircraft crashing – from carrying out a plan he has been carefully nurturing for weeks.

Many of his aides believe John Paul is taking the most calculated risk of his pontificate. A number of them close their eyes in silent prayer for him as the jet touches down.

OKECIE AIRPORT, WARSAW
Same Day: Early Evening

Fr Robert Rush, a greying 55-year-old American Jesuit, describes the spectacle in a voice which still bears traces of his birthplace – Brooklyn, New York.

Rush is six miles from the airport. But the scene is literally unfolding only inches from his eyes. He is seated before a monitor in the headquarters of Poland's State television service, where he will spend most of the next six days, broadcasting reports back to the Vatican.

The Jesuit pulls no punches in his scene-setting. He has already described the overwhelming 'lack of vitality, a quiet and a sadness which is disturbing' as his first impression of Warsaw. He has mentioned bare shop windows and long queues for the few goods available. Then he changed mood to weave a word tapestry of mounting expectancy. 'One can see white and red national flags, yellow and white papal flags, and blue and white flags of Our Lady appearing everywhere along the tree-lined route the pope will travel from the airport to Warsaw Cathedral.'[24]

Now, he notes the time is five-thirteen P.M. as the pope kneels and kisses the ground.

The first part of the ceremonies end with John Paul shaking hands with the diplomatic corps.

The Polish president's speech is polite and guarded. It is received in total silence.

The pope's response draws a sudden round of applause.

'I ask those who are suffering to be particularly close to me. I ask this in the name of Christ's words: "I was sick and you visited me. I was in prison and you came to me." I myself am not able to visit all the sick, the imprisoned, the suffering. But I ask them to come close to me in spirit.'

Rush reminds his listeners this is an unmistakable allusion to those gaoled under martial law. The experienced broadcaster knows that battle lines have been drawn.

16
Roman Responses

It is both a deliberate decision and a gamble – our choosing to observe the Polish pilgrimage from a distance. One of us remains in Rome, with side-bar trips to Paris and London, while the other travels to the United States and Canada to launch *Pontiff*. We both find it possible to maintain contact with the papal caravan as it rolls – perhaps steam-rolls is a better word – across Poland; we have been given a sequential list of private telephone numbers where we can usually get in touch with some member of the entourage. We also talk regularly to each other in spite of our respective movements in Europe and North America.

Our decision not to become directly embroiled in the Polish cauldron quickly pays off.

Twenty-four hours into the visit we get the first whiff of trouble – and not just from the Jaruzelski regime. It is coming from inside the Apostolic Palace, the offices of *L'Osservatore Romano* and Vatican Radio.[1]

A number of monsignors are saying with unusual forcefulness that the pope is going too far in his demands for 'workers' rights', including the restoration of free trade unions. He has just delivered this second bombshell of the tour in a televised meeting with Jaruzelski. On the video cassette we have of the meeting, the general stands there, transfixed, frozen-faced, with just a trace of a depressed smile on his lips. He looks like a man who is about to have a bilious attack as John Paul imparts what amounts to a lecture.

Nobody can claim the pope's choice of language is anything but careful; not a word can be construed as calling Solidarity out on to the streets. There is no need to: the cries and banners which greet John Paul wherever he goes, along with his very pointed references to 'solidarity' – a word we cannot find in the Scriptures to support the quaint idea this is just a pastoral visit – are sufficient evidence that the trade union movement is very much alive and beating strongly in the hearts and minds of the Poles and their pope.

His speeches in Warsaw and later at Czestochowa are a startling condemnation of much the regime represents; in many ways they are all the more stunning because the rejection has been wrapped in copious quotations from the Scriptures; the pope seems to be reminding everyone that he not only has the full moral authority of his office behind what he is saying, but that God Himself undoubtedly approves.

John Paul has bitterly challenged martial law, defended the right to protest against injustice and presented his visit as a shining witness to the Christian faith – and also as an act of support for a nation's people bowed down by agony and suppression.

We expected – and it has come – the regime's spokesmen to protest. What we did not anticipate is the ferocity of the response from within the Vatican. It is the nearest thing we have seen to a palace revolution. Normally reserved and cautious prelates are fulminating that John Paul is overstepping the line between legitimately advancing the gospel message of human dignity and justice, and plunging into secular politics.

One priest-diplomat in the Secretariat of State who has served the two previous popes says this one 'is acting more like he's Primate of Poland than head of the Universal Church'.

On the other hand there is this to consider. John Paul can hardly protest about violations of human rights in Central America and ignore the same issue in his homeland.

Our video of his formal address to Jaruzelski shows John Paul physically far tougher than we had expected. There is a pugnacious thrust to his chin, a jabbing stab to his right index finger, a vibrance in his voice. Judged purely on performance, the pope is an intimidating figure. But a careful listening to his words – all that ultimately matters – shows an underlying reality. Behind the call for the return of independent trade unions, collective bargaining and a real 'dialogue' between the workers and the regime: behind all this there is also John Paul's clear guidance that it would be fatal to force change. He is talking about 'peaceful resolution' and 'patient discussion', not militant confrontation with an unpopular Communist government. Clearly, the last thing he wishes is to be responsible for some mass psychodrama leading to bloody revolution in Poland. His words, then, are equally intended for the Solidarity leadership.

In Vatican Radio, experienced broadcasters like Henry McConnachie believe the pope is 'being too defiant. He's getting too entangled. What is he trying to do?'[2]

McConnachie poses the sort of questions others are asking around the Vatican. Was 'a deal' made beforehand for the pope to go 'only so far'? Is the pope attempting to establish a 'new role' for the papacy in Poland?

There is no evidence, at least yet, or answers for such questions. But perhaps this is not really the issue. The point is they are being asked *inside* the Vatican.

It is almost impossible not to find someone who does not have a query, or an opinion, about what the pope is doing. Priests who normally concern themselves with matters far distant from Poland are now consumed by events there. Transistor radios have appeared on a number of desks to follow broadcasts. It's said that Marcinkus delayed lunch with an American banker to listen to one report.

Work, of course, continues. A monsignor is patiently keeping track of Italy's election campaign, which will result in the forty-fourth government for the country since 1945. The Latin America Desk has a report saying President Rios Montt has brushed aside the Guatemalan hierarchy's pastoral letter – issued with the full approval of the pope – attacking Montt's use of military tribunals and secret executions for those even suspected of terrorist activities. The Middle East Desk is preparing a summary for Casaroli of the Iran–Iraq war, almost three years old and showing no signs of resolution. Mgr Audrys Backis has received two reports on the outcome of the British General Election, which resulted in a sweeping victory for Prime Minister Margaret Thatcher. The first is from London, the second from Dublin – prepared by Nuncio Alibrandi, who has concentrated on assessing the likely effect Mrs Thatcher's return to office will have on Northern Ireland, where the Holy See continues to probe for a way to help bring about a peaceful solution.

All these, and scores of other matters, go on being processed. As a Secretariat of State priest put it: 'At this level we don't really need the pope. We can between us perfectly well take care of matters for months.'

Perhaps so. But he's probably one of the first to tune to Vatican Radio's next broadcast from Poland.

By the time the trip is in its fourth day – the convocation at Czestochowa where the pope says mass for more than a million people at the Shrine of the Black Madonna, and afterwards hands over the blood-spotted sash with its bullet hole from Agca's gun to the monks at nearby Jasna Gora – by then the questions are proliferating. They now almost have a life of their own: one question spawns a score; they produce another batch. It's quite extraordinary.

There are priests like Lambert Greenan who say what happened in Czestochowa 'was a straight fight between Communism and Marianism. Marianism won.'[3] He is clear about that. But he is less certain about other things.

Has there been, as McConnachie suggests, a prior arrangement between the Holy See and the Polish regime? Has Glemp, perhaps even Casaroli, slipped away for serious talks with Jaruzelski's people about reviving Solidarity under the tutelage of the Church? And has perhaps Poggi been devoting himself, when not co-celebrating mass, to some hard bargaining over lifting martial law and having at least a partial amnesty declared?

Greenan gives another Gallic shrug. He says he really does not know.

'Not my field, crystal-ball gazing. I'll tell you something, though. There's probably nobody left in the Vatican who can answer those questions. Things are moving so fast. This morning I have one impression. Now I have another. I'm sorry. I just don't know. It's like listening to reports from another world.'[4]

He is right about that. From what we have been able to glean, what is happening in Poland is coming as something of a surprise even to those on the spot.

'The pope' – a prelate tells us during a late-night call to the monastery at Jasna Gora – 'is pedalling his own bicycle.'

It is perhaps a measure of this priest's own exhaustion that, normally a gifted phrase maker, he has resorted to the sort of lingua franca some of the tabloids are using to report the trip.

We make another call to Poland. This time our source is more articulate. He says John Paul is raising the quality of public debate; he is also reminding the people of the Church's role as 'the supreme teller of the truth. That is not easy when the police are everywhere.'

We briefly discuss his impression of what happened in Czestochowa. He says the million who turned out for mass presented probably the most successful Solidarity demonstration yet.

The union's banners were everywhere, making it impossible to disentangle where religion stopped and politics began. The occasion – to call it merely a religious service is nonsensical – gives Solidarity a kind of sacramental blessing the organization has never before possessed.

This, too, creates unease in the Vatican. From every side voices can be heard declaring it is all very well to say such gatherings are the stuff of which a nation, particularly Poland, is made. But can they ever be more than stirring spectacles? What will be the eventual outcome – when the altars have been dismantled, the popemobile shipped back to Rome and the Holy Father has gone? What then? More repression, no doubt refined, yet in the end repression? Is that what lies ahead? Is Jaruzelski the sort of narrow-minded leader who will seek retribution – may indeed be ordered to so do from Moscow – for the way the pope has bulldozed his way across the country?

There are many in the Vatican who now increasingly fear this could happen. They are asking themselves, and others, whether the pope expects the Polish government to commit *felo-de-se* by doing what amounts to a political cartwheel at his behest. Surely not – not after Gromyko's deliberately timed reminder of Poland's place in the Soviet firmament? Isn't there a growing danger that some of those 5,000 tanks in East Germany and twenty-eight Soviet divisions sitting on the eastern border of the Polish frontier might be sent into Poland after the pope returns home – when his kith and kin feel unable to shake down to reality in his absence?

No one can offer real answers. Only time will tell. That is what now makes the questions so disturbing.

On the morning of the fifth day of the tour – helicopter from Jasna Gora Monastery to Poznan, then on to Kato-wice and later back to Jasna Gora, 400 miles of juddering travel, a score of ceremonies – one thing is clearly emerg-ing. The pope is doing exactly what he planned to do. His entire trip is a paradigm of the relationship between John Paul and the Communist system he so clearly abhors.

Equally, it is emerging that the Polish Church is frankly astonished at its new-found strength, and may not know how to use it.

This speculation has led to more questions. How far should the Church in Poland go in co-operating from now on with the government at the highest level? How far should it increase help to worker-activists at parish level?

In the meantime, at Katowice, the pope is delivering his

twelfth major sermon. Like every other, he uses this one to attack martial law.

Finally John Paul reaches his birthplace, Cracow. Tomorrow is to be the climax of his triumphal tour. Here he intends to execute his final master stroke. In spite of all the official opposition, he intends to meet Lech Walesa.

But even now trouble is brewing over this encounter – and once more it is coming from inside the Vatican.

WAWEL CASTLE, CRACOW
Thursday
Early Morning

Camillo Cibin is camping out in a room little larger than a broom cupboard.[1] His body aches from another restless night spent on a hair-stuffed mattress. Here, in the rear of the rambling palace, conditions are spartan. The floors and walls are bare stone. Overhead the single bulb casts shadows of the tallboy and the security chief's suit hanging on a wire hanger. Now, a little after six o'clock, there is an insistent knocking on the door.

Cibin knows who it is. They generally come at this hour, the two officers who have been acting as his liaison link with the regime on security. Cibin still has difficulty pronouncing their names, but they have surprised him with the fluency of their Italian. He pulls on a bathrobe and lets them into his cubicle.

This morning the elder of the pair – a short, fat colonel with bulging grey eyes – is mournful. He explains he has spent most of his night drafting a report on what he repeatedly calls 'the unfortunate incident in Wroclaw'.

He is referring to a clash between demonstrators waving Solidarity banners and riot police at the end of a huge turnout for the open-air mass at Wroclaw racetrack; at least a million had come to pray.

John Paul had barely left the altar when trouble erupted. Demonstrators on the edge of the crowd started to march towards the city's cathedral, calling on other worshippers to follow them. Truckloads of riot police – western reporters counted at least thirty vehicles – began to attack the marchers. There had been shouts of 'Gestapo'. Foreign pressmen were rough-handled. Tension on both sides had run high for a time.

Now, once more, the colonel is conveying his regrets.

Cibin nods, anxious to be done with the matter; he is tired of the man's handwringing.

The colonel's companion – physically so nondescript Cibin will later have difficulty recalling his appearance[2] – is equally solicitous. The Holy Father, he trusts, was not alarmed by the behaviour of a handful of extremists? The trip has gone so well, so very well. There has been tension at times, of course. But this is only to be expected when radical elements are always trying to disrupt relations between Church and State.

After a week, Cibin knows he will have to endure yet another lecture. Both officers never miss a chance to promote the regime's position.

But, in a way, Cibin has admitted to his own *vigili*, he has grown to rather like the pair. They can make the most preposterous demands without blinking. Cibin hasn't quite got over the colonel's polite request to search the pope's bedroom 'for explosives'.[3] And the man asked the security chief unfailingly every time they met whether John Paul was wearing his bullet-proof vest. If not, perhaps Cibin could arrange to let the colonel examine it?

Their behaviour has provided Cibin with the only light relief he has had since coming to Poland. Otherwise the trip has been the toughest he can remember. Thankfully he will be back in Rome in time for dinner this evening, provided nothing untoward happens during the next twelve hours. He can't wait for item four on the day's schedule to come round: '5.15 Papal flight departs Cracow-Balice airport'.

The colonel looks at Cibin, this time all smiles.

He says the meeting is on.

Cibin begins to ask questions.

Where?

The pope will meet Lech Walesa and his wife and children at a monastic hermitage south of Cracow, in the Tatra Mountains. The pope had frequently gone there when he was the city's archbishop.

When?

The colonel consults a piece of paper. The meeting will take place at eleven-thirty this morning. It will last for thirty minutes.

What about security arrangements?

The colonel reads aloud. The audience will be strictly private. Just the pope and the Walesas. There will be positively no press, and especially no photographers –

Cibin interrupts.

– The pope may want a personal photographic record of the occasion –

– No photographs. The colonel is firm. The smile has gone.

He continues to read. The pope will travel in an unmarked government limousine to the hermitage. The Walesas will be waiting there for him. They have been brought overnight in a military aircraft from Gdansk. All roads in the area for a distance of ten miles around will be closed and guarded. Anybody attempting to pass will be arrested.

Cibin makes a decision. He tells the colonel he is going in the car with John Paul.

The officers exchange looks. The colonel bridles. He says he has no order covering this.

Cibin is adamant. He is going – or the pope will want to know why.

The pair excuse themselves, saying they will be back.

Cibin quickly dresses, putting on the dark grey suit he's worn most days. Several times he had been astonished at the way some of the plainclothes Polish security men had come up to him and touched the cloth admiringly.

The officers return. Once more the colonel is all smiles. Cibin can go.

They arrange to meet after breakfast.

Cibin packs his suitcase, ready for the entourage's baggage handler to send it out to Cracow's airport. But before doing so he slips a loaded Minox camera into a pocket of his jacket.

* * *

At seven o'clock, John Paul hosts a breakfast for forty members of his retinue and the Polish hierarchy in the castle dining-room.

Many of those seated at the long baronial table show signs of lack of sleep. Even physically fit men like John Magee have found the pace gruelling. It is not just the distance travelled, but the continuous strain. The papal party has never lost a feeling that trouble could erupt at any time; that the emotional fervour could turn into violence.

Magee is himself anxious not to overstate the position. 'All papal trips are demanding. This one just a bit more than most.'[4]

In common with everybody else around the table – the cold sausages and dark bread remind Magee of his days in the papal apartment when he regularly ate such breakfast fare with John Paul – the Master of Ceremonies has his own memories of this trip.

There was that poignant moment at the mass in Warsaw's main stadium the day after his arrival when the pope asked people to go home quietly and not to demonstrate. Magee will always remember John Paul spreading wide his arms, urging, 'Brothers, I want this day and all the days of my stay to be days of peace and calm, days when together we will look for paths towards that future which at times seems so obscure.'

The night before, a crowd of 20,000 had marched past Communist Party headquarters in Warsaw, chanting Solidarity slogans and 'The Pope is with us'. Then they had united their voices in a call Magee can never forget. 'Join us! They are not beating us today!'

Luigi Poggi will tell colleagues on the third floor of the Apostolic Palace[5] that he treasures the occasion in another palace, Warsaw's Belvedere, when John Paul used almost precisely the words the nuncio had suggested. 'I do not stop hoping that the social reform announced on many occasions, according to the principles so painstakingly worked out in the critical days of August 1980 and contained in the agreements, will gradually be put into effect.'[6]

Later the nuncio checked: the response was as gratifying as he had hoped. Poles who heard the televised address recognized the reference to August 1980 as a reminder of the agreements which gave birth to Solidarity.

Even Casaroli, so inscrutable in public, rarely permitting himself more than a brief scholarly smile, had been moved to nod his approval after the pope suggested, in the form of a prayer at one of the Czestochowa masses, that it was possible to forgive the regime: 'To forgive does not mean to give up the quest for justice. It means to *aim* for truth and justice.'[7]

For the Poles at the breakfast table, the visit, in Glemp's words, 'is a fortification of the population. Old values have been reborn. Now nothing can remove them.'[8]

To help strengthen that feeling, John Paul means to brief the prelates present on his long meeting with General Jaruzelski the previous night. He had asked the Polish leader to come and see him.

But before he explains what they discussed, he asks those around the table to review the trip as they see it. He listens intently as Casaroli, Somalo, Glemp and then others begin to speak.

Throughout the visit the CIA – via the US Embassy in Warsaw – has kept John Paul abreast of the Soviet Union's reaction.

Even those in the papal party who are not privy to the pope's intelligence briefing are now aware – due to the rumour stock exchange which has been bullish for the entire trip – that the Russians are clearly very concerned.

Yet their efforts to limit the impact of the visit on the Soviet bloc have been only partially successful. Although Voice of America broadcasts to the Soviet Union have been jammed and the pope's speeches censored in the Polish press, there has been no way for Poland's state radio to do anything but broadcast in full the pontiff's words, including his biting references to the government.

Yet those around the pope's breakfast table concede that John Paul should leave Jaruzelski with some vestige of prestige.

It turns out he has.

TATRA MOUNTAINS;NEAR CRACOW
Same Day:Late Morning[9]

Lech Walesa glances around. Immediately behind him is the hermitage, its towering stone walls warm in the full splendour of this summer day.

He looks to his left, as he has done several times, peering towards a clump of fir trees. Beneath them the soldier has parked the car which brought the Walesas here; he is leaning against the bonnet, smoking. Danuta and the children are seated in the back. They have been told they must wait there until the pope arrives.

Walesa stares down the road which leads from the hermitage into the valley. He won't be able to remember how many times he glances at his watch, straightens his tie, tugs at the jacket of a suit which is now too tight-fitting and checks that his shoes are not scuffed. Later, when reporters ask him these sorts of questions, Walesa will be irritated. He does not like being personalized; he thinks it takes away from the real purpose of his life. That purpose is epitomized by his presence in these lonely, lovely mountains. He sees this morning as another step along the long and heroic struggle he is engaged in.

He continues to stand alone, waiting.

Walesa is thirty-nine years old, yet looks older. There is a greyness to his skin which the sun has not been able completely to tan away. His eyes, constantly searching the valley road meandering below him, are equally suspicious and alert. There is not only intelligence there, but also fearlessness. Like the pope he is waiting for, the trade unionist long ago came to terms with dying. He is, he has told Danuta, quite prepared to be killed for what he believes. She has said she understands. This somehow makes it easier for them both to bear what they have to endure.

All the time he has stood here, Walesa has been wondering whether it could be a trick, another form of the psychological pressure the regime maintains on him.

Since the pope arrived in Poland, the harassment has increased. As many as fifty police and militia have followed his every move: they have trailed him to work, to church, when he's gone fishing, even while he played with his children in the park. The guards just stand there, saying nothing, threatening by their mere presence. At night they have been posted near the Walesas' apartment door, in the building's lobby and outside in the street. Next day, when he has gone to work, the procedure started again: policemen ahead of him, beside him, behind him.

Walesa thinks it crazy that the State is spending so much money this way. And, he can remind himself this morning, even so the regime has not beaten him. He is here. That is all that matters.

Not that he can fully believe it. Only twenty-four hours ago the Gdansk police chief sent word there would be absolutely no meeting with the pope. Polish radio carried the same depressing news. Then, late yesterday afternoon, a security police car parked outside the apartment building. Two majors marched to the Walesas' door, were let in, and told the family they had fifteen minutes to pack.

Danuta had smiled – pointing to two suitcases already prepared.

She made hurried arrangements with a neighbour to mind the three smallest children.

Then Walesa, his wife and their four eldest children were driven off.

He'll remember how Danuta had smiled as they sped through the streets to Gdansk's military airport. She put into words what he felt. 'Lech, God has answered our prayers.'

The family were flown in a Russian-built transport plane to Cracow. There they spent the night in a hotel with the usual guards outside their door. The room's telephone had been isolated, reinforcing the warning to Walesa that he must not contact anybody, least of all anyone from Solidarity. The children slept in one bed. Walesa and Danuta spent the night talking and dozing.

At dawn they were awakened, given breakfast, and then driven to this mountain fastness under heavy guard. Escorting their car were two trucks of militia. As the convoy drove into the mountains, the Walesas saw how extensive was the security: road blocks had been placed at regular intervals and more trucks filled with troops were packed along the route.

Danuta had turned to her husband and whispered. 'It must be true. They would not do all this for nothing.'

Walesa reminds her of a simple truth he has come to live with. 'The authorities would do anything if it suits them.'

When they arrived here, an officer in Polish Army security was waiting.

He had asked them politely to see any presents they may have brought.

The children showed him pictures they have painted. One is of their father going to work. He is surrounded by stick-like figures. The officers ask who they are supposed to be.

'Soldiers,' say the child.

The officer hesitates, then hands back the painting. Danuta produces a rosary she wants to present to the pope; Walesa unpacks a small piece of sculpted steel he and his workmates at the Lenin Shipyard have made.

The officer examines them and returns them without comment.

He tells Danuta and the children they must stay in the car. Walesa, he indicates, can wait further up the hill. The

317

officer permits himself a brief smile. 'After all, you are the host on this occasion.'

Now, suddenly, a line of cars appears down the road. Walesa looks at his watch. They are on time. He turns and beckons towards the cluster of trees.

Danuta and the children come running. They group themselves about him. His wife puts her arm around her husband. The children stand in front. Danuta is wearing a traditional peasant costume, the children the clothes they wear for Sunday church.

A little distance from them the cars behind the leading vehicle stop and then reverse down the road.

The large black limousine drives slowly forward.

Cibin is seated beside the colonel with the bulging eyes.

John Paul is alone in the rear. He is wearing an unadorned cassock and skull-cap. On his feet are a pair of sturdy lace-up shoes.

The car stops. Cibin gets out and opens the door for the pope. He emerges, smiling.

He walks towards the Walesas. The car reverses back down the road.

Under the fir trees the Walesas' driver is standing to attention.

Cibin follows behind the pope, but to one side.

As the pope approaches the family, Walesa and his wife gently push the children into kneeling positions. Then they, too, kneel.

John Paul extends his right hand with its Fisherman's Ring, the symbol of his papal authority. First Walesa and then Danuta brush their lips against the ring.

The pope motions them all to rise.

His arms around the children, shepherding them forward, Walesa on one side, Danuta on the other, John Paul walks with them into the hermitage.

Here, almost forty years ago, he had hidden from the Nazis. Then he had been a youth and they wanted to conscript him into a labour gang. Much later, when Archbishop of Cracow, he sometimes came here to meditate.

Now, the thick stone walls of the hermitage protect the small group from the prying eyes of Polish soldiers in the surrounding woods.

They spend ten minutes in the hermitage. Gifts are exchanged. The pope gives Walesa one of his personal gold medals and blesses a rosary he has brought for Danuta. The children receive small framed photographs of the pontiff.

John Paul and Walesa emerge from the hermitage and walk on up into the woods.

Waiting nearby is Cibin. He uses his Minox camera to capture the scene. The pope will have his photographic record.

In the sanctuary of the trees the pontiff and the Solidarity leader have another very private discussion.

Then they return to the hermitage.

Moments later John Paul begins his journey back to Cracow.

The Walesas are escorted to Gdansk.

What transpired during those fateful fifteen minutes the two men spent alone in the woods is about to provide reason for a long-serving and senior Vatican priest to resign.

BALICE AIRPORT:CRACOW
Same Day:Later Afternoon

The scene is reminiscent of when John Paul had previously left here for Rome. The sun beats down on the Russian-built aircraft of LOT, the Polish airline. The plane has been given a coat of white paint for the flight and part of its interior has been revamped. Now there is a salon up front with armchairs and a day bed for the pope. The galley is stocked with Russian sparkling wine (which he will not touch), Polish vodka (which he will drink sparingly), as well as caviare and various kinds of fish morsels.

John Paul arrives with his entourage. They look tired. He remains astonishingly vigorous considering all he has done this past week. He has delivered forty-three sermons and speeches, shaken thousands of hands, slept no more than four hours a night – and taken his pontificate into uncharted political areas. He has challenged the Polish government – and, beyond it, Russia.

Vast crowds line the approaches to the airport. Many are unashamedly crying.

Party officials, led by Poland's head of state, bustle around the tarmac.

John Paul is directed towards a podium. The rest of the papal party follow Casaroli into the aircraft.

The pope then does something that staggers the reporters who have found the energy to come this far: John Paul makes a tedious speech. Even more astounding, it contains phrases which could have been culled from a government handbook. For the first time on the tour the pope refers to the State by its formal title, the Polish People's Republic. Until now he had pointedly implied that Poland's independence, and therefore its nationhood, was stolen by the Nazis in 1939 and has never been returned. This time he speaks of his hope that the authorities 'will secure for the Polish State, the Polish People's Republic, the place it deserves among the nations of Europe and the world'.

It is a call for an end to the country's international isolation.

General Jaruzelski has been given a new lease of life. It has made his flight to Cracow, summoned by almost imperious command of the pope, very worth while.

Only when the LOT plane is a speck in the sky does the significance of John Paul's phrases begin to dawn on those who have heard him. They begin to ask themselves what will happen to Lech Walesa.

They are not alone. On the airliner a number of papal aides are quietly voicing the idea that, in the words of one, 'the Holy Father has lassoed Walesa. He probably told him about the possibility of winning the Peace Prize in one breath and in the next read him his version of the riot act.'

The future of the Solidarity leader dominates the talk in the aircraft during the remainder of the two-hour flight to Rome.

SECRETARIAT OF STATE
Friday
Morning

The Polish Desk is involved in a task which will occupy its staff for several weeks.[10] Analysts are starting to trim away the supercharged emotionalism surrounding the trip in order to assess it in cooler diplomatic terms. It is an approach which these priests hope will produce meaningful answers to such questions as: will the long-term view of the visit be seen as conferring a seal of approval on the regime or emphasizing its failings? Who will be the main Polish beneficiaries from the visit? How will the pilgrimage be received in Moscow and, equally important, Washington?

It is far too early for the desk's staff to make final judgements. But pointers are emerging. These have surfaced by the diplomats on the desk doing what they are good at: asking questions, listening and reading.

Throughout the entire week they have received their usual bundles of newspapers from Poland. These have been gutted. They have also received, among other journals, *The New York Times*, *The Times* of London and a selection of European periodicals. Additionally, the Polish-language service of Vatican Radio has sent over transcripts, and the office of the Polish language weekly edition of *L'Osservatore Romano* has delivered data.

In between assessing it all, the desk's monsignors have kept in close contact with the Polish Mission to the Holy See.[11] From other desks – notably the North America and European Desks – have come continuous assessments of how the trip was regarded in the capitals of Europe and in the United States.

On the flight back to Rome, Polish Desk staff who travelled with the pope were kept busy preparing their own reports. By this morning their colleagues have read and weighed them against the other information they have.

From all this the first tentative conclusions are emerging.

At one level the trip was a success for both the Polish Church and the regime. Trouble had been kept to a minimum. The hierarchy had demonstrated the truth of its promise: to be able to mobilize massive gatherings and also to control them. This could pave the way for a more malleable relationship between the Church and State; in no way should this be perceived as compromise by the hierarchy but rather a continuation of the Church's wish to preserve the integrity of Poland's nationalism and faith, allowing the country to survive that much better until its next historic opportunity.

It seems probable the visit will help to reduce the divisions within Poland's hierarchy.[12] The desk's priests are well aware the Polish Church has its groupings. On one side are the extra cautious, anxious to do nothing which might cause the regime to take punitive action against the Church. In the middle are the moderates, motivated by a wish to cling to what has been achieved in recent years, men satisfied for the moment not to push hard. On the far wing of the hierarchy are the radicals, mostly young priests who believe the Church must be more militant, otherwise it will lose its moral authority and could in the end become stifled by the State.

John Paul has somehow, at least for the moment, fused these disparate elements into a cohesive body.

The most heartening conclusion the desk's staff come to

this morning is that the visit has reinforced what they consider one of the critically important functions of the Polish Church: to be to all intents and purposes the repository of statehood in Poland, for, 'without the Church there would simply be no nation'.[13] Guided by the pope's words, the radicals can be curbed while the ultra cautious elements should be encouraged to be bolder. In the coming months the Polish Church's political acumen will be tested as seldom before.

The desk staff know it is far too early to gauge the eventual impact of the visit on Jaruzelski's future. The reports from Washington, in particular, suggest he could be removed if the Kremlin judges that Russia's control of the country has in any way been loosened. Only a week ago – a long time in politics, as the desk's priests readily concede – Luigi Poggi assessed Gromyko's blunt warning over Poland as no more than posturing.

Now, there is another perception by the Polish Desk. The pope has rallied Solidarity's leadership and infused members with a new commitment, hope and confidence. The danger will come if their rekindled militancy goes too far. Then the Soviet Union might well decide to intervene. It could remove Jaruzelski, replacing him with a leader more acceptable to them, one even more iron-handed when carrying out Moscow's will. The ultimate possibility is that Russia invades Poland. In either event there would be horrendous consequences for the country's people and Church.

A prime function of the Polish Desk is to continue to provide the pope with as much advance warning as possible of Soviet intentions towards his homeland.

While the chance of Soviet intervention can never be ruled out, it is probably less likely now than three months ago, due to the persistent reports of a crisis in the Kremlin leadership.

In all the wealth of information they have assembled, the desk's priests are unable to detect any clear indication of Lech Walesa's future role.

'L'OSSERVATORE ROMANO' OFFICES
Same Day: Noon

It is coming up to edition time – always a time of tension in any newspaper. But this is not the only reason for the undercurrents running through the offices of *L'Osservatore Romano*.[14]

Everybody on the staff now knows what the paper's deputy editor, Fr Virgilio Levi, has done. In the entire 122-year history of the daily – over a century of reporting pivotal papal happenings – its present staff nervously wonder whether there has ever been a more dramatic story than the one the 53-year-old Levi proposes to publish today.

His colleagues are certain that, at three o'clock, when the presses roll out the first copies of today's issue, a print run of 50,000 in all, the world's media will undoubtedly seize upon Levi's story.

Some of the staff wonder if, even at this late stage, Levi will reconsider what he has done – and scrap the leading article.[15]

Others – openly critical and even hostile to the deputy editor – hope he will publish. That could create a situation they have made no secret of wanting for months: publication might lead to Levi being forced to relinquish his post.

Behind this wish is a tale of bitter rivalry which has hopelessly divided the staff into two warring factions.

There are those who believe Levi should be the paper's editor-in-chief, a position which would allow him to advance further the liberal editorial policies he has been advocating ever since Pope Paul VI brought him down from Milan. In Paul's days Levi had been given virtually a free hand to write what he liked. Now, under John Paul, he has felt increasingly constricted. On several occasions he has reportedly received tart rebukes from the 'Polish Mafia' over what he has written on Eastern Europe. Levi broadly believes there should be an accommodation between the Church and Communism; he is convinced that, in such a dialogue, the moral superiority of the Church would win the day. It is not a view to which either the pope or his closest aides subscribe.

Other members of the paper's staff staunchly support the present editorial director, Valerio Volpini. He is an academic and a layman. During the nine years he has held the post, Professor Volpini has shown himself to be both conservative and ever mindful that ultimately he is answerable to the Secretariat of State – even to Agostino Casaroli himself on particularly important matters of policy.

Levi has not concealed his close relationship with Casaroli. They frequently dine together in the Secretary of State's palace inside the Vatican, discussing world events and leaders over dinner. From these meetings has come the stamp of authority Levi's articles carry. Often present is Fr Robert Tucci, the Jesuit director general of Vatican Radio. Like Levi, Tucci's views are nowadays sometimes seen in the Apostolic Palace as antipathetic to the pope's.

On the other hand, Professor Volpini is known to be devoted to John Paul.

The tension between the two factions reached the point where the pope recently asked the highly respected Fr Alfons Stickler, Prefect of the Vatican Library, to conduct an investigation into a feud which has turned the paper 'into an armed camp'.[16]

Stickler's report, now on the pope's desk but still officially secret, is widely believed in *L'Osservatore Romano* to recommend that both Volpini and Levi be dismissed. Technically, there is no problem in sacking them; their contracts have not been renewed – either man can be let go at a moment's notice.

Now, almost as if in anticipation of Stickler's recommendation, Virgilio Levi has written an editorial which is bound to have wide repercussions.

325

It concerns Lech Walesa.

The deputy editor has positioned the article on the front page. He has signed his name to it, and then selected the headline: 'Honour to Sacrifice'.

Shortly after noon he finishes proofreading the editorial. Satisfied, he sends it back to the printers.

The story will appear just below the paper's masthead with its two mottoes: *Unicuique suum*, To each his own, and *Non praevalebunt*, They shall not prevail.

Levi goes to lunch. He well understands the newspaper is regarded as a valuable indication of papal thinking.

THE PAPAL APARTMENT
Same Day: Mid-Afternoon

At three-fifteen a copy of *L'Osservatore Romano* arrives in the Secretariat.

Kabongo, for one, enjoys reading the paper.[17] He likes its layout and authoritative analyses. The secretary knows many of the unsigned editorials are 'inspired' either by a very senior cardinal, such as Casaroli, or at times even the pope.

He recognizes at once that John Paul cannot be the 'inspiration' for what Levi has written.

The deputy editor claims Lech Walesa has 'lost the battle' and will give up politics.

'Sometimes sacrifice is necessary for inconvenient people because a greater good can come from it for the community. Walesa seems to have entered into this spirit, even though in his soul, painfully, the hope will not diminish that things may change in the future.'

Kabongo immediately places the article on John Paul's desk. It will be the first thing the pope sees when he returns to work after his afternoon rest.

* * *

At four o'clock the pope reads the editorial. His reported response is one of fury.[18]

He makes several internal telephone calls, including to Casaroli, Stickler and Volpini.

John Paul spells out his position. He is not interested in how Levi came to write the editorial or who may have 'inspired' it, or for what motive. Nor does he mind whether Levi resigns or is fired.

But he must be gone before the next edition appears.[19]

At four-thirty Camillo Cibin appears in the pope's office. He is here to discuss the next move in a matter which happened while the pope and the security chief were in Poland. It involves papal messenger Ercole Orlandi.

His daughter, Emanuela, has been kidnapped.

Once more John Paul is caught up in international terrorism.

18

THE VATICAN
Monday
Morning

Sister Severia Battistino pushes a button on the switchboard console and says, '*Vaticano.*'

The voice in her headset belongs to a stranger; he sounds both young and nervous. She asks to whom he wishes to speak.

'Casaroli.'

She sighs. Every day the switchboard gets its quota of crank calls for the pope or well-known cardinals like the Secretary of State. There is a routine response to these requests. Sister Severia says His Eminence is not at present available, but perhaps the caller would like to write him a letter.[1]

'I want to talk to Casaroli about Emanuela.' The voice is suddenly angry. 'Give me Casaroli – otherwise she is dead.'

Sister Severia stiffens. Cibin had warned the switchboard staff to expect such a call, and devised the procedure she now urgently implements. Each nun-operator on duty has a notepad beside her. Sister Severia quickly scribbles the word 'Cibin' on hers and shoves the paper in front of one of her companions. The nun immediately dials the extension – 4617 – which the security chief has reserved exclusively for this moment.

The number rings one of four telephones on Cibin's desk. It is answered by an aide. He says Cibin is out. The nun remembers: the security chief had earlier called to say he was going to the Holy Office.[2]

She dials one of its extensions, 3296. Fr Bruno Fink answers. The secretary says Cibin has just left.

While these calls are being made, Sister Severia is following to the letter the instructions Cibin had given.

328

She notes the time, nine fifty-seven A.M., and asks the caller his name.

His anger is more pronounced. 'Stop wasting time. You can't trace this call. By then I'll be gone – and so will Emanuela. Give me Casaroli!'

On the other side of Sister Severia another nun is swiftly telephoning each of the five *vigilanza* guardhouses in the Vatican, asking them to track down Cibin.

Sister Severia is trying to placate the angry voice in her headset. 'Please understand. No one is tracing this call. But I must have a name.'

A nun further down the board has dialled 352496, the number of the *carabinieri* station in St Peter's Square. The duty officer there promptly placed a call to the *Questura* in Via Genova, Rome's police headquarters. He is connected to Captain Nicola Cavaliere, head of homicide in the Squadra Mobile, a division which also handles kidnappings. Cavaliere listens without comment while the duty officer at St Peter's reports that the Vatican switchboard is talking with someone claiming to be holding Emanuela. There is nothing Cavaliere can do until Cibin makes a formal approach for assistance; it is one of the many factors which annoy him whenever he has dealings with the Vatican. There is, he knows, no way he can even begin to trace the call. He must wait and see what develops.[3]

Sister Severia senses she cannot hold the voice on the line much longer.

The nun she has asked to find Cibin thrusts a note before her. It contains one word: *connettere*.

The security chief has been located and is on his way to the Secretariat of State; he has ordered the caller be put through to Casaroli's office.

All three lines are engaged.

Sister Severia tried the *Sostituto*, Mgr Eduardo Martinez Somalo. His first two lines are also occupied. The third extension, 3125, rings.

Somalo answers, then hurries into Casaroli's office.

The Secretary of State terminates his conversation and is at once connected to the caller.

Casaroli motions for one of his staff to listen on an extension. The priest takes a shorthand note of the conversation.[4]

It is brief – and shattering. The voice tells Casaroli Emanuela Orlandi will be released unharmed to her family only if the Italian government arranges for Mehmet Ali Agca to be freed.

Casaroli asks a question: 'Whom do you represent?'

The answer is evasive. 'We are persons interested in the release of Ali Agca.'

The Secretary of State begins to explain the matter is outside Vatican jurisdiction; that Agca is imprisoned in Italy; that the caller should discuss the question with the Italian Ministry of Justice; however, if he has any news about Emanuela –

The voice interjects. 'Italy knows. We have called ANSA' (the Italian wire service). 'It is a straightforward exchange. The girl for Agca.'

There is a click in Casaroli's ear. The man has hung up.

Moments later Cibin arrives.

After hearing what has happened he immediately calls another meeting of the special task force which had been formed at John Paul's request to handle the most bizarre crime in living Vatican memory.

Ten days have passed since Cibin sat in the pope's office and first briefed him on the kidnapping. On that Friday afternoon, the security chief's file contained only the sketchiest of details. Now it is filled with over a hundred sheets of paper. These include procedural reports indicating what steps he has initiated, which officials he has spoken to, what actions he has authorized.

The file also contains a rapidly growing number of personal statements. Cibin has taken depositions from each member of the Orlandi family. He has questioned all of

Emanuela's friends he was able to trace. He has spoken to her teachers. He has retraced her movements right up until the moment she was kidnapped. Yet the net return for this intensive enquiry is, Cibin readily concedes, woefully small.

Until this morning all he was certain of could easily be contained on a single sheet of paper.

On that Friday afternoon ten days ago, after John Paul had recovered from the shock – it is the first kidnapping of a Vatican citizen anyone can recall, and doubly distressing in that it involves a young girl – the pope had begun to explore with Cibin a salient question: motive.

The Orlandi family have no money to meet any ransom demand; the pay, like the position of a papal messenger, is relatively insignificant. In any case the anticipated telephone call demanding many millions of lire in exchange for Emanuela did not come. And indeed, if money was the issue, was it not likely the kidnappers would have addressed their demand to Ercole Orlandi's employer – the Vatican? That would surely be more logical.

Nor, concluded the pope from what Cibin had said, did it seem a case of *crime passionnel*; the security chief had quickly established Emanuela did not have any boy-friends. There is just a chance she has been taken by a gang specializing in snatching young girls and smuggling them to the Middle East where they are sold into the bondage of Arab brothels.

John Paul instinctively doubts this is the fate of Emanuela. The pope is convinced that the kidnapping of the girl is connected with the fact her father is a Vatican employee.

He had outlined a possibility on that Friday afternoon which now seems only too likely.

Emanuela, the pope reasoned, could well have innocently boasted to her friends that her father worked for the pontiff. To outsiders, the words 'papal messenger' might suggest a position in which Orlandi was actually privy to papal secrets – a person of importance.

Was it therefore not probable, John Paul had asked

331

Cibin, that Emanuela was being held for political purposes? That the intention behind the kidnapping was not to extract money from the Orlandis, but something far more important from the papacy?

Waiting in his office for the other members of the task force to arrive to discuss this morning's sensational twist of events, Camillo Cibin does again what he has done many times these past ten days; the security chief goes over Emanuela's file, searching for something he may have overlooked.

Emanuela had gone for her usual flute lesson at a music school in Rome. Afterwards she telephoned home to tell her sister she had been offered a job with Avon – selling the company's products at fashion shows.[5] She explained this could be just the break she so badly wanted: there was every chance she would be discovered by either a photographer or model agency scout at one of the shows – and be put on the way to fulfilling her dream of becoming a top fashion model.

Cibin had spent time with her father, trying to reassure him he should feel no guilt over what had happened. But the messenger had not been persuaded. The crime physically and mentally changed him. He aged overnight, going about his papal duties with bowed head to hide tears which welled in his eyes; his voice, once firm, is now tremulous.

Published coverage of the case began with Emanuela merely described as a missing person. But Cibin had known it would only be a matter of time before the publicity storm broke. He had counselled the Orlandis what to expect – and urged them to say nothing to the press.

Then, with John Paul's approval, the Vatican took its first public step to trace Emanuela when printers ran off 2,000 posters carrying a large photograph of the girl; beneath it was her physical description. The posters were plastered on billboards throughout the city.

The Vatican switchboard was soon flooded by calls from newspapers. But not a word was heard from the kidnappers.

Media interest was further heightened by a deliberate decision of John Paul's. After consulting Cibin, and alerting the family on what he intended to do, the pope had stood at his third-floor window and devoted part of a Sunday Angelus address to a passionate plea for Emanuela's safe release. His voice booming out over the square's loudspeaker system and relayed to more than a hundred countries by Vatican Radio, the pontiff addressed himself to the kidnappers.

'I share the anxiety and the anguish of her parents without losing hope for the sense of humanity of those responsible for this case.'

Afterwards, John Paul had word sent to the family he was optimistic his appeal would bring a response.

No one anticipated there would be a request for the release of Agca.

Cibin knows the diplomatic and legal position. The Holy See cannot possibly become involved in an exchange; it is out of the question even to consider raising the matter with the Italian government. Nor is there any possibility, should the demand arise, of the Vatican paying a ransom.

In these respects, Emanuela Orlandi can expect little from her father's employers. But in every other way the Vatican will do everything in its power to help. And Camillo Cibin will continue to use his own considerable contacts to try and locate the girl.

John Paul has personally ordered the security chief to spare nothing in those efforts.[6]

THE SECRETARIAT OF STATE
Thursday
Morning

It is now fourteen days since Emanuela was kidnapped, and the matter no longer intrudes on the business currently in hand within the Secretariat of State. While priests there remain considerate whenever Orlandi appears, they generally do not have the time to offer more than quick sympathy before turning back to their work.[7]

In three days John Paul will travel by helicopter to his summer palace at Castel Gandolfo. The Secretariat staff is under tremendous pressure to complete a number of briefing papers he has asked to see before he leaves.

A German prelate is preparing an assessment of the future of *die Grünen* in West Germany. He begins with a concise history of how 'The Greens' became a new phenomenon in Federal politics. As well as participating in seven of West Germany's eleven provincial legislatures, it is now represented in the national parliament in Bonn. There, the party has followed a policy consistent with its previous stance: 'participation without responsibility'. *Die Grünen* argues this is the only method which allows it to remain apart from the charges of careerism, bureaucracy and compromise its members level at opponents.

Many of them are disillusioned members of the German Left – the SPD, the German Communist Party and the trade unions.

This may account, argues the monsignor, why after less than three months in national politics, the future of the party seems debatable.

The reason is not hard to find. The prelate has a stack of reports from which he has abstracted an inescapable conclusion: the party is now hopelessly divided over how best to challenge the deployment of the NATO missiles, the very springboard from which it had launched itself upon the Federal national consciousness. Those members of *die Grünen* who have been elected to the Bundestag believe the most effective way to oppose deployment is to abandon 'participation without responsibility', and instead manipulate the parliamentary committee system to their own end.

The party's rank and file members are demanding vigorous action in the streets; they want to see more follow-ups to the 'International Nuremburg Tribunal Trial Against First-

Strike Nuclear Weapons', an impressive-sounding charade the party had held to no great effect.[8]

The monsignor's conclusion is that this factionalism could allow the Communists to dominate the party, perhaps even to the point where they gain an influence in the Federal parliament they have not so far achieved.

His recommendation is that the German Church should maintain its distance from *die Grünen*.

Clarissa McNair's broadcast on China has brought a spate of news to the Asia Desk.

By far the most important is confirmation of what its staff have until now only suspected. There is a thriving underground Catholic Church in the People's Republic. At least half of an estimated 100,000 Catholics in Shanghai are part of this 'loyal' or 'house' church, so called because believers vow loyalty to the pope and worship at home. It also seems that Catholics make up eighty per cent of all Chinese Christians. In the past year over a hundred Catholic churches have reopened, several in the wake of McNair's broadcast, a further sign her documentary was well received.[9]

The Peking government has approved the printing of a million Bibles in the current year. They cost $5.60 a copy, a high price in a country where factory workers earn $45 a month. But demand exceeds supply.

Yet serious difficulties persist for Catholics in the People's Republic. A number of those who have heard McNair's broadcast have written to the Vatican to explain that, although they are not discriminated against in such everyday matters as getting a job or an apartment, they have little chance of playing a political role in the country, and almost certainly their children will not be able to get into university.

A common fear among many correspondents is that the relaxing of religious freedom will be swiftly curbed the moment the authorities view it as a threat. Therefore, conclude the Asia Desk analysts, the greatest threat to a Catholic revival could be its own very evident appeal to young Christians.

Only a week after McNair's broadcast, the Peking *People's Daily* published an article calling for increased efforts to promote atheism, and stressed that religion must not be allowed to entice the young.[10]

The desk staff are patiently trying to place the relaxation of religious freedom in China within the context of the nation's life as a whole; there are, after all, only about four million Christians of all denominations in the country – about one-third of one per cent of the population – though the number has been growing since the Communists took power in 1949.[11]

The question which preoccupies the priest-mandarins is how far religious tolerance is part of the general loosening of constraints since the days of Mao Tse-tung's dictatorship.

They believe nowadays religious freedom in China can be equated with political self-expression: both are more than window-dressing but fall short of having serious practical application.

The country's eight minority political parties had faded from sight under Mao. Now they have been allowed to function again, although there is no possibility of this opposition being allowed to present policies to the electorate.

It is equally not permissible for any form of religion to challenge the Party, especially over questions of moral authority.

The Asia Desk diplomats believe, despite some encouraging pointers this past month, the People's Republic will continue to rebuff any suggestion that John Paul visit the country.

The conclusion they know will disappoint the pope – though they will attempt to disguise it in the same ambiguous language which so often confronts them when assessing information from the People's Republic.

* * *

Lebanese-born Mgr Mounged El-Hachem is pondering a familiar question: the future of Yasser Arafat.[12]

El-Hachem has charted the growing number of PLO fighters who reject Arafat's more moderate policies in favour of a pure holy war against Israel.[13] The Arabic-speaking monsignor is one of several diplomats who have been discreetly encouraging Arafat to maintain his moderate stance, urging this as the only way the PLO can hope to achieve their dream of nationhood. During the past month – in the face of mass desertions – Arafat has become increasingly resistant to the Holy See's views.

Arafat recently told the pro-nuncio in Syria that Arab moderation had been misunderstood in Israel as impotence, and has allowed the Israelis to act as they please on the West Bank, in the Lebanon and elsewhere in the Middle East.

The report had arrived on El-Hachem's desk shortly after Arafat had been expelled from Damascus to Tunisia for spreading 'continuous slander' against Syria.

Since then, El-Hachem has received two further reports. Both trouble him deeply. The first argues that the expulsion of Arafat is the precursor to something far more serious. Syria will mobilize the radical elements of the PLO into a powerful force, capable of launching its holy war against Israel. The Middle East could go up in flames.[14]

The second report is from the Chinese-born secretary who runs the Holy See legation in Tunis City. The secretary had spoken to Arafat soon after he arrived in Tunis. Arafat, too, believes Syria is poised to take over the PLO and use it as a torch-bearer against Israel. The secretary has been unable to obtain any clear impression of Arafat's own future intentions; he expressed the opinion the PLO chairman had, for once, appeared irresolute, 'long on rhetoric but short on objectives'.[15]

These two reports go some way to confirming what yet other briefings are saying: the conflict in the Middle East may now be entering its most dangerous phase.

All the evidence El-Hachem has received suggests that

the intensity of the pressures and the inherent indecisiveness of the present ruling order in the Arab world are the two factors which will combine to topple the existing Arab equilibrium. In its place could come a radical, populist Islamic ideology – more dangerous than anything the region has seen since the first days of Nasser.

Yet El-Hachem remains uncertain this is what the future holds. 'The situation is like two different jigsaw puzzles which have become mixed together.'

Nothing, he has told colleagues, when it comes to Middle East power-plays is quite what it seems. That is why he refuses to come to any firm conclusion about the future of Yasser Arafat.

El-Hachem knows that a man who has survived as long as the PLO chairman has, can never be written off.[16]

The flow of reports going through the Secretariat of State and the Council for the Public Affairs of the Church includes the almost obligatory accounts from all six nuncios stationed in Central America. In El Salvador the regime's forces have begun a new drive against rebels – and those priests who comfort them. In Costa Rica, American diplomats are pressurizing the government to take tougher measures against its guerrillas – and those prelates who condone rebel actions. In Honduras there is growing anxiety that neighbouring Nicaragua will invade. In Nicaragua there is an identical fear, only this time the United States is cast in the role of aggressor – the theme is being actively promoted by the five priests in the Marxist government. In Guatemala, the Rios Montt regime is becoming more hostile towards the Catholic Church.

Each report emphasizes that the local hierarchies are trying to find more effective roles in these crisis situations. But for the moment the Holy See's influence in the region seems to be at its lowest point this year.

★ ★ ★

From Geneva Nuncio Edoardo Rovida has confirmed what Casaroli has been hearing from other quarters.

The arms limitation talks are deadlocked.

After talking to both the Russian and American negotiators in Geneva, Rovida is certain that there is absolutely no prospect of a summit meeting in the foreseeable future between the Soviet and American leaders.

The news is confirmed in the latest CIA weekly briefing to John Paul.

ROME POLICE HEADQUARTERS
Friday
Evening

Captain Nicola Cavaliere knows what is happening, and does not like it. To the homicide chief the situation reeks of something he has no patience with – *politica*.[17]

The whole case, he has grumbled to his detectives, is steeped in politics. From the moment he became involved in the kidnapping of Emanuela Orlandi, the slim and hard-eyed Cavaliere has been embroiled in *politica*.

For a start there is the political question of who is actually in charge of the investigation. Normally, Cavaliere would have complete jurisdiction over any crime he investigates within the city limits. Not this time. Geographically the Vatican may only be 108 acres on the edge of downtown Rome but, as Cavaliere has found out, it is also a world apart – one which he cannot ever enter without invitation.

Cavaliere had wanted to question not only the Orlandi family, but also their neighbours and the papal messenger's colleagues; he wanted to talk to Vatican priests who know Orlandi, to wander through the Apostolic Palace, to conduct his business as he usually does: without fear or favour, going where he pleases, being refused by no one on penalty of hindering a police officer in his enquiries.

Within the Vatican, Cavaliere was allowed to question Emanuela's immediate family. But other than that, his efforts have been ham-strung.

These interviews, and those he has done with Emanuela's school friends, produced very little. The exceptional thing about Emanuela's life is that it had been so unexceptional. Apart from her wish to be a model, there was nothing of substance for Cavaliere to follow. His detectives had checked the city's model agencies. No one has ever heard of the missing girl.

Typically, he growled to his aides, he had only been told at the last moment that the posters of the girl were going up. And the first he'd heard about the pope's appeal to the kidnappers was on the one-thirty television news.

Next day had come the demand that Agca be released in exchange for the girl. Then, at least, he had been immediately alerted by the Vatican. And then, too, for the first time Cavaliere could take complete command of the case.

He called Judge Martella's office and said he wanted Agca brought down to headquarters for questioning.

Martella agreed.

Both had also agreed it should be kept a close secret.

Standing at an office window in the *Questura*, Cavaliere wonders again how this agreement has been wrecked. Below, in the large square courtyard around which the police headquarters is built, he can see television crews, radio reporters and print-media journalists.

Agca was still on the way from Rebibbia prison – to which he has been moved again from Ascoli Piceno – when ANSA, the Italian news agency, announced he was coming.

What perturbs Cavaliere is who tipped off the wire service, and why?

The police chief thinks it no coincidence that not just the Italian but also foreign media are present in the square. Somebody wants to make very sure Agca gets the maximum of exposure.

Yet what he had said when questioned about Emanuela's kidnapping has proved of no value whatsoever.

Agca arrived at police headquarters at seven-forty P.M., minutes ahead of the first journalists. He had been brought up to the third floor, to an interrogation room close to Cavaliere's office. There, two judge-prosecutors had questioned Agca for twenty minutes. By then it was clear he had no connection with the kidnapping of Emanuela.

Now, at eight-fifteen, Agca is escorted from the room by half a dozen *carabinieri*. They are taking him to the truck which will return him to Rebibbia.

When he reaches the courtyard, the sunset gives an ethereal glow to Agca's electric-blue track suit.

Spotting him, the reporters converge. The *carabinieri* make no effort to head them off.

Astonishing as it seems, several journalists will later think Agca and his guards appear to be acting in concert.

Agca raises his handcuffed wrists and begins to bellow at the delighted pressmen.

'Leave this poor girl!'

He is referring to Emanuela. His voice sounds slurred.

The *carabinieri* obligingly move aside to let the television cameramen get better pictures. Reporters record and scribble furiously as Agca continues with this extraordinary press conference.[18]

'I have nothing with criminals, with terrorists. I am with Italy! With the Italian people!'

Agca punctuates his sentences by opening and closing his hands in gestures of prayer.

'I am with the Vatican! I repeat again: I condemn this criminal act!'

There is a curious quality about the words. They sound almost rehearsed.

So do the actions of the *carabinieri*. Slowly – 'painfully slowly', one reporter notes – they begin to edge Agca towards the truck.

A reporter asks: 'Who are the kidnappers?'

Agca stops in his tracks. So does the escort. They stand aside to give an unobstructed view of Agca.

'I have no idea! No knowledge! It's only a dis-human act! I condemn it firmly. I am against each thing with terrorists. The Italian state has to respond with firmness!'

This last sentence is delivered in fluent Italian. It is one frequently used by government spokesmen when condemning terrorism.

Agca glances around at the cameramen and reporters. Later they will recall the dark circles under his eyes, his oddly slurred syllables, the gestures which seem almost conditioned. But now it is his words which electrify them.

'I am repentant for the attempt on the pope! I admire the pope! I thank Italian justice and the Italian state. I am very well in the Italian gaols! I appeal again: leave the poor innocent girl!'

The escort again start gradually to move Agca towards the van.

A reporter, June Dexter of NBC, remarks, 'He is now finished what he has to say.'

She is wrong.

Another reporter shouts, 'Was it the Bulgarians that sent you to Italy?'

Agca pauses in his stride. The escort once more halts. Agca appears to be concentrating. He nods.

'Yes. I said Bulgarians.'

A gasp sweeps the reporters. Another question. This time Agca does not hesitate.

'Yes! I said the attempt on the pope was done by the Bulgarian Secret Service!'

Agca is again shouting, and appears intent on emphasizing his words. He stresses 'attempt', and 'Bulgarian Secret Service'.

June Dexter asks in English a question: 'And the KGB?'

Agca responds in English. 'Yes! And the KGB. I said I have been trained especially by the KGB! International terrorists!'

'Where?'

There is a babble of questions from other reporters. The first words of Agca's reply are lost. Then his voice roars above the others.

'I have been trained also in Bulgaria. I have been in Bulgaria. I trained. Several travels . . .'

The police are pushing him into the van now. Agca is anxious not to go. His eyes rake the reporters. One of them asks who had trained him.

'I have been trained by special experts of international terrorism!'

'From which country?'

'Syria. Bulgaria. I stayed several times!'

June Dexter fires another question. 'Were you ever in the Soviet Union?'

'No! I have not been in the Soviet Union! But it doesn't matter. Soviet Union doesn't have any direct connection by the terrorists! It uses in the Middle East, Syria. In Europe, Bulgaria. I say this many times! I have enough proofs for assassination, for every actions.'

Dexter asks whether Antonov was involved in the papal assassination.

Agca cannot disguise the triumph in his voice. 'I say Sergei Antonov was with me during attempt!'

At last the truck begins to roll slowly forward.

Agca's final words are shouted through a window.

'Antonov my friend!'

The Bulgarian Connection has been resuscitated almost immediately after the Holy See and the CIA have concluded that there will be no summit between the leaders of the United States and the Soviet Union.

19
Roman Responses

We should have remembered. Midsummer in Rome is not a good time to ask questions, let alone expect sensible answers.

The weather is no help. More so than other years the city is like an unattended furnace. Most Romans have fled to the surrounding hills and beaches. It's *Ferragosto,* an annual holiday which involves shuttering up public buildings and private dwellings as if plague were about to descend in the wake of the heat.

Those who must remain – they include Cardinal Casaroli and most of his diplomats, the staffs of Vatican Radio and *L'Osservatore Romano* and ourselves – exist in an environment where there is hardly a shop or trattoria open. Lambert Greenan is right: it does something to the mind when a haircut seems impossible to get in a city of almost four million persons.

John Paul, along with his personal retinue, is out at Castel Gandolfo in the Alban Hills, for a long papal retreat from the debilitating Roman high summer.

We have been there a couple of times this month, still trying to chart the balance of power in a pontificate where the slightest tremor or the subtlest nuance, however fleeting, is to many unsettling. At Castel Gandolfo it can come down to this: who is allowed to use the pool after the pope completes his morning thirty laps of mixed crawl and breast-stroke; who gets invited to stroll with him through the gardens, and for how long; who not only walks but also sits down with the pontiff for lunch. And where is a guest positioned at table? By John Paul's elbow or further away? Those close to the pope would have us believe such matters are significant. Naturally we note them, though it's frankly

344

not always easy to fit such signs into the wider picture we are attempting to assemble.

Officially the pope is on holiday. This means he grants few audiences to foreign emissaries or bishops and nuncios who are visiting Rome. In practice a secular diplomat or a prelate with sufficiently urgent business is able to drive out and see John Paul. And on Friday evenings, without fail, a US embassy car arrives at the villa with the weekly CIA briefing.

As Kabongo says, 'We have simply moved the centre of the Church, not closed it down!'[1]

John Paul, for his part, continues to work harder than most senior corporation executives. He is up at five every morning, celebrates mass in the chapel adjoining his bedroom, and then ploughs his way through a couple of hours of paperwork before breakfast. In the Summary File he generally notates a number of items on which he wants fuller briefings. Afterwards he studies any reports from the Secretariat of State, the Public Affairs Council and the various Congregations that may have been left over from yesterday.

Following breakfast he swims for an hour. He had the pool specially built. When someone joked about the cost – rumour says it was Marcinkus – John Paul reportedly replied the pool was far cheaper than the price of a papal funeral and the ensuing Conclave.[2]

The remainder of the morning he devotes to more paperwork and receiving important callers. Casaroli has been out most days, Poggi twice and Tucci of Vatican Radio once; among other things they briefed the pope before his short pilgrimage to Lourdes.

After lunch John Paul naps for an hour. Then follows four further hours of uninterrupted desk work, divided between Church affairs and matters of State. It is during this period that he prepares, approves and revises the directives for his nuncios on the steps they are to take.

Dinner, usually with Dziwisz and Kabongo, is from

eight-thirty to ten. There is almost always discussion about events on the evening television news.

Later John Paul will spend up to two more hours reading and working with Church and State documents. He is rarely in bed before one A.M.

It is an arduous schedule for both the pontiff and his staff. Kabongo insists they are motivated by a common desire which has sustained them during a year that has already proved unusually demanding. The secretary describes it with a simplicity which is succinct and poignant. 'The Holy Father is trying to make peace enter the minds of every person on earth. We are all here to try and help him.'[3]

But are they coming anywhere near to achieving this laudable aim?

Driving back and forth to Castel Gandolfo or visiting the Apostolic Palace – with the pope and his Secretariat absent the place appears strangely deserted and more overpowering than ever – we remind ourselves of some basic truths about the role of this pontificate in international politics.

John Paul, probably more than any other modern pope, has made sure the activities of the Roman Catholic Church are known in nearly every nation and have a bearing on most aspects of human life.

Eugene Rostow, Reagan's adviser on arms control until peremptorily removed, once argued the Vatican was not only the focal point of a vast spiritual and cultural community, and the highly visible symbol of a living system of ideas and values, but also a well-developed governmental machine: a co-ordinated body for a far-flung multinational bureaucracy. Rostow maintained that any discussion of the Church's international role must include both its spiritual and temporal dimensions.[4]

John Paul's actions perfectly illustrate the point. In the wake of the assassination attempt he has shown renewed determination to promote the Holy See's sway at an international level. Building on the truism that the Church has for centuries exerted a profound and incalculable spiritual and cultural influence in many parts of the world, shaping the minds of men and the impulses which govern their decision-making, he has inextricably entwined Catholicism and modern-day politics.

At Castel Gandolfo the pope and his men continue to employ every permissible expedient in the diplomatic book to perform what they insist is their age-old function as peacemakers.

On the pope's desk in his summer palace is a framed quotation bearing the words Paul VI used when addressing the United Nations General Assembly in October, 1965: 'No More War, War Never Again! Peace, It Is Peace Which Must Guide The Destinies Of People And Of All Mankind.'

The question which concerns us is: how successful is John Paul in forwarding this aim?

He is not working alone, of course. Great though his personal influence is, it remains small when compared with the power of the Church as a whole. Not only is its organization dedicated to the moral and spiritual education of Catholics and indeed western society at large, the Church is also a powerful voice in the political awareness of the West.

Yet the same question applies: how well is it succeeding?

There is, to be sure, a Catholic vision of reality which is refreshing. In this pontificate that vision is intensely spiritual and highly practical. The pope and his prelates exude a feeling they really believe in heaven and in hell; that there is as much evil in the world as there is good. They seem more than ready to give the Devil his due.

It is clear to us their rules of engagement have not basically changed since the beginning of the year. The target that dominated their thinking in January persists: the need for sanity over the nuclear arms issue, the need to abolish the threat of war. They are, as Kabongo says, endeavouring to achieve peace not only for the rest of this century, but for all time.[5] It is a powerful thought. Yet how much does it take into account the abiding moral weaknesses of mankind?

★ ★ ★

In West Germany, secularization shows no sign of abating; there is a decline in Church attendance, particularly among young people, many of whom feel the Federal hierarchy should be more militant in its opposition to the siting of Cruise and Pershing missiles.

From the Irish Republic Nuncio Gaetano Alibrandi continues to report on the increasing number of what he has termed 'lip service Catholics', whose who attend Church solely for form's sake. The nuncio is also concerned over the growing problem of unemployment among Ireland's youth; many when they leave school have little or no chance of finding work. This, he thinks, could provide a breeding ground for unrest. We have been told that in one recent report Alibrandi argued that in many ways the Irish Republic should be regarded as 'part of the Third World' – impoverished in a material sense, ineffectually governed, having social services which cannot cope, and a population increasingly involved in 'the black economy, avoiding their taxes and social responsibilities'. The nuncio seems to fear the Irish hierarchy is not providing the sort of leadership needed.

At another level he has been having discreet and informal discussions on Northern Ireland with the new British ambassador in Dublin. Presumably they are sounding each other out. One of the nuncio's friends quotes Alibrandi as saying, 'Whenever we get into delicate areas, His Excellency talks to me about Sicily. He's very knowledgeable about the place. It isn't quite what I have in mind for a serious political discussion on Ulster.' Alibrandi remains as firmly committed as ever to getting British troops out of the North.

There is a persistent rumour, one that priests from Dublin bring with them to Rome, that Alibrandi is again out of favour with the administration of Dr Garret Fitzgerald: it seems some of his cabinet still view with suspicion the nuncio's continuing contacts with members of Sinn Fein, the political wing of the IRA.

Members of the 'Irish Mafia' in the Vatican tell us that it would take more than the present Irish government to remove the nuncio. One of them put it bluntly. 'He's a bit like J. Edgar Hoover. He knows many of the cupboards where the skeletons of Ireland's political life are stored. It's good insurance.'

This certainly fits the picture of the Alibrandi we know. Of all the papal nuncios we have met he is assuredly most like a diplomatic squirrel. He has an insatiable curiosity and a remarkable memory; he can recall in minute detail lengthy conversations, never forgetting a nicety. No doubt he has a number of enemies, but he also has some powerful friends, including Charles Haughey, the former Irish prime minister. With support like that it would take a great deal of leverage to move Gaetano Alibrandi from a listening post which Rome regards as of considerable importance.

Archbishop Bruno Heim, recovered from his operation, is back in London and has also had 'a very private dinner' there with Sir Mark Heath. Both no doubt reported to their respective governments their exchange of views on Ulster. While the exact details remain firmly locked away in the Foreign Office in London and in one of Mgr Audrys Backis's filing cabinets in the Council for the Public Affairs of the Church, a little digging, coupled with some intelligent guesswork, leaves us with the feeling that Mrs Thatcher does not favour the suggestion of an United Nations peacekeeping force replacing British troops in the province. Nor, it seems, does the view now raise much interest in Dublin government circles.

The entire future of the United States' Church is one which continues to cause grave concern in the Vatican. Archbishop Pio Laghi's recent reports paint a dismaying portrait of disobedience across virtually the entire ecclesiastical spectrum of the country. And in Central and South America the theology of liberation movement flourishes.

In terms of papal observance, it seems to us the Church, under John Paul, is being challenged from within as perhaps never before.

All this makes it that much harder to give the Holy See its correct placing on the current international political chessboard.

It views itself not as a political but an exclusively religious organization; the force it applies is spiritual and moral, certainly not economic, financial or military. Yet Stalin missed the point when he derided the pope's lack of divisions. The Holy See has a universal mission which transcends political borders. That experienced Curialist, Fr Robert A. Graham, contends that the Holy See 'does not want to be identified with any political bloc, but seeks constantly to maintain its own freedom of action in the interests of the supernatural mission which it considers to have received directly from Christ, its founder'.[6]

In the same breath, Graham concedes the Church leadership cannot 'operate in highly sensitive areas without drawing to itself the judgements and criticisms that befall those who deal with human problems'.[7]

Another difficulty is the continued stereotyping of the role of the Holy See and the Church in the general world order.

The Left see John Paul's policies, in Graham's terms, 'as the religious arm of reaction, frantically obsessed with fear of Communism and moodily resentful of this rival ideology of salvation. It is ready to support the status quo in the name of order. It is ready for war, if need be, to save the world from Communism.'[8]

For the Right, argues this distinguished historian – Graham is the associate editor of the Vatican's World War II papers – the stereotype is more flattering. The Right places the Church in the van of the fight against Communism, 'a bastion of order standing firm against the revolutionary waves of our times. It has never been taken in by the slogan of false progress.'[9]

Like Graham, we feel these polarized assumptions hardly reflect reality and are no proper basis for understanding the complex forces which dictate so many of the present papal initiatives.

Because of its traditional position – a universal not a national church, sufficiently determined and powerful to resist strongly pressures from secular powers which infringe its sacred evangelical mission, and with a pronounced record of opposition to Communism – governments in both the East and West have historically paid serious attention to popes and their pronouncements.

Up until the days of Pius XII, governments of the free world almost automatically assumed they could depend upon the moral authority of the pope to support them. Communist regimes, in turn, looked upon the papacy as implacably hostile.

John XXIII and to some extent Paul VI blurred these demarcation lines; their policies seemed those of the genuinely 'non-aligned'. Outwardly, Pope John Paul appears at times to be making calculated effort to be acceptable to both superpower blocs. His criticisms of western consumerism can be just as harsh as his condemnation of abuses of human rights in godless societies. In that respect he does indeed fit the ideograph of Kabongo's spiritual Hercules.

And, as Fr Graham says, 'These moves, though motivated by human considerations, are political in implication and take their place in the political history of the contemporary world. Does the pope have any choice?'[10]

At the best of times it would not be easy to find the answer. In the enervating heat of a Roman high summer it's just that much harder.

We go along to the Secretariat of State. One of our sources there suggests we stroll with him through the Vatican Gardens. In spite of the baking heat the grass is lush and the foliage green. A lot of attention, and water, must go into creating the effect.

Our monsignor is glum. He speaks of the Holy See being 'in a nadir when it comes to making world leaders see sense'. He keeps saying, 'they don't want to listen'. He thinks there could be a 'real war' in the Middle East, that Chile is in 'a dangerous state', that 'South Africa is simmering' and that the Russians 'might yet try something in Poland'.

It is mid-afternoon when we leave this depressed prelate and walk back into Rome. Only then does a question strike us. Why, in his catalogue of pessimism, did our host mention neither the kidnapping of Emanuela Orlandi nor the revived Bulgarian Connection?

Two weeks later, Rudi offers an answer. We have joined him for dinner. He says our priest, and indeed the Vatican, has taken up a well-prepared position over both the missing schoolgirl and the born-again *Pista Bulgara*.

With a touch of malice which so often gives an edge to his observations, the intelligence officer claims that, 'God's little men like it both ways. They are doing a lot of hand-wringing. But they're careful to remind everybody both events are Italy's problem. God forbid anybody should think they have any influence on the matter – apart from the pope doing some praying for the return of the girl.'

We are sitting in Galeassi's, in Rome's Trastevere district. Rudi says Mussolini used to come here. It's an unpretentious restaurant. But the fish soup is reputed to be the finest in town.

Tonight is Rudi's treat, his way of bidding farewell. He has been posted. He would not want us to say where. But in a week's time Galeassi's, and everything else in Rome which now preoccupies him, will be only a memory; over *Negronis*, we agree our paths are unlikely to cross again.

It is almost a month since we last saw him. Then we had glimpsed him dining in the Excelsior with a French diplomat, stiff and formal in their business suits. Rudi had given no sign of recognition. For Galeassi's he's wearing a

Hawaiian shirt, Levi's and sandals; he looks as if he's been born and bred in this raffish quarter of Rome.

He is as gregarious as ever, and a cliché goldmine so far as information goes. He plunges straight into the Emanuela kidnapping. Like the Moro case of five years ago, the snatching of the girl has been of prime interest to his service.

'In Pullach they've got the idea the *Wunderkind* of our terror groups could have been involved in the snatch.'

He explains it is the demand for the release of Agca which has worked up the interest of the BND and probably half a dozen other western intelligence organizations.

Rudi, in our experience, is anything but anti-Italian when it comes to assessing their security services. But this time he is scathing.

'The whole lot of them have made an absolute shambles.'

The fish soup arrives: mounds of lobster tails, flat fish, shrimps, squid, octopus, sea trout, all on a bed of freshly baked bread in a rich garlic-flavoured sauce.

Rudi partially empties his bowl before he resumes. We take turns to make notes, but he is going at such a pace that, like the soup, it's the flavour rather than the details which we mostly catch.

Tonight he's more Italian than ever: he shrugs and gesticulates; he sends for Giuseppe, the owner, and holds an animated discussion on the merits of a Sardinian wine. That settled, he wants extra pieces of lobster. A steaming plateful is brought. Then he wants garlic bread. It really is a performance. In between he keeps up a flow of views on the Orlandi kidnapping.

'A month ago I thought she was just another nice kid. Now I'm not sure. There's a lot of talk, she kept some very fancy company. Guys in the drug scene. That kind of thing. Maybe she is just a nice kid. But she sure as hell was playing close to the fire. Probably that's why the Vatican is keeping a distance – doesn't want to get mixed up in anything with the faintest sniff of embarrassment.'

From anybody else this would be too hard to accept. It flies in the face of almost everything we have been told. Later, we both realize we had reminded ourselves several times during dinner that Rudi does have, so far as we can check, a remarkable record for getting the facts straight.

He spread his hands. 'Two weeks after she disappears, DIGOS suddenly turns St Peter's Square into a maximum security area. They stop everybody and everything. A kid could hardly take his bike there without the thing being stripped. What was all that about? Window dressing. Letting the pope know the Italians are taking the case seriously!'

Rudi doesn't hide his disgust as he reminds us what led up to this show of activity in the square.

'A reporter – *Mensch!* a reporter! – gets a call to go and collect Emanuela's ID card right under the noses of half a dozen policemen. One of the kidnap gang had just left it there, right by their boots. The whole thing's covered with the girl's handwriting.'

Rudi shakes his head.

'Then the pope makes another appeal. That's the craziest thing I've ever known. God knows who advised him to do it. Getting the pope involved gives the case a whole new cachet. The kidnappers know now they don't have an ordinary kid. They've got somebody special. Somebody the pope wants back! That gives them bargaining power. My God, the basic rule of any kidnapping is you play it down; you don't get someone like the pope involved. That just gets everything out of hand.'

Had he offered any advice to anyone on the matter?

He shrugs. 'You ever tried to advise the Vatican?'

But he does say the West German ambassador to the Holy See has conveyed 'certain advice' from his government to Casaroli.

'The pope makes another appeal. More messages turn up. And all those phone calls come to newspapers and television. Madness.'

He swallows another spoonful of soup and refills our glasses.

'I told my people. This has to be an Italian-only job. Not even our dumbest terrorists behave like this. Especially after that business with the tape.'

Nearly a month after Emanuela disappeared, a purported member of the gang had directed the police to a corner of St Peter's Square, by the Bronze Door. Near one of Bernini's columns they were told they would find a cassette tape containing positive proof Emanuela was alive, as well as fresh demands from the kidnappers.

DIGOS combed the place. No tape was found. Another apparent member of the kidnap gang called Rome newspapers and accused the Vatican of stealing the tape.

'Crazy!' says Rudi. 'Absolutely crazy! It's crazy to publish such nonsense. That just stirs up everybody. The press scream "conspiracy". The Vatican get more paranoid than ever! And the pope gets more advice to make more appeals. Crazy! *Mensch!* Absolutely crazy!'

Rudi goes on shredding the investigation: the Vatican for not giving full access to Italian investigators; the pope for continuing to make public appeals. So far John Paul has made seven, including reciting an Ave Maria for the missing girl before a crowd of 50,000 in St Peter's Square. He had flown by helicopter from Castel Gandolfo especially to do so.

The fish soup finally finished, Rudi orders gorganzola. He has the wheel of cheese brought to our table and begins taking slices to serve us. A bottle of port is ordered.

While he is preoccupied carving the cheese, we question him about Agca's involvement in this bizarre story. Following that first telephone call to Casaroli there have been four additional demands that Agca be freed. We suggest their timing is interesting, coming as they did when Judge Martella was in Sofia, exploring the Bulgarian Connection at its very source. Coinciding with the demands, a barrage of further tape recordings and written messages surfaced in various parts of Rome.

The tapes contain gruesome sounds allegedly of Emanuela being tortured, but exhaustive police laboratory tests have been unable to confirm they are genuine. Some of the other voices on the tapes, according to linguistic experts, could be Turkish, Russian, Bulgarian, Latvian or even South American. The words they use – like the written messages – are the meandering inventions of the authentic lunatic fringe.

'Except one,' says Rudi. 'That was written in German, good *Hochdeutsch*. And logical. My people believe it was written by somebody who knows the ropes. No crazy threats. Just a promise of "punitive action". In other words, the girl's life was forefeit unless Agca is freed. That's crazy, of course. Nobody is going to trade Agca for Emanuela.'

Then, we ask, what is the point of these repeated demands he should be freed?

Rudi surprises us. Most of the tables nearby are now empty. It's late even for Trastevere. He hunches himself forward and lowers his voice as he outlines a scenario which he prefaces by saying he expects we will find it hard to believe.

'Agca was, is, and will remain the one exploitable element in all we have spoken about this year. That you accept?'

We nod.

He goes on. His tone is measured, almost lecturing. 'In our opinion – and I want you to understand I am speaking for my people in this matter – in *our* opinion, there is a definite link between the kidnapping and the revival of the Bulgarian Connection.'

This time he waits while we write down his words.

'A definite link,' he repeats. 'Most certainly.'

Rudi begins to develop his theme. 'The girl was kidnapped at the very time the pope was riding high in Poland. By the way, we are confident he knew when he was in Cracow she had been taken. But he had advice on that.'

'From Cibin of course,' one of us says.

A look of annoyance crosses Rudi's face. 'Not at all. Cibin

doesn't have that kind of influence. Probably Casaroli and the pope together decided to keep the thing quiet until they got back to Rome. They wouldn't want anything to detract from their Polish trip.'

We continue making notes.

'But the business with Levi partly ruined it. That was no coincidence the way he went out on a limb like he did. He got a nudge. Our feeling is it was an American.'

'Come on, Rudi!' One of us can't resist interrupting.

'Come on, nothing! You just listen! Not everybody in Washington likes the idea of the pope and Walesa being as close as they are. Neither do a lot of people in the Secretariat of State. That you accept. OK?'

We say OK.

'So Levi goes public, and finds out he's been set up. It almost worked. The Vatican had to sit on it hard.'

We wait. This is highly interesting – and highly speculative too. But what if anything has it to do with Emanuela and Agca?

Rudi's answer is ready.

'Everything we know points to the girl being snatched for straightforward kidnapping purposes. Maybe for sex. Maybe money. Maybe for both. Every kidnapper in this city works on the basis that in every family there's a relative somewhere who can raise enough lire to make it worth while. A few million. So that was the idea at the beginning. Straightforward kidnapping. OK?'

We nod. Rudi is taking his time, making sure we follow.

'So the kid goes in the car and is taken off somewhere, probably by a bunch of amateurs. But news travels fast. Somebody more professional hears what has happened. "Uh-uh," they say, "here we have something." The original kidnappers are contacted by the professionals. A deal is struck.'

Rudi shrugs. 'Or maybe no deal. The original kidnappers get wiped out. No problem. It happens. Check the crime figures.'

Another shrug. 'Maybe not. Maybe the girl is sold to the professionals. It doesn't matter. Now she's theirs. OK?'

He pours more coffee from the pot he ordered.

'They know the real value of the girl. That her papa works for the pope. It makes no difference what he does. He works for the *pope*. That's the point. They also know a lot of people would like Agca back in the news. I don't mean the newspapers. I mean people in my business. When Agca is on the front pages the conspiracy theory is there as well. And that suits a lot of people.'

One of us again interrupts. 'Come on, Rudi, what are you trying to say?'

'*Mensch!* Will you *listen*! I'm not "trying to say" anything. I'm just telling you what I think is the likeliest reason Agca is involved. And he is. You don't get five demands for his release from a bunch of disorganized crazies. Crazy they may be. But there's method in their craziness. Without Agca, Emanuela would be nothing great. But Agca gives it a new dimension. If you think that's coincidence, you'll believe anything.'

We suggest a brief pause. Putting down on paper what he is saying while trying to evaluate its worth is exhausting.

Rudi is impatient to continue. 'Six weeks ago the Bulgarian Connection was dead. So much so the Bulgars allowed Martella to visit Sofia. He goes there last month. They sweet talk him and show him all kinds of things. But, like the CIA have been suggesting, the Bulgars claim there is no connection. Martella comes home and finds his star witness, Agca, back on the front pages as a trade-off for Emanuela. If you think that's another coincidence, you *will* believe anything!'

There's no anger in Rudi's voice, only confidence.

'No. The timing was deliberate. Nobody expects the girl will be returned for Agca. That's not the point. What was wanted was the Bulgarian Connection, through Agca, brought back from the dead in the most dramatic possible way. What's happened is a sort of modern-day Lazarus.

The question is: who would want Agca, so to speak, to take up his bed and walk back into the limelight?'

Rudi does not wait for a response.

'Not the Bulgars. For them he's bad news. The Turks? Maybe; his old terrorist friends, the Grey Wolves, might like him sprung. The KGB? Could be – to kill him. And there's one other prospect. The CIA.'

We both look at the nearly empty bottle of port. Rudi has drunk most of it. Yet he doesn't seem drunk. But the CIA? We shake our heads. Rudi, one of us says, you've got to be, if not actually joking, then wide of the mark.

Now there is anger in his voice. 'I didn't say it *was* the CIA. I said it *might* be. Who the hell do you think tipped off the press Agca was on his way to the *Questura*? I'll tell you something. One of the RAI radio guys told me their call came from a source the CIA always uses!'

Rudi pushes aside the bottle of port. He is hunched over the table, his head thrust forward towards ours.

'If you don't think the Company has its claws into the Italian underworld, then it's time you gave up!'

A thought strikes him. 'You ever see the transcript of the Sindona trial? It's stacked with evidence he was a money man for the Mafia and a financial conduit for CIA operations while working with the Vatican. Read it. That will give you any proof you need!'[11]

Rudi suddenly looks tired. He's been talking almost non-stop for a couple of hours. Even so, his eyes reveal he remains uncertain we are convinced.

'Listen. You can take it or leave it. But my people have a pretty good idea that dragging Agca into the Emanuela case has at least the blessing of the Company. It's a great new start for the *Pista Bulgara*. And the Company seems again to have decided the Bulgars were behind Agca all the time. Behind the Bulgars – who else? – the KGB. And ultimately, Andropov, who of course is not going to sit down with Reagan and settle the missile question man to man. Interesting, *ja*?'

It is hard for us to think of a more stunning way for Rudi to bid us farewell than the one he has chosen.

We walk with him out of Trastevere, hardly exchanging a word.

He gives us a telephone number in Frankfurt to call should we ever need him in future. He explains the person there can always get a message to him. Quick handshakes and he is gone.

We are too preoccupied with our own thoughts to do what we normally do: compare notes. But next day we decide the only proper course is to report Rudi's comments as he gave them. There is no way we can check all – or even most – of what he said. Equally, we know he is not the sort of person to waste both his time and his government's money. Besides, his words have the ring of truth. Yet there is always the nagging possibility that we have been misled, consciously or otherwise.

Not for the first time we find Rome, even in sunny August, a chilling place in which to work.

20

THE SECRETARIAT OF STATE
Thursday
The Early Hours

The first minutes of a new day see no interruption in the flow of telex traffic arriving on the third floor of the Apostolic Palace: 2024 DIRGENTAL VA, the Vatican's telex number and answer-back, has rarely been busier.

There are a dozen machines receiving and transmitting messages. Technicians operate them, feeding in the punch-tapes and tearing off the reams of incoming information. At frequent intervals these messages are sorted and placed in trays for the various desks. The most urgent are routed at once to diplomats who are on duty.

From Beirut, Nuncio Luciano Angeloni is sending news he has just received. Lebanon's President Amin Gemayel intends to commit virtually his entire army to try and recapture those sectors of the city held by Soviet-supported Druze and Shiite Muslim militias.[1]

Angeloni believes this will once more bring Lebanon to the verge of full-scale civil war.

To urgently alert the Holy See of this grim prospect, the plucky nuncio has had to brave almost constant sniper fire in Beirut's streets to first visit the president and then drive to the Intercontinental Hotel, one of the few places left in the city which has a working telex link with the outside world. The hotel is Beirut's press headquarters.

Angeloni has waited in line with news correspondents to send his coded report. Talking to newsmen, he gleaned a fuller picture of the latest fighting than he was able to get in his embattled nunciature in Rue Georges Picot; days ago his telephones were cut by shell fire and his actual living conditions have worsened.

The nuncio's telex contains nothing of his personal plight. His words are as restrained as ever. But behind the

361

diplomatic phrase-making is a clear concern that unless the United States increases its military support for the Gemayel government, Lebanon could shortly be dismembered into enclaves controlled by Israel, Syria and the feuding Lebanese factions.

Angeloni is careful to avoid saying so in as many words, but his evaluation will be seen as a clear-cut warning this is not the time for the Holy See to contemplate stepping up its own involvement in Lebanon.

When the day staff of the Polish Desk report for duty in a few hours, at eight A.M., they will find it has been a busy night.

From Warsaw, Cardinal Glemp has sent news about the latest outbreaks of violence by government forces against Solidarity.

Yet, despite the brutality, Glemp does not feel it heralds a return to the tensions of the pre-papal visit. He sees no wider implications in what has happened; he expects the trouble to die down as quickly as it flared.

His assessment has already been flagged for inclusion in the Summary File – the first document John Paul will read when he starts his working day. The pope still insists that any turbulence in Poland must be drawn to his attention.

For weeks a small task force on the Latin America Desk has been preparing a comprehensive report on Central America.[2] Overnight, copies of the final draft have been mimeographed and now stand in a neat stack in the office of the desk's section head. The report analyses the current crisis in terms of the area's economic roots and history, and predicts what options are presently open to the United States in a region it regards as critical in both a political and military sense.

To help them, the original task force has had to call upon a number of other experts to guide its deliberations. All the nuncios in the region have contributed data; so have the staffs of Central American nations with embassies accredited to the Holy See. Still further information has come from Washington.

From there the industrious Pio Laghi has submitted a comprehensive evaluation of a Reagan decision. The president has just appointed Henry Kissinger to chair a twelve-member bipartisan commission to study all aspects of the administration's policies towards Central America.

News of Kissinger's return to power – for almost seven years the great strategist of the Nixon–Ford administrations has been diplomatically out in the Washington cold – caused almost as great a furore on Capital Hill as the departure of the naval force.

Laghi's conclusion, wrapped as always in the most circumspect of language, is that Kissinger's appointment may be seen as a sign of the growing frustration President Reagan feels over Central America.

The nuncio knows Kissinger has scant first-hand knowledge of the area. During his eight years as Secretary of State, Kissinger visited Central America fewer than a dozen times, including honeymooning in Acapulco in 1974. Throughout much of the South American continent he is best remembered as the architect behind the destabilization of Salvadore Allende's Marxist regime in Chile.

His views on Nicaragua and El Salvador nowadays reportedly coincide with those of President Reagan: they see both nations as posing a significant threat to the United States because of their deepening involvement with Cuba and the Soviet Union. Kissinger has recently been vocal in his support for aiding Nicaragua's counter-revolutionaries to overthrow its government and remove Soviet-Cuban influence.

In assessing the effect Kissinger's involvement could have, Laghi has tapped his own considerable circle of contacts to try and answer an important question: what is the personal relationship today between Reagan and Kissinger?

The president once described Nixon's chief adviser as the

diplomat 'most responsible for the loss of United States military supremacy'. Clearly this does not reflect Reagan's current thinking; and indeed, in their well-publicized meeting in the White House when the president invited Kissinger to head the commission, the two men had behaved like old and close friends.

But Laghi knows this does not necessarily reflect the true position. Many regard both men as opportunists, ready to enter into an accommodation but also prepared to exploit each other. In the nuncio's view, the president needs Kissinger's undoubted prestige, still considerable in spite of recent revelations about his role in the downfall of Richard Nixon, whereas Kissinger remains sufficiently hungry for power to see chairing the commission as a means of re-establishing himself in North American politics.[3]

The political effect of Henry Kissinger on Ronald Reagan's Central American policymaking – will it provide something new and positive or merely generate controversy? – is one of the many factors the Latin America Desk task force has tried to calculate in their report. In spite of Laghi's well-reasoned caution – which the study takes note of – there is a feeling the Kissinger commission will act as a brake on the more hawkish elements in the Reagan administration. The view of the priests who authored the report is that it would be inconceivable for the president to order an invasion of Nicaragua while the commission is sitting. They express the belief the commission, after examining the US position towards Central America in realistic terms, may come to conclusions similar to those advanced in the Latin America Desk report.

Another factor which has influenced those conclusions has been the sudden removal of Rios Montt as president of Guatemala. Sixteen months of Montt's bizarre dictatorship have ended with a short gun battle outside the National Palace in Guatemala City. Montt has been replaced by a devout Roman Catholic, Oscar Humberto Mejia.

Yet, Mejia's close ties to the Catholic Church notwithstanding, the country's apostolic nuncio has sounded a cautionary note, one which has found a place in the final drafting of the Latin America Desk report. The papal envoy fears Mejia may turn out to be no more than a creature of the military. The country's Catholics could be as proselytized as before.

The study also judges that while Cuban intervention in particular has undoubtedly stoked the fires of Central American revolution, it did not actually ignite them; and almost certainly the removal of Cuban and Soviet influence from the region would not now extinguish the flames.

What needs to be grasped, argues the report, is that the revolutionary movements in Central America feed off anti-imperialist feeling as epitomized by the United States itself. Citing Honduras as an example, the report makes the point that in the past twelve months the local Church hierarchy estimates the revolutionary Left in the country has attracted more members than in the previous thirty years, almost certainly due to the client status of the Honduran government in relation to the United States.

The final section of the report – *The United States and Central America: An Analysis of Options Available* – begins with the unequivocal statement that the president sincerely believes it is his paramount duty to defend the United States against what he sees as 'the creeping paralysis of Communism' which is permeating the region. The report suggests the president sees the region 'as the backyard of the United States': anything which occurs there is of legitimate concern to the US.

While the priest-diplomats who have prepared the study agree that the president is quite correct to sound a clear warning about the dangers of Communist infiltration, the present US emphasis on military involvement in the area may be both misguided and counter-productive; the days of old-fashioned gunboat diplomacy are past.

What is needed is a more sophisticated approach, a recognition 'of the realities of the revolution', rather than persisting with a policy which drives revolutionaries towards Marxism-Leninism. Only when this attitude changes will the policies of the Soviet Union be seen for what they are – repressive and no better than the worst of the right-wing dictatorships.

The United States should be encouraged to 'normalize relations' with Cuba, so lessening its present total dependence upon Russia. It should be urged to seek 'dialogue' (the very word the pope used most frequently during his tour of the area in March) with left-wing groups, rather than try to cow them by military force or exclude them from participation in the political processes.

The report accepts this will require a reassessment by the United States of its current attitude towards Central America.

In a judgemental paragraph the authors argue that while there can be no doubt President Reagan wants to avoid his strategies leading to Central America becoming a second Vietnam, equally all the evidence available strongly indicates he has no desire to be remembered as the leader who 'lost' Central America.

Implicit in the report is the resoundingly held view that the Holy See has no need to alter its traditional role in contributing to the solution of social and economic inequalities in Central America.

The same spirit which animates its initiatives elsewhere, applies here – a belief it can promote on earth by preaching love, justice and freedom.

The last thing the authors of this report will accept is that, exemplary though that spirit may be, it has little to do with the realities of one of the most turbulent arenas in the world.

Waiting on the Middle East Desk is a series of new reports concerned with Libya's relentless drive into Chad. Colonel Muammar Gaddafi's well-equipped air force and army have begun to use the latest Soviet-built weapons to attack Chadian government forces – a serious escalation.

Behind this latest move by Gaddafi, reports the apostolic

delegate from Algiers, is once again the Libyan leader fostering his dream of heading a pan-Islamic empire stretching from the Atlantic-swept shores of Morocco right across this vast continent to where the Red Sea laps against the Horn of Africa.

The papal envoy had sounded the first alarm of Gaddafi's intentions towards Chad. Since then, he and other nuncios throughout Europe, the Middle East and Africa have continued to try and predict Gaddafi's intentions.

His attack on Chad has been halted by the arrival of a thousand French paratroopers. President Mitterand's aides informed Nuncio Angelo Felici – along with other Paris-based foreign diplomats – that he is determined to honour France's traditional support for its African allies, even if this means full-scale confrontation with Gaddafi.[4]

Felici's report details the political storm Mitterand's words and actions have caused on both sides of the Atlantic.

His Communist partners in government, along with certain members of his own Socialist party, are accusing Mitterand of 'neo-colonialism', a sensitive accusation in French political circles.

Despite this, Felici believes Mitterand will rally popular support. Further, the nuncio interprets France's military action in Chad as the forerunner of a diplomatic initiative – one where the Holy See might be able to use its good offices, if only to ease any tension between Paris and Washington over Chad.

Mitterand's aides intended their remarks about the president's willingness to act firmly against Gaddafi to remain private. But within hours of foreign diplomats, including the US Ambassador to France, being briefed, the White House announced that after consultation 'at the highest level' with the French government,[5] the United States had sent AWAC surveillance planes to overfly Chad as part of the continuous and close 'co-operation' with France.[6]

The French president has furiously denied that consultation – over the surveillance aircraft or anything else – ever took place. He is especially angered because his administration is now accused by the Soviet Union as 'being a tool of American imperialism'.[7]

Mitterand has been forced to take the unusual step of publicly denying what his aides had privately told Felici and other diplomats.[8] The president is insisting his commitment to Chad is no more than fulfilling France's pledge to protect its territorial integrity. In no way, maintains Mitterand, can any action France has taken be seen as a move to overthrow Gaddafi.

The president pointedly added that if the United States wishes to see the end of the Libyan leader, it should not use France as a surrogate. The French press was quick to inform readers that Reagan has had what one Paris daily calls 'a phobia' about Gaddafi ever since December 1981, when he claimed the Libyan leader had sent a 'hit squad' to America to assassinate him. The CIA subsequently said it could find no evidence to support this.

In Washington, reports Pio Laghi, the Chad crisis is perceived differently. Defense Secretary Casper Weinberger remains adamant that Mitterand knew full well there had been prior consultation between his government and the Reagan administration.[9]

Laghi does not believe 'at this stage' that the Holy See can help diffuse the situation.

But still further reports – from papal envoys as far apart as Lagos in Nigeria and Nairobi, Kenya – suggest the Chad war has produced a mood of guilt and impotence among African nations, feelings which stem from their inability to intervene in any practical sense. More than one nuncio and apostolic delegate indicate this mood could be assuaged by the Holy See offering diplomatic and moral support, a move which could also help improve its relations with those states which continue to keep their distance from other Church initiatives throughout the continent.

* * *

Shortly before two-thirty A.M., a telex machine in the Apostolic Palace accepts a message from VVOUN 429502, one of two teleprinters in the mission headquarters of the Holy See's permanent representative to the United Nations in New York. From a room in the rear of his residence at 20 East 72nd Street, Archbishop Giovanni Cheli, the apostolic observer to the UN, is transmitting a brief but important advisory.

It is nine-thirty in the evening in New York and Cheli has just come from a cocktail party in midtown Manhattan. There, among other diplomats and their staffs, he had met an aide to Jeane Kirkpatrick, the US Ambassador to the UN.

The two men spent time discussing the reaction of the Reagan administration to the assassination of Benigno Aquino. The leader of the Philippines' only credible opposition to the repressive regime of President Ferdinand Marcos had been murdered in cold blood moments after arriving at Manila international airport from exile in the United States.

Aquino was the only political opponent to Marcos with the charisma and dynamism to unite the splintered spectrum of political opinion in the Philippines and, it was hoped, guide it back to democracy. Instead he has fallen to the violence which the Marcos regime fosters.

At the cocktail party Cheli had noted that Kirkpatrick's assistant was hinting what other foreign diplomats are saying more openly around the UN Building: the assassination was almost certainly plotted and executed by men close to Marcos.[10]

This possibility, confides the aide, has caused high embarrassment in Washington. Publicly, Reagan has called for a full and thorough investigation into the cold-blooded killing. Privately, his advisers have urged the president to say or do nothing which could jeopardize 'the special relationship' between the United States and the Marcos regime. To even hint, they have insisted – according to Cheli's cocktail party source – that the Filipino president was in any way involved in the murder could endanger two vital US bases in the Philippines – those at Clark Field and Subic Bay. Between them these bases act as an advance surveillance shield against any Soviet manoeuvre in the Pacific.

Reagan's advisers fear if the United States so much as raises an admonishing finger towards Marcos, the unpredictable Filipino president could reconsider the position of those bases. A recent psychological profile of Marcos prepared by the CIA suggests he is both physically ill and mentally disturbed; nobody can any longer predict how he might react to even some mild questioning from Washington.[11]

Cheli has been told that, in spite of calls by Congressmen such as Senator Edward Kennedy to condemn the Marcos regime – in the way Cardinal Jaime Sin of Manila has done for years – the Reagan administration must take the long view of what ultimately is in the best interests of the United States. There can be no condemnation of Marcos in public. Regardless of the universal outrage over Aquino's assassination and the distaste in the US for what Marcos stands for, President Reagan will do or say no more than he has done already – welcomed the appointment of an independent enquiry into the killing. Just as he personally has consistently avoided making any comment on what – or who – was behind the attempt on John Paul's life by Agca, so now the president will say what occurred at Manila airport is properly left for those on the spot to deal with. The bases at Clark Field and Subic Bay are safe.

Important though this assessment is, it is not the prime reason Cheli has hurried from the cocktail party to transmit the telex to Rome.

Moving from one small group of diplomats to another, the papal envoy has learned of a matter of even more portent, one which fits into the jigsaw of diplomatic titbits he has been acquiring for a month.

The message he sends to the Secretariat of State is short

and is prefixed for the immediate attention of Casaroli. It reads: 'Reliably informed Nitze due Santa Barbara today to receive new negotiating brief from President Reagan.'[12]

Cheli believes what he has been told is proof that carefully timed and calculated pressure from Europe – particularly from West Germany – for 'a movement in Geneva' has paid off.

The possibility that Nitze could return to Geneva with fresh orders is, as Cheli knows, all the more remarkable in view of the indecision, bureaucratic jockeying and clash of personalities which have bedevilled so much of US negotiations on arms control – a situation which has unhappily allowed the Soviet Union to continue with its deviousness, intransigence, crude intimidation and often double-crossing.[13]

Whereas West Germany's Chancellor Helmut Kohl and Mrs Thatcher's government firmly remain the Reagan administration's most powerful supporters for deploying missiles in Europe, they have both recently expressed through their ambassadors in Washington the thought that the United States should perhaps consider again the much-promoted idea – one until now looked upon in the White House with scant favour – of a 'nuclear interim solution'. In this the Russians would be allowed to keep a reduced force of SS-20s trained on Western Europe, while America would reduce its new NATO deployment correspondingly.

Clark, Kirkpatrick and Casper Weinberger lead the administration's opposition to the idea.

Cheli had reportedly been dismayed by Weinberger's uncompromising words. 'We don't want to look as though we are letting the West German Left push us around.'

On a previous occasion, when Nitze asked Reagan for guidance on how to respond to his Russian counterpart in Geneva, he had been advised: 'Well, Paul, you just tell the Soviets you're working for one tough son of a bitch!'

While that still undoubtedly held true, Cheli's contacts

have alerted him these past weeks to the fact the president is beginning to pay more attention to the moderates in his administration. They believe that an arms control settlement which is minimally acceptable to the United States would be an invaluable booster to the president's hopes of re-election. Reagan's decision to stand for a second term is a decision the papal diplomat thinks is bound to make the president look more critically at some of the hard-line advice he has been getting these past months.

Nitze's summons to the Reagan ranch at Santa Barbara could therefore presage a new American impetus at Geneva when the next round of talks begin.

But even as Cheli's telex is arriving in the Apostolic Palace, an incident has just taken place six miles above the Pacific which will dramatically crush any such hopes.

VATICAN RADIO
Same Day:Dawn

From all over Rome the early shift of broadcasters, technicians and secretarial staff are arriving on the second floor and punching their time cards.

Clarissa McNair thinks it more reminiscent of a factory than a broadcasting station. But on this bright sunny morning – the high summer heat has eased and the city is once more habitable – she is preoccupied with other matters.[14]

McNair has recently produced a documentary on the situation in the Philippines which she knows could not be more timely – or more calculated to cause a response from the Marcos regime with its current siege-mentality. The programme was sharply critical of the way the Church is treated in the Philippines.

She has also written and narrated a programme dealing with another highly contentious topic – the war in Chad. Drawing on her considerable first-hand experience of the region, she made what amounted to a powerful plea for France and the superpowers to keep out of the situation.

Although both programmes have been carefully reviewed in the Secretariat of State by numerous diplomats, including Kabongo and Sepe, there has been no complaint from either the Marcos regime or the Chadian factions.

McNair takes this as a sign her programmes have again demonstrated the balance she seeks to convey.

Her card punched, she makes her way to the *Quattrovoci* offices on the fourth floor – her thoughts alternating between work and a pressing personal problem.

She has been awake most of the night dealing with a new set of tiny emperor turtles. They have gone blind. She called a gynaecologist friend to seek his advice. After establishing that the turtles are male – and therefore even further outside his competence – he suggested she move them from their swimming pool to another watery location. McNair placed them in a bidet. During the night she has regularly removed the turtles and bathed their eyes. To no avail. Before she left her apartment, two were dead – destined for burial in geranium pots – and she is certain the others have not long to live. She does not know whether she should call the gynaecologist again.

McNair is also hesitating over a number of new programme possibilities.

In a couple of days the Jesuits will begin their conclave to elect a new Superior-General. She knows it could make an interesting documentary.

A group of American bishops is in Rome. In itself she knows this is hardly newsworthy. Yet perhaps it might be worth exploring with some of them their thoughts on the US pastoral letter. The report has lost none of its controversial impact.

The Catholic Left is exultant because it believes it scored a major victory over the exchange of the verb 'curb' for 'halt'. Other American priests have called the pastoral a 'bowl of mush'.

Still other bishops argue the letter states principles, caveats, contingent judgements and balanced counter arguments which are a masterful display of text-writing.

It certainly, McNair knows, would be interesting to explore the issues with the visiting bishops. But a look at their names discourages her. Most of them would be too verbose, unable to confine their thoughts to minutes rather than sermon length. She decides to drop the idea.

McNair ponders a third possibility. She has learned that Archbishop Luigi Poggi is going to Bulgaria in a few days. She is sure his trip is connected with the plight of the country's Catholics; they are among the most oppressed in the Soviet bloc.

She is still contemplating on how best to approach the nuncio for an interview when she reaches the fourth floor and enters the room where the wire-service teleprinters are positioned.

McNair casually grabs at the unfolding copy on the AP machine.

She stands, transfixed.

There is a flash report that a Korean Airlines 747 has disappeared off Japanese radar screens on a flight from New York via Anchorage to Seoul.

'My God,' says McNair to a colleague. 'I bet this is no accident. Not there!'

Working at top speed she begins to assemble the copy on the fate of Flight 007 and its 269 passengers.

In an hour – at eight-twenty A.M. in Rome – she will be one of the first newscasters to announce to the world the first details of an outrage which will freeze East–West relations for months to come.

THE VATICAN
Tuesday
Pre-Dawn

Shortly before five o'clock, Camillo Cibin's bedside telephone rings.

The last time he received a call this early was on that memorable September morning five years ago when the newly elected pope Albino Luciano of Venice had calmly walked out of the Vatican past a dumbfounded Swiss Guard on duty at the Porta Sant'Anna and stood for some minutes on Italian soil, looking up and down a fortunately deserted street. In so doing Luciano had not only committed a diplomatic gaffe – pontiffs are not permitted to stroll into another country unannounced and unescorted – but created a security problem which even Cibin had not anticipated. His memory of the occasion still induces shudders in the security chief.

Reaching for the telephone, Cibin's instinctive reaction is that there has been some incident involving John Paul.

The number of threats to the pope's life in the past nine months stands at over one hundred.[2] Cibin has been forced to take each one seriously, putting a strain on his manpower resources and his relationship with John Paul, who continues to resent being hemmed in by *vigili*. The threats have markedly increased in the wake of the kidnapping of Emanuela Orlandi. The motive for that crime – like almost everything else about the case – continues to baffle Cibin. The pope himself shows no signs of losing interest in the matter; every week his security chief submits a résumé of the current state of the investigation.

Answering the telephone Cibin wonders whether perhaps he is about to hear some dramatic news from the Rome police about the fate of the girl. The caller is indeed a senior *capo* from *Questura* headquarters. But he is not telephoning about Emanuela. Instead he is both apologetic for calling at this early hour and for being so late with the news he has to impart.

Cibin listens to what the *capo* says. The security chief does not put any of the questions which immediately spring to his mind: why had the Vatican not been informed much earlier of what is to happen; has anyone considered that the drama about to be staged is precisely what the pope does not wish to be involved in; what is the point of it all?

Instead, Cibin thanks the *capo*, springs out of bed and starts to get dressed.

Then he remembers. People must be warned.

He calls the senior *vigile* on duty in the Vatican and briefs him. He instructs the man to alert all the guard posts around the Vatican perimeter. Nobody involved in the forthcoming drama must be allowed to set foot on Vatican soil without Cibin's personal authority.

Cibin next dials extension 3204, the number of the commandant of the Swiss Guards. This is the Renaissance-costumed army of a hundred officers and men, all of whom wear dark blue and yellow-striped uniforms which give them the appearance of toy soldiers off to save Humpty Dumpty rather than to protect the pope and be responsible for 'the defence of his territories'. In practice, Cibin's men have the job. The Guards are essentially ceremonial. Nevertheless, as the Holy See signed the 1966 non-proliferation treaty on nuclear weapons, the Swiss Guards are annually inspected, under the terms of that agreement, to check whether they are in possession of any illegal nuclear weapons. An official comes all the way from the Atomic Energy Commission in Vienna to perform this duty; he gets a good lunch at the Vatican and a pleasant day out.

Next Cibin calls Stanislaw Dziwisz and tells him what is about to happen.

The pope's Polish secretary immediately goes to his bedroom window and peers down into St Peter's Square. It

is still too dark to see anything in detail. Dziwisz calls
Kabongo and explains what he has been told. Both agree
that John Paul is not going to like what is about to occur.

THE BULGARIAN EMBASSY, ROME
Same Day:Same Time

First Secretary Vassil Dimitrov continues to lecture his two
companions.[3]

They are older and, within the Bulgarian Communist
Party hierarchy, far more senior than the diplomat. Judges
Jordan Olmakov and Marcov Petkov are members of the
Bulgarian Supreme Court, the country's most powerful
judicial organization. Physically they are dumpy men,
wrapped in shapeless overcoats with fedoras pulled low over
their foreheads.

Dimitrov is dressed as though he is going to the races: tan
trousers, navy jacket and a startling maroon tie. He has
brogues on his feet. Between trouser cuffs and shoes there is
a glimpse of bright yellow socks. He looks more like a
bookmaker's runner than the embassy's ranking officer: the
Bulgarian ambassador is back in Sofia having 'consultations'
with his government about the Bulgarian Connection.

Matching his clothes, Dimitrov is doused in overpowering aftershave, and there are traces of talc around his shirt
collar.

Perhaps this explains his bouncy confidence, and the
blithe way he continues to address the judges. Only a man
very very certain of himself would turn out like this and, in
spite of his appearance, the judges listen to him carefully.

Following Martella's visit to Sofia in July, the pair have
come to Rome to examine for themselves the Italian evidence for holding Sergei Antonov.

Each night, after spending most of the day in Martella's
office, the judges return to the Bulgarian Embassy and brief

Dimitrov on what they have learned. He then feeds them the latest instructions he has received from Sofia.

This morning, as they emerge from the embassy, Dimitrov again tells the judges to say nothing during the event in which they are about to take part.

Dimitrov adds that keeping silent will help remove the risk of them being misquoted by the 'capitalist press jackals' who are certainly going to learn what is under way. With a smile which reveals his nicotine-stained teeth, the diplomat adds he has already made a number of calls to reporters to make sure they will be present. The judges look at him with open respect.

'But no quotes,' insists Dimitrov. 'Not a word. All that matters is the Bulgarian Connection has worn itself out. Sergei Antonov is as good as free.'[4]

There is new basis for his optimism. A month ago, Martella publicly announced Antonov had been 'slandered by Agca'.

The 'slander' dealt with Agca's allegation that Antonov had helped him with a plot to kill Lech Walesa in 1981 when the Solidarity leader came to Rome to visit the pope.

Martella now accepts there is no truth in Agca's claim, and has delivered a judicial ruling to that effect which exonerates Antonov on this count.

Now a further move is about to begin to try and further destroy Agca's credibility.

'Remember,' reminds Dimitrov yet again as he leads the two judges to a waiting embassy car, 'say nothing. Martella is on the defensive. We must keep him like that.'[5]

Seated in the rear of his armour-plated car, escorted by the usual squad of heavily armed *carabinieri*, Judge Martella peers out into the near deserted streets of Rome. Even so, to avoid the possibility of a terrorist ambush, the convoy is taking a circuitous route to its destination: it roars down the Viale Giulio Cesare, a broad avenue which leads to the Tiber, then turns right, passing Margherita Bridge and Ponte Cavour, before speeding past Castel Sant'Angelo.

Martella believes he has made all possible preparations to meet two interrelated considerations: maximum security and the minimum of publicity.[6]

The idea for what is to happen had not been his, but the Bulgarian judges'. They pushed him hard before he agreed. Martella has no great hopes it will decide anything, one way or the other. But he wants to be especially co-operative where the Bulgarians are concerned. He does not wish anyone later to say he was obstructive or unwilling to explore every possible avenue.

Equally, he has to admit that after ten full months working on the case, he has yet to begin writing his final report, the document which will decide whether Antonov and the others under investigation should stand trial for complicity in the plot to kill the pope.[7]

The problem, as Martella well knows, is Agca. It is becoming increasingly clear that, despite all the help of psychiatrists and the most careful handling, Agca remains in many ways a mysterious figure. It is difficult for even the experienced judge to know how far he dare believe his star witness.

But he is certain Agca is telling the truth when he continues to insist he is in no way involved with the Emanuela kidnapping.[8]

Yet the pope, the girl, and the terrorist remain inextricably entwined in the case.

During past weeks Martella was forced time and again to question Agca about further bizarre developments.

A mysterious Turkish terrorist group had surfaced demanding John Paul make a statement saying, 'Ali Agca is a human being and should be treated as such.'

The Vatican agonized over the request. Eventually the pope had described Agca as 'a person', for 'whom I always pray'.

The lawyer retained by the Orlandi family claimed the Turkish group was 'phoney'. But Rome homicide chief Nicola Cavaliere, a police officer Martella respects, thinks the Turks should be taken seriously.

Next, a message posted in New York arrived in Rome saying Emanuela was about to 'be terminated'; the text was full of gibberish which Agca, when questioned, could not begin to unravel. There then followed several other messages, post-marked Phoenix, Arizona, making even more disjointed statements about Agca and Emanuela.

Apart from these developments, the Vatican has begun to exert pressure on the Italian Ministry of Justice. Senior members of Casaroli's office have called to ask whether there is indeed any connection between the kidnapping and *Pista Bulgara*.

They hint John Paul may be behind the enquiry.

Martella is aware the question has surfaced at the same time as the CIA renewed its support for the Bulgarian Connection. The agency has indicated it is at Martella's disposal to help in any way he might think suitable.

Not for the first time the hard-working judge wonders where all this is leading. Nothing would surprise him any more.

Yet, he is about to be astonished. All his carefully laid plans to keep secret what lies behind this early morning dash through Rome have been wrecked.

At more than fifty miles an hour, swaying under the speed, a blue-painted police truck, armoured with nearly a ton of steel giving it a squat and tank-like appearance, rushes southwards through Rome.

The truck has fenders sufficiently strong to smash through a road block. Its driving cab is covered with reinforced steel mesh. The porthole in the rear is similarly protected.

There are nine men in the vehicle. One sits by the driver. Both are wearing flak jackets and steel helmets with visors. Lying on the bench seat between them are Uzi machine pistols. Six of their companions in the rear are similarly attired and armed. Together, they have enough fire power to deliver 4,000 rounds a minute.

The ninth person in the van is Agca.

He is wearing a sky-blue turtle-neck sweater. The designer's emblem – Stefanel – is over his heart. Stefanel sportswear is among the most popular in Italy. The sweater has been especially purchased for Agca from public funds for this occasion. He is also wearing blue jeans and white running shoes.

The prison barber at Rebibbia has shaved Agca, but made no attempt to improve his close-cropped hairstyle. Agca looks like a campus student from the 1960s. It is an appealing image which the psychiatrist who still treats him has pronounced himself satisfied with.

As the truck enters one of Rome's great arteries, Corso Vittorio Emanuele, police cars, lights flashing and sirens wailing, take up position before and behind the truck.

In other parts of the city, yet more cars with police escorts are racing towards a common destination – Via della Conciliazione, the broad boulevard which leads directly to St Peter's Square.

THE PAPAL APARTMENT
Same Day:Dawn

The position is frustrating for Kabongo.[9] From his vantage point, a top-floor window in the Apostolic Palace, he can hear sounds of increasing activity but can actually see nothing. The tall buildings lining either side of Via della Conciliazione effectively block the secretary's view.

But twice in the last thirty minutes Cibin has reported what he is able to see. He is standing in St Peter's Square, looking straight down the wide street. To make his reports he goes to the guardhouse inside the Bronze Door and telephones from there.

Dziwisz has already informed John Paul what is happening. The pope had sharply asked the question others are posing: why *now*?

381

Meanwhile he has closeted himself in his office, dealing with a workload even the apparently indefatigable Kabongo finds exhausting.

The secretary knows that even at this early hour he can barely afford the time to stare out of the window; every minute of Kabongo's day, and well into the evening, seems to be crowded with meetings and paperwork.

The pope and his secretaries – aided by a stream of advice from the Secretariat of State – are embroiled in the full horror of the shooting down of the Korean airliner by a Russian fighter. The first question John Paul raised was whether Andropov could be implicated in the massacre of those on board. Kabongo has lost count of the number of times Poggi came and went from the pope's office with news which might throw some light on the matter.

Kabongo was one of a team who helped to suggest, draft, revise and edit John Paul's all-important crucial first words on the incident.

The secretary is quietly pleased to see a phrase he had suggested – that the shooting down of the airliner brought the world closer to a 'pre-war posture' than anything else – had been included by the pope. John Paul had also passionately urged that the entire world should pray to avoid a nuclear catastrophe.

Kabongo also helped to clear a separate statement from the Vatican's Academy of Science which called for, in unusually strong language, 'a total disarmament by all nations'.

The Vatican's response, in Kabongo's view,[10] was a firm and finely judged rejection of the Soviet claim the Korean airliner was on a spying mission and that the entire incident, while regretted by the Soviets, was the inevitable result of some CIA-inspired plot. The agency's Station Chief in Rome, on direct instructions from Director William J. Casey, had personally assured the pope there was no CIA involvement whatsoever in the affair.

Completely satisfied with this, John Paul had also stated the world's political equilibrium was dangerously out of balance; he had spoken of 'the precarious condition created by greed for material goods and transgressions of moral laws and the permanent danger of a nuclear slaughter'.

John Paul's words on the shooting down of Flight 007 were among the toughest he has uttered in condemning the actions of the Soviet Union.

Kabongo had hardly finished with an incident he still sees as 'horrendous in every implication',[11] when he was plunged into events in the Lebanon.

Cardinal Franz Koenig of Vienna had called with news of a desperate appeal he had just received from the Lebanese hierarchy. The cardinal has spent a lifetime developing the Church's links with the Middle East and has been closely monitoring the tragic events in Lebanon, often reporting directly to either Casaroli or John Paul. Koenig's input provides a useful check on the reliability of other information the Vatican receives from the area.

Koenig told Kabongo he had been asked by the leaders of the Christian community in Lebanon to appeal to each of the billion baptized Catholics in the world to pray for the safety of all Christians in the area.

The secretary conveyed the request to the pope. John Paul has asked for yet another briefing paper on the Lebanon to help him frame a suitable pronouncement. But he had made clear to Koenig he would only issue one if he felt it would be beneficial. In Kabongo's cautious words, 'The pope is very careful in how he uses his office to the best effect in such delicate matters.'[12]

Koenig's call came at a time when Kabongo was also preparing for a series of meetings between the pope and a number of nuncios. Discreetly billed on the daily Audience List as 'exchanges of information and ideas', in reality these were lengthy discussions on a wide range of foreign affairs involving the Holy See in, among other places, France, Mexico, Syria, Kenya and Columbia.

Once these meetings were under way, Kabongo found himself concerned with perhaps the most important event in the year's Church calendar – the month-long international Synod of Bishops.

Over 200 of the Church's most senior prelates have assembled in Rome to deliberate on issues stemming from the theme of the conference: Reconciliation and Penance in the Mission of the Church. The title was sufficiently general to allow for discussion to range from sacramental and doctrinal matters to debates on international situations.

The Synod is now in its third week. Part of Kabongo's current workload is to ensure the pope is fully appraised of what the bishops are saying.

Staring pensively down into St Peter's Square, the secretary wonders whether the drama unfolding in the Via della Conciliazione will delay those overseas bishops who have early morning appointments in the Vatican.

VIA DELLA CONCILIAZONE
Same Day: Early Morning

Dawn has broken. A cold breeze is blowing off the Tiber, setting the red and white ribbons quivering on the road blocks which close off the avenue from the rest of Rome. Uniformed and plainclothes police are everywhere. There may be as many as two hundred. More are arriving by the minute.

Capi are directing them to set up further barriers across every street intersecting with the Via della Conciliazione.

But, Martella furiously tells a *capo*, the road blocks are too late.

Already the investigating magistrate can count 'at least' forty members of the press inside the barriers. There are television teams from the major US and European networks, radio reporters and print media newsmen and women. Even as he watches they continue to brush past the police, shouting 'Press!'

Martella glares at the *capo* beside him. 'This is not possible! Who told them?'

A passing reporter cheekily responds. 'This is democracy, judge. Nothing is secret or sacred nowadays!'

The truism in this instance does nothing to improve Martella's mood. Just as he has been unable to discover how the press learned beforehand of Agca's visit to the *Questura* when he spoke about Emanuela and Antonov – Martella refused to discuss a widely held theory that it was CIA Rome who tipped off the media – he will be unable to establish how all these reporters milling around him have managed to ruin his carefully laid plans.

He has briefly considered calling off the whole operation. But that, he suspects, could lead to even more problems with the Bulgarians, with the Ministry of Justice and with the Rome authorities, who anyway are bound to complain about the way the closure of Via della Conciliazione is causing traffic chaos during morning peak hour. No: he will just have to go through with it in the full glare of the media spotlight.

Martella pulls up his jacket collar against the cold wind and walks down to the main barrier across the broad avenue. Reporters are still crossing it.

Once more Martella's fury boils over. He turns to the nearest *capo* and yells, 'Can't you at least stop them? What is the point of these barriers if everybody can cross them?'

The officer shrugs. 'What can we do? They are all bona fide press. Imagine the bad publicity if they filmed us throwing them out.' He nods towards the Vatican. 'This is Holy Year. Some of these reporters say they have appointments in the Vatican. There would be big trouble from there if we stopped the press doing their job.'

Martella simmers. 'How can I do mine?'

The *capo* shrugs.

Further up the boulevard Olmakov and Petkov sit in the back of the embassy car, studiously ignoring the television crews circling outside, their portable lights bathing the vehicle in a cold glare as they film it and its occupants from every angle.

Other photographers are roaming the area snapping anybody they think is important.

A *capo* directs them to block access roads into the square. The *capo* shouts louder. He is still ignored.

Martella goes over to the officer. 'Don't bother. Not now.'

The judge walks away in disgust.

ST PETER'S SQUARE
Same Day: A Little Later

Like a besieged general, Cibin continues to prowl the perimeter of his territory. Behind him every entrance to the Vatican is manned by armed *vigili* and Swiss Guards.

In the piazza itself there are some thirty city of Rome policemen. A *capo* directs them to block access roads into the square.

The Vatican is now virtually sealed off.

Cibin hurries once more to the guardhouse inside the Bronze Door to report this latest development.

VIA DELLA CONCILIAZIONE
Same Day: Same Time

A strikingly handsome man – tall, blond-haired, blue-eyed, debonair enough to be an actor – reaches the barrier the reporters have been crossing.

A nervous policeman points his Uzi at the intruder. A *capo* snarls at the luckless patrolman to put down his gun.

Still smiling, Giuseppe Consolo steps past the road

block, courteously telling the policeman he has behaved perfectly properly. Consolo winks at the *capo* and strolls on up the avenue.

From time to time he smiles for the cameramen and pauses to have a word with reporters.

They are all glad to see him. Sergei Antonov's lawyer is always ready to oblige with a good quote, a skilfully phrased opinion, each designed to shaft yet further Martella's investigation.

Consolo looks around, openly amused by everything he sees. He stops by a group of reporters.

'Martella must be getting desperate to stage such a show.'

The reporters smile. This is the Consolo they know: ever prepared to manipulate a situation, always careful to ensure he stays within the bounds of legal propriety so far as Italian law goes.

He is widely held to be not only one of the best but possibly the most expensive lawyer practising in Rome. His fee for defending Antonov, provided by the Bulgarian government, is said to be the highest ever paid to an Italian attorney. Some reports suggest he is getting the equivalent of $5,000 a week. Consolo will neither confirm nor deny such figures. Now, he indicates the police activity.

'This is overkill,' he says. 'All this to try and make my client seem more important than he is. Pure psychological warfare against the defence.'

A reporter asks what is about to happen.

Consolo shrugs and points dramatically back down the avenue.

The barriers are being pulled aside just enough to let pass the armoured police truck and its escort.

The lawyer moves to another group of reporters. He gives them his caustic opinion of 'this nonsensical circus'.

Consolo reaches the embassy car. He beckons the two

judges to join him. They listen respectfully as Consolo briefs them. He ends by saying they must do or say nothing – simply observe.

The armoured truck has parked some thirty yards inside the police barriers.

Martella stares moodily at the vehicle's reinforced rear door. He might be debating whether even now he should call off the entire episode.

Beside him is a diminutive, bespectacled figure; Pietro D'Ovidio barely tops five feet. His ill-fitting clothes make him appear even smaller. With a nervous habit of seeming to peer all ways at once, he has the mournful face of a clown off duty. He is Agca's lawyer.

D'Ovidio tries to smile encouragement at his client when Agca's face suddenly appears in the back-door porthole.

A *capo* steps forward and raps on the truck. The rear doors open. The flak-jacketed *carabinieri* spring out and form a tight cordon around the door.

Agco emerges.

A radio reporter starts to describe the scene into a microphone.

'Agca looks like a lonely animal filled with wonder and fear. He appears both terrified and pleased. Terrified because of his escort who are tensely gripping their weapons. But pleased by the media presence. He seems to be saying to us, "You are all here for me". But how does he really feel, back here, within yards of the pope? And how does the pope feel? Knowing the man who tried to kill him is back on his doorstep?'

Consolo strolls up to Martella. They watch as D'Ovidio walks over to Agca and begins to talk earnestly to him. The lawyer keeps punctuating his words with, 'Do you understand?'

Agca nods each time.

Martella looks at his watch. He beckons the two Bulgarian judges forward. With Consolo by his side the four men join Agca and his attorney.

The radio reporter continues to describe what is happening.

'Martella is explaining what this is about. He wants Agca to retrace every step he took on that afternoon he shot the pope. This is very dramatic. But how is Agca going to remember after all this time? Two years is a long time. And why has it taken so long to have this reconstruction? But these are not questions for now. They can come later.'

The judge takes Agca aside. Martella's voice is calm and encouraging as he gives Agca his final instructions. 'Ali, remember now. Take your time. Don't worry about all these people. Just take yourself back to that afternoon.'

Agca nods.

Martella gives an order to a police *capo*.

The truck moves further up the Via della Conciliazione. The tight cordon of policemen around Agca parts, fanning out to form a loose circle of about fifty feet in diameter. Inside are Agca, Martella, the two lawyers and the Bulgarian judges.

Agca looks about him. It is a cue for the radio reporter to pick up the scene.

'He seems uncertain which way to turn. That's understandable. It has been a long time. It must be difficult for him. No: he is certain after all. He is walking forward very confidently.'

Agca strides on steadily. Martella and the others are a few feet behind him, careful not to impede his direction, or suggest where he should be heading, or when he should halt. Like the police cordon and the press corps behind it, everybody is keeping pace with Agca's measured tread.

The sun is bright now. But the television crews still have their battery lights on, casting shadows against the buildings.

Agca reaches the Caffè San Pietro. It is here, he had claimed in an earlier statement, that he stopped for a coffee with Antonov on the way to shoot the pope.

He pauses outside the café. Martella and the others join him. The police cordon closes in. A *capo* shouts at the reporters. *'Dietro! Dietro!'* They refuse to retreat.

Martella turns and beckons into the crowd behind the cordon.

A tall, short-haired woman and a man step forward. She is an interpreter. He is one of Martella's aides.

The judge addresses the woman. 'Ask him what happened here.'

She turns to Agca and repeats the question in Turkish.

Agca answers volubly, his voice loud and confident.

Consolo waits, poised.

The woman translates Agca's words into Italian. Her voice is crisp and clear.

'He says he bought a roll of film here.'

Consolo relaxes. He smiles broadly at the Bulgarian judges. Agca has added a new element to his original version of events.

The radio reporter interprets the scene. 'Martella looks grim. Agca now appears to be concentrating hard. He is turning and starting to walk again.'

Once more everyone takes up their previous positions. The group moves on, almost as if choreographed.

Agca reaches the Credito Italiano Bank in the avenue. He stops, seemingly uncertain.

Consol makes a joke loud enough for reporters to hear. 'This must be where he keeps all the money he says he got for the job!'

Agca scowls at the lawyer.

Martella stares warningly at Consolo. The judge is making clear he will not allow this reconstruction to get further out of hand.

Agca is walking again.

Next door to the bank is a bar. He pauses before it.

Martella explains to the Bulgarian judges this is where Agca claims he made a second stop on the way to St Peter's. The translator is switching non-stop from Italian to Turkish, to Bulgarian and back again. The judge's assistant is scribbling furiously.

The procession moves on, this time to halt before the Canadian Embassy to the Holy See.

It is here, Agca has claimed, that Antonov and another Bulgarian had left him on the afternoon he went on to shoot the pope. Agca has also said he arranged to meet his fellow conspirators at this very spot after he completed the assassination.

The radio reporter is once more taking up the thread of the story, raising questions that must be in the minds of many witnessing this extraordinary event.

'Why choose this place? It is at least 200 metres from St Peter's Square. On that afternoon it would have been filled with crowds. It would have been impossible for Agca easily to have made his way back here. These doubts have been expressed before. Perhaps today we will see them resolved.'

By now the noise of the backed-up traffic at the barriers is so loud even the directional microphones of the television sound crews can barely pick up the exchanges between Agca and those around him.

Martella is gesticulating again. Consolo is moving from one foot to another. The Bulgarian judges continue to nod solemnly. The interpreter looks flustered.

'You crossed here?' Martella has to shout to make himself heard above the traffic roar; hundreds of engines are being revved and horns blown. 'Was it here you crossed?'

Agca wrinkles his forehead. He nods.

Consolo shakes his head in disbelief.

Martella steps back. There is no way of knowing from his expression what he feels. He says something to a *capo* and walks away. He does not speak further before getting into his car and being driven off.

Agca is bundled back into the truck. It speeds away with its police escort.

Within minutes the road blocks are removed and the Via della Conciliazione becomes jam-packed with vehicles.

It will take a full two hours to clear the backlog of traffic.

ROME
Wednesday
Morning

From the civilized hour of nine o'clock onwards in various buildings – almost all at least two centuries old, but superbly renovated by their governments – ambassadors accredited to the Holy See begin another day in the never-ending process of interpreting for their foreign ministries the latest diplomatic subtleties they have gleaned in and around the Apostolic Palace.

In his magnificent mansion in Piazza di Spagna, His Excellency Don José Joaquin Puig de la Bellacasa y Urdam-pilleta, every inch as splendid a figure as his name, is busily engaged writing in longhand – the final draft will later be typed – his assessment of how the Vatican has responded to the moves by Spain's Socialist government to head off a major confrontation with the Spanish hierarchy and possibly John Paul himself.

After a great deal of nudging both within the Secretariat of State and by the Spanish ambassador – who naturally prefers to use the phrase 'consultation with those in appropriate places'[13] – the pope had finally agreed to an audience with Prime Minister Felipe Gonzalez.

They had spoken for thirty minutes. There was, by all accounts, hard-boiled realism on both sides.

The pope had expressed his disquiet over Spain's new liberal laws on abortion, drugs and the Gonzalez government's demands for greater supervision over the country's Catholic schools.

Gonzalez had listened politely, and then offered to increase State aid to Catholic schools and institutes.

Throughout his report today to Madrid, based on recent almost daily visits by either himself or his staff to the Vatican, the ambassador reflects cautious optimism that there will be no support from the Vatican for any move by the Spanish hierarchy to mobilize those two other great pillars of Spanish society, the military and the business community, against the government.

In the Lebanese Chancellery on Via Emilio de' Cavalieri, the country's ranking diplomatic representative to the Holy See, First Secretary Chucri Abboud, is preparing a lengthy dispatch on a private audience he had with Casaroli yesterday. For an hour the two men had discussed how best the Holy See could intervene in Lebanon. Abboud had wistfully wondered if even now, at this late stage, John Paul could consider making a visit to the area. Casaroli explained the reality of the situation: the presence of the pope would not halt the carnage. What was needed, the Secretary of State suggested, was a new diplomatic initiative behind which the Holy See could throw its full moral authority. For the remainder of their meeting they had explored a number of possibilities that Abboud is now trying to frame into clear-cut proposals.[14]

Inside the Polish Mission offices on Via Castiglione del Lago, Consul Jerzy Kuberski is piecing together what he has gleaned from his Vatican contacts about the just announced news that Lech Walesa has won the Nobel Peace Prize.

Kuberski is 'personally astonished' that Walesa has been given the award.[15] Equally, he knows his government will not be interested in his personal reaction. What is needed from Kuberski is clarification of an intriguing report circulating in Warsaw. This strongly suggests there is a split within the Apostolic Palace on how far the Holy See should go in endorsing the award. John Paul reportedly would like to invite Walesa to Rome, calculating that the Polish government could not refuse Walesa the right to return home, so sending him into exile. But Kuberski has been told members of the Secretariat of State do not favour such a move.

Yet, try as he might, this astute Communist has been unable to find one source to support the story. At the moment the best he can do is to write a response suggesting not everybody endorses the pope's enthusiasm for the trade unionist. To do so he will cite the continuing controversy over Levi; the former deputy editor of *L'Osservatore Romano* has been telling friends, 'My days in Rome are numbered'.[16]

Kuberski has picked up the story – from two Polish priests he is friendly with – that Levi was given the option of either resigning or being fired. Only now does Levi realize it would have been better had he chosen dismissal; by resigning he forfeited any right to compensation. In the Vatican's view he left his job by choice and so is not entitled to recompense.

It's titbits like this that the Polish government uses to try and sow discord within the Catholic Church in Poland.

His Excellency the Turkish ambassador, Sulhi Dislioglu, made one of his infrequent visits to the Vatican a few days ago. He returned to his chancellery on Piazza delle Muse with the definite impression that Mgr Battista Giovanni, *Assessore* at the Secretariat of State, was content with his briefing on Turkey's forthcoming elections.

The ambassador had explained that the creation of 400 members for a single-chamber parliament would effectively end rule by the military which had taken power in 1980 to stop, among other things, the anarchy which spawned men like Agca.[17]

High up on Via Giacomo Medici is the magnificent Villa Spada which houses the residence and office of Ireland's ambassador to the Holy See. For three years Francis Coffey has conveyed his government's views on Irish affairs to the papacy. More than most other ambassadors, Coffey sees his country as enjoying a special relationship with the Holy See. Catholic Ireland, at least on paper, remains one of the main fiefs of the Church in Europe. And, unlike other foreign diplomats, Coffey has no problem persuading the reluctant John Magee to come to dinner; the Master of Ceremonies is still one of the most powerful figures in this pontificate. Indeed Coffey's table is renowned in Vatican circles for its fine food and guests carefully chosen for their insights into Church matters.

But it is not planning another dinner party which preoccupies the urbane Coffey this morning. He is concerned with finding suitable words to convey to Dublin the result of the latest informal discussion he has had with his Vatican sources.[18] They have strongly hinted that, in the words of one, Britain is bankrupt of ideas over how to resolve the plight in Northern Ireland.

For weeks there has been a modicum of optimism that between them London and Dublin could create an acceptable solution now Mrs Thatcher's favourite Irish politician, Dr Garret Fitzgerald, is back in office and has survived the political fallout from the abortion referendum which had turned out to be a further divisive episode in Ireland's turbulent political life.

Those Vatican sources told Coffey that Mrs Thatcher's government is almost certainly going to remain as determined as ever to maintain its present strong stand over Ulster – and she believes she can count on the continued support of Dr Fitzgerald in this.

Since nine-thirty William Wilson has been seated at his desk studying the latest batch of State Department briefings.

One deals with the Reagan administration's decision that, in spite of the shooting down of the Korean airliner, there will be no rupture in trade between the United States and the Soviet Union in such a critical area as America's supply of grain to Russia. A new agreement was signed in August between the two countries on the subject, and Reagan's intention to honour the commitment in the wake of the airliner outrage continues to attract bitter comment at home and bewilderment abroad.

The State Department briefing is intended to prepare envoys like Wilson for any questions their host governments might pose on the matter.

Wilson's reading will allow him to absorb a number of set arguments which, should the occasion arise, would allow him successfully to debate the case *against* a grain embargo with even the lynx-eyed Casaroli.

He is still absorbing the document when his assistant, Don Planty, saunters into the office.

In Rome's bitchy diplomatic cocktail party circuit, Planty is known as 'Mr Shotgun', the professional who attempts to guide Wilson away from diplomatic pitfalls. Nowadays Wilson happily accepts that Planty 'knows the ropes'.[19]

'They want us over at the Secretariat at once.' Planty's voice conceals any excitement or special interest he may feel.

Wilson is more open. He wonders if this unexpected summons could be to receive further news about something which nowadays is seldom out of his thoughts. It is the possibility the United States will establish full diplomatic relations with the Holy See. Among other benefits this could elevate Wilson to full-scale ambassador.

The matter has been under serious discussion for several months in Rome and Washington. Wilson has been told that, while the Holy See will welcome this upgrading, the first formal approach must come from the United States.[20]

Walking the few yards from his office to the Vatican, Wilson discusses with Planty the prospect of such a move coming before the envoy leaves Rome for a lengthy winter break in the California sun. They are still discussing the matter when they reach the Secretariat of State.

A monsignor meets them and takes them at once to Casaroli.

The Secretary of State wastes no time coming to the point. He hands Wilson a letter which the pope wants urgently delivered to President Reagan.

396

The envelope is open.

Casaroli invites Wilson to read the letter. The envoy extracts the single sheet of paper and does so.

John Paul has decided to intervene personally in the nuclear arms reduction debate.

The letter is a direct appeal for President Reagan not to abandon negotiations with Russia.

Wilson folds the letter and replaces it in the envelope.

Casaroli has one last piece of information to impart. An identical letter will be given later this morning to the Soviet ambassador to send to Moscow.

The letters provide the Soviet and American leaders with a stark vision of the pope's fear that Armageddon is closer than they realize.

22
Roman Responses

Judge Martella wants to see us.[1]

We take a taxi to Piazzale Clodio where he has an office in the Tribunale. In design the building is authentically proletarian: it might have been uprooted from a Soviet bloc country – their cities are filled with similar examples of the Tribunale's concrete ugliness.

Armed police are everywhere. The steel entrance gates are reinforced to withstand (it is hoped) a kamikaze-type attack on the building by one of those bomb-filled trucks which have caused such havoc in Beirut and elsewhere.

Inside the gate is a metal detector. Not even Martella can enter this building without being scanned. Security, he happily admits to us, is even better than in Rebibbia. There, Agca and Antonov are presently located only a few cells apart. Both are held in solitary confinement in the maximum security wing.

It is now a year since Martella took charge of the case, we remind him as we sit down in his office. How is it coming along? Will he meet the deadline he has given himself and produce his report within the next six weeks?

He smiles and shrugs. 'It's coming along.'

Just as dealing with Vatican priests requires a degree of interpretation, so, we see, understanding the judge needs a similar skill. It is not only what he says but how he says it, and the gestures which accompany his remarks are equally significant.

This morning it is hard to recognize him as the man who had been so enraged by the presence of the media on the Via della Conciliazione. He not only sounds but looks very different. Then his hair was uncombed and his clothes seemed in need of pressing. Today he wears a custom-made blazer, flannels and expensive loafers. His greying hair is carefully brushed and his trim figure enhances his sportsman-like appearance. The way he moves his hands he could have been a boxer. He is all smiles, and all business too.

He repeats he is glad to see us. He adds he will be even happier to study our copy of the Austrian Security Service file we were given in December 1981, in Vienna. After glancing at it, he says, a trifle bleakly, this is one file the Austrians had not shown him: he wonders whether there may be others.

A large part of the file deals with the activities of Horst Grillmeir, the arms dealer who actually purchased the gun which Agca used to shoot the pope.

Before studying the file in detail, the judge says he is also interested to hear what we know about Frank Terpil.

We explain the unresolved issues our own investigation has raised: Terpil's connections to the CIA before, and possibly during and after, the assassination attempt raise doubts about the agency's claim to know almost nothing about the matter. How much reliance should be placed on that strange Irish brother and sister, John and Marie McCarthy, and their allegations about Terpil? Where did Gary Korkola fit into the picture, apart from being a CIA agent who had worked with Terpil in the Middle East?

Martella listens carefully. He agrees the questions are indeed troubling, and perhaps may never be fully resolved.

He hopes there is evidence in the Austrian file which will show not only whether Grillmeir was in Syria in 1978/79, but also Terpil and Agca.

The question that interests Martella, and ourselves, is: could they have met – *did* they all meet?

The first part, we agree, is easy to answer: they may well have met.

He is eager to get into the file to see if he can solve the second part. The documents are in German, a language he cannot read. But he is looking for persons he can identify.

There are a great number of names: Turks who were members of Grey Wolves' cells in Austria, the terrorist organization to which Agca belonged; Austrian intelligence officers whose reports fill the file; Interpol officers, BND and BKA agents. And Horst Grillmeir. His name turns up time and again. Martella begins to take notes of dates and places. Once in a while he nods; if he is not openly excited, he is clearly deeply interested.

We look around the office. The case files on the assassination attempt have overflowed his desk on to another. Agca's own file is at least ten inches thick. It is broken down into years. This impressive collection of material has pride of place on Martella's desk, standing close to his telephone.

The office is cluttered, the accumulation of documents staggering. There must be several million words stored in this room.

Martella asks whether he can photocopy our file. We agree.

He makes a surprising admission after his year of investigation. 'My problem is to establish who actually passed the gun to Agca.'

There is an engaging frankness about Martella's words; for a moment he sounds like somebody Agatha Christie might have invented.

The judge hopes the Austrian file will give him a clue: a name he can recognize and follow up, the movement of some person he may not have known about. He wants to back-track over Grillmeir's travels in Syria, from that time he had served with the United Nations peacekeeping force on the Golan Heights. Could that have been the occasion he might have met Terpil and Agca?

We ask whether the Austrians were being helpful in providing background on Grillmeir.

'Helpful?' He savours the question, nods and smiles. 'Oh, yes, helpful.'

What about the CIA?

He looks at us but does not answer.

What had Rudi once said: poor Judge Martella; he has no chance with the Company.

We talk on, exploring the ramifications of *Pista Bulgara*, or as far as legal propriety allows him to go.

He has a curious manner when offering information. It comes in staccato bursts, the words tumbling one after the other at speed. Then just as abruptly as he starts, he stops, watching to see the effect of what he has said. It is the technique of a born advocate, never releasing more than can be properly absorbed. He is clearly concerned that everything he says is well understood.

He explains that once he has finished his final report it will be thoroughly checked by another investigating magistrate. That might take months. Then, almost certainly, it will have to be submitted to the Foreign Ministry and the Minister of Justice.

'It is a long and laborious process,' he says wearily.

Nor is the case made easier by its political undertow. Martella knows that if he proves the Bulgarian Connection he is implicating Yuri Andropov; he concedes there is simply no way around that. And *that* could have the kind of repercussions not even Martella likes to begin to imagine. He merely confines himself to a simple truth. 'I am an investigator of crimes, not a politician.'

He turns back to our file on Frank Terpil. It contains not only a wealth of material on Terpil, but also his associates. Martella seizes upon the data relating to Gary Korkola which John and Marie McCarthy had provided.

We explain the entire story to the judge. He shakes his head. 'Incredible. I have never heard of this from the Irish police authorities . . .'

He gives the impression he may wish to find out why he has not been shown the material.

The magistrate asks whether we are able to say when Terpil had been in Lebanon and Syria and where he may have met Agca.

We refer him to the tape-recorded statements of John

McCarthy and our detailed notes of his sister's account: both claimed Terpil told Marie he trained Agca in 1980.

Martella presses. 'When exactly? I must know *when*. The dates are very important.'

But a review of the McCarthys' evidence does not provide the specific dates he wants. He cannot hide his disappointment. 'It's always the same. Often when I want dates they are not available. Agca is very good with dates.'

The telephone rings. Martella looks irritated. His secretary comes running into the office. She says a colonel from Italian military intelligence is on the line.

Martella sighs. He rises to his feet and takes the call. He listens a great deal, grunts once, and then abruptly hangs up.

One of his assistants enters the room. He is in his late twenties, sports a droopy moustache and has the sort of hands bad novelists call capable.

Martella indicates the files we have brought. The younger man begins to study them.

'Terpil,' he says, thoughtfully. 'Yes. An interesting man.'

We talk on, reviewing with Martella our enquiries in Europe. He listens and now and then nods.

Suddenly he looks at his watch. He is sorry, but he has another appointment. Can we return the following Tuesday to continue our discussion?

A time is fixed. Martella seems genuinely pleased.

'Terpil,' he murmurs, echoing his assistant. 'Indeed an interesting person . . .'

We are early on Tuesday – but Martella is waiting. He is almost effusive. He explains he has had an opportunity to go through the Austrian file. He adds, again, he cannot understand why he has not seen it before.

Once more he begins a careful review of the topics we discussed before: Korkola and his connection with Terpil; Marie McCarthy and her connection to them both; Agca and Terpil – what exactly had Marie McCarthy claimed?

How much was supported by her brother? How credible did we think they both were? Could we say for certain that Terpil and Korkola still had contact with the CIA?

We could not.

Had Marie McCarthy any link to the CIA?

We did not know.

How do we estimate the role of the CIA in the matter?

We mention certain misgivings, explaining on what they are based but being careful not to implicate sources like Rudi.

He smiles an understanding smile.

Martella then says the discussion we are about to have must remain privileged. We agree. But after spending a further two hours with him we are sure of one thing. It did not need the CIA to revive the Bulgarian Connection. During all these months Judge Martella has never forsaken it. And, just as a year ago he had startled the world with his allegation that it really did exist, so he is now preparing another bombshell he hopes to explode shortly.

THE SECRETARIAT OF STATE
Thursday
Morning

The black mood of last month carries over.

Kabongo expresses it poignantly. 'We shall continue to pray. That is all, in the end, we as priests can do.'[1]

He is referring, among other serious matters, to the arrival of the first NATO missiles in Europe, at Greenham Common in England; to the latest bloodbath in Lebanon where the PLO appears on the brink of extinction and Yasser Arafat is fighting for his own life; to the news that the newly elected Argentinian government is boasting it now has the technology to manufacture enriched uranium for making nuclear bombs; to the United States invasion of Grenada; to Africa's worst famine in a decade; to the heightened tension in Nicaragua between the Marxist government and the Church; to the latest earthquake to ravage eastern Turkey, killing alone over 1,100 children; to the growing discord between the American Church and the Vatican.

These and a score of other equally demanding situations continue to preoccupy, distress and sometimes depress not only the pope's usually cheerful secretary but also many diplomats in the Apostolic Palace. All are well used to the vicissitudes of the world, but none can easily recall a month which has been as grim as this past one.

For Kabongo, 'the reek of war was never more pronounced than now, nor the need to work for peace more urgent'.[2]

Outwardly there is no sign of strain among those engaged with Kabongo in trying to stave off the apocalypse they detect. They have time for the usual whispered conversations when they meet in the corridors, during lunchtime strolls through the Vatican Gardens or when they gather to pray at appointed hours in one of the many chapels in the palace.

But behind this routine there is a tension which is a direct carry-over from the International Synod of Bishops. It had concluded deliberations on a doom-laden note, deploring 'warlike aggressiveness, violence and terrorism, the building up of arsenals of both conventional and especially nuclear arms, and the scandalous trade in all weapons of war'.[3]

When closing the Synod John Paul declared himself 'very troubled' at the international situation,[4] and had sent those urgent messages to the Soviet and American leaders.

Their responses have provided little reason for optimism. The pope was unable to conceal his disappointment from his staff.

For the first time in months events in Geneva, not Warsaw, now dominate the pope's thinking. The top item every morning in the Summary File is the latest report from Archbishop Edoardo Rovida, the Holy See's apostolic nuncio to the United Nations in the Swiss city.

Rovida says there are now only sporadic contacts between the Americans and Russians, and these take place in an atmosphere of 'stark unreality'. The nuncio describes 'a pretence all is normal while even a glance at the television news or the newspaper headlines tells the opposite'.[5]

That looming uncertainty has caused Cardinal Basil Hume, Primate of England and Wales, to speak out about 'complex and threatening issues', which have 'been brought home to people much more sharply than before'.[6]

Hume stressed that his contribution to the nuclear debate was his personal assessment; nor should it in any way be seen as a response to Mgr Bruce Kent's recent remarks to the Communist Party of Britain's congress.

The leader of the Campaign for Nuclear Disarmament had once more managed to attract a clutch of headlines while causing pained surprise in the Vatican. Casaroli has reputedly criticized Kent to his staff as being politically naïve. Others in the Secretariat of State say Kent is not merely foolish but dangerously so, and should now be dealt with quickly and firmly.

It is not just that Kent has appeared at the Communist congress. He continues to generate more controversy than any other Catholic prelate in the present British hierarchy. He has indicated that servicemen who handle nuclear weapons might be tried as 'war criminals'; he has maintained a sustained attack on many of the policies of the Conservative government.

There is disagreement in the Secretariat of State whether Kent is simply accident prone in terms of his reported remarks, or whether he is determined, whatever the consequences, to force a showdown with Hume and, ultimately, the pope.

Indeed, during the summer Kent publicly questioned John Paul's judgement. He appeared almost to be calling for the removal of the pope. He subsequently expressed regret that he had not emphasized his great admiration for the courage of John Paul.

Since then Kent has continued to entangle the Church with nuclear politics, culminating in his appearance at the Communist rally.

Nobody doubts his views are sincerely held, but the feeling among many in the Secretariat of State is that he is going too far in his zealousness to promote unilateral disarmament.

Hume, who already carries the media scorchmarks from his involvement in that earlier dispute between papal nuncio Bruno Heim and Kent, is anxious to make clear he has been formulating his views on the nuclear issue for months.

He insists he wants to 'show a way forward', to offer guidance on the dilemma resulting from 'the moral imperative not to use such inhuman weapons and a policy of nuclear deterrence with its declared willingness to use them if attacked'.

Hume endorses what he says is emerging as the most widely accepted view of the Catholic Church on the matter: nuclear deterrence can be morally acceptable on strict conditions and only as a temporary expedient leading to progressive disarmament.

The cardinal regards deterrence, 'because of the world situation', as the lesser of two evils, 'without in any way regarding it as good in itself'.

While accepting that the peace movements play an important role – 'they bring before us the terrible questions we might otherwise ignore, but which must be answered; they rightly alert us to the dangers of nuclear escalation and proliferation; they compel us to question whether new weapons are intended to deter or whether they serve an aggressive purpose' – he firmly puts the movements in perspective. 'They bring pressure to bear primarily on the governments of the West and not on those of the East. In Communist regimes, movements critical of official policy are rarely tolerated. There are different perceptions in the East and in the West about the threat to peace.'

He argues there must be 'a firm and effective intention to extricate ourselves from the present fearful situation as quickly as possible'.

The acceptance of a policy of nuclear deterrence, although in some respects 'an untidy view, risky and provisional', gives rise to a number of serious considerations.

Hume enumerates four: any government not taking steps to reduce its nuclear weapons can expect to be increasingly alienated from its citizens; nuclear deterrence should not be morally condemned in the same way as the actual use of nuclear weapons against civilian targets; service personnel may be commended as defenders of security and peace, but 'they, too, face grave moral issues'; deterrence must always be viewed as a means of preventing war, not of waging it.

The cardinal challenges the sheer size of nuclear stockpiles; he sees expenditure on them as 'out of balance and should be cut back'. Acknowledging 'state secrecy on security matters' further complicates an already unclear condition, in his opinion this does not 'give us the right seriously to defy the law in the present situation. We must have due regard for democratic processes and for the institutions of a free society.'

Basil Hume's thought-provoking intervention ends in a mood as sombre as the one which prevails nowadays in the Apostolic Palace.

'The present situation is grave. Those with political power must have the will to discover a better way to achieve peace than through the amassing of nuclear weapons. The future of humanity depends on it.'

The Middle East Desk staff are largely concerned with the fate of Yasser Arafat.[7] The PLO leader is in the Lebanese port of Tripoli, surrounded by Syrian armour and those members of his organization who have not deserted him. Arafat and his meagre force have in the past month been driven virtually into the Mediterranean. But there is no easy escape by sea. Israeli gunboats are waiting off shore. No one on the Middle East Desk knows if they really will snatch Arafat, the man they continue to name as their most wanted terrorist.

For the past three weeks the papal diplomats responsible for Middle East affairs have been engaged in desperate negotiations with Israel and Syria to allow Arafat and his men passage to safety.[8]

A plea has been conveyed directly from the Apostolic Palace to President Assad's mansion in Damascus; it indicates he has already dealt a mortal blow to Arafat's leadership, and ruthlessly to pursue him and his dwindling army is an act of genocide.

Sometimes working through its own nuncios, at others using intermediaries, the Holy See's views have also been presented to virtually every Arab government except Libya's.[9] Gaddafi has made clear he fully supports Syria's determination to remove Arafat from the Middle East cockpit in which he has been such a dominant figure for so many years.

Day after day the Holy See's initiative – working in tandem with the efforts of the United States and France – has continued while Arafat's perimeter in Tripoli shrank and shrank, as he lost one refugee camp after another, and saw his decreasing forces finally cornered in a small area of the port.

Archbishop Angelo Pedroni, the pro-nuncio in Damascus, has shuttled endlessly between President Assad and his ministers, and the papal embassy at 82 Rue Musr. From there Pedroni has telephoned Rome with the same depressing news: the Syrians remain stubbornly unresponsive to any appeal on humanitarian grounds – or the mounting political pressure not only from the West, but also from the East.

Then papal diplomatic persistence began to pay off.

Luigi Poggi tapped his contacts in the Soviet bloc to enlist the Russians to reason with Assad. There was a guarded promise from Moscow that it would have words with its client-state in the Middle East.[10]

In the meantime Casaroli has suggested Pedroni advance a new argument to Assad. For the Syrians to butcher Arafat will only ensure what Assad does not want to occur – that Arafat becomes a martyr, perhaps capable from the grave of one day inspiring a successor to create a new PLO bent on vengeance against Syria for his death. But, to allow Arafat to live, and escape with a greatly reduced following, would assuredly demonstrate the total power and confidence Assad now has in the region.

This time Assad had listened.

He agreed that his foreign minister and that of Saudi Arabia, whom the Middle East Desk regard as the most moderate of the Arab states it has been secretly dealing with on the matter, should meet in Damascus to explore the situation further.

Meanwhile other papal envoys have continued to examine in the utmost secrecy another initiative which preoccupies the Middle East Desk.

Archbishop William Aquin Carew, apostolic delegate in Jerusalem since 1974, had originally reported that Israel might be willing to exchange thousands of Arab prisoners in return for just six Israeli soldiers captured by the PLO and now held in their battered redoubt in Tripoli.

Using Carew as the fulcrum, the Holy See has been delicately conducting a diplomatic see-saw back and forth between friendly Arab states urging them to bring new pressures on Syria to seize this golden opportunity to have their men freed.

President Reagan has brought his own authority to bear on Israel's new prime minister, Yitshak Shamir. And Casaroli, in a highly unusual move, has strengthened his personal standing in the matter by telephoning Shamir and congratulating him on his election. Implicit in the call is the clear understanding that the Holy See might draw closer to Israel.

Pio Laghi has learned in Washington, where Shamir has met with Reagan, that the Israeli leader was guardedly impressed by Casaroli's intervention. Laghi has himself been in constant contact with the State Department over the crisis, feeding news of American moves to Rome and receiving, in return, the latest information on what the Holy See was doing.

Throughout Western Europe nuncios received an identical briefing: they must be on the alert for any news of a breakthrough in the situation. It was possible, based on past experience, that such sensitive listening posts as the nunciatures in Vienna and Bonn could be the first to know of any positive development.

That done, there was no more the Middle East Desk could do, except wait for the next report from Pedroni in Damascus. He has gleaned very little of what is happening in the negotiations in the Syrian Foreign Ministry.

Then, from Paris, Nuncio Felici telephoned. The Israeli government had just placed an order with Air France to fly a number of jetliners to Ben Gurion International Airport in Tel Aviv.

Shortly afterwards Carew reported from Jerusalem that more than one thousand Palestinians, most of them held at

410

the Ansar prison camp in southern Lebanon, were on their way to Ben Gurion airport.

Within an hour the Middle East Desk has full confirmation of the deal from Pedroni.

Arafat will allow the six Israelis to be ferried to a French ship waiting outside Tripoli port. There they would be transferred to an Israeli naval boat. Once they were known to be safe, Israel would release, all told, 4,500 Palestinians and Lebanese captured in the war in Lebanon. They will be flown to Algeria on those Air France planes.

The PLO leader has also accepted a joint Saudi Arabian-Syrian proposal, monitored and approved by the Middle East Desk, for 'a permanent' ceasefire in Tripoli and the evacuation of all PLO forces from the battered port.[11]

Yet what seemed so clear-cut a few hours ago – in the wake of the exchange of prisoners – has now suddenly gone back into the melting pot.

Both Pedroni in Damascus and Carew in Jerusalem report ominous signs Syria and Israel are having second thoughts about letting Yasser Arafat escape.

The Middle East Desk diplomats have begun urgently to discuss how best they can handle this new and totally unexpected development.

The Holy See's response to the latest Middle East crisis has, in part, been affected by its attitude towards the US invasion of Grenada. The Caribbean incursion came as a complete surprise – and shock – to the pope and his men. The first John Paul knew of it was several hours after the action began.[12] He was not pleased either with the turn of events or the fact there had been no prior warning of what was about to happen from either CIA Rome or William Wilson.

Accordingly the early discussions regarding Arafat between the Holy See and Washington were conducted under a certain strain.

411

Since then both the CIA and the envoy – Wilson always accompanied by the vigilant Planty – have kept the pope and the Secretariat of State briefed, the latter informed at what Wilson calls 'the working level'.[13]

John Paul and his diplomats learned why President Reagan felt he must invade Grenada. Eventually they were convinced of the validity of the president's decision.

There is regret within the Apostolic Palace that the pro-nuncio in Cuba, who reported on the position in Grenada earlier in the year, was hoodwinked by the Marxist regime on the island when he reported that, in his opinion, there was little to support the idea of Grenada posing a military threat to the United States.[14]

The evidence Wilson continues to obtain from Washington, and the even more damning data CIA Rome provides, shows that Grenada had become yet another client-state of the Soviet Union.

Now accepting this to be the case, papal diplomats who deal with Wilson have made clear in future they expect some advance notice of any further US intention to go to war.[15]

In spite of this request, the priests on the Latin America Desk are so far unable to obtain reliable comment from Washington on an astounding report they have heard from a number of usually reliable Central American sources. It centres on what these informants claim will be President Reagan's next move in Nicaragua.[16]

There, the Church's own relationship with the Marxist government has reached a new nadir. The last semblance of the fiction of co-existence which followed the pope's visit in March has been torn away. The Sandinista regime no longer bothers to disguise its harassment of any priest who speaks out against its policies. Daily reports from Managua reaching the Latin America Desk describe crude threats towards even senior members of the Nicaraguan hierarchy.

The extent of those threats has increased in direct

proportion to the intensity of that persistent rumour about American intentions. On the surface it is both plausible and logical. But the implications, if true, are far reaching and go well beyond anything previous US administrations have attempted in the region.

This report claims President Reagan hopes to see a 'provisional government' set up in a town captured from the Sandinistas in Nicaragua by some of the 12,000 *contras*, the right-wing guerrillas which the United States finances, equips and trains in the latest techniques of subversive warfare.

According to the scenario which has reached the Latin America Desk, the intention is for the *contras* to establish the provisional government in the captured town. That government would receive almost immediate diplomatic recognition from Washington and other US-backed regimes in Latin America. To ensure its survival there would also be a massive increase in military aid from the United States, including, if necessary, the direct involvement of US troops in Nicaragua.

The papal diplomats readily recognize that such a plan is fraught with horrendous problems. It could create a super-power confrontation in the region if the Marxist regime enlisted the support of Russia.[17] It could engulf Nicaragua in civil war. It could turn the whole of Central America into a killing zone.

For any of these reasons, when they first heard the rumour, the desk's analysts discounted it. But after what happened in Grenada, the priests realize they cannot be so dismissive.

Pio Laghi has indicated there is a mood in Washington for punitive action against the Sandinistas. His colleagues on the Latin America Desk realize the reason Laghi has been unable to obtain firm confirmation – or denial – that the plan exists, could well be because it is under active consideration, and shrouded in secrecy similar to that which preceded the invasion of Grenada.

413

Nuncios in El Salvador, Guatemala, Panama and Honduras have separately suggested the plan was almost certainly discussed at a highly secret session in October of CONDECA, the Central American Defence Council. Like the Eastern Caribbean group which 'invited' the United States to intervene in Grenada, CONDECA has close links with the Reagan administration.

Indeed, on Pentagon orders, the US Army Southern Command ranking officer, General Paul Gorman, attended the CONDECA meeting to discuss, according to one report, the plan to remove the Sandinistas.[18] The general reputedly even gave the operation a code-name: Pegasus. Gorman had also helped formulate the invasion tactics which were so successful on Grenada.

He is said to have been the guiding force at the CONDECA meeting where, again according to a subsequent report, it was agreed CONDECA would militarily support an appeal from the 'provisional government' to help fight off the vastly superior Sandinista forces.[19]

Between its regular army and militia the regime commands some hundred thousand troops. This figure is one of the very few facts CIA Rome has confirmed to the Vatican. Otherwise, the Station, like envoy William Wilson, is showing an unusual degree of reticence to discuss any possible US moves in Nicaragua. This has increased the foreboding on Latin America Desk that something could be afoot.

Still concerned that any military move against Nicaragua would have dangerously escalating consequences, the desk's analysts concede that such an action could work. CONDECA forces, supported by the US naval task force which has been cruising for some months off the Nicaraguan coast, could overcome the Marxist government forces; if there was any doubt, the matter would be settled by President Reagan committing the 4,000 US troops sailing with the task force.

Another sign such an operation might be under active consideration is that nuncios in the region are reporting the

CIA has managed to persuade the various anti-Sandinista factions outside Nicaragua to accept a *contra* government composed of, among others, a millionaire businessman, a former Sandinista ambassador to Washington, the ex-president of Nicaragua's Central Bank and a couple of former ministers in the Sandinista regime.

On paper it could make a credible provisional government. Most important of all, from the Reagan administration's standpoint, if it is to be installed this should happen in sufficient time for the political dust to settle, at least within the United States, before the presidential elections.

To complicate further its analysis of the situation, the Latin America Desk has also just received the equally startling news that the Sandinistas have begun to send home the first of over a thousand Cuban 'advisers' – and have made totally unexpected and sudden overtures to mend the regime's relationship with the local Church hierarchy; its first move in this direction has been to ease the rigid censorship of Nicaragua's only opposition newspaper, the Church-supported *La Prensa*.

These new developments raise more questions for the priest-diplomats to ponder. Do the moves indicate a genuine change in the regime's appalling record of abuses of human rights? Without the departing Cubans, is the Sandinista army powerful enough to repulse an invading force? And are the overtures no more than the regime trying to buy time – knowing that every month which passes will lessen the chance of President Reagan daring to launch Operation Pegasus as the US elections approach?

The pope's experts on Central America, men who for the past years have been remarkably right in their reading of the situation, are now unsure; part of their uncertainty stems from that lack of genuine information from Washington.

Some of the priests feel this position must be expected – in view of what is happening to the relationship between the Vatican and the Roman Catholic Church in the United States.

This is not only affecting the decision-making process on the Latin America Desk but has sent what amounts to a collective shudder throughout the entire Apostolic Palace.

THE PAPAL APARTMENT
Same Day: Late Morning

Papal messenger Ercole Orlandi leads three American bishops down a long corridor patrolled by Swiss Guards and through the first of the two antechambers which give access to the apartment.[20] The prelates are on their *ad limina* visit, come to report to the pope on the year's events in their dioceses and to hear his views on what troubles him about the state of the Catholic Church in the United States; no American priest nowadays can escape being lectured.

Orlandi walks slightly ahead, pushing open the double doors which lead from one vaulted-ceilinged reception room to another. One of the bishops closes the doors behind them and then falls back into step with his companions. They continue a murmured conversation among themselves.

The messenger is lost in his own reverie. He is trying to comprehend what Cibin had told him.[21]

The pope is planning to visit Agca in Rebibbia prison. John Paul hopes that by doing so the kidnappers of Emanuela will finally reveal the girl's fate.

Orlandi's initial response to this latest initiative by John Paul had left him almost in tears. Now, as he leads the prelates towards the pope's office, the messenger has begun to accept the matter in a more objective manner.

Certainly the pope's proposed action seems a further indication that his daughter is dead. During the past few weeks the police hunt has been steadily scaled down. The pope has stopped publicly appealing for Emanuela to be returned. But, on more than one occasion when they have met in the corridors of the Apostolic Palace, John Paul has told the broken-hearted messenger that he continues to pray for the soul of the child.[22]

The pope has also promised Orlandi that if Emanuela's body is found, she will receive a funeral in one of the basilica chapels before being laid to rest within the Vatican walls.[23]

As a final resort John Paul is now prepared to come face to face with the man who tried to murder him. From what Orlandi has been told – news he will later share with his family – the pope intends to go completely alone into Agca's cell. There they will speak privately. Though he has lost a great deal of his fanaticism, Agca remains a Muslim; even so that will not stop John Paul giving him a papal blessing.

The messenger believes the pope is prepared to do this to try and assuage the grief the Orlandi family feels. Ercole Orlandi finds, once again, tears welling in his eyes.[24]

He is visibly relieved to hand over the bishops to Kabongo and hurry away.[25]

The secretary is waiting outside the pope's office door. He welcomes the bishops and then escorts them in to see John Paul.

THE PAPAL SECRETARIAT
Same Day: A Little Later

Kabongo returns to his own office and prepares for the next two audiences.

The pope will first receive the Italian prime minister, Bettino Craxi. Then he will welcome Melina Mercouri, the actress-singer who is now Greece's Minister of Culture and Science.

John Paul's briefs for both audiences have been prepared well in advance.

But even while Kabongo was waiting for the American bishops, two more questions – one for Craxi, the other for

Mercouri – have been sent across from the head of the Middle East Desk with a request they should be inserted at the top of the respective briefs.

The question for Craxi will, in all probability, produce a straightforward 'yes' or 'no' response. Does the Italian government intend to remove its peacekeeping force from the Lebanon if, and when, the PLO is successfully evacuated from Tripoli?

Earlier today the Middle East Desk received news the Italians intend to withdraw. The priest-diplomats urgently want to pin down the facts as these could affect their own plans to mount a new initiative to save Arafat and his men.

The question for Mercouri is closely linked with that initiative. But no instant answer is expected from her. Instead the Middle East Desk will be satisfied with a commitment from Mercouri to return to Athens and immediately discuss with her government the question the section head suggests the pope asks: Will the Greek government provide ships, sailing under the United Nations flag, to evacuate Arafat and his men from the Lebanon?

The Middle East Desk staff believe that not even the avenging Israelis would dare attack ships so protected.

But, to make doubly sure, Nuncio Felici in Paris is exploring with the French government whether it would provide the Greek transports with a protective screen of warships, capable of keeping at bay any threat from the Israelis.

Kabongo places the questions at the top of the briefs. He has a shrewd idea John Paul will devote a large part of the audiences discussing the situation in the Lebanon with Craxi and Mercouri.

It is one of the significant changes in emphasis in the pontificate that whereas earlier in the year the pope was preoccupied with the possibility of Poland being the likeliest flashpoint for serious confrontation, perhaps even all-out war between the United States and the Soviet Union,

John Paul is now convinced the Lebanon is the most serious danger to world peace.

A strong and united Church, he has reminded his staff, is a pre-requisite for the crucial role he sees it playing not only in the Middle East but everywhere the interests of the United States and the Soviet Union conflict. This is why, he adds, he is especially concerned about what is happening with the American Church.

Almost daily it appears to be falling further out of kilter with Rome. There is hardly an hour which now passes when there is not some new shock, some fresh piece of dismaying news, some additional disturbing indication that the American Church, while believing it remains authentically Roman Catholic, is actually 'becoming more and more distinctly American'.[26]

Such judgements provoke a sharp response from the pope. If the Vatican can no longer control the religious attitudes of the richest and fourth largest national branch of Roman Catholicism – with 52 million adherents, the US Church rates behind Brazil's 111 million, the 67 million in Mexico and Italy's 56 million – then, retorts John Paul to his equally troubled aides, how can the Holy See expect to be taken seriously when advancing its only weapon, moral authority, as counter to potential nuclear confrontation?

During his audience this morning with the trio of American bishops, the latest in a procession of US prelates the pope has been seeing these past weeks, John Paul will explore once more what is happening to traditional Catholic teachings in the United States.

Just as he seems never to tire of hearing the latest reports on Agca, *Pista Bulgara* and all the other events associated with his assassination attempt, so nowadays John Paul is prepared, when it comes to the American Church, to go over familiar ground, perhaps in the hope someone will produce a justification for what at the moment seems incomprehensible behaviour by large numbers of US Catholics.

But now, he has asked his equally baffled staff, can any American Catholic bishop explain – let alone justify – what has just happened in Chicago, except in terms of flagrant disobedience?

No fewer than 1,200 nuns and laywomen from thirty-seven states have held a successful rally in Chicago to oppose the limitations placed on the role of women in the Church. They founded what they described as 'a new women's Catholic movement'. Some nuns left Chicago with buttons on their habits announcing: 'I'm Poped Out'.[27]

A sample button has been sent anonymously to the papal Secretariat. Nobody there was amused by this emblem of protest.[28]

But what really angered the pope is an account of another recent gathering in the US. One-third of the country's Catholic bishops have lent support to a consortium demanding ordination for women by attending a meeting in Washington sponsored in part by these activists. The bishops went despite John Paul's clear directive to each of them three months ago that they withdraw 'all support' from anyone promoting the idea of female priests; many of the ninety-seven bishops in Washington made no secret of the fact that they were sympathetic to the women's demands.[29]

John Paul at first wanted publicly to rebuke them for their open disregard of his directive. He decided not to do so; it might further widen the rift between Rome and the United States.

But nobody was able to stop him going ahead with one action. Currently, each of America's 500-plus religious orders and its 300 seminaries is under 'investigation'. Bishops known to be totally loyal to John Paul's thinking have been directed to research the over 800 Church establishments and report to Rome anywhere teaching has strayed from the religious orthodoxy John Paul is determined to enforce.[30]

Each investigating bishop has received an identical brief,

typed in the papal Secretariat and air-couriered to Laghi in Washington for distribution.

Yet even now, as he closely questions the three American bishops about their views on what is happening in the American Church, another shock awaits the pope.

During the morning Fr Bruno Fink has brought from the Holy Office to the papal Secretariat a copy of a report which shows how far one senior American prelate has departed from what the Vatican regards as acceptable.

This particular document has rocked even Cardinal Ratzinger's proverbial composure. The tough-minded Bavarian who heads the Holy Office has himself reread the account several times; each time it produced the same response in His Eminence: an incredulous shaking of his head.

Fink has handed over the report to Stanislaw Dziwisz. He intends to place it before John Paul as soon as the audience with Melina Mercouri ends.

Just as in the Holy Office, an incredulous ripple has surged through the Secretariat as news of the report's contents percolates.

It concerns the Most Reverend Raymond Hunthausen, Archbishop of Seattle since 1975, and the way he ministers to his flock of 287,000.[31]

From the beginning of the year – from that day in January when news of what has become known in both the papal Secretariat and the Holy Office as 'the balloon funeral' first came to the Vatican's attention – there has been a wave of complaints about the goings-on under the greying, bespectacled and avuncular Hunthausen; to opponents he seems bent on rewriting Canon Law to suit his own ideas of Catholicism.

Nobody in the Apostolic Palace can remember such a controversial American prelate since the days of the late Cardinal Cody of Chicago.

As with Cody, Ratzinger and John Paul have held several meetings to decide what should be done about Hunthausen. There is the fact that his reputation as the 'peace archbishop' is spreading across the United States as he peppers his preaching with appeals for unilateral disarmament – placing himself in opposition to what the pope advocates. There is the fact that Hunthausen is directly involving the Church in civil disobedience by refusing to pay half his income tax as a protest against the Reagan administration's hard-line nuclear policies. There is the fact that the archbishop verges on the border of incitement when he takes every opportunity to denounce the nuclear submarine base in his diocese, even describing it as the 'Auschwitz of Puget Sound'.

These facts are not in dispute. Yet both the pope and the Prefect of the Holy Office realize that to remove Hunthausen on what amounted to secular political grounds would create more problems. To ninety per cent of his priests, the archbishop is a hero. They have just signed a public document saying so. And among an impressive number of his parishioners, Hunthausen commands similar loyalty.

But it is his position on religious matters which has concerned both John Paul and Ratzinger; so much so that the pope decided to take action.

He signed a papal order authorizing Archbishop James Hickey of Washington, DC, to make an 'apostolic visitation' to Seattle to establish precisely what had occurred at the now notorious 'balloon funeral', and to sample the views of Hunthausen's followers on other liturgical rituals the archbishop has condoned.

Hickey's account of the 'balloon funeral' episode is far worse than expected. It took place in St Michael's Church in Olympia, one of the parishes within Hunthausen's archdiocese. The service was for a 37-year-old man who had left a wife and two young children – and devoutly Catholic parents who grieved deeply over the loss of their only son. Their sorrow had turned to shock when they entered St Michael's.

The priest who was to celebrate the mass, Fr Paul

Dalton, was dressed in modish vestments; he stood on the altar steps cheerfully urging worshippers to introduce themselves. To the distraught parents, it smacked more of 'a Chamber of Commerce luncheon' than a sacred occasion.

They were in for further shocks. During his breezy homily, Dalton revealed that as the husband was dying, it was the man's wife, not a priest, who annointed him with sacramental oil.

Hardly had the parents recovered from this disturbing break with tradition than they were assailed by Dalton inviting everyone in the congregation – Catholic and non-Catholic alike – to come forward to receive Communion.

Then had come the most extraordinary moment of all, one even Hickey's careful and restrained reporting cannot disguise as anything but an offensive infringement of the normal Catholic rites for the dying.

As the Communion ended a dancer suddenly began to pirouette through the sanctuary. Behind her came a figure in clown's garb, carrying a bunch of inflated balloons.

The clown began to prance around the coffin, keeping up a continous chant. 'Today my brother and sister are dancing together in heaven.'

The dead man's mother recognized the voice. It was that of her own daughter.

The distraught parents watched in stunned silence as their daughter tied the balloons to the brass handles of her brother's coffin. Then, still chanting, she whirled out of the church.

Her place around the coffin was taken up by the pallbearers, half-a-dozen men in work shirts.

They hefted the coffin out of St Michael's and placed it on the dead man's pick-up truck.

His parents had written to the pope detailing what they saw as an outrage.

Hickey's report confirmed the veracity of their reporting. The investigating archbishop spent a week in Seattle speaking to priests, nuns and parishioners.

Yet, many of them had fervently repeated their support for Hunthausen. They described him as 'a man of Vatican II', and reminded Hickey that 'the culture in the US is different from Rome'. Hunthausen's archdiocese was portrayed as a 'paradigm of a nationwide tension between liberals and conservatives'.[32]

Those in the papal apartment who have seen Hickey's report firmly believe it exemplifies the gulf between the Vatican and the Catholic Church in the United States.

There is mounting dismay in the Apostolic Palace that, after a year of almost constant discussion with the US Church, some of its senior members show no signs of abating their dissent.

Only a few days ago, Archbishop Rembert Weakland of Milwaukee joined the growing chorus of criticism. Many American Catholics think Rome continues to treat them as though they were members of a Third World 'mission church'; because of the pope's Polish background, Weakland believes he 'probably doesn't quite understand the American approach to dialogue and pluralism'.[33]

While other American bishops have been quick to dissociate themselves from such personal criticism – notably Cardinal Bernardin of Chicago and Archbishop Roach of St Paul – all agree on the gravity of the situation in one key area of the US Church. The number of American nuns continues to decline: more than 60,000 have left religious life in the past seventeen years and replacements for them have not been found. Further, the figures for men entering the priesthood is totally inadequate to cope with the increase in the number of baptized Catholics in the country.

And, this very week, the pope has issued yet another order demanding that those priests and nuns who remain in the American Church must, like their counterparts everywhere else, abide fully by the new code of Canon Law which has taken twenty-four years to produce. Among the rules which John Paul insists they obey are that all priests and nuns live in convents or religious communities whenever possible; that they do not hold public office; that nuns, in particular, should wear some form of distinctive clerical garb.

One of the reasons the pope is seeing so many American bishops is that he wants to make clear, in the reported words of one of his staff, that 'there could be a real housecleaning' unless his commands are adhered to in full.[34]

Nobody, least of all Kabongo, relishes such a possibility. He sees the influence of the American Church as being 'very considerable in these troubled times. It can do so much in so many places.'[35]

The secretary is thinking of starving Africa.

Twenty-two nations in the continent are now in the grip of famine.[36] From Somalia to Zambia, from Mozambique to Mauritania, starvation stalks the land. A combination of drought, crop disease, cattle plague and the dreaded harmattan wind – powerful enough to suck the last drop of moisture from the soil, leaving the land a parched wilderness over which bush fires can rage unhindered – has taken its toll.

A large proportion of the 150 million Africans living in these afflicted areas face hunger and malnutrition.[37] In Chad and Ethiopia the presence of civil war has furthered the natural devastation.

Finally, there is the fundamental fact that Africa's 'baby boom' far outstrips its capacity to feed those extra new mouths. The continent has the greatest population growth rate in the Third World.

The Vatican monitored a recent meeting in Rome attended by representatives from those impoverished twenty-two African states plus thirty-five donor nations and international relief organizations. There had been recognition of the need for urgent and concerted action.

Kabongo has seen no real evidence this has been implemented.[38]

Less than twenty per cent has been pledged of the three

million tons of grain and other staple foods needed. Certain of the countries which have promised supplies say they cannot in addition afford the transport to take them to the stricken areas.[39]

The Vatican – through the Secretariat of State, numerous Congregations and local African hierarchies – is heavily involved in attempts to alleviate the plight of the hungry. Every available Catholic organization has been mobilized. Money has been made available through Vatican Bank to purchase essentials – and the means to get them to the needy. But it is not nearly enough.[40]

Kabongo, for one, accepts that the powerful influence of the American Church, properly directed from Rome, will be needed to help persuade the Reagan administration to make a renewed effort to stave off the real possibility of Africans dying in their tens of thousands.[41]

But if influential members of the US hierarchy continue to be at odds with the pope, then it will not be easy for the American Church to appear to be speaking with the full authority of Rome in the matter. This is one more reason why the compassionate black secretary wants to see everything possible done to avoid further confrontation between 'head office and a key branch'.[42]

THE SECRETARIAT OF STATE
Friday
Late Afternoon

Luigi Poggi begins to write. Hunched at his desk, an old-fashioned fountain pen – a gift from Paul VI – firmly gripped in his right hand, the nuncio who more than any other papal envoy keeps track of the power plays in the Kremlin and throughout the Soviet bloc is finally satisfied he can commit to paper the answer to a momentous mystery.

For the past three weeks Poggi has concentrated his considerable personal energy and mobilized every source he has behind the Iron Curtain to establish the answer to a question which is being repeatedly posed in every western capital. Is Yuri Andropov really dead – or alive?

In hot pursuit of the truth the nuncio had flown to Warsaw, Budapest, Prague and Vienna. There, he probed his contacts to try and discover what is happening in Moscow.

Before him, on his desk, Poggi has the few facts which are not in dispute. These barely cover a single sheet of paper. On other sheets are the notes of his own researches. This information gives him confidence that what he writes will be as accurate as anybody can be.

The two commonly known truths are: Andropov has not been seen in public for a great many months; and he failed to appear on the reviewing stand above Lenin's Tomb in Red Square to take the salute at the parade marking the 66th anniversary of the Russian Revolution.

This scanty data has spawned a growth industry of rumours, innuendoes and black propaganda.[43] The weekly reports from CIA Rome to the pope have, in recent months, contained a fair sample of the stories in circulation: Andropov is dead; Andropov is dying of cancer; Andropov has a terminal kidney disease; Andropov has gone mad; Andropov has been shot by Brezhnev's son and is critically injured; Andropov has deliberately gone into retreat to plan a sudden attack on the West.

None of these stories, the CIA reports hasten to add, can be verified.

But they have alarmed John Paul. He has asked Poggi to try and establish Yuri Andropov's fate.

With the Geneva arms control talks finally collapsed, and the two superpowers at dagger-point, the pope is anxious to know whether the Soviet leader is dead or alive.

John Paul's interest is an indication of how, in the past weeks, there has been a re-evaluation of his own feelings about the Reagan administration. While he would undoubtedly prefer to hold the view that envoy William Wilson fosters – namely, 'there are no fundamental disagreements between the Holy See and Washington on all important matters'[44] – John Paul has grown concerned, say his aides, that the continued speculation over Andropov's absence from the international political arena could lead to a situation which President Reagan might decide to exploit.

The network of nuncios in the Middle East, reinforced by news from Laghi in Washington, suggest there is a growing fear the United States may wish to deliver a stunning blow against Syria in retaliation for the recent massacre of hundreds of Marines in Beirut; it is a crime which continues to outrage and bind American opinion to the view that it would be justifiable to strike back. Syria has been identified by the CIA as playing a role in the massacre.

Papal envoys scattered throughout Central America are still insisting there is a possibility the United States will take offensive action against Nicaragua, in spite of recent conciliatory noises by its government.

With Andropov's whereabouts a matter of conjecture, the pope is concerned not only that the United States could make further military moves in the Middle East or Central America; what troubles John Paul equally is how the Soviet Politburo might respond to such action if Andropov, for whatever reason, is no longer in control in Moscow.

Poggi is confident he can now state certain opinions without fear of contradiction. Based on everything he has been told, he feels sure Andropov is alive. The nuncio further believes the Soviet leader is entirely in command of Soviet affairs, exercising his authority through nominees on the Politburo.

Yet, though alive, Yuri Andropov is certainly seriously ill, confined to a sick bed in a sanatorium near Moscow.

Poggi admits in his report to the pope that the nature of Andropov's illness remains a matter of considerable speculation; the nuncio merely notes the most commonly repeated cause is nephritis, a serious kidney condition. Poggi adds that some of his sources have told him Andropov's condition is so serious it is unlikely he will appear at the annual Supreme Soviet meeting in Moscow.

While his absence then would doubtless fuel further speculation, the nuncio is careful to point out his trusted sources are insisting it is too early to give credence to reports, mostly emanating from the CIA, that a search has already begun for a successor to Andropov.

Luigi Poggi doggedly holds to the belief that until the Soviet leader is actually declared medically dead by his doctors, Yuri Andropov will cling to office. In the nuncio's view this alone makes him 'the most dangerous Russian leader since Joseph Stalin'.[45]

THE PAPAL SECRETARIAT
Same Day: Early Evening

At six o'clock Casaroli arrives and is shown into the pope's office.

John Paul has set aside the next half-hour to review with the Secretary of State matters arising from their failure to save the life of a convicted murderer, Robert Sullivan.

Thirty-six-year-old Sullivan had spent his last ten years on death row in Florida state prison. During that time he persuaded many Catholic bishops, priests and nuns who visited him not only of his genuine religious faith but also of his innocence.

Partly as a result of this the American Church had been trying to save Sullivan's life since 1981. During that year a Florida bishop arranged for a priest in Boston, Mass., to see a local homosexual whom Sullivan said was with him in a gay bar far from the scene at the time of the murder.

The man, under the secrecy of the confessional, confirmed Sullivan's alibi. But he refused the priest's request to sign an affidavit to this effect which would almost certainly have resulted in a new trial for Sullivan. The man claimed his family did not know he was a homosexual and he did not want to make the fact public – even if this meant Sullivan would die.

Since then Sullivan's case had become a torch-bearer for intensifying the American Church's opposition to the death penalty.[46]

This campaign coincided with the hierarchy's renewed efforts to show its concern for life in other ways: by vigorously opposing abortion and euthanasia.

The fight to save Sullivan's life had been waged with the full approval of the Vatican. Casaroli personally endorsed the four separate statements opposing capital punishment which had been issued by the Catholic bishops of Florida. When the Secretary of State visited Miami last month – for the consecration of his private secretary as an archbishop – he had listened sympathetically to influential local Catholics who urged him to involve the pope in the case.

Back in Rome, Casaroli received a formal request through Pio Laghi for John Paul to make a personal plea to Florida's governor to save Sullivan.

The pope had immediately sent the governor an appeal for clemency on 'humanitarian grounds'.[47]

It was to no avail. A few days ago, Sullivan – his skull and right leg shaved for better contact with the electrodes – had been strapped into the electric chair.

A last-minute telephone call was made from the death chamber to the state governor. He would not change his mind and accede to John Paul's request. He insisted to the executioner there were no grounds for him to do so.

Sullivan was allowed to make a final statement to the world. They echoed Christ's own words on the Cross. 'I hold malice to no man. May God bless us all.'

The executioner then pulled the switch which sent thousands of volts coursing through Sullivan's body, cutting off his terror in mid-stream.

Neither the pope nor Casaroli now dwells on Sullivan's brief death agony. They are concerned with how to handle future cases; they have little doubt the time will come when John Paul will again be asked to intervene. The question is: should he do so – and risk further refusal?

John Paul is clear. Providing there are sufficient grounds to believe that guilt is in doubt, he will be prepared to make further appeals for the lives of other convicted murderers.

VATICAN RADIO
Wednesday
Morning

Walking through the second-floor corridors of the station, where the executive offices are situated, Clarissa McNair wonders how she can persuade Fr Quercetti, the vice director of programmes, her immediate superior, to tell her all he knows about the very strange happenings surrounding a recent broadcast of McNair's.[48]

They include: Vatican Radio issuing an unprecedented apology to its world-wide English speaking audience;[49] the possibility The Mad Mentor has struck, as he once vowed to do, to cause McNair the maximum embarrassment; the involvement of both Casaroli and Cibin in what has become known as the Case of the Doctored Tape.

Even now, as she heads for Quercetti's office to discuss the matter once more, McNair feels, 'I am tilting at windmills and the blades are coming around behind me to clout me on the head.'[50]

She has been feeling like this virtually from that afternoon three weeks ago when Thomas Siemer walked into the station, seeking air time to promote his anti-nuclear views.

Siemer brought with him a sheaf of press clips confirming his story of having spent twenty-three years working for Rockwell International in Columbus, Ohio. Siemer, a systems engineer, had helped the corporation develop a whole range of weapons – including nuclear missiles – for the American defence industry.

The newspaper stories spoke of his guilt-ridden feelings about his work; how the strain of making 'death weapons' turned him into an alcoholic; how he had developed cirrhosis of the liver and a heart ailment. They also describe how he suddenly quit his $80,000 a year job at Rockwell, emptied his bank account of its $100,000 deposits, sold up his three homes and the hundreds of acres they stood in, and used all his cash and energy to found a 'peace center' attached to the Holy Family Catholic Church in Columbus.

Siemer had gone on to establish contact with Cardinal Bernardin's committee, then drafting the US pastoral letter. One of the bishops suggested Siemer should go to Rome to lobby the Vatican with his views.

The burly, bearded, intense and blue-eyed Siemer, a Catholic of forty-two years, the father of seven children living in reduced circumstances with their mother in Columbus, had taken the advice.

McNair had listened carefully while Siemer argued why Vatican Radio should give him air time. He was passionate and eloquent. But McNair hesitated.

In recent weeks she had broadcast a series of reports which could be labelled controversial. She chose to put Siemer's case to her programme editor, Fr Ricardo Sanchis, a Spaniard who speaks no English.

Sanchis decided Siemer's views were sufficiently important to be spread over three separate programmes. The decision made, McNair interviewed Siemer. He bitterly attacked the Reagan administration's nuclear position, graphically described the effect of a Cruise missile landing on target, and drew the familiar apocalypse scenario of all nuclear disarmament debaters.[51]

McNair frequently challenged him, hoping to make clear she was 'only asking the questions, not agreeing'.[52]

Sanchis sat in the control booth during the entire interview. He expressed himself satisfied with 'the editorial balance'. McNair was wryly amused by this, as she was certain Sanchis had not actually understood a word of her interview.

She spent two days editing the tape into three programmes. She gave them to Sanchis. He placed them in a sliding-door cabinet. It is the regular storage place for tapes awaiting broadcast. The cabinet is locked only at night.

The first Siemer programme – broadcast to every English-speaking country in the world – caused considerable anger among US diplomats based in Rome.[53]

William Wilson, by then back on holiday in the United States, was reportedly furious that Vatican Radio had once more transmitted a programme that was anti-American.

The second Siemer programme was aired two days later.[54] After a few minutes it began to make no sense. Siemer's responses bore no relation to McNair's questions.

McNair knew what had happened: 'The tape which was broadcast was not the same as the tape I had edited. Mr Siemer's views in the broadcast tape did not properly represent what he said nor did the tape reflect my position. I was horrified to hear that one portion had been excised. I gave no authority for anybody to tamper with this tape.'[55]

Furious, she went to Quercetti. He told her to write 'a memo'. When she returned to place it on his desk, she found he had suddenly left the station and would not be back for some days.

Baffled, she sought, and obtained, an interview with Fr Pasquale Borgomeo, the station's director of programmes – answerable ultimately to Casaroli for what is broadcast. Borgomeo was placatory, insisting there must be a 'simple explanation'.

But when Siemer's secretary visited him demanding a full apology, Borgomeo quickly agreed. He personally wrote it. This was transmitted immediately prior to the third Siemer programme.[56] The apology spoke of a 'technical error' distorting the views of Thomas Siemer.

433

The matter, outwardly, seemed over.

Behind the scenes, in McNair's words, 'the mud was alive with alligators'.[57]

In spite of Borgomeo's initial nonchalant attitude, he was badly rattled by what had occurred. Casaroli was informed. The Secretary of State ordered Cibin to begin an investigation.

Within forty-eight hours Cibin established that the tape had almost certainly been tampered with, during the afternoon preceding transmission the following morning.[58] By interviewing the station's technicians and programme staff, the security chief concluded this could not have been done within the station.

By now Vatican Radio's apology had attracted the interest of a number of Rome-based reporters. They began to chase the story.

Al Troner of the London *Daily Express* had little doubt what had happened. 'McNair and Siemer are victims of CIA dirty tricks.'[59]

Troner claimed he had information, 'from good DIGOS sources', that the tape had been 'whisked out of the radio station by a CIA mole working there, doctored in a Rome studio by a Company professional and then slipped back into the station without anyone being the wiser'.[60]

His newspaper published a report about the hunt for the Vatican Radio mole and concern over a serious breach of the station's security.[61]

Security, as such, at Vatican Radio is almost non-existent. Tapes to be transmitted are easily accessible to anybody. Nor would a thief who had removed a tape for secret re-editing need fear this would be discovered before the tape was actually broadcast. Unlike most radio stations, no final pre-broadcast check is made at Vatican Radio on what is about to be aired.[62]

Cibin was not the only person astounded by the casual way the station conducts its affairs. Other reporters followed up Troner's story. They, too, discovered how simple

434

it could have been for someone to have snitched the Siemer tape and tampered with it.

One of the newsmen investigating the story was Andrea Purgatori of *Corriere Della Sera*. Both reporter and newspaper are widely held to be the best in Italian journalism. Indeed, Purgatori's reputation for investigative sleuthing has placed him among the top journalists in Europe.

After recording telephone interviews with Borgomeo and Quercetti, who had suddenly reappeared at the station and reminded McNair not to talk to reporters, Purgatori concluded that each priest was 'engaged in the sort of cover-up the Vatican is famous for. My questions scared the hell out of them. I could almost hear Quercetti falling off his chair.'[63]

Purgatori's questions were designed to probe further the station's laxity over security.

After his call, Borgomeo sent for McNair and tried to persuade her, 'for the good of Vatican Radio', to admit that, just as his apology stated, there had been a 'technical error' and she alone was responsible for it.[64]

Clarissa McNair steadfastly refused to accept the blame.

Since then she has been under increasing pressure to do so.

Reporters continue to contact her. Though she has firmly refused to speak to them, she has listened to what they have discovered.

They support Troner's contention: 'It all points to a professional intelligence job.'[65] He believed 'the Company badly wanted to destabilize Siemer since he left Rockwell. What better place to do it than on Vatican Radio? And there would be the extra bonus of being able seriously to embarrass McNair.'[66]

This morning, as she enters Quercetti's office, she cannot help but feel, 'The Mad Mentor has once more returned to plague me.'[67]

Despite reporters like Troner calling her alleging the CIA was involved in doctoring the tape, the broadcaster realizes no one – least of all she – will ever be able to prove it, especially if it was The Mad Mentor. He had once boasted to her he could get away with anything.

Standing before Quercetti's desk, she is aware he is watching her closely. She is trembling slightly. She decides not to tell him why.

Instead she begins to answer his questions. Though they have all been asked many times before she is no longer angry about this.

She has come to view the whole episode as 'a game: pointless and nasty, but a game. It's the best way to look at it.'[68]

This is perhaps her best defence against a shivery feeling she also has: that the CIA is continuing to impinge upon her life.

24

Roman Responses

We can pinpoint the exact time the threatening telephone calls began. It was three-thirty in the afternoon just nine days after one of us saw Judge Martella in his office.

That first caller – a woman with a soft American accent – sounded as if she was reading from a prepared script. She could have been an actress, the careful way she delivered her message: 'You shouldn't have given that file to Martella.'[1]

Since then the telephone calls had become more threatening. They were not only from that mysterious woman; in the past three weeks we have identified no fewer than six different voices making these calls to us and our families in England and Ireland.[2]

One of the callers, another woman, has a distinctive English accent. A man has an Irish brogue. A third could be Italian or Spanish. A fourth, Australian or South African. A fifth, claiming to be calling from Vienna, introduced himself: 'This is Kadem – Agca's friend.'[3]

In *Pontiff* we documented how Sedat Siri Kadem, a classmate of Agca's in their village school in Yesiltepe in Turkey, had become a terrorist, trained in Syria, and had first taken Agca there on 10 March 1977. The two men had become lovers. Their homosexual relationship lasted until February 1980. That was the month Agca made his first visit to Sofia in Bulgaria. Kadem had then dropped out of sight.

We have no way of knowing whether the person allegedly phoning from Vienna is the real 'Kadem'. But the man's warning was clear enough: 'We don't like what you are doing. Be careful.'

Such threats are relatively rare in our work. We normally

dismiss them as crude attempts to try and divert us from our writing.

But these calls appear different. For one thing the voices are aware of many of our movements: when we fly in and out of Rome; a chance meeting in the street with someone from Vatican Radio; sometimes they even seem to know the gist of telephone conversations we have had with each other.

We moved out of the Albergo Santa Chiara some months ago and are now in separate apartments on opposite sides of Rome. We spend a lot of time on the telephone discussing a whole range of topics.

Experienced reporters like Andrew Nagorski of *Newsweek* and John Winn Miller of the Associated Press say that telephones in Rome are frequently bugged. Neither of our telephone numbers is listed in our names. Yet the callers were able to find us at once.

And Kadem, if he was calling from Vienna, seemed up to date on a telephone conversation one of us had only an hour previously with Judith Harris at NBC's Rome bureau.

We have sought advice. Mgr Kabongo suggested one of the security services might be interested in our work. Sir Mark Heath, Britain's Ambassador to the Holy See, warned us not to take the calls lightly. Judge Martella offered to alert DIGOS. We declined the suggestion. The prospect of working with DIGOS agents shadowing us is not appealing.

All those we have spoken to agree that for so many separate voices to be involved needs considerable resources and money.

A recent caller – the man with an Italian/Spanish accent – made no bones about whom he represents. 'I'm a friend of Frank Terpil and Gary Korkola. They don't like the way you are involving them and the McCarthys with Martella. That's bad news for you.'[4]

Others are quite clear what they want – that we recover from Martella the material we have given him. Even if we wished to do that, it is beyond our power. The judge has formally entered into his investigation the Austrian Intelligence file and all the documentation on Terpil and Korkola which Marie and John McCarthy handed over in Ireland of their own free will.

Other callers are melodramatic with their threats of physical violence – 'You could fall under a car very easily'.

Yet, when we try to analyse the pattern of our respective calls, they become more confusing than ever.

If, in the parlance of one of those telephoning us, we are to be 'hit', then why should we be given advance warning? Either some intelligence agency is using its 'frighteners', or we are being harassed by an entirely different group. Perhaps more than one. We don't actually believe there is a 'Friends of Frank Terpil' team on the loose. But we suppose anything is possible.

We hear that two Austrian intelligence men, both known personally to us, have been in Rome, in the words of another caller – again that Italian/Spanish voice – 'to get back all the stuff you were so unwise to give Martella'.[5]

The reported arrival of the two Austrians prompts us to look back over the notes of our meetings with them in Vienna in December1981. And there we find at least a clue as to what might be behind the calls.

An Austrian intelligence officer who had helped arrange for his service's file to come into our hands had told us then that his organization was riven with interservice rivalry. This, in part, had led him to decide to co-operate in handing over the file to us. He had spoken, repeatedly, of a 'cover-up' in the early stages of the Austrian Security Service investigation into Agca's attempt on the pope's life. He had hinted that some of his colleagues made efforts to block enquiries into Horst Grillmeir's involvement in providing the actual gun for Agca to shoot the pope – and that they had done so with the support of the West German BND.

With Martella now in possession of our copy of the file, it would be that much harder for the original to be conveniently 'lost' in the labyrinthian headquarters of Austrian Security on the Schottenring in Vienna.

The question we now face is this. Accepting that the Austrian Security Service knows we have a copy of the file – we actually published the fact in *Pontiff* – do they now fear we have also been passed other even more secret documentation which we are about to publish?

We, of course, possess no such material. But some of these telephone calls begin to make sense if we set them against the possibility that members of the Austrian Security Service believe we hold such data.

The calls would then be intended to panic us to the point where we decided to keep any further Austrian information away from people like Judge Martella.

We cannot be sure this is the situation. But enough of the pieces fit together to make it plausible.

Accepting this, we feel more relaxed about the calls. We begin repeatedly to tell the callers we have no hidden information of interest to them.

Suddenly the calls stop as mysteriously as they started.

But we begin to receive other calls which are equally surprising.

Giuseppe Consolo, Sergei Antonov's lawyer, is making them.

He says, his voice brimming with confidence, that Antonov will be released from Rebibbia prison by Christmas. He has lit the fuse to Martella's bombshell.

We ask him how he can be so certain. Consolo claims 'a deal has been done which is nothing to do with the guilt or innocence of my client. He is, of course, innocent. But that is not the purpose of this deal.'[6]

He then explains what is behind it.

In Consolo's version there are involved two Italians and some very adroit footwork on the international stage.

This is the lawyer's story. The two Italians have been held for some months in Bulgaria on alleged espionage charges. As an 'act of compassion', the Bulgarian government will release them soon after Antonov is freed. Freeing Antonov will effectively collapse the Bulgarian Connection.

That will also certainly sever any damning links between the Bulgarian Secret Service – the DS – and the Soviet KGB. So will end a full year of intense speculation that Yuri Andropov must accept ultimate responsibility for Agca's attempt on the pope's life.

Consolo claims – with the aplomb of a born advocate who can either make two and two add up to four or sound like twenty-two – the way will then be free for Reagan and Andropov to meet.

He gives us the date Antonov will walk out of Rebibbia – Wednesday, 21 December. Technically, Antonov will be under 'house arrest'. But, insists the lawyer, for all practical purposes 'he will be a free man'.[7]

If correct, this is truly shattering news. We check urgently with Martella's office. We are further stunned to hear that the judge is in the final stages of writing his report, and hopes to deliver it to his superiors in a few days.

Yet, only a month ago, the judge had indicated to us it would be well into next year before his report was ready.

What has suddenly happened to make it now possible for Martella to produce a document which will include some 20,000 pages of evidence? And why has he agreed that Antonov can be released to house arrest?

In another telephone call Consolo tells us – again accurately as it turns out – that Antonov will be released for 'health reasons'.[8] But the lawyer also admits he first petitioned on this account back in March. 'It's interesting that it's convenient now to accept such grounds.'[9]

It is indeed interesting.

But, we persist to Consolo, Judge Martella has a reputation second to none for fearlessly pursuing justice. Surely he could be no part of any cover-up? The question is almost unthinkable to ask.

Consolo is expansive. He says he, too, has the highest regard for Martella, 'but what will emerge is that the judge, after all his investigation over a year, will state there is, after all, no evidence to send my client for trial'.[10]

It is clear that a new chapter has opened in the plot to assassinate John Paul, one which may substantially confirm what we have suspected for so long: at the very minimum some western governments would rather not know the true background to the plot, and certain western intelligence services, among them CIA and BND, have deliberately tried to conceal the facts to avoid a confrontation with the Soviet Union.[11] Martella, and his determined search for truth and justice, has of course no part in such machinations.

Our telephone calls begin to make even more sense.

THE SECRETARIAT OF STATE
Thursday
Morning

The hard-worked diplomats on the Middle East Desk barely have time to notice the giant Christmas tree in St Peter's Square, a gift from Austria, being decorated by *sampietrini*, and other Vatican workmen putting the finishing touches to the Manger scene in a replica of that original stable in Bethlehem.

Nearly two thousand years after the birth of Jesus an event of a very different kind continues to preoccupy the priests.

For the past twenty-one days they have mounted a heroic diplomatic drive to get Yasser Arafat and his men safely out of Tripoli, Lebanon.

Their efforts have not been made easier by the response Premier Bettino Craxi gave during his recent audience with the pope about the position of Italy's peacekeeping force in the Lebanon.[1]

Craxi had said that whether or not the PLO was extradited from Tripoli his government intends steadily to reduce its commitment in Lebanon – and would consider an immediate complete withdrawal if it suffered casualties on the scale which had decimated the French and American forces in Beirut during recent weeks. But in spite of this, matters had looked optimistic.

Melina Mercouri had taken the pope's request for ships back with her to Athens. The Greek government agreed to make available five transports. Nuncio Felici in Paris helped persuade the French government to provide a naval armada, including the aircraft carrier *Clemenceau*, to protect the evacuation of Arafat and the dispirited remnants of his once-powerful force.

Then Israel broke a firm undertaking not to intervene.

The agreement had been negotiated jointly by the Reagan and Mitterand administrations and supported by the Holy See.

The Israelis sent a flotilla of gunboats to bombard the PLO redoubt in Tripoli. In Jerusalem government officials made plain to apostolic delegate Archbishop Carew that Israel did not propose to let Arafat slip away without further punishment.

Their naval bombardment continued, forcing the Greek ships to remain well clear of the area and leaving the French naval force riding frustratedly at anchor; their rules of engagement specified they could attack the Israeli gunboats only if the Greek transports were threatened. There was no provision for the vastly superior French warships to drive away the gunboats from Tripoli. The Israelis continued to pound the PLO trapped in the port.

Carew and papal nuncio Luciano Angeloni in Beirut learned virtually at the same time – and transmitted the news with similar speed to the Secretariat of State – that Israel apparently did not intend to stop at a full-scale bombardment.

With the consent of Prime Minister Yitshak Shamir and his new cabinet, special military and intelligence teams were being prepared to infiltrate Tripoli under the protection of the incessant shelling. Their task was to assassinate Arafat.[2]

Casaroli had acted at once. Pio Laghi in Washington was informed. He discovered the State Department already knew of Israeli intentions.

President Reagan also moved swiftly. He publicly condemned Israel for impeding the evacuation and demanded the blockade be ended.[3] The State Department arranged for a senior official to reinforce the president's words by summoning Israel's ambassador to Washington, and telling him the United States expected to see every Palestinian who wished to leave Tripoli do so at once without hindrance.

Israel withdrew its gunboats.

Soon afterwards the Greek ships, escorted by the French

flotilla, arrived in Tripoli. Before they docked, a small Lebanese boat toured the inner harbour dropping sticks of dynamite to explode any mines the Israelis might have planted under cover of darkness before departing.

The evacuation passed without incident. To the very end Arafat remained confident. 'We are not giving up the struggle. No one has cut off our head and we are not on our knees. I resign only when I am dead.'

Still exuding optimism, Arafat has turned up in Egypt, seeking the support of Egyptian president Hosni Mubarak.

News of Arafat's arrival was telephoned from the nunciature in the Cairo suburb of Zamalek by the papal pronuncio to Egypt.

His vast experience of Middle East affairs continues to serve the Middle East Desk well this morning.

He informs its section head that Arafat's appearance in Egypt could have considerable significance and should be seen as more than another of those unexpected moments of diplomatic fluidity which so often bedevil any attempt to gauge what is happening at the bottom of the cauldron of Middle East politics.

The nuncio's assessment is that in meeting Mubarak, Arafat has not only scored a new personal triumph in the wake of his removal from Tripoli. Almost certainly during their meeting the president and the PLO chairman discussed the prospect of establishing new ties between them. For Egypt there would be a definite attraction in such an alliance. Egypt has been virtually isolated within the Arab world since the late President Anwer Sadat formulated the peace initiative which led to the accord between Egypt and Israel.

If Egypt's new president was now to establish a proper link with Arafat's segment of the PLO, then – the nuncio argues – the way could be open for joint Mubarak/Arafat approaches to the moderate governments of Saudi Arabia and Jordan. If these were successful an even more momentous step might be contemplated: rapprochement between Arafat and King Hussein of Jordan. It had been Hussein who, all those years ago, expelled the PLO from Jordan, so beginning the organization's bloodthirsty progress throughout the Middle East and beyond.

The nuncio believes if all these links are forged, it would create a powerful new alliance for any fresh discussion with Israel on President Reagan's presently moribund 1982 peace initiative. The cornerstone of that plan was to establish links between Jordan, the West Bank and Gaza, areas occupied by Israel since 1967.

Somewhere in this area could be founded the homeland for the PLO which the Holy See has striven hard to see established.

In a few hours the Vatican will give a rare public boost to the covert diplomatic manoeuvring it has been engaged upon during much of the year on behalf of the PLO. With the full approval of John Paul and Casaroli, *L'Osservatore Romano* will publish a commentary in its next edition which will laud Arafat as 'an able and open-minded politician'.[4]

However, on the last-minute advice of the Middle East Desk, the commentary will add that, evacuating Lebanon, Arafat 'leaves the scene with a new humiliation'.

The desk's diplomats have started to receive news that Syria and Israel – themselves mortal enemies – have intensified their desire, though for very different reasons, to see Arafat destroyed.

Israel regards Mubarak's support for Arafat a serious breach of its own agreement with Egypt; this, very properly, forbids the Egyptian government from encouraging terrorism. Where Mubarak and Shamir disagree is over the status of Arafat. The Egyptian president sees him as a patriot; the Israeli premier regards him as a murderer. There have been bitter words between Cairo and Jerusalem.

Syria's President Assad simply looks upon Arafat as a traitor to Arab radicalism.

Both Shamir and Assad want to see the PLO chairman finally finished.

The Middle East Desk staff know that, like so many other diplomatic moves the Holy See is engaged in, the questions surrounding the future of Yasser Arafat will not be neatly solved by the end of the year. Even this time next year these diplomats recognize they could still be dealing with the problems of the PLO.

Yet they see a gleam of hope. Arafat has indicated in Cairo he may be prepared to give up the role of revolutionary leader and become head of a PLO government in exile. In all likelihood it would be based in the Egyptian capital.[5]

While the Holy See could not itself formally recognize such a government, it would, in the words of one of its senior priest-diplomats, Mgr Mounged El-Hachem, 'look sympathetically on it and encourage it to flourish for the purpose of stabilizing a very dangerous situation'.[6]

As Christmas preparations continue in St Peter's Square, the Middle East Desk priests begin to ponder how best they can help to achieve the birth of that government in exile – something which will ensure Arafat's 'humiliation' will be short-lived, and that he will finally unbuckle his gun-belt in favour of a more reasonable form of persuasion.

Some of these diplomats cautiously concede that if they do succeed in elevating Yasser Arafat from a streetwise politician to a world-ranking statesman, it will be coming close to the miracle of Christmas itself.

Same Day: Noon

Shortly before midday Archbishop Guido Del Mestri telephones from Bonn with news which further hardens a feeling among Secretariat of State staff that the release from Rebibbia prison of Sergei Antonov the previous day – exactly as his lawyer Giuseppe Consolo had predicted – had less to do with the Bulgarian's health than with high political stakes.

The nuncio in Bonn has learned from his contacts the contents of a letter President Reagan recently sent Chancellor Helmut Kohl. Reagan has written to him saying he is 'very interested in meeting Chairman Andropov in the near future'.[7]

Normally Del Mestri could count on his information as a major diplomatic coup. However, he has also been told that Kohl intends to take the highly unusual step of making the letter public in a Christmas Eve television address to the German people.

A former West German chancellor, Helmut Schmidt, has also this morning made an intriguing pronouncement in the country's mass-circulation daily, *Bild*, that 'neither Washington nor Moscow is thinking about having a war. There is no danger of war.'[8]

To hammer home the message, Pio Laghi has gleaned from his White House sources what the president has just told *Time* magazine in another carefully planned interview to be published immediately after Christmas.[9] Reagan intends to reveal he has hitherto unsuspected 'channels', which he has kept open during the blackest moments of US-Soviet confrontations during the year. These 'channels', says the president, allow him to make private contact with the Soviet leadership should the public bellicose rhetoric between Washington and Moscow appear to be indicating something close to physical action between the superpowers.

Poggi has been informed that Yuri Andropov is on the mend – though still not fit to attend the Supreme Soviet and Party Plenum. And, in another unprecedented move, sources in the Party Central Committee, normally so wary of publicity, have started to tip-off foreign correspondents in Moscow about Andropov's return to better health. Reporters are being told that while the nature of his illness must remain a 'State secret', it is definitely not kidney disease.[10]

In Brussels the European Economic Community announces it will not continue beyond the end of the year with trade sanctions imposed almost two years ago against Soviet exports as a protest against the imposition of martial law in Poland. From 1 January, Soviet shrimps, caviare, upright pianos and farm tractors will be among the fifty-nine items again available in Western Europe.[11]

From Warsaw comes news that the Polish government – freely admitting bowing to 'popular opposition' – has postponed for 'at least several weeks', increases in food prices. They were planned to range from ten to fifty per cent.[12]

All the nuncios in Central America are reporting what seems to be an open secret: the commission led by Henry Kissinger is about to recommend a $1.5 billion fund for the region.[13] Even Nicaragua will be included in the package if the regime gives Washington guarantees about holding free elections. Aid to Guatemala will be linked to an improvement of human rights by the government the Reagan administration has unswervingly supported throughout the year. The commission is expected to tell the US president he would be wise to reduce the present strength of the American military presence in Honduras.

In many ways the report follows the recommendations the Latin America Desk prepared for the pope in the late summer.

If the Kissinger commission verdict is accepted it will go a long way to stifling Soviet charges of American 'imperialism' in the region.

And, among this agreeable plethora of reasonableness, there is one other piece of good news – although not welcomed by everybody.

It involves William Wilson.

Following a Congressional decision to end an 1876 law which banned the use of Federal funds to maintain a diplomatic mission to the Holy See, it has finally been decided that the United States will be the 108th nation to have full diplomatic ties with the Vatican city-state. Further, President Reagan has earmarked his good friend Wilson as ambassador in the knowledge that 'the Holy See is an international focal point of diplomatic contact'.[14]

Yet, opposition to the move persists. In Rome, Wilson's past behaviour towards Vatican Radio and his lack of formal training still rankle with some. And in the US, a leader of America's Baptists thinks the establishment of relations a 'blatant violation of the principle of Church-State separation'. But the president of the Catholic Conference strongly disagrees. 'It is not a religious issue but a public policy question.'[15]

The question has now been settled. For the first time in 117 years, the US will have a fully accredited ambassador to the Holy See.

There is a feeling within the Secretariat of State that just as the sudden release of Antonov could have wider political significance, so the creation of formal diplomatic ties may not be unconnected with the matter of who will govern the United States after the 1984 election.

THE BULGARIAN RESIDENCE, ROME
Same Day: Early Evening

Vassil Dimitrov lurches to his feet and proposes yet another toast.[16] It is identical in spirit, if not words, to the others he and his colleagues have been offering all afternoon. They had started with the very best of Russian vodka. Then, over lunch in the residence's normally cheerless dining room, they switched to vintage Italian wines, usually offered only to senior visitors coming from Sofia.

Now, chairs pushed back from the table, ties loosened, the dozen men are raising glasses filled with a fiery Bulgarian brandy.

Dimitrov looks at his watch and begins to count off aloud the seconds. At five forty-five he shouts, 'Comrade Sergei is now beginning his second full day of freedom! We salute him!'

The others stand unsteadily and raise their glasses towards Sergei Antonov, seated in the place of honour at the head of the table.

Exactly twenty-four hours have passed since Antonov emerged from Rebibbia prison and has been driven, his car escorted by a posse of police cars, to this apartment building on Via Galiani which houses many of Rome's Bulgarian diplomats.

His release had been the bombshell Martella prepared – the detonation of which caused shockwaves not only in the Apostolic Palace but in a dozen western capitals.

Against all the betting, Martella decided, just as Consolo predicted when speaking of 'a deal', that the evidence was no longer strong enough to hold Antonov in custody.

Shortly before Antonov left the gaol, the judge departed Rome on vacation. Behind him he left questions the scores of reporters awaiting Antonov's return have passed the hours speculating on.[17]

Martella's year, which had begun with such certainty he would prove conclusively the facts about the Bulgarian Connection, was ending on a note of doubt. Those who gamely hold to *Pista Bulgara* point out Antonov has only been released to 'house arrest', that he is still effectively under indictment. Yet the consensus among the waiting newsmen outside his home – rightly or wrongly but reinforced by some of Rome's diplomatic corps – is that, in the words of one European ambassador, 'It's all over bar the shouting.'

The prevailing view is that Antonov's release puts paid, at least for the time being, to any serious prospect of officially linking in public the attempt on the pope's life with Andropov.

The newsmen have noticed that although certainly thinner, Antonov looks healthier than they had expected. He is also more handsome than in his photographs. His moustache is neatly trimmed and, in true Balkan style, waxed and curled upwards at the ends.

Consolo, debonair as always, nevertheless stood beside

his client long enough to inform the media mass Antonov was 'not well', and 'cannot eat'.

There was no evidence of either this afternoon in the residency.

Antonov has eaten and drunk his fill. He is wearing the blue suit of the previous day. But he has a crisp white shirt and a dark red tie to go with it. His moustache is immaculate.

He does not look like someone who has spent over a year in one of Italy's maximum security gaols. Nor, Consolo reminded him before they parted late the previous evening, need Antonov fear ever returning there.

The lawyer has by now also left Rome, for a vacation on an Indian Ocean island, an exotic holiday he has postponed three times since he began defending Antonov in November 1982.

So far – in legal fees and a sustained world-wide publicity campaign which has also spawned three Bulgarian state-subsidized books – the equivalent of nearly a million American dollars has been spent to make possible this increasingly unrestrained celebration.

For Vassil Dimitrov it is a climax to a year which started so bleakly. Ten months ago he had been a diplomatic pariah among his colleagues in Sofia. Now, every Bulgarian minister with access to a telex is conveying his congratulations to Dimitrov.

This evening as he prepares to deliver yet another toast – 'to Italian justice; long may it always be so' – the dedicated Communist diplomat can also raise his glass to that old capitalist proverb about nothing succeeding like success.

THE SECRETARIAT OF STATE
Saturday
Morning

The overnight telex traffic this Christmas Eve is light. It includes a lengthy message from VVOUN 429502 in New York. Archbishop Giovanni Cheli is reporting on the outcome of his meeting with Jorge Illueca, president of the UN General Assembly.

Illueca has just written to Reagan and Andropov urging them, 'as a gesture of goodwill during this great holiday season, a season of peace, to desist voluntarily from any further expansion of the nuclear confrontation, and to sit around the Security Council's table determined to put a stop to this madness'.[18]

The assembly president sent a copy of his letter to Prime Minister Indira Gandhi in her capacity as head of the non-aligned movement. The Holy See had also been informed of its contents.

According to the UN charter the fifteen members of the Security Council are required to hold periodic meetings. Only one has in fact ever been held, in October 1970, to discuss the Middle East and southern Africa. Then, only foreign ministers rather than heads of state had participated.

Illueca's letter was warmly welcomed by John Paul, coming so soon after his own appeal to the superpower leaders. Cheli had been instructed to convey the pope's support to Illueca, and to see how best the Holy See can help further in arranging a meeting.

Cheli's report on this request is so confidential it is encoded. The telex is taken to Casaroli's office where it will be unscrambled by one of his staff.

Two other reports, each in plain language, also find their

way to the Secretary of State's room. Both are from West Germany.

The first is a copy of an address to be delivered by the country's foreign minister, Hans-Dietrich Genscher. He calls for the building of a long-term East-West relationship based 'on mutual trust and military equality'. The West, he adds, is ready to consider the Warsaw Pact proposals – repeated throughout the past year – for 'a mutual renunciation of force', if the Soviet Union gives up attempts to dominate Europe with its arms arsenal.[19]

The second statement, by a member of the Bonn government's junior coalition party, goes a great deal further.[20] This demands that West Germany disarm unilaterally, removing from its soil all tactical nuclear weapons.

The attitude is a far cry from the papacy's position on arms control.

Nor does it correspond with the judgement of Paul Nitze, a man whose patience and tenacity Casaroli personally admires.

Nitze shares the Holy See's growing concern that the anti-nuclear movement in Western Europe can, without intending to, provide a very serious obstacle to the resumption of negotiations in Geneva.

Nitze, like Casaroli, accepts Cardinal Hume of Westminster's implied judgement: while there is no actual proof that the peace movement is Soviet *directed*, there can be little doubt that the Russians have *sought* to inspire it.

Therefore, for the Soviet Union to depart from its rigid position and sanction in any form the presence of Pershing and Cruise missiles in Europe would, in Nitze's view, 'undercut seriously their supporters in Western Europe'.[21] Put at its simplest, the peace movement members would feel betrayed.

However, Casaroli is coming to the conclusion that Nitze could be correct when he argues that the deployment of the first missiles, endorsed by majorities in the parliaments in

London, Bonn and Rome, have removed what Nitze calls a 'psychological barrier' to the arms control talks resuming.

But these two West German reports are almost certainly going to provide a new boost for the peace movements, making it that much harder for the American and Soviet leadership to agree on cuts.

During the morning Casaroli receives further unsettling news. It arrives in his copy of the monthly *Bulletin of the Atomic Scientists*.[22]

Since 1947, on Christmas Eve, the *Bulletin* has published a symbolic doomsday clock. It had originally been set at seven minutes to midnight to show graphically how close the world was to a nuclear Armageddon.

In 1953 the clock's hand was moved to two minutes to midnight. That was the year Russia exploded its first hydrogen bomb. In 1972 it was put back to twelve minutes, after the United States and the Soviet Union ratified SALT, the arms-limitation agreement.

But now the forty-seven scientists – eighteen of them Nobel Prize-winners – after carefully considering 'the inclination of the leaders of the nuclear powers to talk and act as though they were prepared to use these weapons' – have moved the hand forward one full minute from where it stood a year ago.

The clock's hand now stands at exactly three minutes before midnight. This is the closest it has been to doomsday for thirty years.

THE PAPAL APARTMENT
Same Day: Early Evening

Wrapped in topcoats against the chilling fog which is drifting up from the Tiber, Ercole Orlandi and his wife, Maria, hurry down the Via del Belvedere. The narrow Vatican street is deserted.

Behind them looms the outline of the Vatican library and the Secret Archives. Ahead they can see the silhouette of the Church of Santa Anna dei Palafrenieri. Built 410 years ago for the papal grooms to worship in, it is now still used by Vatican staff. Every day the Orlandis come to this pretty oval church to light a candle for Emanuela.

To their right rises the Leonine Wall, the massive construction which isolates Vatican City from Rome.

The Orlandis pass a blue-caped Swiss Guard patrolling Porta Sant'Anna, and make their way through the rear entrance to the Apostolic Palace.

At regular intervals they meet more Swiss Guards and Cibin's men patrolling the almost deserted palace corridors. Apart from them, the only other persons the couple encounter are a few priests going about their business.

Utilizing the elevator he normally uses, Orlandi takes his wife up to the papal secretariat.

There, Kabongo is waiting. He leads them to the door of the pope's office. The secretary knocks, opens it and steps aside.

John Paul comes forward to welcome the Orlandis as Kabongo softly closes the door.

Twenty minutes later the messenger and his wife emerge. They are visibly moved. The pope has once more shared with them his own grief over their missing daughter. He has also explained what he hopes to achieve by going to Rebibbia to meet Mehmet Ali Agca.

ST PETER'S BASILICA
Sunday
Late Morning

At John Paul's request the tall windows leading on to the balcony from which he will address the Christmas Day crowd in the square are kept closed until the last possible moment. Icy fog wreathes not only the piazza but has settled like a pall over the rest of Rome.

Gathered in the large room behind the central balcony above the main entrance to St Peter's are Casaroli and other curial cardinals, his secretaries and Jacques Martin, the prefect of the papal household.[23]

Despite the weather, the piazza is filling up. Many thousands are pouring out of the Basilica in which John Paul has just concluded morning mass. As noon approaches, Martin, who has an eye for such things, estimates there could be 50,000 in the crowd.

Moments before midday, Kabongo and Dziwisz open the window doors on to the balcony. In the square two matching bands blare out first the papal and then the Italian anthem. The bells of St Peter's begin to toll the hour.

Adjusting his mitre, flanked by Casaroli and Cardinal Ugo Poletti, the vicar-general of Rome, John Paul steps out on to the balcony to deliver the annual *Urbi et Orbi* – to the city and the world.

He wastes little time before coming to the core of his message.

His voice is suddenly raised, thundering through the banks of loudspeakers positioned around the piazza and causing the technicians of Vatican Radio rapidly to adjust the sound levels on their apparatus; the speech is being relayed to nearly 200 countries. For the first time, too, the fledgling Vatican Television is filming the occasion. Only a few weeks old, and still in its experimental stage, the television unit is part of the Vatican's expanding communications programme.

'Look with the eyes of the newborn child upon the men and women who are dying of hunger, while enormous sums are being spent on weapons.'

One of the reporters shivering in the press pen close to the balcony makes a note. 'He's just given his first order. The crowd is quiet and still. A group of Filipinos, vivacious and noisy only a moment ago, freeze like petrified rocks.'

The pope moderates his voice while allowing its tone to become even more impassioned.

'Look upon the unspeakable sorrow of parents witnessing the agony of their children imploring them for that bread which they have not got but which could be obtained with even a tiny part of the sums poured out on sophisticated means of destruction, which make even more threatening the clouds gathering on the horizon of humanity.'

A wave of applause sweeps over the square.

'Listen, O Father, to the cry of peace that rises from the peoples being martyred by war, and which speaks to the heart of all those who are able to contribute, through negotiations and dialogue, to equitable and honourable solutions to existing tensions.'

Another roar of approval. The hand-clapping sounds like a barrage of small-arms fire.

'Look upon the anxious and often troubled path of so many, who toil to win the means of subsistence, to progress and to rise. Look upon the anxieties and sufferings that afflict the souls of those who are forced to be away from their families or who live in a family divided by selfishness or infidelity, of those who are without work, without a home, without a country, without love, without hope.'

The journalists, following their supplied scripts, exchange excited comment.

One records: 'He's speaking in Italian – but it's double-Dutch to the tourists who don't understand the speech. Yet he holds them with a word, a phrase. "Pace", "dialego", "angosce e le sofferenze", "famiglia", "egoismo", "infedelta", "amore". He fires these key words, and others, at the crowd like bullets.'

The pope continues to speak, his voice filled with ringing conviction.

'Look upon the peoples that are without joy and without security because they see their own fundamental rights trampled upon. Look upon the world of today, with its hopes and disappointments, with its high aspirations and its vile deeds, with its noble ideals and its humiliating compromise.'

A reporter, framing her story, notes, 'Not only is it a great speech, but a realistic one. Its profound idealism is balanced by an accurate perspective. He defines the world today as one of aspirations, disappointments and compromise, instead of the usual catch-all, "Good versus Evil". He is asking for divine inspiration to give us strength and wisdom, and that may be all that is left to us – the Hand of God.'

Behind her, in the square, photographers are snapping several nuns weeping as John Paul comes to the traditional closing of his *Urbi et Orbi*. First he appeals for help for the Third World. 'Assist your Church in her efforts on behalf of the poor, the neglected and the suffering.'

The thought has been shaped by Kabongo; his year is ending with commitment to the Third World as strong as ever.

Finally, John Paul delivers his Christmas blessing in no fewer than forty-three languages.

There is a renewed murmur of speculation among the reporters as he comes to deliver his greetings in Bulgarian. They note that the words 'ЧЕСТИТО РОЖДЕСТВО ХРИСТОВО' are in capitals on their copies of the list from which the pope is reading. And, before he delivers them, he stresses this is 'The Bulgarian Expression'.

What can this mean? wonder the journalists. Is the pope somehow signalling that he, too, now recognizes *Pista Bulgara* has almost run its course?

And is the day after tomorrow, at Rebibbia, to be the end?

459

26

THE PAPAL APARTMENT
Tuesday
Pre-Dawn

At four-thirty – almost three hours before the lights on the Christmas tree in St Peter's Square will be switched off, coinciding with the dawn of another day – John Paul's valet knocks and enters the pope's bedroom. He turns on the overhead light and opens the curtains.[1]

The surprisingly small room, square, with a high ceiling, has barely altered during the five years John Paul has slept here.

The walls are still covered with the pastel linen cloth which Paul VI favoured.[2] In a corner is the same mahogany chest of drawers where the former pope stored his shirts and underwear; John Paul uses it for the same purpose. Opposite the chest is a large hanging closet filled with John Paul's cassocks.

As in Paul's days the wooden floor gleams from being electrically polished. But the Afghan rug the old pope treasured has gone, replaced by one spun and woven by Polish nuns.

On the wall above John Paul's old-fashioned brass bed – in which four of his predecessors had lain, waiting for death – is a crucifix.

On another wall is a fine painting of Our Lady. Both crucifix and portrait are also gifts from Poland.

The bedside and occasional tables around the room hold other reminders of John Paul's birthplace: among these are Polish-language books and framed photographs of Cracow.

Pride of place on the bedside table is given over to a Bible in his native language; it is the one which John Paul was given when he was ordained.[3] Beside the Bible is a telephone, extension 3102, the pope's night-line. While he sleeps it will be rung only for the gravest of reasons.

As they do most mornings, the pope and his valet exchange a few words, mostly about the weather. This morning the servant has no need to predict the prospect.

A strong wind is rattling the bedroom shutters, drowning out the distinctive *tufo*, the unique sound of Rome, a vibrant hum produced as a result of the city being built on hardened volcanic ash.

The wind has blown away the fog which has all but shrouded the Vatican these past two days. Now, the sky is speckled with stars.

Below, in the otherwise deserted piazza, the patrolling policemen shelter from the harsh wind behind the pillars of Bernini's colonnade or stand in the lee of the replica of the Manger.

It is not a morning to be about.

Yet, every night he has slept in this bedroom, no matter what the weather, John Paul has begun his next day at this hour.

Even in bed – its predecessor's pastel blankets have been replaced by a Polish featherbed John Paul brought with him from Cracow – the pope is an imposing figure in his pyjamas.

Those who see him at this hour – his valet, sometimes his secretaries with news that cannot wait, very occasionally one of the nuns who run the papal apartment – insist he has regained much of his old vigour and vitality.

Today, as always, he begins by going to his prie-dieu to kneel and say his private prayers.

Then, while he shaves and bathes, in a bathroom as functional as any designed for Hilton or one of the world's other hotelkeepers, his valet returns and lays out John Paul's clothes, white clerical shirt, cotton vest and shorts, knee-high white stockings, brown shoes and white skullcap.

None of the garments bears a label. It is one of the cachets of the House of Gammarelli that they never mark any of the items they make for the pope.[4] After nearly two centuries of

461

cutting and sewing papal garments, Gammarelli's believe there is hardly a priest in the Church who cannot recognize the distinctive cut of an article tailored by them for pontiffs who go all the way back to Pius VII in 1800.

The valet leaves when he has laid out the clothes.

Shortly after five o'clock John Paul is dressed and ready to meet Agca.

REBIBBIA PRISON
Same Day: Later

At five-fifteen one of the guards unlocks the door of Agca's cell, T4, the fourth on the left behind the electronically controlled steel grille which isolates the maximum security wing from the rest of the prison.[5]

Until a few days ago, Antonov had occupied T3, across the corridor from Agca. Sometimes they hurled abuse at each other.

Now, Agca is once again the wing's solitary occupant. He is guarded at a cost of a million lire a week, about 700 US dollars, making him not only Rebibbia's most notorious but also its costliest inmate.

One of the guards opens the door of Agca's cell; though the door is reinforced with steel plating thick enough to withstand gunfire, it swings silently open. The other officer carries a bundle of bedding.

Agca is in bed. The frame of his iron cot is painted a bright orange. Its single blanket is almost threadbare and the sheets and pillows are patched.

The guard who opened the door motions for Agca to get up. His companion lays the bedding on the cot.

The cell is uniformly white. A mirror is embedded in one wall.

Behind the door is a cupboard. Here Agca keeps his prison uniform, and the clothes he was allowed to wear for those visits to Martella and his extraordinary public appearances in Rome earlier in the year.

The red tiled floor is bare. But the cell is warm from the old-fashioned iron radiator beneath the two bullet-proof windows. Their bars are reinforced by steel mesh. The windows look on to a small courtyard roofed in by the same mesh and cut off from the main prison exercise yard by a high brick wall. Within this area Agca can exercise when he likes.

Out of bed he stands in a pyjama top and the boxer shorts he prefers to sleep in.

His dark-skinned body is without an inch of fat. Agca's close-cropped hair with its jagged fringe – the result of an unscheduled haircut he has had for this occasion – gives his lean, swarthy face an ascetic look. In spite of pressure from the gaol governor, Agca has refused to shave. He says he wants to grow a beard so as to look 'more biblical' for the pope.

One of the guards tells him to undress. His companion tosses Agca's top and shorts into the clothes cupboard.

Agca is ordered to turn and face the wall, arms extended, feet splayed, while his body is inspected in case he has somehow secreted a weapon; it might be inserted in his rectum, taped to the soles of his feet, curved to fit into an armpit.

Satisfied, one of the guards escorts him to the bath-house at the end of the isolation block. Agca showers and towels himself, under the watchful eyes of the officer.

He is then marched back to his cell. His bed has been stripped and remade. It is now covered with a brown and white striped blanket and fluffed pillows, encased in laundered cases. The sheets are neatly turned down. The guard who has performed this transformation stacks the old bedding in the cupboard behind the door.

Both prison officers watch carefully as Agca selects the clothes he will wear. He chooses a close-knit crew-neck blue woollen sweater, jeans, black socks and black and white jogging shoes. Before he puts on the shoes he is ordered to remove the laces. They could make a potential garrotte. For the same reason Agca is not allowed to wear a belt.

Dressed, he is forbidden to lounge back on the bed, as he does every other day. Instead he is instructed to sit on a black plastic chair, almost identical to those provided for favoured guests at Wednesday audiences in St Peter's Square.

THE POPE'S STUDY
Same Day: Later

His first mass of the day celebrated and breakfast over, John Paul continues going through the overnight Summary File, marking items on which he wishes to be further briefed.

Once more Lebanon fills the opening pages of the file. The Middle East Desk thinks the fighting will, if anything, worsen. Radical Palestinians who have deserted Arafat to remain in Lebanon are almost certainly going to escalate their guerrilla war in the Israeli-occupied southern sector of the country. This is bound to bring the usual swift and severe retribution from Israel.

A similar response – albeit a political one – is virtually certain to come from the Israeli government if Egypt does go ahead and provide Arafat with a home for his proposed government in exile.

Archbishop Carew has travelled from Jerusalem to Amman to explore with the Jordanian government its reaction to the idea. Carew found the response sympathetic. The mood in Amman is one of cautious relief that perhaps no longer will King Hussein have to represent Arafat in any future discussions with Israel, but instead could treat the PLO leader as a fully fledged partner, a fellow head of state.

Carew is cautiously optimistic the Israelis will in the end sit down with Arafat – though it might be this time next year before that occurs.

The Latin America Desk has two items the pope marks for further perusal. The first is a report from Archbishop Lajos Kada in El Salvador. The nuncio has information that the left-wing guerrillas are planning to wreck the country's presidential election, due to be held in three months. The event, important for the future stability of the country, has in part come about through the patient and discreet manoeuvring of Kada and that segment of the local Church hierarchy which recognizes the only hope for El Salvador is a semblance of true democracy.

The year in Central America is ending as it began – in a mood of uncertainty and looming renewed violence.

Yet, several thousand miles further down the generally troubled continent, from Buenos Aires, papal nuncio Ubaldo Calabresi has good news. In spite of its unwelcome decision to manufacture enriched uranium, the country's fledgling democratic civilian government is not flinching from facing up to the problem Calabresi identified months before in another report to the Secretariat of State.

It concerns the fate of 'The Disappeared', thousands of victims of the death squads operated by the military junta during nearly eight years of brutal suppression.

One of the first acts of President Raoul Alfonsin following his inauguration seventeen days ago was to order no fewer than nine junta members to stand trial for mass murder and torture of civilians.

The pope indicates he will want to know the outcome of the trials.

He also ticks the Asian Desk submission – itself based on Cardinal Sin's report – describing the latest developments in the assassination of Benigno Aquino.

A commission appointed by President Marcos, the second he has been forced to authorize in three months after damning criticism from Sin, has suddenly unearthed two witnesses who cast the gravest doubt on the government version of how Aquino died. In this, Aquino is killed by a terrorist who is then instantly gunned down by

Marcos's soldiers, conveniently removing the alleged killer.

The new witnesses claim it was one of the troopers who murdered Aquino in cold blood.

By eight o'clock John Paul has worked his way through the Summary File. The last item is a report from the Polish Desk that Cardinal Glemp has been successful in having a number of Solidarity members freed from prison.

Six months ago such a report would almost certainly have been near the front of the Summary File. Now the Secretariat of State staff have given the news from Warsaw what they see as appropriate weighting.

His reading over, it is time for the pope to turn his attention to Agca.

John Paul begins to study a red-covered folder which contains the latest news clippings on the man he is about to visit. The pope sees it as a deliberate and carefully thought-out act of forgiveness and redemption.[6] By embracing and again pardoning his enemy, John Paul hopes to pave the way for the kidnappers of Emanuela Orlandi to show that they, too, possess a spark of the profound Christianity which ultimately motivates all John Paul says and does.

REBIBBIA PRISON
Same Day: Later

By eight-thirty the supporting players in the melodrama have assembled.

Near the gaol's entrance stands a group of off-duty guards and their families.

Opposite them, kept in place by *carabinieri* and armed prison guards in distinctive blue berets, are some fifty journalists. Only twelve have been selected to accompany the pope into the prison. Afterwards they will brief their colleagues, an arrangement which pleases no one.

Further down the road, the public are held at bay by a cordon of police.

On the prison roof as well as along the entire route from the Vatican, police marksmen are alert to deal with any attempt to harm the pope.

Inside the gaol the focus of attention is increasingly on Agca's cell. Its door is now permanently open. The two prison officers stand just inside the cell, staring silently at Agca, only stepping outside into the corridor when more senior staff enter.

Shortly after nine o'clock Nicolo Amato, Director of Penal Institutions – the prosecutor who had sent Agca to prison for life before taking up his present appointment – arrives with Mino Martinazzoli, Minister of Justice.

Agca quickly takes the right hand of each man in turn and presses it to his forehead in a Muslim gesture of respect.

Amato asks him what he intends to say to the pope. Agca looks uncertain.

Martinazzoli frowns. Surely he has had sufficient time to think the matter over?

Agca shrugs. In Italian he says he will express his regret over what he tried to do to the Holy One.

'The pope,' says Amato sharply. 'Not the "Holy One" but His Holiness, the pope. Understand?'

Agca nods. He is told to sit down.

The two men inspect the cell. Amato stops: there is something wrong. He turns to one of the officers in the doorway.

'The pope's chair. Where is the pope's chair?'

Moments later a tubular steel and plastic chair is carried into the cell.

Amato positions it immediately opposite the seated Agca.

It is Martinazzoli's turn to continue the briefing. He reminds Agca he should rise when the pope enters and greet him with a handshake; he should only use the traditional Muslim forehead gesture at the end of his audience. Agca should wait for the pope to be seated before he sits. He must not make any sudden movement; at all times he should keep his hands clasped between his knees. He must positively not petition the pope on any matter to do with his sentence. Nor must he volunteer any views he might have on his prison conditions; if the pope asks, he should merely say he is 'content'. Otherwise he should answer any questions put to him in a polite and deferential manner. Was all this understood?

Agca nods.

Amato and Martinazzoli leave.

Outside in the corridor the cameramen from RAI, the Italian network, and Vatican Television are testing their equipment. Between them is Arturo Mari, a photographer from *L'Osservatore Romano*, who has been given the exclusive right, and responsibility, to provide still pictures of possibly the most dramatic confrontation in the entire history of the papacy.

One of the many conditions surrounding the encounter is that no sound record should be made. But already one of those in the hallway – they include not only the cameramen but prison officers – had secretly taped the exchanges between Amato, Martinazzoli and Agca. The man plans to do the same when pontiff and prisoner come face to face.[7]

SAN DAMASO COURTYARD
Same Day: Later

Two black Vatican limousines are drawn up before the massive John XXIII entrance to the Apostolic Palace.

Stanislaw Dziwisz and Emery Kabongo are among the group of prelates standing inside the doorway, sheltering from the wind which whistles around the courtyard. During the Christmas holiday the secretaries sat with the pope and watched videos of Agca.[8] Both men wanted to accompany the pope to Rebibbia. In the end it was decided the entourage should be kept to the minimum.

Dziwisz is going. So is Cardinal Ugo Poletti in his capacity as Vicar-General of Rome. Mgr Jacques Martin, the prefect of the papal household, has claimed the ancient right of his office to accompany the pope anywhere he chooses to go. Cibin completes the party. His presence, he knows, is purely symbolic. Not a single *vigile* or Swiss Guard will accompany him. The prison authorities have insisted they alone must have total control over the protection of the pope inside Rebibbia.

At precisely nine-thirty John Paul gets into his car, chauffeured by the very man who was at the wheel of his popemobile in St Peter's Square when Agca had shot him.[9]

Outside the Arch of the Bells, a Rome police escort waits for the papal convoy. At comparatively high speed they all head north-eastwards across the city.

Twenty-nine minutes later the pope's sedan glides to a halt outside Rebibbia prison. John Paul sits on his throne seat, smiling and waving at the half-frozen group of prison officials and their families.

He virtually ignores the journalists. Yet many sense their presence is an integral part of what the pope intends. They feel he wants them to convey this very visible demonstration of reconciliation – coming as it does at the climax of the Holy Year of Redemption – to a world, in the words of one of the correspondents present, 'filled with nuclear arsenals and unforgiving hatreds, with hostile superpowers and smaller, implacable fanaticisms'.[10]

Once the car's hard-top is electrically lowered – making it easier for John Paul to exit gracefully in his cassock – Mgr Curioni, Chaplain of Prisons, and Fr Dante Mele, Rebibbia's padre, greet the pope.

Gusts of wind tug at John Paul's cassock and threaten to dislodge his skull-cap. Bending into the near gale he hurries across to meet the guards and their families. He kisses a few babies and blesses the parents before Dziwisz eases him towards the entrance to the prison.

Amato and Martinazzoli welcome him. Then, tightly bunched together, the papal party and prison escort make for the gaol's chapel.

The congregation of some 500 criminals – a cross-section of the gaol's murderers, terrorists, drug peddlers, arsonists and gang leaders – burst into spontaneous applause as John Paul enters.

He moves slowly down the centre aisle, pausing and extending his ring hand to be kissed.

The guards escorting the party scan the prisoners. They have one instruction: to use any force necessary to stop anyone who makes an unexpected move towards John Paul.

The walk to the altar is the time everyone in the pope's entourage most fears. This is when John Paul is in the greatest danger. Though the prisoners have been searched before entering the chapel, somewhere among the tumultuous throng could be one now holding a weapon.

Cibin keeps as close to the pope as he can, without edging Poletti or Martin out of position. He knows what he will do if there is trouble: hurl himself on the pope, ready to take any blow aimed at John Paul.

In the meantime he follows a basic rule of his work: Cibin constantly watches the eyes of the prisoners nearest the pontiff; eyes are the giveaway which can provide him with that vital split-second warning.

John Paul is outwardly unconcerned, moving from one side of the aisle to the other, stopping for a brief word, his ring hand always extended.

The procession moves slowly, far more so than Cibin wishes. But John Paul specifically requested there should be no unseemly hurry. He reminded his staff that the Church has always relied upon evocative imagery – paintings, sculpture, architecture – to implant a lasting visual memory in the minds of those it wishes to impress. He firmly believes this measured, majestic progress through the ranks of many of the most dangerous men in Europe fits perfectly into the pattern, and also the theme of forgiveness he believes is at the very centre of the Christian message: that no one is beyond redemption; that by openly exposing himself to the risks either side of the aisle he is also proclaiming a larger exemplary message to the world.

One of the handful of reporters squeezed into a corner beside the altar jots a note which may come close to explaining what the pope has in mind. 'Can his actions here today have a political application? Can they serve as an example to reconcile political enemies? If the pope can come here and by his presence forgive those who have committed some of the worst crimes against society, can leaders of that society use forgiveness to bring about reconciliation? Can Shamir forgive Arafat in the way Begin did when he met Sadat? Could the American and Soviet leaders put the past behind them and, in another sense of the word, "forgive" each other?'[11]

The reporter has no answers. Nor does he expect to find them amidst this cacophony of sound.

The pope reaches the altar, venerates it, and turns to face the congregation. Abruptly, as if drilled to recognize a signal, there is utter silence.

John Paul makes the sign of the Cross. Then he pauses and closes his eyes. His face suddenly seems filled with pain and anguish.

The mass proceeds to the homily. For a moment John Paul stares out across the rows of convicts. His eyes alight on a face, pause and move on again. Few can hold his gaze. Hardened men bow their heads. A reporter scribbles: 'It may be the light. But I would swear some of the prisoners have tears in their eyes.'[12]

Nobody can doubt the emotion in the pontiff's voice. There is a power and sincerity behind his words which carry to every part of this modern prison chapel, a place to which the pope says he brings 'the warmth of a friendly word along with an invitation for hope'.

471

Some of the prison guards in the aisle seats move uncomfortably as the pope swiftly conjures up a succession of images: 'These are days in which the memory of your dear ones is more alive and the desire to unite in the intimacy of your own homes invades your hearts with strong nostalgia.'

He produces a moving reminder of the hardships the early Christians faced. Then, he focuses on the birth of Jesus. God, he said, had sent his only begotten Son to ensure, among other things, 'the freedom of the slaves and the liberty of prisoners'.

He reminds those who may have forgotten – and there is not a trace of a smile on his lips – that they can find these words in Isaiah.

The Word of God, he continues, has improved prison life. 'The message of the Gospel has throughout the centuries promoted a better respect for the human dignity of the prisoner. It has given him rights to equal treatment and the possibility of a return to society.'

He promises them that the Church will continue with this policy.

But for those who may have too literally interpreted his words, John Paul inserts a qualification.

'Christ came above all to liberate Man from his moral prison in which his passions are locked. Sin is Slavery! That is what is meant by the freeing of slaves. There is no man who is not, in one form or another, a prisoner of himself and his passions.'

The reporters who have covered so many of his sermons sense the pope is coming to his climax. There is even more certainty to his delivery; the pauses are spaced carefully. He wants every word to be remembered.

'God is love. And remember you too are loved by Him. Do not await love and forgiveness from your earthly brothers. Turn towards Christ. He will free you from your Sin. I stretch a hand to all imprisoned persons and, with profoundly felt affection, wish one and all a year much better than the one that is ending. It will be a better year if in our hearts we find space for God who "is love". I give you all my benediction.'

There is a profound silence in the chapel. Nobody moves.

Then very slowly, the prisoners rise and begin to file silently past John Paul seated on the altar throne. The first man carries a gold-plated plaque. He hands it to the pope.

John Paul reads the inscription. 'In our humility and solitude, a token of a happy day, 27 December 1983.'

The pope gives the prisoner a rosary and one of the boxed Christmas cakes stacked beside the altar.

The prisoner bends and kisses the pontiff's ring. He turns and walks away, misty-eyed.

It takes almost an hour for all the inmates to file past, present their gifts – they include a ship, a banjo and a Cross, each fashioned from toothpicks and matchsticks – and receive, in turn, identical rosaries and boxes.

At five minutes after noon John Paul leaves the chapel. Father Mele leads the way to the maximum security wing.

The electronically controlled barrier has been opened moments before the pope appears.

Including reporters, there are, all told, eighteen persons in the company of the pope. They all stop just beyond the barrier.

John Paul walks on alone down the corridor towards the open door of cell T4.

In the corridor just past the door, their cameras angled to give them perfect close-up pictures of the scene inside the cell, the two TV cameramen and Mari begin work.[13]

The pope turns and pauses in the doorway of Agca's cell, his broad back to the cameras.

Agca behaves exactly as instructed. He rises and waits.

The pope walks forward, ring hand extended. Agca moves to shake hands, hesitates and then bends down to kiss the Fisherman's Ring. He takes the pope's hand and raises it briefly to his forehead.

'*Lei, è Mehmet Ali Agca?*' The pope frames the question softly.

A quick smile flits across Agca's face. He might almost be embarrassed to admit who he is.

'*Si.*'

'*Ah, lei abita qui?*'

The pope looks around him, genuinely interested that this is where his would-be assassin might well spend the rest of his life.

'*Si.*'

John Paul sits, grasping the chair's arm rests.

Agca sinks on to his seat, clasping and unclasping his hands.

'*Come si sente?*' The pope's question as to how Agca feels is almost paternal.

'*Bene, bene.*' Suddenly the words pour from Agca; voluble, excited, tumbling one after the other. '*Volevo chiedere perdono . . .*'

He is asking so intensely for the pope to forgive him that the skin on the back of Agca's clasped hands turns white as he squeezes his fingers tighter together.

The three cameramen in the hall adjust their lenses to get closer on the two faces in the cell.

The pope is now as intense as Agca. His voice is low, urgent and emphatic. He turns his head so that only Agca can see his lips.

Agca begins to nod. Once he seems about to smile, then changes in mid-expression, his lips pursing. There is a sudden troubled look in his eyes. Then it is gone. And this time he does smile.

John Paul nods and inches his chair forward so that he can be even closer to Agca. Their knees are almost touching.

They look at each other. Now it is John Paul who smiles.

Agca hesitates, then gives a boyish grin. It lights up his whole face.

He knows that the pope has really forgiven him. It is

there in the way John Paul extends his arms in a gesture of embrace.

Agca leans forward and John Paul's hands quickly touch his shoulders.

The pope leans back as Agca starts to speak. His voice is no more than a whisper. He is explaining, using his hands to reinforce his points.

John Paul looks pensive.

Agca stops talking. His hands drop between his knees; he clasps and unclasps them.

The silence stretches.

The pope once more leans forward. As he moves, so Agca starts to speak.

'. . . *Italia* . . .'

The pope's face shields Agca's. The rest of his words are muffled.

Agca is once more whispering, almost into John Paul's ear.

The pensive look returns. The pope gives an almost imperceptible shake of his head.

Agca pauses.

John Paul indicates, with a quick wave of his right hand, that Agca should continue talking.

Both men are so close that their heads almost touch.

Agca starts a new explanation. His lips barely move.

John Paul cranes forward. There is a pained look on his face. He closes his eyes, as though he is concentrating even harder.

Agca unexpectedly stops in mid-sentence.

John Paul does not open his eyes. Instead he leans an elbow on Agca's knee.

The pope's lips move. But only Agca can hear the words.

Agca resumes speaking.

Abruptly, the pope lifts his elbow from Agca's knee and begins to make a chopping motion with his hand.

Agca stops talking.

John Paul once again bends his head in a priestly posture.

Agca resumes talking.

The pope places his hand on his forehead, shielding his eyes from Agca. He begins to speak.

Agca laughs; a brief cut-off sound, come and gone so quickly his lips barely change shape.

John Paul reaches forward and grasps the younger man's upper arm. He squeezes it, as if in a gesture of support.

The two men begin to talk at once. But again, their voices are so low that no full sentence carries. '. . . *Gesù* . . . *Dìo* . . . *Madre*.'

And so, in this manner, twenty-one minutes pass.

At last John Paul rises to his feet. He holds Agca by the hand, helping him to rise.

Pope and assailant stare into each other's eyes. There is a certainty in John Paul's as he brings this near perfect drama to its end.

He reaches into a pocket of his cassock and produces a small white box '. . . *piccolo regalo*.' He hands it to Agca.

There is a sudden confused look in his eyes. He has not been told to expect this. He turns the box over in his hand.

The pope waits, the gentlest of smiles on his lips.

Agca opens the box. It contains a rosary crafted in silver and mother-of-pearl.

Holding the rosary in his left hand, Agca shakes the pope by the hand with the other.

'*Ti ringrazio*,' thanks Agca. '*Ti ringrazio*.'

John Paul nods. '*Niente. Niente*.'

He half makes to go and then stops. He turns back to face Agca, completely blocking him from view. John Paul leans forward and utters some whispered last words. He steps back, waiting.

Agca bends low, reaching for the pope's right hand and kisses again the Fisherman's Ring. He raises his face and smiles.

John Paul turns and walks quietly from the cell.

The cameras remain focused on Agca. Watching the pope depart, the sudden look of uncertainty is back on his face. It is as if he cannot yet believe that the man he tried so hard to kill has been to him as a friend.

Outside in the corridor, surrounded by relieved prison staff that this historic confrontation has passed without incident, John Paul explains all he intends to reveal.

'What we talked about will have to remain a secret between him and me. I spoke to him as a brother whom I have pardoned and who has my complete trust.'

Without another word he begins to walk out of the maximum security block.

Minutes later, when the cameramen have been escorted from the area, the two prison officers return and order Agca to strip his bed and replace the original sheets and blankets. The other bedding is neatly folded and taken away. The door of cell T4 is locked.

But Mehmet Ali Agca is allowed to keep his rosary.

27
Towards Tomorrow

For us it is almost over.

Twelve months have passed since we stood in St Peter's Square, observing Camillo Cibin going about his business and Archbishop Luigi Poggi arriving with news that The Year of Armageddon was about to be launched on a course no one could predict.

Now, standing once more in the piazza we have visited a hundred – and more – times since then, outwardly little seems to have changed. The graffiti scratched on Bernini's colonnade are as mindless as ever. The Swiss Guards at the Bronze Door and other Vatican entrances seem, if anything, younger. The *vigili* have the same disparaging collective face; the Rome police something which falls between a swagger and a slouch. The priests, nuns and tourists continue to give the impression they have come from some central casting agency.

Yet behind this timeless dimension there have been changes. Many of them are far reaching; a few irrevocable.

Papal diplomacy, the political core of a highly centralized bureaucracy, has more than at any other time in its 500 years of very active history, become involved with international events.

The procedures for doing so remain the same – a well-established mixture of international, constitutional and canon law, theology and conscience.

But under John Paul, papal politics no longer oscillate between conservatism and liberalism. They are firmly committed to the right. Just as in the matter of his religious beliefs – an abhorrence of divorce, contraception and the ordination of women priests – so John Paul is determined that his political views should prevail.

This became evident after his return from Central America.

Something *had* happened to him there; something which is impossible to define with certainty.

Maybe it is related to that awful day in Nicaragua, when the Sandinistas had screamed at him: '*Queremos la paz!*' –We want peace!

And John Paul had finally thundered back at them: '*La primera che quiere la paz es la Iglesia!*' – The Church is the first to ask for peace!

In Guatemala he had been forced to shake the hand of Rios Montt, the now deposed and barely remembered dictator who spurned John Paul's appeal to spare the lives of men whose guilt was disputable.

In Haiti he had endured politically slanted speeches and ostentatious self-serving manifestations.

All this had shocked him. It was the first time he had been publicly defied and his office insulted.

Following his Central American pilgrimage new furrows appeared in John Paul's face. His deep-blue eyes remain penetrating but they seem more troubled. Kabongo could be right: the pope indeed appears to be a man who has glimpsed Hell on Earth.

John Paul's public voice has lost little of its timbre: perhaps a trifle harsher at times, it is still remarkably powerful for a man of his age.

In the pope's sermons, addresses and speeches and impromptu asides, the spirit of reconciliation remains as strong as ever. His visit to Agca was the ultimate manifestation of this.

Yet in the privacy of his own household, John Paul has become more introspective, more withdrawn. These are the times when he appears not only at his most human, but also at his most vulnerable. These are also the times when he feels he has failed to convince his listeners of the grand design of Christian humanism in which he so deeply believes.

Nevertheless, he remains equally committed to exercising

in full what he sees as the traditional rights of the papacy. There is no shilly-shallying: he wants his diplomats fully involved in all those areas he believes are politically important.

He is motivated by a declaration he made early on in his pontificate: before he had been shot, before he travelled on those eighteen subsequent pilgrimages covering the equivalent in distance of six times around the world.

The declaration climaxed his visit to the Irish Republic in 1979.

He had proclaimed that 'violence is evil. Violence is unacceptable as a solution to problems. Violence is unworthy of man. Violence is a lie, for it goes against the truth of our faith, the truth of our humanity.'

This was acceptable papal intervention in secular political matters. Here was the pope displaying his traditional religious character, making full use of his moral authority.

Since then he has added another crucial element, what his staff call 'spiritual sovereignty'. It is a convenient label for John Paul's belief that Church and State can have equal responsibility in settling secular matters; that papal diplomacy should not be seen as an exercise in influence but rather as one of pure service and love.

Yet within the Church the religious divisions grow deeper; new convictions become more firmly anchored; the forces of change multiply inexorably. More and more Catholics make clear that they will not abide by every view expressed from the Apostolic Palace. These dissident voices call for increased autonomy, freedom and power of choice in all aspects of religious life. The pope they had once thought would loosen the shackles has done nothing of the kind – nor will he.

Indeed, in his pontificate traditionalists find favour. Consequently, there will be increasing internal polarization. The question of religious democratization will produce even more intense pressures. Conflict and crisis could deepen to the point where it is impossible for John Paul and his officials to cope with the mounting challenges to papal authority.

Faced with such internal religious strife, the possibility of this pontificate continuing to exercise effective external political influence is also complicated by a number of other factors.

There is no evidence that the Holy See desires to establish a full diplomatic relationship with Israel during the foreseeable future. There persists, unhappily, a powerful anti-Semitic lobby in the Secretariat of State. Many members of this pressure group are young. They could still be in office at the start of the next century. While they remain in authority, there can be little prospect of the situation changing.

Conversely, sympathy for the 'moderate' Arab position grows, and will continue to do so, not least because John Paul has maintained his personal links with Yasser Arafat through all the PLO chairman's travails. The pope sees Arafat assuming the role of elder statesman in Middle East affairs – provided he physically survives.

And the Middle East itself, along with Central America, will continue to remain the focus of intense Holy See interest. In the first arena, the pope and his diplomats will continue actively to pursue a search for a homeland for the PLO; in the other they will seek a means to unite the Latin American Church so that it once more becomes a unified voice within the Third World which the Vatican sees as being increasingly important.

In its relations with China the Holy See will move cautiously, attempting to go no faster than Peking will permit.

Over Poland the pope will continue to display his personal emotional commitment. But increasingly his diplomats – especially Casaroli – will try and moderate his position. They will continue to remind John Paul that the most turbulent part of Vatican diplomatic history involved areas now largely under Russian control, and that he must not expect too much.

No one can be confident what course Vatican–Kremlin relations will take in the wake of the death of Yuri Andropov;

like so many other issues, it is complicated by John Paul's deliberate decision to continue to allow his political perspective of the world to be formed, if only partly, by the Central Intelligence Agency.

The most powerful, and perhaps best informed, spy organization in the western world has, if anything, drawn closer to John Paul.

While many will see the close ties the CIA has with the papacy as the misbegotten offspring of religion and politics, others will draw comfort that it is the CIA, and not the KGB, which briefs John Paul.

Nevertheless, it is arguable whether the Holy See needs such intimate links with any intelligence service. After all, papal diplomats insist their efforts are still directed towards simple objectives; to maintain the liberty of the Church; to defend human rights; to try and create a better world.

It was the CIA which gave John Paul the first news that Andropov would not recover. The pope learned this from the CIA's station chief in Rome soon after returning from visiting Agca. And it fell to the intelligence officer to be the first to inform John Paul, in February 1984, that the Soviet leader was actually dead.

Among other things, Andropov's death put an end to John Paul's wish to know – one way or another – whether the Soviet leader was implicated in the papal assassination plot.

Instead the CIA told the pope – in one of the weekly Friday evening briefing reports CIA Rome continues to send over to the Apostolic Palace – that the end of Andropov took much of the sting out of the Bulgarian Connection. Shortly afterwards John Paul instructed papal diplomats around the world to stop collecting press clippings on the attempt on his life.

Yet on a wider scale the violence continues unabated.

It dominates not only John Paul's own thinking, but that of his staff: those who run the Secretariat of State desks; those who occupy the nunciatures and papal missions scattered to the far corners of the earth. And it has affected not only them, but the local Church hierarchies: their cardinals, archbishops, bishops, and on down to the humblest parish priest and nun.

To many of this vast spiritual army – in size it approaches a million and a half souls – carnage undoubtedly remains the most disturbing image they see for the future; there is continual violence not only in the Middle East and Central America, but almost anywhere. A person or a building can be shattered by explosives, the innocent blown to pieces in the defamed name of nationalism.

Who is to know how many times in the future the pope's celibates will be called out to comfort the dazed survivors of an outrage, or pray before rows of flag-draped coffins for the souls of those pointlessly murdered?

Other priests and nuns, in defiance of their pope, will continue to protest for unilateral disarmament. Still more will continue to believe their time is better spent giving succour to those who could not protest – because they are the victims of political systems which forbid it, trapped by regimes which prefer instead to gaol, torture, suppress and arrange to make 'disappear' anyone who opposes their creeds.

For his part John Paul will continue to speak out for the basic rights of man. His will remain the authentic voice calling for true freedom of action and thought; it is his words which will highlight mankind's inexcusable inability to feed the starving and restrain the hostility between differing ideologies while at the same time trying to convey hope for a world now all too capable of destroying itself.

In John Paul's mouth, words like 'truth' and 'justice' and 'freedom' have not become debased. When he speaks of 'salvation', it is not a tired noun but a reminder of the dignity of man.

Yet in many ways this is both a moving and mysterious concept for reducing global tensions. It presumes a great deal: that all societies have the spiritual capacity to accept the pope's ideals.

But where is the dignity of man in the religious turmoil which characterizes the regime of the Ayatollah Khomeini?

Where is the evidence that it is alive – let alone flourishing – under Marxism?

Where is the dignity of man to be seen in the retributive hatred of Northern Ireland?

Where is it present in Lebanon, where senseless acts are followed by equal response?

In these and so many other places the past seems to influence the present – ever ready to devour the first sign of the dignity of man.

Yet this total and passionate commitment to human dignity is the ultimate weapon at the pope's disposal; it is this concept that is behind every move he and his diplomats make on the international stage.

The signs are, however, that while the Holy See will undoubtedly remain an authoritative international agency concerned for human rights, it will become more cautious as to where and how it will commit itself.

This is almost certainly partly due to such potent influences on the pontificate as the CIA, Opus Dei and a general return to religious conservatism.

While clinging to its purely religious image, the Holy See, when it does so, will plunge ever deeper into international politics – encouraged by forces without and within the Church.

Holy See initiatives will still display a degree of independence. But the entanglement of John Paul and his diplomats with so many powerful and disparate forces can only endanger the acceptable and traditional role of papal diplomacy. This sees itself exclusively devoted – both in the spiritual and secular sense – to the central issue of man's survival on Earth.

It may indeed seem a fragile enough weapon to ward off the self-destructive impulses of a world which steadily darkened during the Year of Armageddon.

Notes

CHAPTER 1

1. Undoubtedly the best recent study of modern Holy See politics is the masterly *Eastern Politics of the Vatican 1917–1979* by Hansjakob Stehle (Ohio University Press, 1981). Stehle is a German historian who has covered Vatican affairs since 1970. His work has established a benchmark for students of papal politics, an area which is not generally noted for authoritative writings. However, certain older works, such as *Vatican Diplomacy* by Robert A. Graham, SJ (Princeton University Press, 1959), and *The Politics of the Vatican* by Peter Nichols (Pall Mall Press, London, 1968) are also well worth consulting.

2. Nuncios are automatically deans of the diplomatic corps in the countries to which they are accredited; pro-nuncios are not. An apostolic delegate is the Holy See's equivalent of a personal envoy.

3. The view was expressed by Eugene V. Rostow, Under-Secretary of State for Political Affairs in the Lyndon Johnson Administration, at the celebrated Boston College Symposium in 1970. It is one still widely held.

4. We used three professional researchers to assist us: George Waller, Vivienne Heston and Clarissa McNair. We owe much to their very special skills.

5. Graham, op. cit.

CHAPTER 2

1. Details of exigence procedures were provided for us by a German intelligence officer in July 1983 and by a *capo*

in the Rome police. The plan is regularly updated and test runs are carried out to check how quickly police reinforcements can reach St Peter's Square in a crisis. The Gemelli Hospital, where John Paul was taken after being shot in 1981, remains the designated emergency centre. There, too, procedures are frequently checked to avoid repetition of the situation following the 1981 shooting: the hospital received no prior warning that the critically injured pope was on the way.

2. Ibid.

3. In various conversations with us while we were researching this book, Mgr Emery Kabongo emphasized the problem of balancing adequate security against giving what he said was 'the essential freedom for the Holy Father to get around and meet his flock'.

4. Cibin's views and behaviour, including his daily walk through the Vatican, as related here, are based on lengthy personal observation of the security chief, conversations with him, and from information supplied to us by independent Vatican sources.

5. Pioneer investigative journalism into the complexities of the CIA–Vatican relationship has been done by that gifted reporter, Roland Flamini of *Time* magazine. During his years in Rome, Flamini amassed impressive data on the Company and the Church. He is the author of a standard work on intelligence and the papacy, *Pope, Premier, President* (Macmillan, New York, 1980). Additional information was obtained in particular from US Senate Committee Investigations into the CIA, too voluminous to cite here. See also Martin Lee's article in *Mother Jones* magazine (July 1983), pp. 21–7, 36–8.

6. The full story of how the Vatican was bugged was first revealed to us by an employee of Vatican Radio in May 1982. Two other sources subsequently independently confirmed the facts we had been given.

7. Within a few days the news that the CIA was 'in' reached other western intelligence stations in Rome.

The details were passed to selected Vaticanologists, including ourselves.

8. A West German BKA intelligence officer, based in Rome, used these words when speaking to one of us on 24 July 1983 over dinner at the Hilton.

9. Ibid.

10. Clarissa McNair told of her experiences when she agreed to assist us with certain research requirements from April 1983 until the completion of this book. She made it clear that her first allegiance was to her Vatican employers and anything done for us must not interfere with her work or compromise her position with them. This was agreed. Her experiences at the hands of The Mad Mentor, which we detail further in subsequent chapters, have a Kafka-like quality; not for the first time it raises unsettling questions about the mental state of some of those associated with the agency.

11. We visited the Palace of Justice many times during 1982–3, and came to know it well.

12. Giuseppe Rosselli, the respected and veteran Rome reporter on legal affairs, has, since he came to know Martella during the Lockheed scandal investigation, remained one of the few Italian journalists the magistrate will speak to; Martella has had his share of vilification in the national press of Italy and, tough-minded though he is, he has inevitably been wounded by some of the more vicious smears. Rosselli has maintained a position of trust; that is why we trust the background on how Martella took the case which Rosselli provided for us.

13. From the Italian Parliament daily record (20 December 1982, pp. 1,194–8 inclusive).

14. The relationship between the two men is common knowledge on the fourth floor of the Palace of Justice.

15. Twice during this period – on 19 December and 27 December 1982 – one of us spoke to Martella. He was able to confirm certain facts we already possessed while

putting us right on other matters. We incorporated a portion of this data in footnote form in *Pontiff*; space requirements and the inevitable printer's deadline made it impossible to publish it all. The material is now included in this work.

Martella admitted he had not expected the huge amount of publicity resulting from his December allegations about a Bulgarian Connection. When the media storm refused to slacken, he took the sensible course of refusing to speak further to reporters. Two who nevertheless occasionally managed to reach him were Giuseppe Rosselli and then correspondent for the London *Daily Express*, Al Troner. They helped further our knowledge. But almost all the details of Martella's conversations with Agca, on this and subsequent occasions, came to us in a surreptitious but trusted way. To build his case Martella needed the co-operation of numerous foreign intelligence agencies: he had to see their files of depositions and background material. Of special interest to him was the data the West German agencies, BND and BKA, possess. The material was made available to Martella. In return he provided the BKA and BND with copies of his often personally typed transcripts of conversations with Agca. In turn our own sources in these agencies passed certain portions of this material to us. There was no security breach involved; in no way, for instance, could anyone claim Agca's recounting of the influence of the Koran on his life could be a threat to anybody. But to two grateful social historians, this is the sort of prime source material required to help understand the interpersonal relationship between Martella and his prisoner. We do not of course claim to have seen all or even most of the material the Germans have obtained from Martella. We believe that we have, however, seen sufficient to recreate accurately what we have described.

16. Contrary to some reports the *vigili* have no authority to

shoot to kill or maim in circumstances other than during a direct threat to the pope's life. There seems no hard and fast rule as to at what point a threat would become sufficiently serious to justify such action.

17. Our portrait of Poggi is drawn from a number of sources. One is his fellow diplomat, Archbishop Gaetano Alibrandi, the papal nuncio to Ireland. Another was President Reagan's Envoy to the Holy See, William Wilson. A third is Fr Lambert Greenan of *L'Osservatore Romano*. We were also able to form a personal impression of Poggi during a conversation one of us had with him on 3 May 1983. The archbishop had to end it abruptly when he realized he might miss his plane, this time for Budapest. In no way do we wish to suggest that Poggi broke the sacred trust the pope has placed in him by providing us with details of his diplomatic journeyings. But we did learn something of them from sources knowledgeable on such matters: the Soviet, Bulgarian and Polish embassies in Rome. They monitor his movements with the greatest of interest, and if they think there is political gain to be achieved, they will talk to the curious. In our case we were curious and they presumably thought there was for them a possible gain.

18. *Time*, 27 December 1982, p. 4; *Newsweek*, 3 January 1983, p. 20.

19. Hansjakob Stehle's indispensable *Eastern Politics of the Vatican 1917–1979* (p. 390).

CHAPTER 3

1. The file was shown to one of us during a visit to the Secretariat of State on the afternoon of 19 April 1983. Our guide was a monsignor whose reticence to be identified again illustrates the problem of not always being able to name those who provide help. Nor are we alone in this situation. Kenneth Briggs, the immensely

capable religious editor of *The New York Times*, succinctly summed up the problem in these words: 'Those in high places rarely speak openly, let alone critically, about Church affairs or the pope . . . hierarchical habits ingrain fierce loyalties in underlings, effectively stifling candour. Outspokenness entails great risk. Prelates keep Church business almost exclusively within the walls of the Vatican and generally grant interviews only on the condition that names not be used' (*The New York Times Magazine*, 10 October 1982, p. 8).

2. Details of the pope's devotions were given to us by Mgr Emery Kabongo on 14 April 1983.

3. Fr Bruno Fink, private secretary to Cardinal Joseph Ratzinger, Prefect of the Sacred Congregation for the Doctrine of the Faith (the old Holy Office), told one of us, on 5 May 1983, a great deal about the Church's efforts to combat secularism in West Germany.

4. Poggi confirmed to one of us, on 3 May 1983, that he writes all his reports in longhand.

5. In one of his many revealing insights into how the papacy works, an Irish Dominican delivered this caustic judgement. Our personal observation tends to suggest he has, if anything, understated the matter.

6. Ibid.

7. The story of John Paul's involvement with Walesa and Solidarity is a contentious one, at least as far as the Vatican Press Office goes. We told part of it in *Pontiff* (pp. 426–30, 465–6). It was based on investigative work done by NBC television and by our own enquiries. The official Vatican response was to deny both what NBC broadcast and we published – namely, that John Paul had written to Brezhnev. In the furore which followed our revelations – in themselves more detailed than the NBC broadcast – we returned to our four prime Vatican sources for our information and asked them to verify what they had previously told us. They did and confirmed we had published the facts as they under-

stood them. Since we had last spoken they had unearthed yet more information which we have used here to develop the story of the papal involvement. In December 1982 Senator Alfonse D'Amato (Republican, New York) said that he had been reliably informed by 'a Vatican source that the pope had threatened to lead a resistance movement in his native Poland in the event of a Soviet invasion'. *The New York Times* felt the story of sufficient importance to run a five-column report, 'Vatican Official Hints That The Pope Wrote A Letter To Brezhnev' (*NYT*, 30 January 1983). Once more the Vatican Press Office issued a denial. By then few took it seriously. This letter quite possibly paved the way for the attempt on John Paul's life. The Vatican Press Office did not deny the substance of our detailed chronology of the pope's relationship with Walesa as outlined in *Pontiff*, now considerably amplified here.

8. The pope's view of Walesa was confirmed for us by two of his closest aides.

9. See note 7.

10. Mgr Kabongo told us during several of our talks with him that the pope has 'long ago made his peace with God and fears nothing. It is we who fear for him.'

11. For a detailed exposition, see *Eastern Politics of the Vatican 1917–1979* by Hansjakob Stehle.

12. Ibid.

13. Professor Stehle made this point to one of us during a lengthy interview on 23 April 1983.

14. Ibid.

15. Dimitrov vividly recalled for us the pressures he had felt when the Bulgarian Connection first broke. In a number of conversations between April and December 1983 the first secretary also provided a fascinating insight into the life and attitudes of an Eastern European diplomat working in the West. During all his discussions Dimitrov consistently held to the view his country was the victim of a western press campaign; the

quotations in this section are, as best he could recall, his own responses at that time.

16. *Newsweek*, 20 December 1982, p. 59.
17. *Newsweek*, 27 December 1982, p. 42.
18. *Economist*, 28 December 1982, p. 12.
19. Dimitrov's fears of being called back to Bulgaria appear to have been groundless; he has remained in Rome, one of the more popular of the eastern bloc diplomats in the capital. He did agree however that some of his colleagues have been recalled or 'moved elsewhere' following the press conference débâcle.
20. We were able to observe Mgr Kabongo going about his work several times between March 1983 and the end of the year.
21. Our impression of the Secretariat of State is based on visits there to obtain from various officials the information which enabled us to write this section.
22. Mgr Kabongo gave one of us, on 12 April 1983, a full account of his life and career. He was engagingly modest and constantly played down his own rather remarkable achievements in Korea and Brazil. Others painted a more realistic portrait of Kabongo's many talents. One of them, Mgr Roland Minnerath, secretary at the nunciature in Brazil, said that in his opinion the pope's secretary was one of the most outstanding of the younger diplomats currently in Holy See service. And Cardinal Franz Koenig of Vienna, a fine judge in such matters, told us Kabongo is 'destined for the upper echelons of Church service'.
23. Two of Magee's Irish colleagues in the Vatican gave us in June 1982 various examples of the friction between Magee and Dziwisz. And a close family friend of Magee, a person of impeccable reputation, told us on 22 April 1983 that 'poor John has suffered quite a lot with the Pole'.
24. Based on a discussion with Mgr Kabongo on 15 April 1983 in the papal apartment.

25. William Wilson, President Reagan's personal envoy to the Holy See, told one of us on 17 April 1983, during a lengthy interview, 'that fellah Kabongo is a tough man, not to fool with'.
26. Based on personal observation.
27. Full text of speech provided by Fr Lambert Greenan.
28. Ibid.
29. Mgr Kabongo's reaction was recalled for us by him in conversation on 12 April 1983.
30. Two sources provided us with detailed information on the network – the generic term for the pope's envoys. An overview was provided by Fr Greenan during one of the many luncheons and dinners we shared with him throughout 1982 and 1983. Before he became editor of the pope's English-language weekly, Greenan worked in the Secretariat. A more immediate view of the workings of papal diplomacy was offered by Mgr Kabongo.
31. On Saturday, 22 May 1982 the pope sent a telegram to Mrs Thatcher and President Galtieri, couched in identical words, in which he spoke of his 'deep anguish' and the threat to international peace the conflict had created. He was further distressed by the unyielding replies.
32. Both cardinals, in the end, shared a common view over the pope's visit to Britain and Argentina during the Falklands War. They were convinced the visit should go ahead. It did, although the pope did not meet Mrs Thatcher. Immediately after his British visit, John Paul flew to Argentina. He was received by President Galtieri. The brief meeting was widely misunderstood in Great Britain; by meeting Galtieri there was a feeling that John Paul was somehow 'taking sides'. In the ensuing public debate it was frequently pointed out that the pope is head of state – and that Galtieri, too, was then head of state. Diplomatic protocol required that the pope meet him, just as he had been obliged,

and delighted, to meet Britain's head of state, the Queen.

33. Mgr Kabongo expressed this hope to one of us in conversation on 12 April 1983.

34. The story would persist during 1983.

35. Mgr Kabongo put the pope's attitude into perspective for us on 9 April 1983. 'It is quite understandable that the Holy Father would like to know the facts. In that respect he is no different from anybody else whose life has been spared after such violence. It has left a serious impression on him. The pope also has a very healthy curiosity about what is being said and written about the background to the attempt on his life. Much of it is nonsense. But sometimes he does learn something that takes his understanding that much further.'

36. Based on personal observation by one of us on 15 August 1983.

37. Information on Agca's prison conditions came to us from two sources. One is an employee with the Italian Ministry of Justice. The other is an intelligence officer. Both evoked the pledge of secrecy before they agreed to talk. Neither knows the other, at least as far as we could establish. Yet their information matched in all important details. Our meetings with them were spread over 1982 and 1983.

38. In lengthy interviews one of us had with the Agca family in Yesiltepe in January 1982, they repeatedly expressed the view that their letters to Agca were intercepted by the Turkish authorities. This was formally denied to us on 16 February 1982 by a spokesman for the Turkish Foreign Ministry.

39. One of our intelligence sources, whom we choose to call Rudi, personally interviewed Agca twice in late 1982. He said that he found the change in Agca quite remarkable: 'he was being well treated by the medical people looking after him at this stage'.

40. See note 38.

CHAPTER 4

1. On 4 January 1983, Rome newspapers carried detailed accounts of Antonov's impending release. Press reports said sources 'close to the investigation' – believed to be some of Judge Martella's more severe critics on the fourth floor of the Palace of Justice – stated that Antonov had stood up to 'more than 27 hours of questioning about his role in the case. They said that although he had engaged two lawyers, he waved [*sic*] their presence during much of the interrogation' (*Rome Daily American*, 4 January 1983). Of more significance was that some lawyers were starting to question Antonov's alleged role in the assassination attempt because 'he remained in Rome more than a year after the shooting. They have pointed out he had free access twice-a-week to return to Bulgaria' (ibid.). Clearly alarmed by what was happening, Martella was relieved to find himself supported publicly by the Israeli government. A MOSSAD official in Tel Aviv told the Associated Press (wire service dispatch 4 January 1983) that Israel 'believed Italy's claims there was a Bulgarian Connection and a link to the Soviet KGB'. The MOSSAD source was quoted as saying, 'Bulgaria does nothing without the approval of the KGB.' The same source was critical of West Germany for continuing to play down the Bulgarian Connection. On this same day there was an unsourced report that 'a key Turkish suspect', Cedar Celebi, presently under arrest in Frankfurt, would be extradited to Rome. The same story claimed 'a Turkish report to the Vatican suggested Celebi may have been one of three gunmen in St Peter's Square on the day of the shooting' (*Rome Daily American*, 4 January 1983). It was the first public indication of how reports to the Vatican on the papal shooting are discreetly leaked after they have been forwarded to Martella. The magistrate has come to

accept this is 'very much the Vatican way of doing things' (his comment to one of us on 19 December 1982).

2. The immediate Vatican response to the news was to have the Polish hierarchy urge all Polish workers to ignore the mini-unions. So successful was the move that PAP, the Polish news agency, was forced to concede that a 'mood of reserve and expectation still holds among the personnel of many enterprises' (UPI wire dispatch, 4 January 1983).

3. Vatican interest in the scandal was keen. Urgent assurances were sought by the pope from Marcinkus that Vatican Bank was not involved in the issue. Marcinkus assured the pontiff this was purely 'a secular matter' (his reported comment was relayed to one of us on 3 January 1983 by one of his staff). Cibin was interested in the affair for a different reason. His own enquiries suggested the source of the *Daily American* report (31 December 1982) headlined 'FAO Official Alleges Agency Rigged Bank Rates' was none other than The Mad Mentor, the elderly CIA operative whose connection to the Vatican had begun to worry the city–state's security chief.

4. A similar accusation was made by the former Director of the CIA on NBC Television (30 December 1982); he stated categorically that the assassination attempt bore 'all the earmarks of a KGB operation'.

5. *L'Osservatore Romano* (24 September 1982, p. 1).

6. *The New York Times Magazine* (10 October 1982, p.7).

7. Numerous Vatican staffers believe that *The New York Times* in recent years has become more critical of the Church. The judgement is hard to justify. In our experience the *Times*, unlike some US newspapers, has maintained a healthy perspective on this pontificate.

8. The only occasion we can recall Greenan revealing a personal glimpse of John Paul was during the Falklands War. The editor explained to us that the seriousness of the situation could be gauged by the fact that the pope

'was adding mineral water to his single glass of white wine per meal and was only picking at his food' (in conversation on 19 May 1983).

9. The papal announcement was on 10 January 1983.
10. Jas Gawronski, an Italian member of the European Parliament, told one of us over dinner on 4 September 1983 that his 'most trusted sources' in the Vatican now believed that any 'real evidence' no longer existed which would 'really implicate the bank'. Gawronski stated that the hitherto close relationship between the pope and Marcinkus had markedly cooled, 'and there would be no way John Paul would keep him on if he had any evidence to move Marcinkus out'. Gawronski added that to shift Marcinkus would also be seen as a tacit admission that he had 'more than made mistakes. In Vatican terms this would be unacceptable. The Vatican has a highly developed sense of what is properly pragmatic.'

CHAPTER 5

1. Sister Severia described her duties to us during several discussions between 3 April 1983 and the end of the year.
2. The pope has his own mini-console on his desk. It has six separate lines which enable him to bypass the Vatican switchboard should he so wish. Through this console John Paul made his now celebrated series of telephone calls to Lech Walesa during the run-up period before the formation of Solidarity.
3. The pope used this phrase several times during speeches on his North American visit in 1979.
4. There was a sensation when Cardinal Bernardin issued the draft document to the media in 1982. He regarded its circulation as an 'opportunity to teach and learn' (*The New York Times Magazine*, 10 May 1983).
5. A curial monsignor informed us of this on 10 April

1983. We put the remark to Wilson on 20 April 1983. He did not discount it.

6. Wilson, in personal interview with one of us on 13 April 1983.

7. Mgr Kabongo painted an evocative portrait of Montalo for us on 14 April 1983.

8. Arafat's stay in Algeria was marred by bitter public squabbling with Gaddafi's representative. In the end Arafat asserted his dominant role. In a fiery speech he promised that the PLO would continue the political and military struggle against Israel, 'until a just peace has been achieved and the Palestinian flag is hoisted atop the mosques and churches of Jerusalem'. He made no mention of the Jewish places of worship in the Holy City. In Jerusalem, he promised 'peace will be achieved by an independent decision of our people, taken through the barrel of a gun' (Associated Press dispatch, 15 February 1983).

9. The nuncio's views became known to us when we met Joseph Harmouche, the Beirut publisher and editor-in-chief of *Middle East Panorama*, a news magazine of considerable status in Arab countries. Harmouche is a Lebanese Christian with close connections to Nuncio Angeloni. During a series of discussions from 23 July to 27 July 1983 Harmouche provided considerable detail on the Holy See's involvement in his country's affairs. His appreciation proved accurate when we were able to check it with our Vatican sources.

10. Ibid.

11. Ibid.

12. The same MOSSAD source expressed an identical view to one of us in Rome on 29 July 1983. He was in Rome to have 'informal talks' on the Middle East with a member of the West German BND.

13. Angeloni's words were quoted by Harmouche on 24 July 1983.

14. Harmouche, 26 July 1983.

15. *Time*, 31 January 1983.
16. Both the pope's and the Secretary's telephones have override buttons which allow them to interrupt each other's calls.
17. The Holy See's influence helped. While the final communiqué of the Managua summit did denounce the 'use of Israel by the United States in its interventionist practises in Latin America', the statement was described by most delegates as relatively mild and fell far short of outright condemnation. Egypt and India still felt the document was too critical of the US.
18. The assessment is in the hands of Mgr Mounged El-Hachem, one of the Secretariat's experts on the Middle East. He admitted to one of us on 5 September 1983 that 'keeping track of all the groups is a nightmare'.
19. *New York Times*, 17 January 1983.
20. Ibid.
21. Wilson, in personal interview, 13 April 1983.
22. Pope John Paul in New Year's Day Message, 1 January 1983.
23. *The Soviet War Machine* by Christopher Donnelly (Salamander Books, London 1981) and *The Final Decade* by Christopher Lee (Hamish Hamilton, London, 1981) provide authoritative insights into the effects of a future nuclear war, as does *The Medical Effects of Nuclear War* (British Medical Association, Chichester, 1983).
24. Quoted to one of us by Mgr Kabongo on 10 April 1983.
25. NATO *Force Comparisons*, 1982 and NATO *Defence Fact Sheet*, February 1983 – both compiled with the aid of western intelligence services, including the CIA.
26. Ibid.
27. Mgr Kabongo, 10 April 1983.
28. The pope's speech, delivered in French in the Apostolic Palace's Royal Hall, also contained criticism of those governments that 'make a certain number of people disappear, without trial, leaving their families in a cruel state of uncertainty'. This was seen as a reference to

Argentina. Further, the pope referred to 'outside inter-ference' in Central America.

29. Between 15 April 1982 and 27 July 1983 we had a series of meetings with Fr Fink. He was cautiously helpful at first, but gradually became more open, though constantly reminding us that he was bound by the oath of secrecy which had been administered to him in Latin. Like Mgr Kabongo, he was modest about achieving such an important position so early in his Church career; he felt he had 'just been lucky'.

30. In *Pontiff* we wrote that Küng was 'ordered to Rome, escorted to the third floor . . . and paraded before its officials. They listened and swiftly pronounced.' This was inaccurate – but the mistake also illustrates the very real difficulties of interpreting what might be called the 'sign language' of our source, Bruno Fink. On Küng, Fink had been unusually circumspect, hinting but never actually saying that Küng had been brought to Rome. When *Pontiff* appeared a number of helpful critics pointed out that although Küng had indeed been asked to explain his position, and though we had been entirely accurate in our description of his censure, he had in fact skilfully avoided walking into the jaws of the Holy Office. When one of us put this to Fink, on 27 July 1983, he said, 'You did not understand my meaning. I did not wish to convey that Küng had been here. I only meant that we had acted in a certain manner over him.'

31. Fink, in conversation, 29 March 1983.

32. Fink, in conversation, 23 May 1983.

33. Ibid.

34. We learned of Fink's methodology from one of his colleagues.

35. Cited by *Time*, 29 November 1982, p. 46.

36. Ibid.

37. Pius XII made his pronouncement in 1954. It had a deep effect on Karol Wojtyla, then a rising young star in the Polish hierarchy.

38. Cited by *Time*, 29 November 1982.
39. Ibid.
40. Krol made his remarks during a keynote speech to the conference.
41. Fink also repeatedly stressed, when recounting his feelings at the time to one of us on 17 March 1983, that he was expressing his own views only and they should not in any way be taken to reflect those of his cardinal or the Church.
42. For those wishing a further explanation of the workings of the Secretariat we recommend George Bull's study, *Inside the Vatican* (Hutchinson, London, 1982).
43. In a lengthy taped interview on 23 April 1982 Alibrandi explained that the 'entire question' of Irish neutrality was of continuous interest to him and, *inter alia*, the Holy See.
44. The Holy See attempted, and failed, to save the life of hunger striker Bobby Sands in 1981. A full account can be found in *Pontiff*. When it was published, Cardinal Hume of Westminster claimed he had no prior knowledge of the secret Holy See initiative, but the four sources who had provided us with information subsequently confirmed that overall our portrayal accurately reflected the unhappy Sands episode. When numerous Irish reporters asked Alibrandi in June 1983 if he wished to challenge the veracity of our reporting he declined to do so.
45. Mitterand will say: 'Whoever gambles on the decoupling of the European continent from the American continent would call into question the maintenance of equilibrium and thus the maintenance of peace.'
46. *Time*, 31 March 1983.

CHAPTER 6

1. Gromyko made his statement in Bonn, where he had gone to attempt to persuade Chancellor Khol not to

accept the missiles on German soil. Kohl refused his request. The timing of Gromyko's repeated rejection of President Reagan's zero option proposal doubtless affected the thinking of the conference.

2. In Washington the feeling was the Soviet Union was about to do the very thing Casaroli's nuncio in Beirut had predicted – increase its presence in the area. CIA sources expressed concern that even one Sam-5 missile could provoke a dangerous new crisis if Israel decided to destroy the weapon which had the capability to reach into Israeli airspace and cover much of Lebanon. There was also a fear that not only other such weapons were en route to Syria from the Soviet Union but they would be accompanied by Russian troops to man them.

3. McNair's detailed diary, which she made available, enabled us to pin-point precisely every broadcast she made. By comparing her journal with the list of alleged complaints that The Mad Mentor had transcribed and which would eventually be submitted to Vatican Radio – and on up to Cardinal Casaroli's office – it was possible for us to conclude which broadcasts had been deemed anti-American.

4. With this particular broadcast we are satisfied the operative used the same procedure he applied on previous occasions: as soon as he recorded and had transcribed McNair's newscast, it was sent along to Wilson's office.

5. Wilson, in a particularly unguarded moment during a very unguarded interview with one of us, 17 April 1983.

6. McConnachie on 11 April 1983.

7. Ibid.

8. A dozen Vatican sources have expressed similar thoughts to us. The situation is not entirely Fr Panciroli's fault. He took over the post when it was *de rigueur* for the Vatican Press Office automatically to conceal the most innocent of facts. Steeped in that tradition, the hapless Panciroli now finds that both the media and

the attitudes of those who work in the Vatican have changed; there is growing contact between the two sides. In any event, Panciroli was not subsequently removed.

9. The full extent of the plot was revealed to us on 6 August 1978, the day Paul died, still fearing, his then personal secretary Mgr John Magee told us, that he might become the victim of a terrorist outrage.

10. While our source was indeed invaluable, we do not believe he should be reproached for explaining to us what was going on. The conference had already generated a large number of leaks, many of which were of doubtful authenticity. Our source was only concerned that we should get it right; for the most part he answered our questions rather than volunteering information. He also spoke to us in the knowledge that when we did publish the immediacy of the event would have passed; doubtless his attitude would have been different if he thought his words would be appearing in the next issue of a newspaper. We did not, of course, pay for the information he gave.

11. Roach quoted in Rome's *Daily American* (19 January 1983, p. 1).

CHAPTER 7

1. Between 24 March and 27 April 1983 we made four separate visits to the papal secretariat to observe something of its workings. During one of these visits Mgr Kabongo remarked that writing 'on all the aspects of papal diplomacy must be very fascinating'. We assured him it was.

2. Personal observations of one of us during a visit to the papal apartment in May 1983.

3. This routine was confirmed for us by Mgr Kabongo on 14 April 1983.

4. The schedule of papal appointments was provided by Greenan.

5. Mgr Kabongo told us on 14 April 1983 that he was 'truly astonished at the ability of the Holy Father to absorb so much material so quickly. He is the hardest worker of us all.'

6. The meeting, according to UPI sources, did not discuss the specifics of the letter; we believe it did.

7. The Czech attack was reinforced by Soviet charges that the pope was running 'an anti-Communist campaign'.

8. Bull, op. cit., describes such formalities in detail.

9. Wilson, 4 May 1983.

10. Ibid.

11. Hornblow, 4 May 1983.

12. Planty, 5 August 1983.

13. A description of the protocol was given to us by Don Planty, who replaced Hornblow in June, on 15 September 1983. He stated: 'they just followed standard procedure. They've done it a thousand times. Secret servicemen have one job – stick closest to the man they are assigned to. Nobody can get in the way of that.'

14. Based on conversation with Mgr Martin in 1982.

15. Bush statement, 8 February 1983, in Rome.

16. Based on a study of Bush's public responses to his trip.

17. Based on a Secretariat of State source who had helped prepare the pope's brief.

18. Bush, loc. cit.

19. Recalled by Wilson to one of us on 4 May 1983.

20. On 4 August 1983 one of our researchers visited Rebibbia.

21. Ibid.

22. Washington Post, 28 January 1983; International Herald Tribune, 28 January 1983; New York Times, 29 January 1983; et al.

23. The meeting was on 8 February 1983. Afterwards D'Amato issued a swingeing attack on the CIA which was widely reported.

24. Los Angeles Times, 1 February 1983.

25. Ibid.

26. The Vatican Press Office described the meeting merely as 'consultations'.
27. Mgr Kabongo's description of preparing for the trip filled a vivid hour for us when we spoke with him on 19 April 1983.
28. The communiqué was issued publicly by President Roberto d'Aubuisson on 1 March 1983.
29. Document dated 3 February 1983.
30. Botta in interview, 21 April 1983. During this, he recalled the dialogue he had used and the precise information he provided.
31. MacCarthy was interviewed by us often. This particular quote comes from the interview of 13 April 1983.
32. Wilson confirmed to us on 17 April 1983 that he had 'tried to put this point as strongly and as often as I could to Casaroli and his people'.
33. This view has been well developed by David Holloway, lecturer in the Department of Politics at the University of Edinburgh, in his excellent study, *The Soviet Union and the Arms Race* (Yale University Press, 1983).
34. Wilson, loc. cit.
35. The exchange between McNair and Quercetti was independently confirmed by them both in two lengthy interviews on 24 April 1983 and 26 April 1983. McNair subsequently made available her detailed journal.
36. Wilson said he could not recall why he did this when we discussed the entire incident with him on 17 April 1983.

CHAPTER 8

1. Alitalia keep a detailed log of all papal flights. The airline provided us with the information for this particular trip.
2. Frazier interview, 24 May 1983.
3. Statement issued in Mexico City by El Salvador Democratic Revolutionary Front, 1 March 1983; the government did not reciprocate.
4. Frazier, loc. cit.

5. Frazier, 3 May 1983.
6. Magee, 23 May 1983.
7. Ibid.
8. Magee, 19 May 1983.
9. Ibid.
10. Ibid.
11. MacCarthy made himself available to us for interview and also provided a wealth of documentary data about the tour.
12. It is unlikely the men were direct employees of the CIA; probably they were members of one of the region's many civilian security agencies, some of whose staff have worked for the CIA.
13. Later the pope sent Cibin a memo congratulating him on the security arrangements.
14. The words were overheard by the doyen of Vatican correspondents, Wilton Wynn, and reported in *Time*, 14 March 1983.
15. Other world leaders were receiving similar calls from their ambassadors in Bonn.
16. *Time*, 14 March 1983.
17. Kabongo, 12 April 1983.
18. Fink, 23 April 1983.
19. The computer predictions were remarkably accurate. Kohl's Christian Democratic Union and its Bavarian ally, the Christian Social Union, gathered 49 per cent of the vote. Vogel's Social-Democrats trailed with 38.3 per cent. The anti-nuclear Green Party captured 5.5 per cent giving it a foothold in the Bundestag for the first time. The surprise of the election was the showing of the Free Democratic Party which, despite predictions of its demise, collected 6.7 per cent. The result for Kohl was a personal triumph. He had gone to the country only six months after assuming office, combining his conservative policies with populism, arguing that the 'silent majority' would more than offset the widespread peace and protest movement.

20. Kabongo, 12 April 1983.
21. Frazier, loc. cit.
22. Details of Agca's writings were made available to us through a prison source whom we agreed not to identify.
23. Kabongo, 12 April 1983.
24. Poggi, in conversation with one of us on 3 May 1983, described his Polish nunciature in these words.
25. There was a rush of stories that Andropov was mortified by Kohl's success. See *Time*, 21 March 1983, *et al*.
26. Weinberger believed acceptance of an interim formula would make it 'more difficult to get the Soviet Union back to the table for the follow-up' (Department of Defense statement, 17 March 1983).
27. Poggi, loc. cit.
28. Kabongo, loc. cit.
29. President Reagan's Speech to the Nation, 23 March 1983; General Secretary Andropov's reply, *Pravda*, 26 March 1983.

CHAPTER 9

1. A full account of our involvement in the story was published in the *Sunday Press*, Dublin, on 27 March 1983 and 3 April 1983. Subsequently the *Express* group of newspapers in London syndicated it world-wide.
2. Excerpt from taped interview with John McCarthy, 20 March 1983.
3. The interview with Marie McCarthy took place in Ashford, Co. Wicklow, on 21 March 1983.
4. The call was made on 23 April 1983.
5. Marie McCarthy, loc. cit.
6. John McCarthy, loc. cit.
7. John and Marie McCarthy repeatedly made such claims, in his case on tape, in their separate interviews on 20 March 1983 and 21 March 1983.

8. Research trips: December 1981, January/February 1982.
9. Kabongo, 23 March 1983.

CHAPTER 10

1. Cited by Bull, op. cit., p. 161.
2. Mgr Kabongo and Mgr Sepe between them gave us these insights into Casaroli's personality during separate interviews on 8 April 1983 and 9 May 1983.
3. Walesa in Gdansk, 3 April 1983.
4. Vatican Radio transcript of broadcast, 15 June 1983.
5. Cardinal Koenig in discussion with one of us, 24 March 1983.
6. Ibid.
7. Vatican Radio, op. cit.
8. *Asian Survey*, December 1983, pp. 1, 206–37.
9. Cited at Joint Economic Committee, 97th Congress, 2nd Session, Washington, DC, 13 August 1982.
10. We discussed the issue on three occasions between April and August 1983 with one of the Vatican's experts on the Far East, Fr Quercetti of Vatican Radio. He believes Peking's goal is to establish good relations with the US and Russia on terms that will enhance China's influence as a world power; this strategy could include a more positive relationship with the Holy See.
11. One of the most informed studies of current Sino-European relations is Dr Douglas T. Stuart's 'The Prospect For Sino-European Cooperation', published in *Orbis*, in its Fall issue, 1982.
12. McConnachie, 11 April 1983.
13. Abu Daoud, who organized the attack on Israeli athletes at the Munich Olympics, in his speech of 22 February 1983.
14. Arafat on ITV's *Weekend World*, 6 March 1983.
15. Some observers believe *lo strappo* a clear indication that the 'reality of the eastern bloc' is unacceptable to the

majority of members in the PCI. Perhaps equally relevant is the fact that three-quarters of the delegates to the Milan conference joined the Party after 1961; for them interest in Soviet ideology runs a poor second to the reforms they want to see implemented in Italy.

16. Alibrandi reported in May 1983 that Protestant reaction in Ulster against the amendment in the South was being greatly magnified. He proved to be right.

17. Brezhnev's failing health was unknown to many Kremlinologists right up to the time of his death.

18. The French had apparently not been more specific than to say an attack on the pope was likely within the following three months. No location was given. Nevertheless, more reliable information was on hand. MOSSAD had informed DIGOS in Rome that Agca and two men whom the Israeli intelligence service identified as KGB operatives were in Perugia. That information should have made the CIA take the French data more seriously than it seems to have done.

19. Part of the reason may have been the cost. To keep a surgical/medical team on standby would be very expensive, especially when the Church was claiming it was in poor financial circumstances. There was also the question of keeping the matter secret – something Cibin said would be almost impossible.

20. McNair, 15 September 1983.

21. King Carlos, according to some Vatican sources, also told the pope that if real proof emerged the KGB was connected with the papal assassination attempt, Spain would take the strongest possible action against the Soviet Union – perhaps even breaking off diplomatic relations. A Royal Palace spokesman in Madrid subsequently refused to confirm or deny whether the conversation had taken place.

22. *Time*, 18 April 1983.

23. UPI dispatch, Geneva, 9 April 1983.

24. Ibid.

25. McNair, 26 April 1983.
26. McNair's Vatican Radio script, seen on 19 April 1983.

CHAPTER 11

1. Magee, 24 April 1983.
2. Kabongo, 19 April 1983.
3. Ibid.
4. Magee, loc. cit.
5. Kabongo, 24 April 1983.
6. The interview with William Wilson lasted over two hours. Our account here is necessarily a shortened version of a very lengthy transcription. But we feel it faithfully reflects the tenor of the envoy's position.

CHAPTER 12

1. During this Sunday, and in the week to follow, we made over a dozen visits in all to the Apostolic Palace to speak to members of the Secretariat of State and the pope's staff. The events portrayed are virtually entirely based on their recall.
2. Kabongo, 1 May 1983.
3. An earlier written request from the Polish Communist Party Politburo had been rejected (*The New York Times*, 1 May 1983).
4. During the meeting a number of people – messengers and more junior members of the Curia – came and went from the pope's office with updates and instructions relating to the developing situation in Poland. Some of them saw and overheard the reactions and responses reported here.
5. We are uncertain how the pope conveyed this guidance to Walesa. One source strongly suggested John Paul made another of his now famous telephone calls to Walesa. To have done so would certainly have been both typical of the pope and a heroic gesture under the

circumstances. But we tend to discount a telephone call. In the prevailing political climate it would have been almost foolhardy to make contact this way. We favour the idea that an intermediary was used, probably Poggi or Glemp.

6. We learned of the telephone call to Dziwisz in October 1983 in Rome; we were in the Apostolic Palace at the time the news came through that Walesa had been awarded the Nobel Peace Prize.

7. On 13 December 1981 we also received a copy of the Austrian Intelligence file. The person who provided it insisted he was motivated by a wish to publicize what he called 'a cover-up among western intelligence agencies'.

8. We first learned of the existence of the two versions during a lengthy briefing, on 9 December 1981, in Wiesbaden, West Germany, from two senior officers, Kommissar Helmut Bruckman and Kriminalhauptkommissar Hans-Georg Fuchs of the BKA.

9. Cahani, in an interview with one of us, 14 February 1982.

10. MOSSAD teletype shown to us in Vienna on 11 December 1982.

11. In the aftermath of the papal shooting, the staff of the DIGOS office in Perugia was replaced; the senior DIGOS officers on duty in Rome over Easter 1981 was also subsequently moved.

12. Bruckman and Fuchs confirmed the episode to us on 9 December 1981.

13. On 29 May 1983 *The Los Angeles Times* published a long story citing Clark and Casey under the headline: 'US Officials Discount "Bulgarian Connection": New Attitude On Attempted Assassination of John Paul Based On CIA Data.' The report said Clark and Casey 'now both lean toward the view that efforts to find a "Bulgarian Connection" between Bulgarian intelligence agents and the attempted assassination of Pope John Paul have

run dry. Their new attitude follows a review of information available to the CIA.'

14. Kabongo, 28 September 1983.
15. Ibid.
16. Kabongo, 1 May 1983.
17. Text of papal speech provided by Fr Greenan.
18. Magee, 1 May 1983.
19. This entire scene is based on several interviews with McNair and full access to her detailed journal for the period; reference was also made to *The World Today*, Vol. 39, No. 2, pp. 68–94.
20. The pope's reaction was conveyed to us by a member of his staff on 2 May 1983.
21. Kabongo, in a comment to one of us on 7 May 1983.
22. Statement issued by Cardinal Glemp in Warsaw, 7 May 1983.
23. Adam Lopatka, quoted by PAP, 7 May 1983.
24. Quoted by PAP, 7 May 1983.
25. Kabongo, in a comment to one of us on 7 May 1983.
26. Reported to us by a member of the Secretariat staff on 6 May 1983.
27. Ibid.
28. Ibid.
29. The possibility for such a force later surfaced in *The Los Angeles Times* (28 May 1983).
30. The nuncio's views were made known to us by a member of the Secretariat staff on 8 May 1983.
31. Ratzinger reportedly found there were insufficient grounds for him to act. But on 20 October 1983 his secretary, Bruno Fink, conceded to one of us that the matter was 'by no means closed'.
32. Excerpt from proposed National Pacification Law, promulgated 15 May 1983; as a sweetener the law also proposed to offer an amnesty to 300 prisoners convicted of terrorist-related crimes by military courts.
33. The pope reportedly deferred making any decisions on the matter.

34. Henry McConnachie in interview with us on 7 May 1983.

35. Events in late October, when the United States invaded Grenada, would prove the priest wrong. See *The World Today*, Vol. 39, No. 12, pp. 468–76.

36. Andropov, in Moscow, 4 May 1983.

37. Kabongo put it very well to one of us on 17 October 1983: 'Papal diplomacy is ninety per cent reading; no, correction – ninety-five per cent reading. A great deal of it does not require more, thank God. How could we cope otherwise?'

CHAPTER 13

1. Dimitrov was one of the persons we chose for regular checking during the entire research period. We were frequently surprised how frankly he would speak; diplomats from Communist countries are rarely as forthcoming as Dimitrov. Nevertheless, he did not tell us everything. Some of the information contained in this scene came from western intelligence officers who as a matter of routine monitor the activities of Soviet bloc emissaries.

2. Dimitrov, 18 April 1983.

3. Dimitrov, 13 May 1983.

4. *The Los Angeles Times* (29 May 1983) provided full details of Soviet anger over the Bulgarian Connection; the *Times*' source was one ever helpful to that newspaper, the CIA.

5. Dimitrov, 13 May 1983.

6. *Il Giornale* (18 April 1983) carried full details of the impending interrogation; their information bore all the marks of being on the inside-track – either there was a leak from Martella's office or *Il Giornale* acquired its material from another source, which Dimitrov believes could have been the CIA.

7. Dimitrov, 13 May 1983.

8. Dimitrov, 14 May 1983.
9. NBC, 5 May 1983.
10. ABC, 12 May 1983.
11. Dimitrov, 13 May 1983.
12. Vatican Press Office communiqué (13 May 1983).
13. Temkov quoted in *On the Wolf's Track*, by Iona Andronov (Sofia Press, 1983).
14. Quoted in Bulgarian Telegraph Agency report of 3 May 1983.
15. Kabongo to one of us on 13 May 1983.
16. During the preparation for *Pontiff* and this book, we were able to observe at close hand Mgr Martin at work. Our impression of him is of a formidable personality capable of overwhelming almost any opposition.
17. Kabongo, loc. cit.
18. Laghi's prediction proved to be accurate. Sister Mansour relinquished her vows, protesting, 'Neither I nor my superiors were ever given the opportunity to appropriately present our case. I do not feel that I should or could give witness to an obedience which, for me, would be irrational and blind.' Her mother superior said the order was 'deeply saddened and profoundly disturbed' by the Vatican's position. After that the matter faded from national interest.
19. More than any other recent Church issue in Britain, the *Affare Inglese* attracted worldwide publicity. On at least one occasion Cardinal Hume's spokesman felt it necessary to deny publicly some of the reporting, such as a *Daily Express* story of 28 April 1983, banner-headlined 'Pope gags CND priest'. Much of the reporting was sympathetic to Kent: see, *inter alia*, the *Catholic Herald* (6 May 1983).
20. Associated Press dispatch (27 April 1983) from London.
21. Cardinal Hume's remarks of 26 April 1983.
22. Mgr Kent gave one of us a full account of his position on 29 September 1983.

23. Cardinal Hume, reported in *The Universe* (20 May 1983), would stress his 'great respect' for Kent. 'We must not underestimate the importance of this debate in which it is vital for us all to listen carefully to each other's arguments. There can be no difference of opinion among Christians concerning our ultimate aim which is to prevent nuclear war from ever taking place. The debate concerns only the means to be adopted to achieve this.'

24. We first learned of this initiative on 23 April 1982 in the course of a lengthy interview with the nuncio to Ireland, Archbishop Alibrandi. He mentioned that 'the Holy See is most concerned to play its part in bringing a proper and just solution to the situation in Northern Ireland'. While Alibrandi would not be specific he did concede that 'the key to our hopes is London; it is there that we are working the hardest'. With the help of the same four sources who assisted us in piecing together previous Holy See initiatives in Ulster, we were able to establish Heim's role.

25. A MOSSAD source reminded us in Rome on 1 August 1983 that Jordan had put Fr Ayad on trial for conspiracy in the 1951 assassination of the country's King Abdullah – murdered presumably because the king was insufficiently steeled in his resolve to quash the new Jewish state. Ayad was acquitted.

26. Fr Ayad, 24 October 1983, in a reported comment to the Middle East Desk.

27. In 1973, Paul VI met in audience the former Israeli premier, Golda Meir, and there were heated exchanges on the subject.

28. Cardinal Glemp speaking in Rome, 19 May 1983.

29. In a comment to one of us on 20 May 1983.

30. Quoted by Kabongo to us on 13 May 1983.

CHAPTER 14

1. McConnachie, 30 May 1983.
2. Greenan, 30 May 1983.
3. *The Los Angeles Times* (29 May 1983).
4. On 1 June 1983.
5. Pope John Paul, on 14 December 1982, to Peter Mladernov; in an audience the pope spoke of *espace vital*, 'living space in order to fulfil the religious mission' in Bulgaria, where he also sought 'a mutual and not a sterile search for solutions of various problems between Church and State'.
6. The latest Vatican figures suggest there are about 65,000 baptized Catholics in Bulgaria. The Holy See has repeatedly tried to ease their plight, and carefully drawn attention to it; during the Belgrade follow-up conference to the Helsinki European Security Conference, Vatican Under-Secretary Silvestrini referred, on 7 October 1977, to 'some serious open wounds that we would like to see healed'.
7. *Stern* magazine claimed to have acquired Hitler's 'secret' diaries. They turned out to be forgeries, an outcome which led to mass resignations at the magazine.
8. Cardinal Koenig, 23 April 1982, during an interview with one of us at his palace in Vienna.
9. Magee to us on 22 April 1983.
10. See *Annuario Pontificio* (1983), pp. 1,169–91.
11. July 1944. Martin A. Lee, a respected American writer specializing in CIA matters, told one of us in Rome in October 1983 that Donovan received his knighthood for assisting the Church during World War II in his capacity as Chief of the Office of Strategic Services, the forerunner of the CIA. Donovan's close ties with the Vatican gave him 'an invaluable insight into the secret affairs of the Vatican, then a neutral enclave in the midst of Fascist Rome'. See Lee's article in *Mother Jones* magazine (July 1983), pp. 21–7, 36, 38.

12. See Bull, op. cit., pp. 198–201. In the aftermath of World War II, the order also assisted, along with the International Red Cross and the Vatican, in helping some of the 50,000 Nazi war criminals escape to South America. They included Klaus Barbie, 'the butcher of Lyons'. In 1948 the order bestowed one of the highest awards in its gift, the Gran Croce al Merito con Placca, on General Reinhard Gehlen, who had been Hitler's main spymaster against the Soviet Union. By then Gehlen had joined the CIA. The agency trained him to set up West Germany's post-war intelligence service. Gehlen recruited mostly ex-Nazis to work under him (Lee, loc. cit.; Flamini, op. cit.).

13. Lee, loc. cit.

14. In a conversation on 24 April 1983.

15. Lee, loc. cit.

16. See, *inter alia*, *The Tablet* (26 March 1983), pp. 286–9, and Lee, loc. cit.

17. To one of us on 6 June 1983.

18. To one of us on 7 June 1983.

19. To one of us on 9 June 1983.

20. To one of us on 10 June 1983.

21. To one of us on 10 June 1983.

22. McNair's journal for 11 June 1983.

CHAPTER 15

1. Annibale Gammarelli, 10 June 1983. The House of Gammarelli, founded in 1786, has dressed all the popes since then. They also clothe most of the cardinals. Since 1981 the firm has accepted credit cards. Gammarelli says 'most of our clients have them. I still have not got used to a prince of the Church offering me an American Express gold card.' He refuses to say how the pope pays for his garments. Almost certainly Prefect Martin takes care of such papal bills, and he abhors credit cards.

2. Gammarelli to one of us on 14 June 1983.

3. Kabongo to one of us on 14 June 1983.

4. Impressions conveyed to us by secretariat staff, 17 June 1983.

5. A view widely reflected. See *International Herald Tribune* (17 June 1983) *et al*.

6. Taiwan's ambassador to the Holy See, Chow Shu-Kai, reiterated this view to one of us on 14 November 1983 when we discussed in Rome the McNair report. He was dismissive of Madame Gong's involvement: 'She is a Communist, and has no official standing with the Holy See. Taiwan is the legally recognized representative of the Chinese people.'

7. The state of emergency in Peru ended three years of struggling democracy in the country. A crushing economic depression and abnormal weather – severe drought in the south of the country, heavy flooding in the north – were advanced as contributing factors for the sudden upsurge of violence.

8. The 32-page document is broken down into hours and often minutes. Two hundred copies have been delivered to the papal party and the Polish hierarchy.

9. Magee recalled the mood for us in a conversation on 24 April 1983.

10. Jas Gawronski to one of us on 24 October 1983.

11. Cibin to one of us on 15 November 1983.

12. Ibid.

13. Press Release, Ministry of the Interior, Warsaw (15 June 1983).

14. Press Release, Ministry of the Interior, Warsaw (12 June 1983).

15. Cibin, loc. cit.

16. Press Release, Ministry of the Interior, Warsaw (15 June 1983).

17. Statement by Polish government, 11 June 1983.

18. In keeping with so many of its affairs, the precise links between Vatican Bank and Poland's financial crisis

remain blurred. Reports continue to surface that the bank has secretly channelled huge sums of money to Solidarity. (See, *inter alia*, Martin A. Lee's report in *Mother Jones*, op. cit., p. 36). Equally, that much respected observer of Polish and Vatican affairs, *Newsweek*'s Rome bureau chief, Andrew Nagorski, is adamant that even Vatican Bank could not cover its tracks totally successfully in such dealings. Besides, say Nagorski, 'the sums speculated about, if true, would totally wreck the Polish financial infrastructure'.

19. We learned of this in July 1983 during briefings from several ambassadors to the Holy See whose nations were represented at Williamsburg.

20. See *The Los Angeles Times* (15 June 1983), *et al*.

21. Jerzy Kuberski, head of the Polish Mission to the Holy See, confirmed these facts to us on 16 November 1983 in an interview. He saw them as 'a sign of the good links between the Church and State in Poland'.

22. Several priests on the trip subsequently told us it had become an open secret how deep was the rift.

23. During a public audience in Rome on 26 May 1981.

24. Vatican Radio transcript of 16 June 1983.

CHAPTER 16

1. Dissatisfied priests were not only ready to speak to us; they nobbled any reporter ready to listen, and with considerable success. See Associated Press dispatches 19, 22, 24 June 1983 and *The New York Times*, 26 June 1983, under the front page headline, 'Pope's Trip Stirs Vatican Debate on Political Role'.

2. To one of us on 18 June 1983.

3. Greenan to one of us on 19 June 1983.

4. Ibid.

CHAPTER 17

1. Cibin to one of us on 15 November 1983.
2. Ibid.
3. Ibid.
4. Magee to one of us on 29 July 1983.
5. Quoted by one of them to us on 4 August 1983.
6. 17 June 1983.
7. 18 June 1983.
8. Glemp, 23 June 1983, in Cracow.
9. This entire account was reconstructed in November 1983 with the help of two wire-service reporters in Warsaw. They asked, because of contractual commitments to their employers, to remain unnamed. Both reporters have a close working relationship with Walesa. We were also helped by information provided by Bogdan Lis, head of Gdansk Solidarity. This help included obtaining for us the direct quotes attributed to Lech and Danuta Walesa in this account.
10. The final analysis of the papal trip was completed on 4 August 1983. It is a document of several hundred pages. Mgr Josef Kowalczyk, a senior member of the desk, told one of us on 19 November 1983 that the documentation had also been turned into a book, published in Polish and Italian, for Secretariat of State staff.
11. Jerzy Kuberski, head of the Polish Mission to the Holy See, to one of us on 16 November 1983.
12. Bohdan R. Bociurkiw, a professor of political science at Carleton University, Ottawa, identified these divisions in *The Los Angeles Times* (29 June 1983).
13. Kowalczyk, loc. cit.
14. A vivid description of the in-fighting within the newspaper appeared in *National Review* (2 September 1983), pp. 1,072, 1,093.
15. Lambert Greenan offered an interesting comment on the matter to us on 19 November 1983. He remains

520

convinced that Levi was astonished at the concern expressed over the article prior to its publication. 'He told me there was really nothing exceptional in it,' said Greenan.

16. *National Review*, loc. cit.
17. Kabongo to one of us on 11 November 1983.
18. *Sunday Telegraph* (26 June 1983), *et al*.
19. Levi resigned on 25 June 1983. He explained the article 'contained my own personal considerations as a journalist'. Announcing his departure, the Vatican statement used the same words.

CHAPTER 18

1. Sister Severia Battistino described the procedure to us in a discussion on 24 October 1983.
2. This nun was one of several on duty who subsequently helped us re-create events in the Vatican switchboard on this morning.
3. On 1 November 1983 in Rome police headquarters, Cavaliere explained his frustrations to a member of our research team, Vivienne Heston. During a remarkably candid interview the homicide squad chief spoke feelingly of his problems with the Vatican. 'We are responsible for security in St Peter's Square. But Vatican citizens are foreigners of a sovereign territory as far as Italian law is concerned. It would not be wise for us to subpoena people of whom we have no material evidence of wrong-doing.' He made it plainly clear that Vatican co-operation in this case had not gone beyond what was essential.
4. Within hours this supposedly confidential record was in the hands of several Rome reporters. Our version is based on what they mutually agree transpired.
5. Avon subsequently issued a statement saying it does not market its products in this manner.
6. While Cibin made clear to us, on 21 November 1983,

521

that he could not discuss – for the record – the investigation, he agreed John Paul continued to take an active interest in the matter, and had indeed told him to do everything possible to locate Emanuela.

7. One of Mgr Audrys Backis's secretaries in the Council for the Public Affairs of the Church told us, on 21 November 1983, that 'it was very hard to do more in this department than express condolences. We are always under great pressure to deal with matters within our competence and kidnapping is not one of them.'

8. See *Der Spiegel* (No. 11/83), pp. 29–34; and *Frankfurter Rundschau* (22 February 1983), pp. 2, 4.

9. The papal representative in Taiwan, Mgr Paolo Giglio, informed the Secretariat of State on 1 July 1983 that the broadcast had been widely commented upon in Taiwan; many Taiwanese saw it as the first step by the Holy See in downgrading its relationship. Giglio was instructed to say this was not the case.

10. 20 June 1983, p. 4.

11. There are also an estimated 140 million Muslims and Buddhists. The Muslim population has been described as China's 'potential political time bomb' (*US News & World Report*, 25 July 1983, p. 38). Most Muslims live in provinces bordering Russia, areas where Peking's influence is marginal, ethnic nationalism high, and Soviet subversion a constant threat. Because of this, Muslims have more freedom and subsidies than other religions. The State, for instance, finances schools to train their priests. And as there is now less fear of contamination spreading from Iran's fundamentalists, Peking has allowed them religious contacts with Muslims abroad.

12. On 22 November 1983 Mgr El-Hachem spoke freely to us about Arafat. In his seventeen years in the Secretariat of State, this diplomat said he had never encountered a more perplexing man than the PLO leader. On a personal note, El-Hachem explained the cost of the

522

fighting in Lebanon for his family: so far forty-six members had been killed. He repeatedly said, 'This is a tragedy which has been foisted on the Lebanese people. I pray for them every day.'

13. El-Hachem to us on 22 November 1983.
14. Ibid.
15. Ibid.
16. By 21 November 1983 El-Hachem had revised his opinion. He told us, 'I believe now that Arafat is finished. It is only a matter of time before they kill him.'
17. Our enquiries into Emanuela's fate have been considerably helped by the investigative talents of Vivienne Heston. Calling on her own impressive range of contacts in the Rome police, including Cavaliere, this tenacious journalist produced a remarkable amount of data which has not been published elsewhere.
18. The complete transcript of what was said was subsequently made available to us by NBC's Rome Bureau.

CHAPTER 19

1. Kabongo on 4 August 1983.
2. On 27 November 1983, Marcinkus denied to one of us he had ever queried the cost of the pope's pool. 'If you listen to every rumour they try and pin on me, you would have time for nothing else,' quipped the archbishop.
3. Kabongo, loc. cit.
4. Rostow, 27 March 1968, at a symposium in Boston on the subject of The Vatican and World Peace.
5. Kabongo, loc. cit.
6. Graham, 27 March 1968 (see footnote 4). His words, he told us on 12 April 1983, still stand good.
7. Ibid.
8. Ibid.
9. Ibid.
10. Ibid.
11. See *Mother Jones* magazine (July 1983), p. 37, for a

lengthy article by Martin A. Lee on the CIA, the Vatican and Sindona.

CHAPTER 20

1. The attack was successful, but victory was short-lived. Within hours West Beirut was infiltrated by snipers making a mockery of Gemayel's appeal 'for a national reconciliation dialogue to chart Lebanon's future within the framework of territorial integrity and total sovereignty' (*International Herald Tribune*, 1 September 1983).

2. Details of the report came to our attention on 10 November 1983.

3. Reagan's aides were amused when Kissinger insisted on an immediate interview with the president. 'Next he'll be commandeering an Air Force jet and be off on a round of shuttle diplomacy,' joked one aide to *Newsweek* (1 August 1983). The implication was that Reagan's Central American policy 'could use the publicity' (loc. cit.).

4. The terms of the 1976 Franco-Chadian military co-operation accord speaks only of logistical support. Article 4 goes so far as to declare that French military personnel in Chad cannot 'participate directly in operations of war'. In an interview with *Le Monde* on 23 August 1983, Mitterand agreed that French action did go beyond the terms of the accord.

5. White House spokesman Larry Speakes on 24 August 1983.

6. Ibid.

7. *Tass* (30 August 1983).

8. *Le Monde* (27 August 1983).

9. Weinberger insisted 'we sent the AWACs only because the French indicated they wanted them' (*Time*, 29 August 1983).

10. Diplomats, not named but based in Manila, told *The*

New York Times (31 August 1983) that Aquino was killed as a result of what the *Times* called 'a high level conspiracy'.

11. We learned of this profile from a Vatican source on 2 September 1983.
12. Telex text conveyed to one of us on 2 September 1983 by a member of the Secretariat of State.
13. A full and authoritative account of this finally appeared in *Time* (5 December 1983).
14. McNair's journal for 1 September 1983.

CHAPTER 21

1. The entire event on this astonishing morning was reconstructed by us by dividing up our research forces and by the generous co-operation of news colleagues like Andrew Nagorski of *Newsweek*, Al Troner, then of the London *Daily Express*, and Judith Harris of NBC. Between us we were able to cover various locations as well as focus in on the central point around the Vatican. It required some very deft foot-work, and again we pay due tribute to our two Rome-based research assistants, Vivienne Heston and Clarissa McNair. Using their well-developed contacts within the Rome police force and the Vatican, they were able to obtain interviews and reactions that almost certainly would not otherwise have been possible.
2. Cibin, 27 September 1983.
3. Dimitrov, obliging as ever, amplified his role on this occasion during an interview with one of us on 22 October 1983.
4. His words, as best he could recall them, were given to us by Dimitrov during the interview on 22 October 1983.
5. Ibid.
6. Martella's views on publicity were very firmly restated to one of us by the judge on 12 November 1983. Then,

a full month after the event described here, he was still seething at the way the press had behaved – perhaps with some justification.

7. Martella, loc. cit.
8. Ibid.
9. Kabongo, 18 September 1983.
10. Ibid.
11. Ibid.
12. Ibid.
13. Urdampilleta, 11 December 1983.
14. Abboud, 11 December 1983.
15. Kuberski, 12 December 1983.
16. Gawronski, 11 December 1983.
17. Dislioglu, 12 December 1983.
18. We spoke to two of them on 11 December 1983 when they confirmed to us their views.
19. Wilson, 10 November 1983.
20. Ibid.

CHAPTER 22

1. The indefatigable Vivienne Heston had spent days trying to fix an appointment. Martella regretted he could not grant one; he had the Bulgarian judges in town. Heston slipped a note under his office door in the *Tribunale* begging a few minutes of his time. Before she had left the building, he called her back. When he heard about the Austrian file and our material on Terpil, Heston recalls 'his eyes lit up'. He arranged for a meeting soon afterwards, during which Heston would act as translator. Martella made her sign an official document precluding her revealing anything of the discussions. We were not asked to sign such a paper. Accordingly we are able to recount what happened, except for that period at the end of the second meeting when he stipulated there could be no reporting of what was said.

CHAPTER 23

1. Kabongo to one of us on 1 December 1983.
2. Ibid.
3. Statement of Synod of Bishops, 29 October 1983.
4. On 29 October 1983.
5. Rovida's views were reported to us on 3 December 1983 by two members of the Secretariat of State.
6. Hume's statement appeared in *Briefing*, Vol. 13, No. 38, insert pp. 2–6, issue of November 1983. *Briefing* is a subscription service containing documents and official news releases of the Roman Catholic hierarchy in England and Wales.
7. Stressing that he was only expressing a personal opinion, Mgr El-Hachem told one of us on 2 December 1983 that he still feared Assad was determined to have 'Arafat's head as if he was John the Baptist'.
8. In piecing together the details of their negotiations we agreed, because of the very delicate nature of what was involved, not to name all our sources.
9. The Libyan leader refused a request to meet Mgr Gabriel Montalgo, the papal nuncio with responsibility for Libya–Holy See relations. The request was made on 24 November 1983.
10. The first appeal to Assad from Moscow was made by Gromyko on 19 November 1983.
11. Communiqué issued by Syrian Foreign Ministry, 29 November 1983.
12. Confirmed by Kabongo to one of us on 3 December 1983.
13. Wilson to us on 10 November 1983.
14. The story was prevalent in the Secretariat throughout November. A number of Rome-based journalists, like Al Troner of the *Daily Express*, also heard it. Troner described it as 'smacking of CIA' to one of us on 14 November 1983.
15. Wilson insisted on 10 November 1983 that he always

tried 'within all possible grounds' to keep the Holy See informed in advance of US moves.

16. See the *Sunday Times*, London (30 October 1983, p. 13); *Newsweek* (14 November 1983, 28 November 1983); *Time* (5 December 1983) *et al*. These included analysts who argued that the widespread prediction of a US-backed invasion was part of a clever propaganda ploy to 'frighten the Sandinistas into behaving in a more democratic fashion'. There were others who noted the regime had been crying wolf over the possibility of a US invasion for more than a year, using it as a pretext to justify a massive military build-up. Certainly the war jitters proved a political godsend to the beleaguered regime, deflecting domestic attention away from the country's grim economic and social problems. The prospect of an invasion also rallied some Nicaraguan moderates behind a government losing popularity. All this accepted, the latest report on the Latin American Desk is still astounding.

17. *Tass* (24 November 1983).

18. *The Sunday Times*, London, loc. cit.

19. Ibid.

20. One of us was in the papal apartment, visiting Kabongo, when Orlandi and the bishops arrived.

21. Two of Orlandi's fellow messengers provided us with the first news of the pope's plan to visit the gaol. Kabongo confirmed it. The official announcement came on 16 December 1983.

22. One of Orlandi's colleagues to one of us on 1 December 1983.

23. Ibid.

24. Ibid.

25. Personal observation of one of us on 1 December 1983.

26. *Time* (28 November 1983, p. 29).

27. Ibid (p. 28).

28. Kabongo to one of us on 1 December 1983.

29. *Time* (28 November 1983, p. 28).

30. Ibid.
31. Ibid (p. 29).
32. William Sullivan, quoted op. cit., President of Seattle University.
33. Quoted op. cit. (p 28).
34. Ibid.
35. Kabongo, loc. cit.
36. FAO Report, November 1983.
37. FAO Director-General Edouard Saouma to one of us on 17 November 1983.
38. Kabongo, loc. cit.
39. Saouma, loc. cit.
40. Kabongo, loc. cit.
41. Ibid.
42. Ibid.
43. See, *inter alia*, *Newsweek* (21 November 1983, pp. 10–12) and the *Daily Express* (17 November 1983).
44. Wilson, loc. cit.
45. Poggi to one of us on 1 May 1983.
46. In 1974 and again in 1980 the US National Conference of Catholic Bishops condemned capital punishment. Six times in the last few years American bishops have intervened in capital cases.
47. The plea was sent on 27 November 1983, three days before Sullivan was scheduled to die. It was relayed from Laghi to Miami's Archbishop Edward McCarthy. He read it to the state governor who said he was 'personally moved' by the pope's concern. But he refused to halt the execution.
48. McNair's daily journal from 16 November to 7 December 1983 is virtually given over to the incident related here.
49. On 18 November 1983.
50. McNair's journal, 7 November 1983.
51. One of us interviewed Siemer on 21 November 1983 in Rome.
52. McNair's journal, 11 November 1983.

53. Broadcast on 14 November 1983.
54. On 16 November 1983.
55. McNair's journal, 16 November 1983.
56. Broadcast on 18 November 1983.
57. McNair's journal, 17 November 1983.
58. Cibin pinpointed the incident taking place between the hours of two P.M. and six P.M. on 15 November 1983.
59. Troner to one of us on 18 November 1983.
60. Ibid.
61. *Daily Express* (18 November 1983, p. 6).
62. Quercetti defended this policy to one of us earlier in the year on the ground that 'the people who work here are all trustworthy' (2 May 1983).
63. Purgatori to one of us on 22 November 1983.
64. McNair's journal, 21 November 1983.
65. Troner, 21 November 1983.
66. Troner told one of us on 21 November that he had spent several days trying to get a second source for what a US diplomat at the American Embassy to Italy had told him: that the Station Chief of CIA Rome had been called in by his ambassador to be briefed on what had occurred. The ambassador was reportedly 'outraged', according to Troner's source, to learn that The Mad Mentor had allegedly played a part in spiriting the tape out of Vatican Radio. Troner was unable to verify the story to the point where he could publish it. We decided to confront The Mad Mentor. One of us, in the presence of McNair, telephoned him on 24 November 1983 at his home. Most of his side of the conversation, which he opened with the somewhat astonishing remark, 'everybody says I am in the CIA – so what?', was given over to attacking McNair's 'anti-American-ism'.
67. McNair's journal, 7 December 1983.
68. Ibid.

CHAPTER 24

1. The call was received on 24 November 1983.
2. The total numbers of calls exceeded thirty during one ten-day period.
3. The call was received on 27 November 1983.
4. The call was received on 30 November 1983.
5. Ibid.
6. Consolo to one of us on 9 December 1983.
7. Ibid.
8. Consolo to one of us on 14 December 1983.
9. Ibid.
10. Ibid.
11. Our view is shared by Claire Sterling, an acknowledged expert on terrorism, a long-time resident in Rome and author of a book, *The Time of the Assassins*. In it she claims that the US Embassy attempted to interfere with her reporting. Her view, expressed in *Newsweek* (2 January 1984), pp. 7–8, is that 'a great deal of information was available to all the major western secret services, but they wanted it deeply buried. When the story of a Bulgarian connection began to come out, they were caught flat-footed.'

CHAPTER 25

1. Craxi's views were given maximum exposure by Vatican Radio on 24 December 1983. Italian government officials saw this as not very subtle pressure to get Craxi to change his position.
2. Details of the alleged Israeli plans were eventually leaked to *Time* magazine for its issue of 2 January 1984 (p. 32).
3. Reagan's intervention was also given maximum coverage by Vatican Radio on December 1983.
4. 22 December 1983.
5. The idea was first proposed by President Sadat.

6. El-Hachem to one of us on 3 January 1984.
7. Kohl, 23 December 1983, in Bonn.
8. Schmidt, 23 December 1983; *Bild*, p. 1.
9. 2 January 1984, pp. 18–19.
10. UPI dispatch from Moscow (21 December 1983).
11. EEC statement, Brussels, 22 December 1983.
12. Polish government statement, 22 December 1983.
13. Again, the information the nuncios acquired through their diplomatic connections quickly became publicly available. This strengthened the feeling in the Secretariat of State that the United States and Soviet Union were engaged upon, not for the first time, an exercise to prepare public opinion for a sudden thawing of relations between the superpowers.
14. Statement of President Reagan's spokesman, Larry Speakes (10 January 1984).
15. Both quoted in *International Herald Tribune* (11 January 1984).
16. Obliging as ever, Dimitrov was happier than usual to provide details of the celebration luncheon. It was widely reported in the Italian press.
17. Among them was our researcher, Vivienne Heston, on whose account this scene is largely based. It was one of her last assignments for us during a year in which she demonstrated the kind of initiative which later made the London *Daily Express* appoint her their full-time Rome correspondent in place of Al Troner when he joined the Associated Press and went to work in Singapore. Heston willingly remained 'on station' for us with Clarissa McNair during the Christmas holidays, helping us to ensure that nothing of significance was missed in and around the Vatican during this period.
18. The letters were sent on 21 December 1983.
19. During a meeting in Prague in January 1983 leaders of the Warsaw Pact first called for the mutual renunciation of force in East–West relations.
20. Burkhard Hirsch, a Free Democrat deputy, argued 'if

one wants to break through the nervousness of both superpowers, which is one cause of armament, then one side must start by signalling the other irrefutably that things can change'.

21. Nitze would reaffirm these views in *Newsweek* (2 February 1984).

22. A member of Casaroli's staff confirmed to one of us on 4 January 1984 that Casaroli is an ardent reader of the *Bulletin*.

23. Our own researchers, Vivienne Heston and Clarissa McNair, were strategically stationed in the Basilica and St Peter's Square to provide the overview on which this scene is based.

CHAPTER 26

1. The start of the pope's day was described for us by one of his staff on 31 December 1983.

2. We first learned of these details on a visit to the papal apartment when researching *Pontiff*, in January 1982. We were accompanied at the time by photographer Peter Thursfield, whose professional eye for detail was invaluable.

3. The details of John Paul's possessions were described to us by a member of his domestic staff during conversations earlier in the year.

4. Annibale Gammarelli to one of us on 31 December 1983.

5. Details of Agca's cell and how he was treated on this particular day come from a number of sources. These include Vivienne Heston, who had toured part of Rebibbia with a lawyer friend earlier on and maintained contacts with several staff. Other prison staff – including one working in the maximum security wing – provided additional information, often invaluable. Further, we had the benefit of details supplied by that excellent reporter, Andrea Purgatori of *Corriere della*

Sera. Two other reporters – who because of contractual obligations wish to remain anonymous – provided more data. On top, we performed our normal function of talking to anybody who could be helpful: relatives of prisoners in Rebibbia; lawyers who visit there.

6. On 4 January 1984, during our farewell discussion with Kabongo, the secretary told us John Paul had kept fully abreast of 'all developments' relating to the attempt on his life. 'So have we all here. We have our very definite ideas.' He would say no more; but it was clear many other members of the pope's staff do not believe justice has been served by the apparent weakening of the Bulgarian Connection.

7. We subsequently were able to hear the recording on 5 January 1984.

8. These we provided. Kabongo told one of us on 4 January 1984 that 'we were especially interested in the one relating to Frank Terpil and Gary Korkola'. It was a film originally made by Irish television.

9. Reuters dispatch (27 December 1983).

10. *Time* (9 January 1984), pp. 7–12.

11. Ibid.

12. Ansa dispatch (27 December 1983).

13. On 5 January one of us was able to view a recording of the entire meeting. This enabled us to provide the account of what transpired between the two men in cell T4.

Index

535